Praise for *Fully Funded*

"As an avid reader and the Treasurer of the Wharton Club of Charlotte, I found *Fully Funded* a tour de force—a must-read, must-own, and, for many events / ideas in the book, a must-do for every alumni club leader. It has inspired me as the treasurer not only to buy insurance for our club but to plan bigger and better events and to give more of my time and talent. Stacie's succinct 'Make It Happen' lists make it easy for us time-strapped volunteer leaders to implement her numerous creative and outrageously successful ideas."

—*David Chu, Senior Portfolio Manager, Equities for Wellingdon Wealth Management, and Treasurer for the Wharton Club of Charlotte*

"As someone who has been deeply involved with running and growing an alumni chapter, I can wholeheartedly recommend this extremely practical book. It is filled with great ideas, best practices, and essential operating processes. I only wish I had known everything it contains before I began leading my local chapter. If you're leading an alumni chapter, this book is your bible."

—*Greg Colandrea, CIO of YPO and President of the North Texas Chapter of the US Naval Academy Alumni Association*

"*Fully Funded* is an invaluable resource for alumni volunteers and leaders who want to build thriving local alumni clubs. Stacie Hyatt has done a wonderful job of presenting the critical role alumni clubs play in engaging alumni and deepening their connection to their alma mater. She then lays out a comprehensive and actionable plan for club leaders to build an engaged group of local alumni by generating and managing the income necessary to build a thriving club. Stacie covers both sophisticated fundraising strategies (including how to utilize crowdfunding, mobile giving, and matching gifts) as well as the key tactical issues around managing expenses. Her insights include numerous helpful tips for club leaders regarding everything from how to negotiate favorable agreements with venues to event promotion, membership dues and benefits, sponsorships, insurance, and alcohol policies. Best of all, she has made it easy for alumni volunteers to put these ideas into action with helpful 60-Second Takeaways and Make it Happen Checklists."

—Drew Clancy, President and CEO of Publishing Concepts; Past President of the North Texas Amherst College Alumni Chapter; and Past President of the St. Marks Alumni Association

"In *Fully Funded*, Stacie Hyatt has created something that previously didn't exist. Gathering success stories from alumni clubs and chapters from institutions of all sizes, Hyatt has created a roadmap to help clubs overcome some the greatest challenges volunteer-driven organizations face. From finances to website and data management, to event planning and leadership transition, she shares proven tips for leading alumni clubs and chapters to success. Both alumni professionals and club / chapter leaders will find this first-of-its-kind book to be a handy resource filled with useful tips and examples."

—Kathryn Greenwade, Vice President of the Association of Former Students of Texas A&M University

"Stacie Hyatt has crafted the most useful and insightful guide to building a successful and enduring Alumni Chapter that you will ever find. *Fully Funded* is the result of more than ten years of impassioned research and interviews, augmented with hands-on management of alumni chapters. Stacie is a tireless champion of success through detailed planning and cooperation. It shows in her writing. I am honored to have had the opportunity to endorse her creation. She has provided the definitive template that will help your organization succeed and remain vibrant into the future."

—Alden McCall, Initiator, Co-founder, repeat Past President and Past Treasurer of the Dallas Business Club; Past President of Thunderbird Dallas Alumni Chapter; and Past Board Member of the Thunderbird National Alumni Board

"*Fully Funded* by Stacie Hyatt is a terrific how-to handbook for a huge, underserved sector: alumni chapters, representing tens of millions of college and university graduates. So many alumni hunger for more meaningful contact with their colleagues, but so many alumni chapters don't have the information on how to set up and run alumni chapters. *Fully Funded* tells alumni in step-by-step fashion how to set up, fund, and operate an alumni chapter that really serves alumni, from interesting events to networking to sustainability. Full of checklists and examples gleaned from the author's years of experience in the field."

—*Stuart Diamond, JD–MBA, Emeritus Professor at the Wharton School and best-selling Author of* Getting More: How To Negotiate To Succeed In Work And Life

"Heartfelt thanks to Stacie Hyatt for sharing her perspective, expertise, and innovative initiatives, gathered from extensive research and personal experience as an alumna and as a humble, transparent and empathetic Alumni Club leader, across the United States. *Fully Funded* is an inspiring gift to all alumni and universities! Our leadership team is excited to learn more and to adopt the valuable advice and effective strategies Stacie generously shares to ensure sustainable growth for our community as we continue to develop and offer our alumnae opportunities to build meaningful relationships!"

—*Dare Rosebery, Vice President of Leadership and Development, People Programs Group, Inc., and President of Colorado Ivy+ Women*

"Stacie Hyatt has caught lightning in a bottle with *Fully Funded*. Vibrant, sustainable alumni clubs are essential entry points for future major gifts donors. *Fully Funded* will empower clubs to grow and thrive, unlocking a tremendous opportunity to match alumni resources with passions, which leads to "development magic.""

—*Derek Dictson, Senior Director of Development at Auburn University*

"In 2016, alumni contributed over $10 billion to higher education, and alumni chapters are a key part of engaging these loyal supporters. Keeping alumni in touch with their classmates and establishing a vital network of professional and volunteer opportunities makes a real difference when it comes time to ask for support. In this groundbreaking book, Stacie has provided excellent and highly practical advice for both chapter leaders and their college and university partners. If you're looking to amp up your alumni-chapter engagement and effectiveness, this is the book to read."

—*Brian Gawor, CFRE, Vice President for Research at Ruffalo Noel Levitz*

"As a leader for over ten years, I truly appreciate Stacie's wisdom and guidance with our 501(c)(3) incorporation, annual state filings, and federal IRS forms.

But after reading *Fully Funded*, I am humbled. Not only does it have these essentials, it truly stokes your aspirations for a successful club, providing a depth of knowledge and breadth of strategies you will find indispensable. It's practical, effective, and inspirational—a must read!"

—Sean Lofgren, VP Business Development, Overwraps Flexibles; CFO and Past President, Northwestern University Kellogg Network DFW; five-time winner of Global "Club of the Year," and 2015 "Kellogg Club Leader of the Year"

"Stacie has written a one-of-a-kind book on financial planning guidance for alumni clubs and associations; however, the principles, tools, and techniques Stacie recommends could certainly apply to other organizations, non-profits, and even small businesses! As a small-business owner, I was captivated by her ideas—she addresses everything from organizational structure to marketing, fundraising, and beyond. I am sure I will apply those ideas to my own business! This amazing book has practicality beyond alumni associations, but I would consider it a mandatory read for anyone serious about creating a thriving and robust alumni group."

—Erin Botsford, CFP, CRPC, Founder and CEO of Botsford Financial Group, and Author of the best-selling financial book The Big Retirement Risk: Running Out of Money Before You Run Out of Time

"Stacie Hyatt has written the first-of-its-kind guide for running an alumni club, with important information for those of us who want to move our clubs to the next level."

—Fred Brown, Partner at Tomlin Investments; Vice President of the Dallas Business Club; President for the Dallas Alumni Chapter of the Graziadio School of Business and Management, Pepperdine University

"Stacie dynamically presented how to engage all generations across multiple alumni networks at our annual leadership conference. Our Seminole Club leaders experienced her passion firsthand and are excited to learn more from this must-have resource!"

—Melissa McClellan, Director, Seminole Clubs at the Florida State University Alumni Association

FULLY FUNDED

FULLY FUNDED

Outrageously Successful
Ways to Fund an
ALUMNI CHAPTER

STACIE HYATT

BROWN BOOKS
PUBLISHING GROUP

Fully Funded
Outrageously Successful Ways to Fund an Alumni Chapter

Brown Books Publishing Group
16250 Knoll Trail Drive, Suite 205
Dallas, Texas 75248
www.BrownBooks.com
(972) 381-0009

A New Era in Publishing®

ISBN 978-1-61254-962-0
LCCN 2017932167

Printed in the United States
10 9 8 7 6 5 4 3 2 1

Publisher's Cataloging-In-Publication Data

Names: Hyatt, Stacie. | Lundquist, Sam, writer of supplementary textual content.
Title: Fully funded : outrageously successful ways to fund an alumni chapter / Stacie Hyatt ; foreword by Sam Lundquist, Vice Dean, External Affairs, The Wharton School, University of Pennsylvania.
Description: Dallas, Texas : Brown Books Publishing Group, [2017] | Includes bibliographical references.
Identifiers: LCCN 2017932167 | ISBN 978-1-61254-962-0
Subjects: LCSH: Universities and colleges--Alumni and alumnae--United States--Societies, etc.--Finance. | Nonprofit organizations--United States--Finance. | Fund raising--United States.
Classification: LCC LB2411 .H93 2017 | DDC 378/.0088379--dc23

For more information or to contact the author, please go to www.SACLeadership.com.

To the countless volunteer alumni chapter / club / group leaders and the alumni relations professionals in the trenches—all giving so much of themselves for the benefit of others and the future of higher education.

Contents

Acknowledgments   xvii

Foreword   xix

Preface   xxiii

» A Network of Acceptance, Mutual Respect, and Timeless Power   xxiv

» Local Chapters, the $17 Billion Prize   xxv

» The Primary Culprits to Chapter Success . . . Are Fixable   xxviii

Introduction   1

Part I: The Basics

Things That Might Need Funding   9

» The Bare Essentials   9

» Website-Related Expenses   10

» Stepping Up the Game   14

» Behind-the-Scenes Enhancements   23

» 60-Second Takeaway   39

» Make It Happen Checklist   40

Coveted Resources from the Central Alumni Association   43

» The Chapter Liaison, Your Fairy Godparent   44

» Glorious Insurance Coverage   45

» The Foundational Website Platform   47

» The Annual Stipend—Great Seed Money   50

» Possible Project or Event Grants for Actual Cash Money   52

» The Ever-Popular Collegiate Merchandise   53

» A Real Gift—The Alumni Leaders Conference   55

» Access to Prominent Guest Speakers   58

» Other Opportunities to Benefit   60

» Keep the Support Flowing   60

» 60-Second Takeaway   61

» Make It Happen Checklist   62

Contents

PART II: The Broadest of Opportunities

Chapter Memberships—Great Foundational Income

Chapter Memberships—Great Foundational Income — 65

» Defining Alumni and the Alumni Community — 67

» Chapter-Specific Membership Benefits — 70

» Membership Types à la Carte — 71

» A Dartboard for Pricing Memberships — 75

» When Local Membership Dues Are Prohibited — 79

» 60-Second Takeaway — 79

» Make It Happen Checklist — 81

Sponsorships Loved Far and Wide — 83

» Cost-Relieving Gifts of Products, Services, or Venues — 84

» A Smorgasbord of Sponsorships — 85

» Sponsor Benefits and Packages — 86

» Danger Zones, Pitfalls, and What Not to Offer — 88

» Sourcing Sponsors — 89

» Weaving a Compelling Story — 91

» Keep Them Coming Back — 95

» 60-Second Takeaway — 96

» Make It Happen Checklist — 97

Traditional and Not-So-Traditional Fundraising — 99

» Cash Campaigns Plain and Simple — 100

» Merchandise Sale—Come and Get it! — 103

» Auctions Interwoven into Other Events or Solo — 105

» Crowdfunding Is a Crowd Pleaser — 108

» Raffles Can Be Fun but Iffy — 111

» Large-Scale Events: Large Work but Large Money — 113

» The Last Act — 115

» Don't Bite Off More Than You Can Chew — 116

» 60-Second Takeaway — 116

» Make It Happen Checklist — 118

Mobile Giving Now for Everyone, Big and Very Small — 119

» The Modern Twist — 120

» How It Works — 122

» Cost Considerations — 123

» Tips for Success — 126

» 60-Second Takeaway 128

» Make It Happen Checklist 129

General Events Are Still the Workhorse 131

» A Sexy Event Subject 133

» A Convenient Date and Time 134

» Determining Attendee Composition 136

» A Venue That Is Right in Every Way 138

» Winning Catering and Beverage Strategies 141

» Enticing Ticketing 145

» Other Elements Not to Overlook 148

» 60-Second Takeaway 149

» Make It Happen Checklist 150

Photo Shoots for Today's Digital World 151

» Headshots—A Must-Have for a Digital Presence 151

» Holiday and Other Themes Spice Up Marketing Efforts 153

» Considerations for Success 154

» Photo Shoot Pricing 155

» Wrapping Up the Loose Ends 156

» 60-Second Takeaway 157

» Make It Happen Checklist 159

PART III: New Horizons for 501(c)(3) Chapters

Giving Days Are Sweeping the Country 163

» Advantages and Compounding Funds Up for Grabs 163

» Important Guidelines for Chapter Leaders 166

» Other Giving-Day Scenarios 167

» Flawless Campaign Execution 168

» 60-Second Takeaway 170

» Make It Happen Checklist 171

Matching Gifts—Big Money Left on the Table 173

» Typical Exclusion Criteria 174

» Executing a Campaign 176

» 60-Second Takeaway 177

» Make It Happen Checklist 179

Contents

Volunteer Grants Are Easy Money for Chapter Leaders   181

»   Grant Allocation Methods   182

»   The Process and Typical Exclusions: Pay Close Attention   185

»   Landing the Grant   187

»   60-Second Takeaway   189

»   Make It Happen Checklist   190

PART IV: Operational Essentials

Promotion for Maximum Impact

Promotion for Maximum Impact   195

»   Know Your Target Audience   196

»   Websites Remain the Anchor   201

»   Surprise! E-mail Is Still King   204

»   Social Media Is Not Optional   210

»   Text Messaging, Not Just Twitter   221

»   Don't Ignore Print Media Just Yet   225

»   Phone Calls Still Have Their Place   230

»   Physical and Digital Third-Party Channels—Secret Weapons   231

»   Blogs, TV, Radio, and Other Alternatives   237

»   Best Strategies by Generation   238

»   Ensure They Show Up   242

»   Integrated Campaigns Are Most Effective   244

»   60-Second Takeaway   250

»   Make It Happen Checklist   251

Collecting and Handling the Money   253

»   A Checking Account—The Most Basic Requirement   256

»   Valid Business Documentation   258

»   Credit Card Payments 101   263

»   Payment-Processing Options   264

»   60-Second Takeaway   267

»   Make It Happen Checklist   268

State and Federal Tax Implications   269

»   501(c)(3) vs. 501(c)(7) and Tax Deductible Donations   271

»   When to Pay Income Tax   277

»   A Closer Look at Tax-Free Purchases   279

»   Total Annual Receipts and Income Thresholds   282

»   60-Second Takeaway   284

»   Make It Happen Checklist   286

Why It's Worth Every Minute   289

About the Society for Alumni Club Leadership (SACL)   293

Appendix

    Free SACL Tools and Resources Available to Readers   295

Notes   297

About the Author   329

Acknowledgments

First and foremost, a special thank you to my father, Robert Hyatt, and my sister, Carrie Counts, for their relentless unconditional love and support from the very beginning, even when they did not quite understand the direction I was taking. Your unceasing commitment to me helped fuel my resolve to stay the course.

I would also like to acknowledge Beckie Allen, Richard Anastasi, David Chu, Linda Higginbotham, Sean Lofgren, R. Shawn McBride, John and Terri Miller, DeWayne Nelon, Junior Ortiz, and Cathryn and Charlie Taylor for going above and beyond when encouraging me to take this leap and never waning in their persistent support throughout the long nights, countless interviews, and extended deadlines it took to make this book happen. Thank you for believing in me.

I am further grateful to the following friends and subject-matter experts who graciously donated their time and talent to reviewing this content for accuracy: Elizabeth Bull, Senior Vice President and CFO at Communities Foundation of Texas; Matthew Coscia, Partner with Montgomery Cosicia Greilich LLP; and Kristin Lonergan, Executive Vice President with American National Bank of Texas.

Lastly, I would like to express my gratitude to my publishing team at Brown Books Publishing Group, who helped make this first book a reality. I could not have done it without: the eternal patience, professional guidance, and content awareness of my primary editor, Judy Hebb; the hand-holding through the daunting process of first-time publishing by the COO, Tom Reale; and, finally, the amazing woman who was there at the start, helped me see what was possible, and brought it all home, CEO—and my friend—Milli Brown.

Foreword

As higher education continues to professionalize alumni relations and fundraising, best practices are continuously being established and refined by college and university administrators. The seamless integration of full-time alumni relations staff and part-time volunteer leadership is an emerging best practice of engagement models around the world. Working well together, all the time and everywhere, is an elusive achievement but one that can be reached when combining solid relationship management with more sophisticated tools and programs for alumni.

Stacie Hyatt has done a remarkable job touching all aspects of the process in this book. It serves as a definitive guide for both volunteer leaders and professional staff who have responsibility for putting the building blocks in place for successful regional alumni programming and service. After all, alumni clubs serve as essential centers of gravity for colleges and universities who want to keep their alumni close to their alma mater, despite distance and time since graduation.

Fundamentally changing the culture of alumni engagement was the highest priority of the Alumni Relations and Development program when I joined the Wharton School at the University of Pennsylvania as Vice Dean of External Affairs in 2010. The School needed to shift from engagement and fundraising programs that were frequently perceived as transactional to programs that were built on core values of relevance and convenience to alumni. If the core values were adhered to and alumni / school relationships were comprehensive, then the fundraising would follow naturally.

My first meeting and conversation with Stacie during a visit to the Dallas area in 2010 touched on these very principles. She was an early adapter, already well underway in thinking about methods that foster alumni-centric practices that strengthened her regional club. The secret to the success of her model? Best practices at the local alumni level made club membership convenient and relevant while supporting the strategic goals of the Wharton School. Gone was the possibility of competing agendas between her alma mater and the Dallas-area alumni, whose needs are unique to the market and industries in which they live and work. Stacie had a vision for the classic win-win scenario that defines a high-functioning club program.

There are many hurdles to overcome in the process of harnessing the power of alumni clubs. They are often characterized as "The Three Ts" (time, talent, and treasure) or "The Three Ws" (work, wealth, and wisdom). Very few of us have an abundance of all three, and if we do, our willingness to give them all in meaningful ways at the same time is even more unusual. It really does come down to the fundamental questions that a volunteer leader would naturally ask herself or himself: "What is in it for me?" and "What has my school done for me lately?" Both are fair questions; the value proposition for both the club leader and the institution needs to be clearly articulated and understood at the beginning of the relationship to be mutually beneficial. The world is a competitive place, and a healthy, fully functioning club network will certainly strengthen the value of one's diploma by strengthening the school brand.

I used to talk a lot about brand value when discussing philanthropy with prospective donors, but I found that was not a compelling message to a group of alumni who already enjoyed the unmistakable power of the Wharton brand that was already backed up by a large institutional endowment. Make Wharton stronger and richer? Really? When there is so much need in the world? Yes, absolutely, by supporting and giving to both. "Do both" is a common phrase heard in the Wharton External Affairs office. It is a call to leadership that recognizes the impact of a Wharton education on positioning its alumni to make a difference in their multi-faceted lives. Inevitably, we trust that Wharton played a role in shaping their personal and professional skill set—influencing who they are today and how they contribute to the world. The message resonates because their Wharton experience was funded, in part, by those who preceded them and chose to "pay it forward" with their own personal resources. In that way, alumni leaders and donors are part of a continuum in the life of a college or university. It is the beauty and uniqueness of American higher education.

Because higher education is a communal and terrestrial experience, it is centered on campus, where students grow intellectually and socially in a manner that causes most alumni, in my experience, to conclude that "I learned as much outside the classroom as I did inside the classroom." So there is value in gathering as a community with common goals. Once you experience it, the value proposition of higher education is never questioned, and the case for support is self-evident. But self-evident does not mean self-fulfilled; the role of regional alumni clubs has two profound imperatives. Alumni clubs facilitate the network that makes lifelong learning possible as a benefit of institutional affiliation, and clubs provide the remote infrastructure that acts as a catalyst for alumni engagement. While technology is changing the way we do business, it is not fulfilling the need and desire to come together as a whole to celebrate and promote a shared experience.

Stacie Hyatt has written a wonderfully practical guide to leading a successful alumni club. Whether you are an alumni club officer or an alumni relations staff member, this book covers all of the essential thinking, planning, and implementing needed to run a best-practices alumni club program.

Sam Lundquist
Vice Dean, External Affairs
The Wharton School
University of Pennsylvania

Preface

Often, I am asked why I would de-prioritize my successful career in medical technology to write this book and support alumni efforts. It is simple. Although I very much love medical technology and the people involved, I also believe in the enormous power of alumni networks and their potential to significantly impact the professional, personal, and spiritual lives of tens of millions of people, as well as the future of education. If alumni Chapter operations are well executed, alumni relations professionals and volunteer alumni leaders have the unique and awe-inspiring honor of setting the stage and watching the magic happen. The next paragraphs will further explain my deep appreciation for those in service to alumni and their communities. We will explore why well-funded alumni chapters are (or should be) important to the three primary constituents—alumni themselves, the college and university leadership, and alumni relations professionals—followed by a revealing look at the struggles and barriers encountered by chapter leaders as they execute their selfless mandates. With these issues exposed, it is likely that my passion and enthusiasm for the cause will become abundantly more obvious.

Let's start with the three identified constituents: the alumni, the academic institutions, and the alumni relations departments sandwiched in between. For alumni, the answer is obvious, as tens of millions actively gravitate toward the local Chapter of their alumni association seeking both professional advancement and personal connection. This population is absolutely enormous, having roughly 90,000,000 living members with at least one degree from a US degree-granting college or university. That number is closer to 125,000,000 when factoring "former students," those that attended but did not graduate, into the alumni base,[1] as do the vast majority of colleges and universities.

The 4,762 US degree-granting institutions[2] also inherently care, though they should care even more. Alumni are the largest primary direct and indirect sources of financial contributions, marketing, volunteer resources, and future students. They represent the past, present, and future. Over $9.9 billion dollars, representing 24 percent of all contributions received, was donated by a mere six million alumni.[3] That is a tremendous amount of money from a tiny percentage of the population (5.8 percent), screaming of a huge untapped opportunity.

The alumni relations departments most certainly care, so much so that they have dedicated their lives to serving alumni efforts. They spend their careers balancing between directly serving the alumni as a critical part of Chapter operations and advocating to university leadership on their behalf.

Unmistakably, the world of alumni relations is critical to all three constituents. Before we launch into the heart of financially supporting and managing local alumni Chapters and networks, indulge me a bit more as we explore the massive impact on alumni and universities and then look at the surprising barriers holding this community back from reaching its full potential.

A Network of Acceptance, Mutual Respect, and Timeless Power

Alumni care deeply for a connection with their alma mater, fellow graduates, and former students. They desire:

- To have continuing educational enrichment.
- To connect with those who share the same bond and loyalty.
- To stay abreast of happenings at their alma mater.
- To give back to the school that gave so much to them.
- To enhance their professional opportunities.
- To expand their social connections.
- To feel the nostalgia of staying connected to the good times and a place that shaped so much of their future.

They seek all of this and more in the welcoming environment of nearly unconditional acceptance and mutual respect. The personal, professional, and spiritual impact that ignites with an acceptance letter and deepens with time is unparalleled.

The most effective way to convey this power is by allowing the magic and potential of the alumni bond to transcend through a pivotal story in the life of two fellow alumni, one of whom is my very dear friend and past Vice President of the Wharton Club of Dallas–Fort Worth. Near the conclusion of this book, I will also share a truly magnificent alumni encounter of my own that irreversibly altered my life from that point forward.

A little over a decade ago, Evan Shelan was travelling from his home in Longview, Texas, through the DFW airport to Chicago when he noticed a well-known alumnus approaching him. It was *the* Robert Crandall, the retired CEO of AMR (parent company of American Airlines, Inc.). At a momentary loss for words, Evan leveraged their unmistakable bond in Wharton and asked if he would speak at an alumni club event sometime. Mr. Crandall graciously accepted the invitation from this total stranger before heading off to catch his flight. A venue was secured, and Mr. Crandall delivered a riveting lecture on the future of the airline industry to a crowd of 200+ attendees and press. It was a wonderful outcome for the local alumni, but the real magic was yet to come.

Representing the club as the quintessential professional he is, Evan circled back around to thank Mr. Crandall through his assistant, Ms. Howell, who had been instrumental in the coordination of the process. In mid-sentence, she interrupted, wanting to know whether Evan had explained his young company's business model to Mr. Crandall yet. Hearing no, she facilitated a request from Mr. Crandall to meet the very next day. For two hours, the men discussed the potential of eZforex using Mr. Crandall's well-read copy of the business plan, littered with notes and ideas in red ink, as a loose guide. When all was said and done, Mr. Crandall, infatuated with the business model, asked to become an investor. He became the best mentor and partner to Evan that any individual or company could ever expect.

Today, eZforex is the nation's leading foreign exchange service provider to 4,000+ financial institutions, enabling easy access to over one hundred foreign currencies with next-business-day delivery. Evan, Chairman and Founder, warmly shares, "Mr. Crandall is one of the shrewdest, gracious, and most brilliant minds in the world. He provided his intellectual support, contacts, and brilliance for the past ten years. eZforex would never have achieved the same level of success without him."[4]

The alumni side of the equation unquestionably knows the network's value proposition, rarely underestimating its timelessness and power. That same power and influence can be leveraged to drive even the loftiest university goals and objectives well past expectations—if only unleashed.

Local Chapters, the $17 Billion Prize

Fundamentally, our second party—academic institutions—consists of educational businesses with stakeholders in which financial motivations and rankings reign. Leadership is held to exceedingly high expectations and strapped with great fiduciary responsibility. Although there is a self-selection bias in which people who value education and care for those in its service end up in administrative leadership, college and university administration must ultimately deliver the numbers at the end of the day. Bearing that in mind, the next paragraphs will arm such leaders with the financial and related arguments necessary to support action wildly favorable to all constituents—the alumni network, the office of alumni relations, and, most certainly, the college or university itself.

Recall that scattered among the 90 to 125 million alumni are the very small percentage directly responsible for donating the roughly $10 billion dollars. As impressive as the figure is, the full story is even more awe-inspiring. We can all see without further explanation how a daunting $100+ billion has been left on the table by the remaining 94.2 percent of the alumni population itself. But what if the pool of donors could be made even larger than that of the alumni? In essence, that is what has been done by empowering outside supporters to become officially recognized members of the family through alumni Chapter networks that embrace the broader "alumni community."

Colleges and universities create alumni by admitting them to the institution. Alumni associations simply play the catcher when students transfer into the association's sphere or responsibility upon completion of the criteria defining alumni. However, alumni represent only a portion of the population the association engages in support of the university. Overwhelmingly, alumni associations openly welcome not only alumni but family, parents, spouses of deceased alumni, friends, and all those with a passion for the school to be a part of the alumni community. This acceptance comes with nearly full privileges through the alumni association and the Chapter networks.

One might ask how that approach has fared for the schools. Well, while alumni contributed nearly $10 billion, individual non-alumni supporters contributed another $7.5 billion. Together, these groups comprise almost 43 percent of the total contributions. If those numbers don't stop you in your tracks, we have yet to touch on the influence alumni had in directing donations from corporations, yielding 16.1 percent of the contributions, foundations at 30.4 percent, or other organizations at 11.0 percent.[5] It is not unreasonable to suggest that the alumni community is directly or indirectly responsible for the vast majority of those contributions. In the higher education world of plummeting state and federal financial support, the alumni community's affinity and resulting contributions are more critical than ever.

Accordingly, the big questions follow. Of the tens of millions of alumni and related supporters, which ones are more likely to engage and donate? And if they and their motivators can be identified, then can the broader group be better cultivated to result in a higher percentage of donors? Published research indicates that current alumni association members are 4.8 times more likely to be current university donors and 11.5 times more likely to be current donors, with cumulative giving of at least $10,000 as compared to non-members. Further, the same research revealed more member donors became alumni association members *before* making their first gift to the university.[6]

Let's take the discussion one step deeper, beyond broad association membership down to the local Chapter level. The Annual Giving Network found that when volunteers were involved in operating the network (Chapters), the number of alumni participating in annual giving was *twice* that of when the central alumni association or university ran the alumni activities.[7]

To summarize the money trail, the most fruitful population of engaged givers is paid members involved in alumni-run Chapters. This is further compounded by the mirrored affinity the broader alumni community has demonstrated in giving—only possible through acceptance and involvement at the Chapter level. A logical conclusion that one might draw is that a college or university would reap by far the most benefit from a large network of many healthy, active, locally run alumni Chapters.

Not only does this sub-group generate the lion's share of the $17.4 billion (and influences far more) that the universities receive, but it also is the primary branding and awareness channel into the broad community. Volunteer alumni act as ambassadors of the university with the public; they unselfishly offer themselves as valuable resources to be interviewers, mentors, and advocates; they serve on boards and as leaders in the university community; they are a conduit for communicating the programs and offerings to potential students and families; they rally support for athletics; they often are the source of senior capstone projects; they facilitate the hiring of its graduates; and so much more.

The local Chapter is the epicenter through which alumni often connect in support of their alma mater, and vice versa. The pinnacle importance of the locally managed Chapter is abundantly clear. So you can imagine how disconcerting it was to learn that two out of three academic institutions reported that focusing on the annual fund revenue is a higher priority than on alumni participation.[8] Based on the data, driving alumni participation *is* the key to growing the annual fund—and it is done best by supporting local Chapters.

As a benchmark, alumni participation in giving ranges from 0 percent to about 48 percent across US colleges and universities, with the average resting at about 8.9 percent and a median of 6.5 percent.[9] If a particular university cannot report participation numbers at the level it would prefer along that scale, there is an exceptional opportunity lying right at its feet, waiting to be recognized.

The Primary Culprits to Chapter Success . . . Are Fixable

Regardless of whether the college or university leadership is solely driven by contribution goals or is truly more altruistic, a thriving network of healthy, active, locally led alumni Chapters should unquestionably be of the utmost priority. With so much interest and demonstrated value for both sides of the equation, why do so many local alumni Chapters fail to launch, limp along, or, worse yet, fizzle out?

I propose that the problem, at its very core, is the system itself. The good news is that it is addressable and can be fixed. To do so, we first need to take a brief look into the characteristics of what I believe to be the cold, hard realities of the ultimate mismatch.

On one hand, you have the central alumni association (to which we are all thankful), typically accessible during standard working hours on standard working days in a single time zone. Then, there are the enthusiastic association personnel (to whom we are also thankful) that have the luxury to be passionate, motivated, and dedicated to the cause. In addition to their personal devotion, it is their job to do so. Further, they come armed with a robust operational infrastructure, including various degrees of support and technical resources.

On the other hand, the equally enthusiastic local Chapter leaders—dispersed around the nation and often around the world—are unpaid volunteers, largely with family and paying jobs both vying for prime time and mindshare. Chapter-focused attention gets squeezed into the off hours. Compounding matters, the volunteers lack the basic infrastructure, support, tools, and financial resources to adequately perform the job. The two sides of the equation could not be more misaligned.

As the central alumni association's side of the equation is largely well positioned structurally, technically, and skill-wise to accomplish its mandates (though often underfunded and understaffed, something this book hopes to help rectify), the primary barriers to success that can most rapidly be remedied rest with the ill-equipped local alumni leadership. It is there that I see the greatest initial opportunity. I have identified four primary underlying reasons alumni Chapters struggle:

- Lack of volunteer, nonprofit leadership training
- Administrative burdens
- Serious financial constraints
- Lack of continuity over time as a result of the above

First, although alumni are by default educated, very few are educated in volunteer or nonprofit leadership in which they wield no actual leverage. As a result, alumni leaders are often untrained and ill prepared for their roles, armed with little more than good intentions.

Second, alumni Chapter leadership is often administratively intensive. Local volunteers—eager to leverage their networks and dazzle their constituents for the Chapter's and personal benefit—find themselves buried by scheduling conflicts, evaluating venues, negotiating menus, collecting RSVPs, printing name badges, sending newsletters, scribing meeting minutes, keeping up with the accounting, compiling expenses and receipts, scrambling to address last-minute special requests, and a mountain of other tasks. When these mundane but absolutely vital tasks are ignored or performed poorly, the event's professionalism, the overall experience for the attendees, and both the Chapter's and the school's images suffer. Repeating this lackluster behavior can result in low attendance, leading to frustrated leaders. The cycle can spiral downward—fast.

Third, more often than not, Chapters are extremely financially constrained. Central alumni associations are often unable to provide enough in the way of resources or financial support to operate a network of professional organizations. Chapters are generally expected to operate each event as a net-neutral endeavor, leaving very little margin for improving overall circumstances or offering relief from the stresses and strains of leading an eternally boot-strapped operation.

Lastly, Chapters suffer from a perpetual lack of continuity from frequent leadership turnover, often as a direct result of the three aforementioned issues. With each person's departure, the Chapter files and operational memory become more fragmented—leaving gaps and loose ends with service providers, accounts, and records. The remaining leaders are destined to unnecessarily face reinventing the wheel, again. The lack of continuity is a serious and perpetual threat to the survival of any Chapter.

The lack of synergy between the intense desire and need for alumni Chapter success and the challenging realities results in an entire sub-population of floundering alumni networks across the country—and globally. The good news is that these culprits are identifiable and can be addressed. That is where the Society for Alumni Club Leadership (SACL) comes in. I founded the organization to address these issues head on, helping to facilitate highly functioning Chapters and thriving networks. More can be learned about SACL at the end of this book.

Research revealed that focusing on just one of the culprits—the financial challenge—could ease the burdens imposed by the others. Further, nearly 40 percent of approximately 400 alumni clubs, serving ninety-one colleges and universities, openly state that more funding would most help the group become more successful.[10] Accordingly, it quickly became the subject of this first book. Research also revealed that some alumni associations share the same understanding of this issue, like the Alumni Association of the University of Mississippi (Ole Miss Alumni Association), which serves 130,000 alumni through its network of one hundred clubs and groups.[11] Not only has it acknowledged the need for raising funds in support of everyday Chapter operations, it makes that one of two primary responsibilities of the Fundraising Committee outlined for each Chapter.[12]

Future books are likely to explore topics such as the broad and creative world of Chapter events and their planning; the complex and widely varying Chapter structures, roles and governance; and the elusive volunteer Chapter leader recruiting, education, training, and cultivation. In the meantime, this first book will focus specifically on helping Chapters to prepare, generate, and manage income—through the participation with or the blessing of the central alumni association. Providing financial relief will enhance Chapter operations, yielding more active Chapters, which in turn heightens the alumni community's affinity for the college or university. We already know what greater affinity begets—greater giving of time, attention, and resources. All parties not only win but thrive.

Introduction

In my experience over the past decade, funding the Chapter's activities is one of the weightiest and most recurring issues the leadership can face. It drives what events can be offered, how many times the Chapter can offer events, and how professionally the events are administered—the very factors that directly influence the reputation and popularity of your Chapter. The results directly influence how aligned alumni feel with each other and their alma mater and how likely they are to give back financially or through other means.

Although an undeniable benefit of leveraging lessons in this book is improved university giving, the immediate and intended audiences for this text are the local Chapter leaders and the alumni associations. This goes out to all those in the trenches who actually plan and execute the Chapter operations.

Upfront, it is very important to acknowledge that various levels of policies and guidelines define the degrees of operational freedom with which a Chapter may operate. In no way does this book suggest that a Chapter should go beyond those parameters set by its own alumni association. Rather, it provides ideas and fodder for discussion that may bring awareness to opportunities not previously realized. Maybe it sparks new thoughts and possibilities. At a minimum, it will offer guidance on how to execute approved activities to ensure success. Regardless of how entwined Chapters may be with their central alumni association, there is value to be gleaned for everyone throughout the book, even if only in the section dedicated to effective promotion.

Chapter networks seem to fall into one of three primary scenarios with respect to financial and operational authority. In the first group, Chapters are legally subordinates of the alumni association, and the association maintains in-house accounts and total control of finances. All payments are made and all registrations are received by the alumni association. Chapters may or may not be allocated any direct funding; rather, it may be available on a first-come, first-served, event-specific basis. Events are typically planned as financially net-neutral. Raising money for scholarships might be the only approved fundraising, or maybe not even that. In this environment, where planning far ahead of an event is especially critical because of the number of people involved, the book section dedicated to *Promotion for Maximum Impact* might be the most valuable. Even when planning a breakeven program, the pricing is based on a specific number of predetermined attendees. Inspiring at least that number to participate is essential.

The second scenario that seems to be fairly common occurs when the Chapter is still a legal entity of the alumni association, only, it is permitted to have Chapter-specific bank accounts. The accounts may be held at an identified financial institution, or they may be opened at a bank of the Chapter's choosing. The Chapter may have the flexibility to deposit and withdraw funds; however, the accounts are legally sub-accounts of the association in which the association performs the tax filings. In some cases, the alumni association provides a small annual stipend in cash and / or event grants for operational expenses. In addition to the presence of unique bank accounts, the other way this category differs from the first is the greater likelihood that Chapters have some ability to raise their own funds, often for scholarships and possibly for operations as well.

An example on point for this category would be the Marquette University Alumni Association (MUAA), supporting more than 200 events annually[1] for over forty Chapters[2] through volunteer leadership in service to its 110,000 alumni.[3] The MUAA acknowledges that a Chapter may generate profits from operating events and that those profits may be used for operating expenses or scholarships by stating:

> Any profits from events should be earmarked for the club's operating budget and the scholarship fund it supports (if applicable).[4]

If your Chapter situation fits into the category just described, your leadership team will be able to benefit at a greater level from the content provided.

The third and final broad scenario that a Chapter might find itself in is when the roles switch and the Chapter maintains primary or total control of finances. In this case, Chapters are independent organizations rather than legal subordinates of the alumni association. They are required to file for their own Employer Identification Number (EIN), file as an entity with the state, and open their own bank accounts—all under the guidance of the alumni association. The Chapters are responsible for managing their own payments and reimbursements. These Chapters are less likely to be allocated funding from the alumni association, as they typically operate as self-sufficient. This model provides the greatest financial freedom for a Chapter; however, it also significantly increases the management necessary to maintain state and federal compliance.

One such scenario-three network belongs to the Nebraska Alumni Association (NAA), serving the 196,000 alumni of the University of Nebraska[5] through nearly ninety Chapters.[6] Chapters are approved affiliates of the NAA, where finances are executed locally with guidance from the NAA. Accordingly, all Chapter leaders—and especially the treasurer—are required to sign the university's Statement of Fiduciary as a safeguard and to ensure integrity of the finances. Chapters maintain responsibility for their own finances, bank accounts, and annual IRS filings.[7] Those that have the passion, the desire, and the category-three freedom to pursue Chapter growth fueled by access to additional revenue will be in a position to utilize the contents to the greatest extent.

Although greater overall change is likely to stem from enhancements to Chapter support by way of higher prioritization by the university leadership, it is at the grassroots level that immediate change can take place. I am reminded of a quote by Margaret Mead:

> Never believe that a few caring people can't change the world. For, indeed, that's all who ever have.

This guide will explore what types of expenses a Chapter faces today and set the stage for those expenses likely to be incurred and / or recommended for the future as it grows. Presented next is an overview of financially significant assistance from the alumni association that may be available to your Chapter. Several methods of generating the income necessary to operate the Chapter at whatever level of professionalism is right for your group will follow, with a special section dedicated to unique opportunities for 501(c)(3)-designated Chapters. Finally, we come full circle by touching on several important and related aspects of promotion, collection, financial management, and tax-related issues not to be overlooked. The last moments of the book are dedicated to the amazing and unparalleled reasons why it is all unquestionably well worth the effort to get it right.

Each section offers insight into a specific topic and is presented in a concise format. Following the topical discussion, which may be subdivided into appropriate subsections, you will find the "*60-Second Takeaway*" for those seeking only sound bites. Next, you will notice a short checklist of to-dos I call the "*Make It Happen Checklist.*" If there are helpful resources available for further insight or clarification, they are listed at the end of the book in the appendix.

One further item before jumping in relates to terminology. As you can imagine, the terminology for various aspects of alumni organizations and groups is expansive. For simplicity's sake, I will normalize a few terms discussed below.

Let's consider the example of Florida State University. Its alumni support organization is called the FSU Alumni Association. In some cases, the group performing such functions may be referred to as the Office of Alumni Affairs, Office of Alumni Relations, or Department of Alumni Affairs. The department titles may also include "Engagement," "Development," or "Advancement." Regardless of a college's or university's alumni engagement team structure, the group performing the primary alumni Chapter support functions will unilaterally be referred to as the "central alumni association" within this text. Other variations will include "alumni association," "central association," and the "association." This will apply even if the alumni association is dedicated to a specific school within the broader university.

The term "Chapter" as used in this book will refer to the local child groups of the central alumni association, generally organized according to geographic parameters. Such groups may be referred to as chapters, regionals, clubs, affiliates, constituents, communities, societies, organizations, spirit groups, networks, or other terms by your central alumni association. They may represent groups of alumni or separately be organizations of parents of students. All such groups will simply be called a Chapter in this text. For example, the regional alumni of Florida State University in San Diego, California, gather under the name San Diego Seminole Club®. Therefore, the San Diego Seminole Club is a Chapter according to this definition.

Much of what is discussed will also apply to groups not structured around geography, such as academic, athletic, or other special interest groups also organized and managed by the alumni association. Examples include Black Alumni, Marching Band Alumni, or the Gay, Lesbian, Bisexual, Transgender, Queer and Allied (GLBTQ+) Alumni. Such groups are often, yet not always, operationally parallel to that of a geographic alumni Chapter. Where the parallels exist, it is more than appropriate to leverage the information presented here. Assume, for efficiency, that these groups are also considered under the term "Chapter."

Other such related entities are the alumni Chapters of sororities and fraternities. Again, much of the information presented will apply to them as well; however, there are important nuances throughout the discussion that would most certainly require some adjustment to be most applicable to fraternal organizations. Such groups may also benefit from and use the concepts presented as a loose guide. Just understand that this writing specifically looks out at the world from the eyes of a more standard alumni association Chapter.

The term "Chapter network" or simply "network" as used in this book will refer to the complete pool of local Chapters under a central alumni association. In keeping with our example, that would mean that the FSU Alumni Association Chapter network represents one hundred+ Chapters in the United States and internationally.[8, 9] Some alumni associations choose to refer to their own individual regional Chapters as "networks." This book will not. The use of the term "network" here will encompass all Chapters collectively within the purview of the central alumni association.

The text may use "university," "college," "school," or "academic institution" interchangeably throughout the book. Consider all of the above to be synonymous. It is important to acknowledge the different types of degree-granting institutions; however, listing them all each time is highly inefficient. Further, no distinction will be made here between type of college or university, such as public or private, religious or secular, or large or small.

This book is offered as a tool to fuel the exploration of a variety of funding opportunities that may be available to your Chapter or Chapter network. It is by no means an exhaustive discussion of all things on the topic. It does, however, take the time to discuss a few additional, related topics that seem to be of importance beyond the direct methods of raising funds. Throughout the text, I will interject actual and hypothetical examples from many colleges and universities around the country, as well as personal experiences from my time in leadership of the Wharton Club of Dallas–Fort Worth or the Dallas Business Club, to drive home a particular point.

As there are many legal relationships and structures defining the organization of alumni associations and their Chapter networks, this book does not suggest that examples presented are best practices. What is exceptionally effective for one may be wholly inappropriate for another. Accordingly, the examples and illustrations provided are, rather, just that: examples. Each one is an isolated set of specifics as to how one college or university approaches a topic. The examples simply serve to illustrate a point, as well as to offer practical applications of concepts to stimulate conversation. The specifics offered may even provide a source for further exploration.

It is always advisable to review new directions for your Chapter with the central alumni association and maybe even with the local professional council prior to acting. This is important. I will state it now and repeat it often throughout the text.

It is my sincere hope that this book will help inspire college and university leadership to seriously elevate the prioritization of the alumni association and the Chapter networks from wherever they are now through financial and other support. When this happens, everybody wins—the donor development team exceeds fundraising goals, alumni relations experiences a far more interactive outcome, local Chapter leaders enjoy greater continuity and ability to recruit, and the alumni themselves further engage with each other and the university.

No university seems to embody this spirit more than the Stanford Alumni Association (SAA) when it states:

> Clubs may make a gift to The Stanford Fund but, since individual members of the club will not be recognized for such a gift, it is preferable for clubs to invest their finds into creating a strong local Stanford community, which will in turn encourage alumni to stay connected to Stanford and support the University.[10]

Would it be any surprise that Stanford University received the highest total contributions of any college or university or that the alumni participation-in-giving rate is approximately 26 percent?[11]

I hope that you find this book to be of real value to your central alumni association and your local alumni leadership team. Have we missed anything? If so, let me know at FullyFunded@SACLeadership.com! I eagerly encourage the sharing of thoughts, examples, and ideas that can be repurposed to help others.

Part I
The Basics

Things That Might Need Funding   9

»   The Bare Essentials   9

»   Website-Related Expenses   10

»   Stepping Up the Game   14

»   Behind-the-Scenes Enhancements   23

»   60-Second Takeaway   39

»   Make It Happen Checklist   40

Coveted Resources from the Central Alumni Association   43

»   The Chapter Liaison, Your Fairy Godparent   44

»   Glorious Insurance Coverage   45

»   The Foundational Website Platform   47

»   The Annual Stipend—Great Seed Money   50

»   Possible Project or Event Grants for Actual Cash Money   52

»   The Ever-Popular Collegiate Merchandise   53

»   A Real Gift—The Alumni Leaders Conference   55

»   Access to Prominent Guest Speakers   58

»   Other Opportunities to Benefit   60

»   Keep the Support Flowing   60

»   60-Second Takeaway   61

»   Make It Happen Checklist   62

Things That Might Need Funding

Funding opens the door to so much for an alumni Chapter. This guide offers awareness of common Chapter expenses by bucketing them into four primary categories: the basics, web-related expenses, external aspects the alumni will instantly notice, and internal enhancements. Walk through the categories with a critical eye, determining what may apply to your Chapter now and in the future.

Although this is called out in the *"Introduction,"* I wish to make one more reference to reading the following with the understanding that only tactics in compliance with your alumni association should be considered for your Chapter. That being said, let's get started!

The Bare Essentials

A few basics are needed to support even the simplest operations. Here are a couple of those things found on even the tightest of shoestring budgets:

- **Office supplies** – Every Chapter needs a few office supplies, such as name badges, pens and / or markers, tape, check-in lists, sign-up sheets, and handouts. Even if the only thing your Chapter might do is watch games together at a sports bar, it can be helpful to have a printout of the team roster and possibly that of the opposing team. A sign-in sheet may also be beneficial, as well as name tags, especially if family members are encouraged to join in. If the Chapter has upcoming events already scheduled, passing out a calendar of events to those who already prioritize event attendance can be effective.

  Several alumni associations provide some office supplies, such as name tags, if asked, like the University of Minnesota Alumni Association, in service to 466,000+ alumni[1] and one hundred Chapters,[2] which offers name tags among others items in activity kits.[3] If a Chapter does not have this option, be prepared to enter some figure for office supplies into the budget.

- **Decorations** – Even simple game-watching parties need decorations! These might include pompoms, streamers, small football helmets, noisemakers, and beads, to name a few. If the event is something more festive, then balloons, color-appropriate service ware, tablecloths, and more elaborate decorations may be desired. Some decorations might also be available through the alumni association.

- **Snacks and food** – Another foundational expense goes to fund various drinks and snacks, including pizza, during officer and other planning meetings. It is the least the Chapter can do for its dedicated volunteers, especially when meetings must be established outside of the typical work and family schedules, like early in the morning or late at night. If meetings are in the mornings, coffee, donuts, kolaches, and / or fruit might be more appropriate. This is the case for several Chapters in Dallas whose leadership chooses to meet at 8:00 a.m. on Saturdays. Food and / or drinks at some foundational level are also a likely part of just about any event.

There are alumni associations that specifically restrict the use of Chapter funds to cover food and drinks for officer and board meetings. If this is the case, Chapters may see language in the Chapter handbook to this effect. The Iowa State University Alumni Association (ISUAA), catering to an alumni population of more than 230,000, of which 50,000+ are members through its network of over forty Chapters,[4] is one such association. It states:

> ISUAA funds are to be used to benefit the greater alumni population in your area. They are not designed to pay for meeting costs associated with Board meetings or the entertainment of the Board or Executive Committee members.[5]

If your Chapter should fall under similar mandates, pay heed and forgo the eats or pay out of pocket.

Website-Related Expenses

A website is important, as it represents the core of a Chapter's identity and communication. It is typically the first place someone will look for information. It is possible that the central alumni association provides website support and maintenance on the Chapter's behalf. In fact, there is very likely to be web support in some capacity, however minimal, since the alumni association typically wants to manage the university brand. The next section, *"Coveted*

Resources from the Central Alumni Association," goes much further into detail regarding alumni association–supported sites.

Some colleges and universities do not offer branded Web pages or websites. Instead, the alumni association may post a simple listing of all Chapters and their contact information. Interested alumni then reach out to connect with that Chapter. Chapter leaders of the Bowling Green State University (BGSU) Alumni Association, serving 176,000 alumni through seventy-five Chapters,[6] might find themselves in this situation. The BSGU Alumni Association[7] provides a basic listing of the Chapter names along with a Chapter leader or two and their corresponding e-mail addresses.

The Florida State University (FSU) Alumni Association, serving more than 330,000 alumni through ninety+ chapters and clubs,[8] offers a directory listing online of the Chapters by geography with links to one or more of the following methods to connect: Facebook, Twitter, e-mail, and / or a website. Since no Web page or website template is provided, Chapters are free to establish and design their own sites. About 40 percent of the Chapters have done so.[9]

If there is no website support established, as is the case for about 47 percent of alumni Chapters,[10] and the alumni association approves of the Chapter working out its own solution, then a couple things to consider include:

- **Domain registration** – If the Chapter is on its own regarding a website, then it will want to own and protect a specific website domain for ages to come. This expense can be purchased in graduating blocks of time, offering greater value per year at each level. The longest window of time that the Chapter can afford is recommended. With as much benefit as it offers, the extended plan also bears one important challenge worth noting. Chapter leadership tends to turn over regularly in most instances. So, should the Chapter decide to pay for an extended plan, make certain to document the provider, the account number, and account contact for future service and renewals.

  It is also important to understand the difference between signing up for a domain with a direct service provider or a domain wholesaler. The wholesaler will likely be the lower cost; however, it limits the Chapter to a stagnant domain. I would recommend choosing a direct service provider instead. This is an issue with which I am dealing as I draft this text.

  Recently, Wharton Alumni Affairs changed alumni web portal vendors and wanted to convert our local Chapter over to the new system. A flurry of e-mails went back and forth between the current Chapter

President, the Treasurer, and the central alumni association to no avail. Confusion existed around who actually controlled the domain and how to get it redirected. Officer turnover and less-than-helpful customer service personnel passing the buck did not improve matters. As the immediate past President, I was called to weigh in on historical activity and to help where possible.

According to the Whois directory, our domain was associated with an individual account—not a business account—under the ownership of a direct service provider. Great! This should not be such a problem. It was then that I learned that our domain was not under the control of the listed service provider, as indicated, but rather a third-party wholesaler masked behind the listed entity. After some reconnaissance, I discovered that the domain account was established with this wholesaler in ten-year increments even before my involvement with the Chapter by someone I had never met. It also came to light that since the domain was actually a wholesale domain, we did not have the ability to redirect it from the current alumni portal to another—it was completely frozen in time.

To redirect the web address, the domain must first be transferred from the wholesaler to a direct service provider. If the account had been initially set up as a business account, we could complete the paperwork and send a request on letterhead. However, since it was established as a personal account, we need either to locate the original person who opened the account and have him make the transfer request or to seek a court order. We were hoping for the path of least resistance by locating the account owner. This went on for weeks. Eventually, the transfer request was submitted, a new account was opened as a business account with a direct service provider, and finally the domain was redirected.

Take this miserable experience, and let it be your gain. Establish the domain as a business account with a full-service provider, and document everything for future leadership. A ten-year .com address might run approximately $100 to $150 paid out up front in full. The bill could grow another $75 to $150 if your Chapter wants any additional features, such as keeping the name and address private or e-mail addresses with the same domain.

- **Website development and maintenance** – Maybe there is a savvy web developer among your Chapter's alumni who will donate the time to build and maintain a website. If so, this is excellent! Otherwise, you will need to consider commercial options, of which there are many. Unless your Chapter website will need to support financial transactions or maintain a linked database of alumni information, any one of many providers that offers a free website-development platform for the average Joe should work fine. There is very little concern related to the website if it is simply informational.

Additional research is recommended for those planning on a more interactive site. Again, sourcing personal experience, our Chapter was provided a professional website that integrated into the university's alumni database. It was nice to have something supported by the university; however, it was not very user friendly, and unless you were working on the site regularly, it was difficult to remember how to get things done. This is when our Chapter outsourced the website postings and event tracking to a third-party administrative person. We learned that even vendor-supported sites can lead to maintenance issues. Our solution was to spend a little money rather than the extra time to manage our issue.

For budgeting, the website itself could range from $0 if using a free service and simply providing information with no transactions to roughly $250 per month plus set-up costs for a fully functional site.

- **Website hosting** – In addition to the Internet web address, the website itself will need to reside somewhere in cyber space. The hosting fee is also likely to be more cost effective over longer periods of time and will require consideration of desired features including robustness of cybersecurity, size of its cyber footprint, and responsiveness of customer service, to name a few. There are free options through several web development providers as part of bundled services. Some are more than sufficient for a simple, informational site.

  Should your Chapter plan to support financial transactions or maintain a linked database of alumni information, further exploration into options is recommended—especially related to cybersecurity and frequency of backups. Costs will grow according to needs. As a placeholder, you might use about $10 per month as a rough approximation for the budget.

- **E-mail distribution service** – This is especially important if your Chapter intends to communicate with alumni via e-mail. With all of the Internet spamware, anti-virus, and mal-ware detection algorithms today, anyone sending many separate e-mails and / or e-mails with many recipients from their own accounts will be tagged as a spammer—regardless of whether the originating e-mail address / server is a corporate or personal one. In fact, it is possible that not only your e-mail address but the entire server will be blacklisted. Once that happens, it is very difficult to get off the list. According to research, 37 percent of alumni Chapters are walking this dangerous line using personal e-mail. When one respondent was asked why, he replied, "They [the alumni association] do not let us send a newsletter, so I send from my own."[11] Don't do it!

This issue is the impetus for the rise of e-mail distribution service providers. If your Chapter does not have the capability to launch communications through the website's platform or another tool offered by the university, it is strenuously recommended to engage such a service provider. The costs are very reasonable—and well worth it! Budget in about $0.01 to $0.03 per recipient per distribution. If your Chapter sends two newsletters a month to 1,000 people, that is about $20 per month.

We will explore this a bit more in the much later section *"Promotion for Maximum Impact: Surprise! E-mail Is Still King!"*

It is likely that your central alumni association already provides a website platform and most of the above that goes along with it. If that describes your Chapter, take a moment to let them know how appreciative you are. Those without it have a little steeper and possibly more expensive hill to climb. Of alumni clubs surveyed, 63 percent reported that they do not pay anything for their websites, for one of three reasons: 22 percent said the association covers the fees, 32 percent use a free web service, and 9 percent benefit from a donor or sponsor covering the costs. Another 22 percent of Chapters pay for their websites at various levels. About 11 percent pay up to $100 annually for their sites, while 10 percent pay between $100 and $500 each year and only 1 percent pay over $1,000. The remaining respondents answered that they did not know.[12]

If you do need to go about it on your own, do so in partnership with the alumni association. In surveying the Internet, I have come across some frightful alumni Chapter websites, even of large, reputable universities, that do anything but enhance the brand. Do not be one of those unprofessional brand killers! If you get stuck, SACL can help.

Stepping Up the Game

If the Chapter wants to step up the professionalism of the alumni experience while enhancing engagement, then an additional list of outwardly visible and / or interactive topics to evaluate include:

- **Speaker gifts** – It is customary and considered good form to present a guest speaker (who has likely donated his or her time) with a token of appreciation at the conclusion of the talk, even if the speaker was organized by the central alumni association. In fact, if the speaker was accompanied by a representative from the central alumni association, offer a thank-you gift to him or her as well.

  The gift rarely needs to be extravagant, but even small- or medium-ticket items have a cost. The gift should also take the recipient into consideration. Is he or she also a graduate of the school? Is he or she local? Does he or she have room to carry something back with them? Depending on the answers to the posed questions, some ideas include an engraved acrylic award-like gift, a coffee-table book of the university, or some other university-related paraphernalia. On a more local front, a regional food item or something with a local flair might be appreciated.

  Here in Texas, we are fortunate to have so many regional options for gifts. One popular standby, especially if there might not be too much room to transport something home, is a nice presentation of pecans or locally made salsa with chips that might be consumed before leaving. Another slightly more expensive option could be a custom belt buckle. There are vendors that will design a pewter or silver belt buckle with your Chapter's logo. This is a small and easy to carry yet very memorable gift that is guaranteed to end up on display in the speaker's office. If several are needed, that helps drive down the individual costs by spreading out a set-up fee over more than one buckle.

  From a budgeting perspective, determine the approximate cost of such a gift, evaluate the number of events with speakers your Chapter might host, and determine how many gifts might be necessary for each one to arrive at a number. Consider a gift to cost somewhere between $15 and $75 to be sufficient.

- **Door prizes** – It always builds anticipation and fun when it is possible to become a winner just by attending an event. Door prizes may be donated or purchased; however, if the Chapter is subject to IRS tax-exemption guidelines, it is far more advantageous to have the door prizes donated. These are typically inexpensive or moderately priced items that are related to either the topic of the event or the university itself. If the event is a seminar, then offering one or several donated books written by the presenter as door prizes could be a nice complement to the evening.

Be certain to make it clear that no additional purchase is required to be eligible for the door prize. All attendees should be eligible to participate just by being there; otherwise, it starts to look like a game of chance. (See the later subsection "*Traditional Fundraising Never Goes Out of Style: Raffles Can Be Fun but Iffy*" for more about games of chance and related issues.)

If your event is held at a restaurant, that can be a great opportunity to request one or more gift cards from the restaurant to use as door prizes. Those are always a winner—unless your alumni association expressly forbids the distribution of gift cards as a prize!

It might be possible to receive something as a door prize from the alumni association. For example, the Georgia State University Alumni Association (GSUAA), serving nearly 200,000 alumni and ten active networks,[13] specifically offers at least one signature door prize for a Chapter along with other logo items as available each year.[14]

Boise State Alumni Association, founded in 1967 and serving 80,000 alumni through its fifteen+ Chapters,[15] offers smaller Chapters an autographed football or basketball that can be used as a door prize. The giveaways are very popular and used as Chapter incentives to grow dues-paying association memberships by three or more per year.[16]

With a little luck, you can benefit from items like the above from your alumni association. However, if you cannot, don't let that stop you. Source your own door prizes to make the event more interactive!

- **Holiday party** – Holiday parties or annual kick-off events are excellent opportunities to engage the alumni and their families; however, they can require an initial investment. Costs might include invitations, the venue, catering, parking, decorations, and entertainment, to get the list started. It is possible to recoup some or all of the costs through ticket sales or other means discussed later in this text, but there is no avoiding the fact that some things will need to be paid up front. The Chapter will need partially filled coffers to operate at this level—or significant advanced notice to organize this with the alumni association.

  For years now, the Wharton Club of Dallas–Fort Worth has thrown an annual cocktail-attire membership-appreciation gala entitled "A Night to Remember" in January or February to kick off the year's slate of events. All active, dues-paying members are invited to attend at no charge, and guests are only charged a nominal amount. The members love it, and it continues to be one of the most highly attended events all year. The gala only works, however, because the leadership has been diligent about budgeting, ensuring that annual revenues produce enough margin to cleanly host the event. Further, the club maintains a healthy buffer in the bank just in case the year's events do not yield the income expected. Events like this are great for morale, but they take careful planning and diligent budgeting.

- **Scholarship fund** – Many alumni associations promote—and Chapters value—the ability to offer one or more scholarships to local students each year. The Wisconsin Alumni Association (WAA), founded in 1861 and now serving 435,000+ alumni through its network of one hundred Chapters,[17] is one such example. In 1967, the University of Wisconsin Foundation established a scholarship-matching program to encourage alumni Chapters to enthusiastically participate in the process. It matches the funds raised by Chapters, dollar for dollar, up to $10,000 per year.[18] The program is certainly working, as Chapters have awarded more than $10 million in scholarships to UW students since the program's inception.[19]

  There are three primary types of scholarship programs in which Chapters typically engage. They are scholarships awarded once a year for only that year, recurring scholarships in which an amount is awarded to the same student for each of four years, and endowments in which a fund is established and the scholarship money is awarded from the interest earned, never touching the principal. Within a one-time scholarship, also known as a one-year or annual scholarship, Chapters award all monies raised each year to some number of recipients. They simply raise their own funds for scholarships and dole them out each year according to an established Chapter process or one set by the university. Other times, a Chapter establishes a recurring scholarship or even an endowment for scholarships.

  The University of Iowa Alumni Association (UIAA), serving 270,000 alumni[20] through fifty+ Chapters,[21] encourages Chapter-sponsored scholarship funding and also incorporates a matching element to make it more enticing. Many Chapters (IOWA Clubs) raise money on their own in order to provide scholarships to local students. Once the money is raised, the UIAA matches the funds up to $1,000 per Chapter per year. The UI Office of Student and Financial Aid selects the winners and submits them to the Chapter for final approval, and then the UIAA notifies the winners. The matching-funds angle can be a strong motivator to embrace raising scholarship funds as part of the Chapter's plan.[22]

An example of a university supporting recurring scholarships would be the University of Arkansas and the Arkansas Alumni Association (AAA), supporting 146,000 alumni[23] through sixty-eight Chapters and societies, generating one hundred events annually.[24] Chapters may engage in awarding one-year scholarships for seniors or recurring scholarships in which a certain dollar amount is provided each year for all four years at the university. Full funding for the scholarship must be deposited with the University of Arkansas Foundation prior to the scholarship being awarded. A Chapter wishing to award $500 per year to a student for four years would be required to have all $2,000 deposited in the scholarship account prior to releasing the money.[25]

The Chancellor of the University of Arkansas has implemented a program to match up to $50,000 in Chapter-sponsored scholarships raised each year through at least 2018. In order to ensure matching funds are applied equally, initial matches will be capped at $2,500 per Chapter. After such a match is applied, should there be any unused matching funds, the AAA Scholarship Office will allocate remaining money across the Chapters in an equitable fashion.[26]

The third approach is through establishing an endowment. Many colleges and universities offer a program though which a scholarship fund may be established with your Chapter in a partnership with the alumni association and the university foundation. With endowments, a large portion of the account is protected, while releasing a small percentage annually to be awarded to a deserving student. Funds generated at the Chapter level often generate the endowment principal, while annual gains supply scholarships for years to come.

Indiana University Alumni Association (IUAA), with its large alumni base of nearly 660,000 alumni involved in more than 180 groups, affiliates, and communities,[27] has a well-developed program in which a Chapter may set up one of a few types of scholarship accounts through a partnership between the IU Foundation and IUAA. When the minimum donations and / or pledges for the endowment are received, a scholarship account may be opened. An annual distribution percentage of roughly 4.5 percent dictates how much may be withdrawn and granted for scholarships each year.[28]

The Chapter determines how many scholarships they wish to award, the value of the scholarships, and which semester they will be awarded. The IUAA scholarship committee will select recipients that meet the Chapter's requirements and provide the contact details to the Chapter so that it may deliver the great news. For the 2016–2017 academic year, IUAA Chapters funded scholarships for 91 students, totaling $101,500.[29]

Another interesting program is through the Mississippi State University (MSU) Alumni Association, which serves more than 125,000 alumni through ninety-five chapters and clubs globally.[30] Scholarships may be funded annually or may be fully endowed. Chapters that choose to establish an endowed scholarship must meet the minimum of $25,000 and are given the opportunity to have the fund named in honor of the Chapter or in honor or memory of a special Chapter member. Annually funded scholarships are asked to start with a minimum contribution of $1,000.[31] Of the Chapter network, sixty-three are participating in the scholarship program to various degrees.[32]

The Iowa State University Alumni Association (ISUAA) encourages its Chapters to support scholarships through accounts created and managed by the Iowa State University Foundation (the Foundation). Scholarship options include expendable (annual) funds and endowments.

The Foundation requires a commitment of at least $1,250 per year for five years to create an expendable fund. In order for an ISUAA Chapter to establish an endowment, a minimum commitment of $50,000 is required, recently increased from the previous minimum of $25,000. Several ISUAA Chapters have embraced endowed scholarships and have established the following funds—some even establishing two:

» ISUAA Club of Black Hawk County Scholarship
» ISUAA Club of Black Hawk County, David Juon Scholarship
» ISUAA Club of Dallas-Fort Worth Visualize Your Adventure Scholarship
» ISUAA Club of Hamilton County Scholarship
» ISUAA Club of Kansas City Sandra J. Chandler Memorial Scholarship
» ISUAA Club of Kansas City Kim Bailey Memorial Scholarship[33]

This next example is an extreme outlier but is so miraculous it had to be included. In approximately 2005, Jerry Finger, one of the Wharton Club of Houston officers, set out to start an unprecedented scholarship endowment with the outrageous goal of raising $150,000. The fund grew incrementally through donations, sponsorships, and peeling a portion of revenue off the top of every event the Chapter hosted. The responsibility was passed from one slate of leaders to the next over the years. It has taken more than a decade, but under the leadership of the current Chapter President, the endowment crested its goal. In 2016, the Jerry Finger Foundation Scholarship from the Wharton Club of Houston was established to provide perpetual scholarships to graduate and undergraduate students from the Houston community.[34] What an amazing milestone for a small group of dedicated alumni to achieve. What a legacy to leave!

Scholarship funds are wonderful ways to access a Chapter's common ground to positively impact a young person, the community, and your alma mater. With many annually funded scholarship minimums beginning at $500 or $1,000, it is easy to get started.

The Texas Exes, the Ex-Students' Association of the University of Texas, supporting 450,000+ alumni around the world through 140+ chapters and networks,[35] makes a significant collective contribution to scholarships. In the 2015–2016 academic year, the Chapters contributed roughly $462,000 to the scholarship fund. The money was raised locally and was awarded right back to the communities from which it was donated.[36]

It may be worth mentioning here that operating an active scholarship program also may help 501(c)(3)-designated Chapters maintain compliance with their charitable purpose of supporting education. Conversely, some Chapters are restricted from raising scholarship money. Be certain to talk with your Chapter's liaison before acting on any such plans.

When it is time for your Chapter to engage in funding scholarships, there are budgeting considerations to acknowledge. Not only does the scholarship fund goal need to be raised but also the costs of the process. Maybe the funds will be raised through sales of items such as T-shirts. Then, costs such as generating the design, buying and printing the shirts, and mailing them to the purchasers should be captured. Maybe your Chapter is embarking on something a bit more ambitious, such as a golf tournament or an auction; then, for the event itself, all inputs need to be line-itemed through budgeting, including giveaways, catering, promotion, and much more.

- **Local third-party charity** – Chapters may also seek to make a contribution in support of a local charity. Raising the money for a charity fund is logistically very similar to how a Chapter would budget for and raise a scholarship fund, discussed above. It is not at all uncommon for a Chapter to either commit to a partner charity or rotate partner charities on some predetermined schedule. There are no rules as to how charities are selected by alumni Chapters; however, there does seem to be a trend to support educational efforts such as reading programs as well as child-focused organizations like the Boys & Girls Clubs of America.

The Kellogg Network DFW, one of ninety Chapters[37] serving 60,000+ business school alumni[38] of the Kellogg School of Management at Northwestern University, provides an outstanding example of a Chapter making a significant difference for a charity in addition to its own university. It has raised money for Big Brothers Big Sisters of America for the past eleven years by throwing a uniquely themed costume party each year, featuring a casino night and the roaring twenties themes on two occasions. In the inaugural year, they raised and donated $1,000, followed by $1,500 in year two. Flash forward nine years to the fall of 2016; the Chapter was thrilled to announce that the Mardi Gras–themed event raised an amazing $53,000![39]

Dartmouth College Office of Alumni Relations affords its 78,000 alumni through nearly one hundred regional clubs and affiliated and shared-interest groups[40] the opportunity to financially support third-party charities, especially if Chapters can do so while still championing the college's mission and values. It has this to say to its Chapters on the subject:

> Organizations [Chapters] should focus on fundraising efforts that support the organization of Dartmouth. Organizations may also raise funds for other organizations where it is consistent with the organization's nonprofit purpose and IRS regulations, especially where the fund-raising activity serves a dual purpose of bringing together organization alumni (such as the Dartmouth Association of the Rocky Mountains bicycling team's efforts to fundraise for local charities).[41]

One last example I could not ignore revolves around the Arizona State University (ASU) Alumni Association, serving more than 400,000 alumni through 170+ academic, international, geographic, and special interest groups.[42] The ASU Alumni Association and its Chapters are strong supporters of Pat's Run, the 4.2-mile signature fundraising event of the Pat Tillman Foundation (PTF), which provides academic scholarships to military veterans and their spouses to various academic institutions. Before diving into the numbers, this is an especially unique relationship that is worth better understanding.

Pat Tillman was an outstanding athlete, scholar, and patriot. As a linebacker, he helped lead ASU to the 1997 Rose Bowl after an undefeated season, earned three consecutive selections to the Pac-10 All-Academic Football Team, and was a 1st team Academic All-American honor, as well as the NCAA's Post-Graduate Scholarship recipient for academic and athletic excellence. He then went on to play professional football for the Cardinals and broke the franchise record for tackles in 2000. As a scholar, he graduated Summa Cum Laude from ASU's W. P. Carey School of Business, graduating in only three and a half years. As a patriot in the wake of the September 11, 2001 attack, he placed his NFL career on hold to enlist in the US Army. He was assigned to the second battalion of the 75th Ranger Regiment in Fort Lewis, Washington, with whom he served tours in Iraq and in Afghanistan. On April 22, 2004, he died when his unit was ambushed. His family created the PTF in honor of his life and to further his commitment to others.[43]

The year 2016 marked the twelfth anniversary of Pat's Run, which is held in Tempe, Arizona, each April with Shadow Runs (also called Tillman Honor Runs), sponsored by the ASU Alumni Association and held across the country, largely by alumni Chapters of ASU. Over 36,000 people participated in Tempe, while the Chapters hosted thirty-two Shadow Runs with a total of 2,600 participants that raised $50,000 for the Pat Tillman Foundation and Tillman Scholars. To date, $14 million has been raised to support 460 scholars at over one hundred academic institutions in which recipients have maintained a 3.6 average GPA.[44]

Although the above examples are inspiring and tug at your heartstrings, do not rush out to make it happen, since not all Chapters are permitted to raise cash for third parties. If the Chapter's college or university is also a tax-deductible nonprofit entity, as it is likely to be, it would not be surprising to learn that raising money for a third-party nonprofit could be seen as a conflict of interest. Accordingly, some alumni associations expressly restrict Chapters from doing so.

As a clarification, if this restriction exists, it applies specifically to raising cash money for other charities, not to donating time or skills. I have yet to see any restrictions on performing charitable acts in the community or on behalf of a third-party charity, such as collecting blankets for the homeless with the Salvation Army or painting a house with Habitat for Humanity.

Among many colleges and universities, the University of Delaware Office of Development and Alumni Relations,[45] serving 170,000 alumni through its thirty+ Chapters,[46] is one such entity that restricts Chapters from raising cash for third-party charities. Another is the University of Tennessee Knoxville (UT Knoxville) Alumni Association, serving 235,000 alumni and sixty-three alumni groups.[47] Its Chapter handbook provides clear direction on the matter by stating:

> Many alumni participate in a wide array of service-oriented activities in their local communities. A chapter is encouraged to lead such activities and may also invite chapter members to be part of a hands-on local effort like a Habitat for Humanity build, staffing a 5K race, or volunteering at an animal shelter. However, a chapter may not sponsor or host an event, raise money for, or direct any chapter funds or event proceeds to another charitable organization.[48]

The Tulane Alumni Association (TAA), founded in 1898 and serving 125,000 alumni[49] through more than sixty clubs globally,[50] is also in the same situation, stating:

> While we encourage Clubs to plan or participate in activities that benefit their communities, Tulane Clubs cannot sponsor or participate in events that raise funds for organizations other than Tulane University.[51]

If your Chapter is considering adding something like this to its program, be certain to gain approval from the alumni association and set reasonable expectations. It takes some time to get it off the ground, but the rewards can be well worth the effort and wait.

Each of these options presented above is visible to the alumni and factors into their perceptions of how likely they might be to participate in the future or even take on leadership roles. The higher the quality and the more organized the events, the easier it is to recruit speakers and volunteers and to generate high participation levels.

Behind-the-Scenes Enhancements

Also under the umbrella of stepping up the professionalism would be several infrastructure items addressing liability protection for the leadership;

improving operational efficiencies, including accounting, banking, and credit card processing; attendance at the alumni leaders conference; notable tax issues; easing the burdens on officers with administrative assistance and SACL support; and making recruiting and retaining leaders far more successful. Here are a few top priority topics to consider:

- **Insurance** – This is very important and often overlooked by Chapter volunteers. If the central alumni association's liability insurance does not specifically cover volunteer Chapter leaders during Chapter activities, then the liability falls to the individual leader's personal insurance. For example, this would include an alcohol-related event after someone who had been drinking leaves an alumni activity or damage that occurs to the venue during an event.

  Gratefully, many alumni associations provide some degree of coverage, most often when the Chapter is a legal subordinate of the association. As expected, such policies are laced with criteria only under which the coverage is effective. The criteria are generally reasonable, such as the leaders maintaining membership in the alumni association and operating within the bounds of established policies. If an insurance policy exists that covers your Chapter, leaders, and / or members, become familiar with it as soon as possible. There are likely to be a variety of circumstances under which the Chapter may want to operate yet might be excluded from coverage. If no such coverage is available, it is advisable to seek immediate guidance on insurance issues.

  From personal experience, our Wharton Club of Dallas–Fort Worth leadership team came too close to facing this issue firsthand when I was acting club President. We threw a summer picnic for the local alumni and their families that was exceptionally well attended by nearly 175 people. The picnic took place on the ranch property of an alumnus, where we offered swimming, a petting zoo, fishing, and horseback riding, along with a proper Texas barbeque. In spite of it being 104° F that day, the entire event was an amazing success with only one hiccup—one person fell off of a horse. Most importantly, she was not injured beyond some bruising. I was gratefully breathing a sigh of relief until another asked if she was going to take legal action against the club. My heart seemed to stop, and shivers shot up my spine as it dawned on me that we were an independent Chapter and did not have any insurance in place.

  Fortunately, the horseback rider healed just fine and did not pursue any action against the club or any other party. If she had, it would have fallen to the personal liability of most certainly me, the club President, and likely the other officers and the homeowner. Shortly thereafter, we established an insurance policy and have never let it lapse!

If no university or association coverage exists—most certainly the case with independent Chapters—or if found in non-compliance with university policies, liability exposures for a person participating in nonprofit organizations may be covered under that person's homeowner's policy with increased limits under a personal umbrella liability policy. It would be a good idea to confirm you are covered. Consider this situation: litigation is brought against not the Chapter but a specific Chapter leader, and that leader was found guilty of gross negligence, willful misconduct, or being not in compliance with the university's policies. In this situation, there could be personal liability. If that Chapter leader is you, your personal insurance needs to measure up.

Consider another scenario. Among the functions, events, and services provided by the University of Nebraska's Nebraska Alumni Association (NAA) is a well-documented, clearly written guide on its impressive insurance coverage—for which it should be commended. Although it may be one of the most comprehensive policies this author has seen, there are still situations in which a Chapter or leader may not be covered. For example, events in which the venue cannot supply a certificate of insurance would not be covered—such as events in parks, on boats, or at a private residence. In this situation, the Chapter would be required to purchase event-specific insurance, often referred to as special events liability. Further, the wonderful NAA insurance coverage does not apply to Chapters that are established as their own independent 501(c)(3) organizations. The NAA does provide guidelines for insurance requirements for such Chapters, however.[52]

Returning back to my experience with the Wharton Club of Dallas–Fort Worth and the picnic, even if I had been the President of the local NAA Chapter with its full liability coverage, we still would not have been covered. The incident took place at the home of an alumnus, falling into one of the standard policy gaps noted above. We would have needed an additional special events liability policy specifically for the picnic.

Insurance coverage is a real consideration for alumni Chapters of the Louisiana State University (LSU) Alumni Association, supporting more than 130 geographic and academic Chapters[53] and nearly 225,000 alumni[54] as well. The alumni association states:

> The LSU Alumni Association and University maintain independent general liability insurance policies. These policies do not provide coverage to the officers, members or volunteers of recognized Alumni Chapters or events hosted by such Chapters in any way.[55]

This is not an unusual situation, and the clarity of the LSU Alumni Association's position and the situation is to be commended. Its policy document goes on to say that although general liability insurance is not required, it is recommended. If the Chapter chooses not to maintain an active policy, the LSU Alumni Association does require event-specific insurance on an as-needed basis.[56]

The Chapter leaders of the 249 Harvard Clubs and shared-interest groups in more than eighty countries around the world[57] fall into the same situation as those of the Wharton School and LSU. Chapters and their leadership are independent organizations and are not covered by any university or alumni association insurance policies. Of the universities taking this approach, the Harvard Alumni Association (HAA) has the most comprehensive explanation and guidance document for Chapters I have seen. Within its club officer handbook, Chapter leaders can learn of ways to handle events in someone's home, as well as how to extend coverage of existing third-party and vendor policies to include the Chapter at no additional cost. It even provides guidance for related vendor contract requirements and negotiations.[58] Nonetheless, any costs associated with annual policies or special event liability still fall to the discretion and budget of the Chapter.

The conversation here has focused largely on general liability insurance; however, I would be remiss if I did not mention directors and officers liability (D&O) insurance. This is a policy that protects the Chapter and its officers from claims alleging failure or negligence by an officer in carrying out his duties as a representative of the Chapter. Make this topic a point of discussion when exploring your Chapter needs.

As can be seen, insurance is an important issue and operational cost consideration for nearly everyone. Whether a solid liability policy exists that seemingly covers the Chapter or the Chapter is completely on its own, there are various gaps that need assessed and addressed. Luckily, this is an issue easily remedied by a little operational cash.

Do not wait until it is too late. Make liability insurance of highest priority. Determine if the central alumni association has insurance that covers the volunteer leaders, and check on the coverage of Chapter members while you are at it. If the association has such a policy, request a copy of the language and ensure you are comfortable with the coverage for you and your team. If there is no umbrella policy or if the existing one is inadequate from your perspective, make it a priority to right the situation.

Insurance policies vary in coverage limits, inclusion / exclusion criteria, breadth of coverage and pricing. From the perspective of budgeting, use $1,000 annually as a placeholder for general liability with D&O coverage. Depending on your Chapter's needs and activities, it could be a lower or higher, but $1,000 is a reasonable place to start. With respect to special events liability insurance, it may range from roughly $250 to about $500. Do note that special event liability is just that—only general liability. It does not typically contain D&O components. Thus, a special event liability policy is not a more economical equivalent substitution for an annual D&O and general liability policy. These are not absolute numbers, merely rough guidelines as you prepare your first draft of the expenses to budget. There is further discussion on this topic in the next section, titled *"Coveted Resources from the Central Alumni Association: Glorious Insurance Coverage."*

- **Accounting software** – This is more important for any Chapters that are required to track and / or manage their own finances, especially if they must complete their own state and federal tax or information filings. The more active a Chapter becomes, the more transactions it will incur, and thus the greater need to organize and be able to reference several years back if necessary. An Excel spreadsheet is an option, and it is certainly the least expensive approach. If your Chapter is not actively performing financial transactions, this might be sufficient.

  For those with a little more activity or more reporting responsibility, there are a few options available today with the basic functionality required by a Chapter that are either free or very cost effective. For any Chapter, including one designated as a nonprofit, there are online tools available for anywhere from no cost to about $15 per month.

- **Bank account fees** – A bank account will be important if the Chapter intends to manage money and / or raise income for its own use. If your Chapter has or plans to open a standard checking account, be aware of the minimums required to initiate and maintain the account. Additionally, understand what penalty fees could be assessed, such as falling below a minimum balance, too much or too little activity, or triggering an overdraft transfer. Do not forget to include these possibilities when budgeting. Managing potential fees is not difficult or cost prohibitive; in fact, most are avoidable. Just be aware of the details and incorporate them into your budget.

Some alumni associations have made arrangements with a financial institution on behalf of their Chapters. One benefit of this arrangement is that typically the monthly fees are waived. Although the fee structure might be reduced to be more palatable for Chapters, it is almost certainly not eliminated. Other fees, such as overdraft fees, may still apply. Keep this in mind as the Chapter develops its expense side of the budget.

The Stanford Alumni Association (SAA) handles bank accounts this way as one option for Chapters. It is partnered with the Stanford Federal Credit Union (SFCN) to offer banking without monthly fees, and it provides debit cards to minimize the need for reimbursements to Chapter leaders and others. As an additional benefit, the required account statements can be automatically sent to the SAA rather than the Chapters having to take responsibility for that step. Although the SAA Chapters are encouraged to take advantage of the arrangement, they are not bound to do so. A Chapter is free to choose any banking partner, as long as the association's signatory and financial guidelines are met.[59] If it does choose another bank, additional fees may be assessed and should be budgeted.

Brigham Young University (BYU) Alumni Association, serving 412,000 alumni[60] and 300 Chapters,[61] provides some guidance related to avoiding fees when setting up a bank account. It states that when a bank account can be established, the Chapter should

> try to find an alumnus who works in the banking industry that might waive the fees for a chapter account, or seek an institution that will waive the fees for a small, non-profit entity.[62]

Further, beyond the standard bank accounts for handling largely cash and checks, there may be a need for a merchant bank account to support accepting credit and debit cards. More about credit cards below.

- **Credit card processing fees** – Should your Chapter support (or plan to support) the use of credit cards to pay for things such as event registration tickets online or at the door, it is important to understand the costs to do so. It is possible that credit card processing is handled by the central association on the Chapter's behalf. If so, the processing fees may or may not be passed through to the Chapter.

In the case of the Arkansas Alumni Association (AAA), it will set up an event registration page on behalf of the Chapter to process credit card registrations. It is important to factor into the budget that use of this central online event registration system carries a cost of 5 percent to be paid by the Chapter to cover the processing and merchant account fees.[63]

The Chapters of the Texas State Alumni Association, serving its 170,000+ alumni,[64] experience a different situation. The alumni association specifically states it will "incur any applicable credit card fees" on behalf of the Chapters for event payments and donations made through the provided association website.[65] Binghamton University (also known as State University of New York [SUNY] at Binghamton) Alumni Association, catering to nearly 120,000 alumni through thirty+ Chapters,[66] also absorbs the credit card processing fees on behalf of the Chapters.[67]

If the Chapter rather than the alumni association is responsible for establishing and maintaining accounts for accepting credit cards, likely both a merchant account (mentioned above) and a gateway provider will be necessary. It is important to keep in mind how much of the incoming revenue is being syphoned off by the vendor to cover processing costs.

This process is much easier today than it was even just two years ago. In some situations, both accounts are offered by the same vendor. Typically, the fees include a percentage of the amount transacted and / or a flat fee per transaction, plus possibly a set-up fee and / or monthly fees. Somewhere around 3–6 percent of revenue is likely to be lost in the process. That is an often-overlooked line item when budgeting.

If you are using an event management website to gain access to a credit card processing option, you have just added yet another vendor to the mix. It is quite possible that the Chapter is paying an additional 3 percent on top of the actual processing fees when using this method. Read the fine print. The combined fees could reach 10 percent or more.

Some credit card processing and online event management vendors offer discounts for 501(c)(3)-recognized organizations. If your Chapter qualifies, take the time to ask about special pricing. For a more detailed evaluation of online and credit card processing issues, look to the section dedicated to *Collecting and Handling the Money* later in this text.

- **Alumni leaders conference (ALC)** – ALCs are not universally offered by all alumni associations to all volunteer alumni leaders, and the ones that do exist vary in audience, intensity, size, and frequency. If the opportunity to attend one is available, do not miss out! These events are true gifts to any committed alumni volunteer and his or her Chapter. Participation enhances the relationship with the alumni association, strengthens affinity with the educational institution, and expands knowledge of available resources and programs—all yielding smoother Chapter operation and Chapter leader retention. It also provides a Chapter leader with much needed moral support and camaraderie with those sharing the same passion and pain.

  As these events are typically held on campus once or twice a year during the week, the majority of Chapter leaders will be required to travel and will likely need to take time off of work. ALCs can run from a half day to three days and may include networking and social events in addition to training. They often leverage a campus event of significance such as homecoming—making the time all in from two to four days. The audience might be as narrowly defined as only Chapter leaders or exceptionally broad, encompassing affinity club leaders, board members, athletic support groups, students, and more.

  With respect to budgeting, your Chapter should be aware of travel costs and registration fees. Assistance with travel expenses varies significantly from none to complete reimbursement, while registration costs tend to be small, ranging from zero to about $100.

  With respect to travel expenses, specifically transit costs, the majority of alumni associations do not offer any financial assistance. Those that do are in the minority. However, a couple such minority alumni associations and their approaches to reimbursement are mentioned in the next section, *"Coveted Resources from the Central Alumni Association."* If you are not aware of your alumni association's reimbursement policy, start by assuming the Chapter will be required to pick up all travel costs. The budget can be revised when more details are known or confirmed.

  The second type of payment that may be incurred is a conference registration fee. Most colleges and universities that offer ALCs do not require payment to attend; however, some do. In general, the registration fees that are charged tend to be minimal. For example, registration for the Wisconsin Alumni Association's (WAA) Building Badger Leaders Conference includes a small $50 fee for the day-and-a-half event that takes place in late October or November.[68]

Alumni association members of the National Historically Black Colleges and Universities Alumni Associations (NHBCUAA), such as Bowie State University National Alumni Association (BSUNAA), serving 30,000 alumni through fifteen+ regional and affinity groups,[69] participate in a collective Alumni Leaders Conference. It is sponsored by the NHBCUAA and hosted by a different member campus each year. Volunteer leaders of the member schools experience two full days of targeted programming annually in August right before the fall semester kicks off. This event carries a registration fee of $95 for members and $125 for non-members.[70]

As the BSUNAA places a high priority on providing support and guidance to its alumni leaders, it also hosts its own Alumni Leaders Conference each year in addition to the collective event described above. Chapters will also want to budget $75 per Chapter leader for the BSUNAA leaders event.[71]

I am a true believer in the value and importance of attending your alumni association's ALC. I also feel it is appropriate for the Chapter to cover expenses not covered or reimbursed by the alumni association, as the volunteer is already sacrificing personal and, possibly, professional time. For budgeting purposes, assess the out-of-pocket costs to attend, multiply it by the number of Chapter leaders your Chapter plans to send, and then subtract expenses reimbursed by the alumni association. That should be a good place to start. This topic is further explored in the next section, titled "*Coveted Resources from the Central Alumni Association.*"

- **State and / or federal taxes** – If your Chapter is a full subordinate of the alumni association or is a recognized independent, nonprofit, tax-exempt organization at the state and federal levels that does not generate any unrelated business income, you can skip this bullet. Otherwise, this might be a line item to budget. There are two situations in which a Chapter would incur income tax: if it is a taxable entity (not recognized as nonprofit or tax exempt) or if it is tax exempt but the revenue generated is classified as "unrelated business income."

  For example, the Purdue Alumni Association, serving alumni through seventy-five regional clubs,[72] is clear with its Chapters. It shares that it is a nonprofit, tax-exempt organization that pays taxes on income from activities unrelated to its tax-exempt status. It further clarifies the following for Chapters:

Local alumni clubs are not part of the legal entity known as the Purdue Alumni Association, and thus are not tax-exempt by virtue of having a relationship with the Association or the University.[73]

This is a challenging topic due to the various state regulations and legal relationships between the Chapter and the association, so I will direct you to a section found near the end of the book entitled "*State and Federal Tax Implications*" for more information. For now, just realize that state and federal income tax may be applicable and might factor into the Chapter budgeting.

- **State and federal filings** – Several central alumni associations allow or even encourage Chapters to become independent, nonprofit, federally recognized, tax-exempt organizations. Of the 501(c) tax-exempt IRS options, Chapters typically fall into either a 501(c)(3) charitable organization or a 501(c)(7) social organization designation based on their mission and guidance from the alumni association. A more thorough introduction of the state and federal filing process can be found in the later sections "*Collecting and Handling the Money*" and "*State and Federal Tax Implications.*" So as not to be repetitive, I will focus solely on a brief and high-level review of the steps with cost implications here.

    From a budgeting perspective, a Chapter seeking tax exemption federally and with the state (two different steps) will first need to file with the state to become a legal nonprofit entity. Such filings have a fee but tend to be small. In Texas, it costs approximately $25 to file the Certificate of Formation,[74] while in New York the fees for reserving the name and filing the Certificate of Incorporation will cost a total of $85.[75] Florida requirements state that designating a registered agent and filing the Not for Profit Articles of Incorporation will total $70—more if additional paperwork is requested by the Chapter.[76]

    There is no fee for any organization when taking the next step of filing an IRS Employer Identification Number (EIN) application, regardless of the state in which the Chapter resides. (See later section "*Collecting and Handling the Money*" for more information on EINs.) As such, we will move on.

    The next fees assessed will be associated with filing either the IRS Form 1023 or the Form 1023-EZ to apply for a 501(c)(3) designation or IRS Form 1024 for a 501(c)(7) designation.[77] Fees are the same for both designations and are based on the Chapter's recent income above or below $10,000. If below that threshold, the charge will be $400; otherwise, pencil in $850.[78] There is one lovely exception. The IRS will waive the need to request a 501(c)(3) determination letter and the fee altogether for Chapters that receive less than $5,000 annually. The Chapter may simply declare its status.[79] More about tax-exemption status and issues can be found in the later section "*State and Federal Tax Implications: 501(c)(3) vs. 501(c)(7) and Tax Deductible Donations.*"

It may be necessary to circle back to the state with your Chapter's shiny new IRS designation letter to qualify for certain state tax exemptions, such as sales tax or other taxes. If so, there may be an additional small fee. This will likely not be more than another $100. Altogether (state nonprofit, federal tax-exemption, and state tax-exemption filings), using either $550 or $1,050 based on income might be a reasonable placeholder for the actual filing fees.

If your 501(c)-designated Chapter intends to send quite a bit of postal mail for which the postage is not covered by the alumni association, it may wish to consider applying for reduced nonprofit postage rates. The process requires a designated post office and adherence to multiple postal mail qualifications, including size, maximum weight, and minimum number of pieces, as well as an additional filing fee of approximately $175. This option is really only attractive to large Chapters sending more than one large mailing per year.

In addition to the initial filing fees, look into any ongoing state filing fees or fees to make changes to documents already filed. Some states will require an annual filing payment related to taxes, for example, even if no taxes are to be paid. In the State of Illinois, a Chapter would need to pay $10 to file its Annual Report.[80] The same $10 amount applies to the California Annual Information Return, but only for Chapters with income over some threshold from $50,000 to $75,000 based on number of years the Chapter has existed. Otherwise, no filing or fee is necessary.[81]

Regarding change fees, some states may charge fees for making changes to the organizing documents, for the change of a registered agent, or for other changes to what is already officially on file regarding the Chapter. For example, the State of Florida charges $35 to remove a director from the filings[82] and another $35 to change the registered agent.[83] If the Chapter is in Kentucky, the fee for changing the registered agent is $10, as is the fee for changing the official address of the Chapter.[84]

Do not forget to factor in any additional professional service-related fees, including legal and / or tax guidance if your Chapter should incur them. In most cases, your Chapter should not need to seek paid outside assistance. Between guidance from the alumni association and any local alumni with the right skill set, your Chapter should be set. The costs related to nonprofit formation and tax-exempt designations may be well worth the long-term benefits (presented later).

Please note that content presented here is in no way intended to substitute for professional legal and tax guidance regarding any topic addressed or the decision itself to seek a federal tax-exempt designation. A very narrow light was shined on only the immediate, high-level elements that incur fees for budgeting purposes. There are many more considerations, including compliance and annual reporting requirements that must be evaluated prior to making any decisions. This discussion purely provides some basic information to initiate and formulate questions for a formal session with a professional.

- **Remote administrative services** – Wow! This service has the potential to be one of the most important factors in recruiting—and, more importantly, retaining—Chapter leadership. So much of Chapter management is simply administrative in nature—and a terrible time sink for those with families, jobs, and community involvement. Gathering RSVPs, coordinating with a venue, making the check-in list and name badges, taking and distributing the meeting minutes, responding to inquiries, and so much more represent the details that are necessary to execute an event worthy of your alumni. However, they also represent the busy work eating up vast sums of time and driving away otherwise willing volunteers. Luckily, outsourcing is an option to handle the administrivia, enabling the volunteers to focus on strategy and building relationships . . . for a long time to come.

  Recently, I heard a declaration made by one Chapter officer, who wishes to remain nameless, who during a monthly officer meeting stated, "Without this [admin] support, I cannot do this anymore." That was the final straw before that Chapter adopted this outsourcing approach.

  Remote administration is a service that I engaged when leading the local Wharton Club of Dallas–Fort Worth and then later introduced to the Dallas Business Club. And I am not the only one—not by a long shot. Many, many Chapters have adopted this strategy due to the undeniable results—a more enjoyable, sustainable experience by leadership and a higher quality experience for attendees when the Is are dotted and the Ts are crossed. According to Harvard Alumni Association (HAA) Chapter best-practices documentation, 23 percent of their Chapters engage a paid administrator.[85]

The United States Naval Academy Alumni Association (USNAAA) of North Texas now uses an administrator for a number of services, including assistance with monthly speaker lunches. The USNAAA of North Texas is one of more than 250 chapters, clubs, and organizations under the United States Naval Academy Alumni Association umbrella, serving 60,000 alumni.[86]

The North Texas Chapter's Vice President of Programs focuses on identifying and securing outstanding speakers through his network, welcoming attendees, performing the introductions, building relationships with and among alumni, and guiding the administrator's activity for the lunches. In partnership with the Chapter VP, the administrator performs the background tasks that do not require the VP's special knowledge, credibility, or relationships. She secures the annual schedule with the venue; generates, posts, and distributes approved announcements / invitations; responds to inquiries from alumni; keeps Chapter leadership apprised of registrations; coordinates the seating, AV, and patriotic requirements with the venue; prepares the check-in list; arrives onsite to welcome attendees and process payments (cash, checks, and credit cards) at the door; takes pictures throughout the event; reviews the invoice for accuracy prior to passing to the VP for signature; deposits cash and checks at the bank; and prepares the first draft of the event summary for the next announcement, among other miscellaneous tasks to make the event a success. The experience enables the VP to consider taking on broader program responsibilities and affords him more time to schedule events further in advance. It has also spurred many positive comments from alumni regarding the improved professionalism and flow of the events. In particular, the alumni really appreciate spending time with the Chapter VP, when, in the past, the VP could not mingle while performing the necessary check-in and administrative responsibilities.[87]

When choosing an administrator, there are a few considerations to keep in mind—and one or two that might incur a cost. Make sure you know who he or she is. If working with a company that provides such services, the administrative resources are more likely to have been vetted and background checked. Confirm this assumption. This is important, as the administrator will likely have access to sensitive demographic, contact and / or financial information for your alumni in order to perform the tasks of the job. The Nebraska Alumni Association (NAA) feels that knowing who the person is that will have access to sensitive information is so important that it even performs background checks on new Chapter leaders.[88] Hats off to them for taking the responsibility to protect the alumni and their confidential data this seriously.

If the administrative person is independent, perform the background check yourself—and budget in that cost (or pass the cost through to the administrator), roughly $55. Know the person you are trusting with highly sensitive, confidential information.

Determine when the resource will be available to you. Will he or she be accessible and available on the weekend? In the early morning? Late at night? Can you reach them by cell phone or only via e-mail? Most Chapter events are executed outside of typical working hours, as are most Chapter planning meetings. Will the administrator be available when you need him or her to be? Can they be on the officer meeting calls Saturday morning at 8:00 a.m. in your time zone when you meet?

It is important to know the backup plans for administrator absence. If it is a company with whom your Chapter is partnering, then there are likely to be backup options available for when someone is on vacation or suddenly takes ill. If the administrator is an independent contractor, the contingency plan is all that much more important to establish up front. Be transparent with your needs and plans so that such gaps might be identified well in advance where possible.

What are the administrator's qualifications? Is he or she experienced with working remotely? How versed might they be on the website platform your Chapter uses? Is there much depth in social media communications? Have they worked with alumni Chapters previously? Have other organizations or companies trusted this person with access to sensitive information? Can the resource provide references? These are good questions to start the conversation. As this person will be working remotely without supervision much or all of the time, you will want to be confident in your selection.

What about payment? Does the administrator require a contract, such as an annual agreement? Might there be a minimum number of hours per month required? What happens if those hours are not used, such as during the summer months? Are they lost, or can they be "rolled over"? Ensure that your Chapter is getting the service it needs in a way that is most convenient for the Chapter. Chapter funding does not fall from trees, so be mindful when using it.

Stepping back a moment, it is important to coordinate this addition to the team with the central alumni association. If a third party will be servicing the Chapter, the association should be aware of the type of activities and access they will have. It is possible there will not be any issues at all, or maybe the administrator will simply be asked to sign paperwork agreeing to uphold applicable policies, such as those related to confidential information. Regardless, keep your Chapter liaison in the loop.

From a budgeting standpoint, start small and consider the number of events planned and how much time would be helpful. Keep in mind things like whether they will be needed at Chapter leadership meetings (likely via phone or Internet), either to simply take notes for distribution or also to help keep them current on plans and what will be needed. I rarely run across an alumni association that does not require or request that meeting minutes are documented, distributed, and filed. If so, calculate the meeting time into the overall need. Should the Chapter wish to take this service to the next level and require physical presence for meeting check-in, bank deposits, and errands, factor that cost in as well.

It may seem like these are lots of questions; however, they are largely common sense. The relief such a service provides when well executed by a trusted resource is beyond expectations. I would suggest that remote administrative services is another high-priority item that is well worth the cost to improve the operation of the Chapter and events, and it directly leads to more successful leadership recruiting and retention. As this relationship would ideally continue for some time, it is also worth the one-time, up-front effort to get it right. References can help immeasurably—just reach out; I am here to help.

- **Travel** – It is not too often that travelling happens on the Chapter's dime; however, there are two cases in which it might: when bringing in an out-of-town speaker or when sending Chapter representatives to an annual or periodic central association leaders workshop such as discussed above. The vast majority of Chapters do not pay speakers for their time nor require them to travel in from out of town. When that does happen, it is often under the coordination of the central alumni association and on its tab. On the rare occasion that an amazing opportunity presents itself and a

Chapter wishes to bring someone in who requires travel reimbursement, the Chapter may need funds in the bank to cover it.

There are a few opportunities to receive coveted financial support from the alumni association for travel, such as in the case with Penn State Alumni Association, founded in 1870 and serving 658,000 alumni. Today, the chapters and affiliate groups number more than 300[89] with a membership of 175,000+.[90] The Penn State Alumni Association does specifically offer speaker grants to Chapters. According to their guidelines, travel expenses and honoraria for speakers are the responsibility of the Chapter. However, it will provide assistance up to $500 each year to help offset some of the expense.[91]

- **Membership in the Society for Alumni Club Leadership (SACL)** – SACL has been developed *by* experienced alumni Chapter leaders *for* alumni Chapter leaders and associations. It offers important back-office infrastructure and instruction, such as a Chapter server, guidance documentation, sample documents and ready-to-use templates, remote Chapter administration support, credit card processing, and so very much more.

  By default, alumni of academic institutions are educated and intelligent. They are only missing the infrastructure and guidance to make the nonprofit, alumni, volunteer leadership experience truly enjoyable and sustainable. SACL provides just that. Building SACL access into the budget early on will yield a significantly easier plan to operate a more enjoyable and more successful Chapter. Access to SACL's subscription-based services varies by level of support, starting with a basic access for free and spanning several levels of increasing support. In general, most Chapters should find that their needs could be met for less than $10 a month.

Determining the costs of running your Chapter at the level your leadership team deems appropriate is an excellent budget-building exercise that should be executed as a team, gaining buy-in and commitment from each of the leaders. Although the ideas presented here do not generate an exhaustive list, they provide some of the most important infrastructure considerations for today and tomorrow.

To support your efforts and help get the process started, a broad template for budgeting, the **Chapter Budgeting Template**, is available to those purchasing this book. Reference the appendix titled *"Free SACL Tools and Resources Available for Readers"* for instructions on how to access it.

Most likely, the Chapter will not be able to afford everything it would like to today, nor may it have the authority to do so. Developing the expense component of a budget reflecting the Chapter's ultimate goals is a place to start. Planning a complete budget and working with the alumni association is an iterative process. The information in the next sections will provide many ideas of how to operate the Chapter and raise the funds to meet any goals. By blending some of the ideas presented with your own, develop a graduated plan to bridge from today to the ultimate goal over a period of several years.

60-Second Takeaway

Although operating a local alumni Chapter can be done on a shoestring, access to a bit more capital can greatly improve the breadth and quality of activities, ease the burden on volunteers, enhance the Chapter's reputation, and increase participation. Beyond the essentials, a website and communication tool rank among the most notable needs.

When the Chapter leadership is ready to take it to the next level, speaker gifts, holiday parties, and scholarship awards can help increase professionalism and participation. Internally, very important considerations include insurance, bank accounts, ability to accept credit card payments, the alumni leaders workshop, income tax, nonprofit tax-exemption filings, travel, and outsourced administrative assistance. The support of SACL becomes important for guidance and streamlining day-to-day operations, as well as more successful recruiting and retention of volunteer leadership.

Additional services will be necessary to help the Chapter grow and mature as an organization, nearly all at a cost. It is advisable to develop a budget for the near term and also for the future, with a graduating plan bridging the two to achieve the Chapter's full potential, working in conjunction with the central alumni association.

Make It Happen Checklist

☐ Generate an initial schedule of anticipated Chapter events and activities over a specified time interval, ideally for the Chapter's official fiscal year. Include officer meetings, game-watching parties, speaker events, a holiday party, and any other plans. This will evolve as you progress through this book.

☐ Determine the Chapter's infrastructure, operational, and charitable goals for the short term and the long term.

☐ Discuss the initial plans and ideas with the central alumni association.

☐ Determine how much should be allocated for general office supplies, decorations, and meeting snacks.

☐ If a website presence is desired but not offered by the central alumni association, determine what level of functionality is appropriate and what it will cost.

☐ Determine if an e-mail distribution vendor is appropriate and the associated costs.

☐ Include any costs, such as travel or honoraria, for bringing speakers to the Chapter.

☐ Factor in the cost of anticipated speakers' gifts and door prizes.

☐ Establish the Chapter's scholarship funding goals, if any.

☐ Determine if the Chapter will support a third-party charity and to what financial level.

☐ Determine if and when general liability and D&O insurance is appropriate—or if gaps in existing policies require event-specific coverage. If so, gather quotes and select one.

☐ Assess the need and applicable cost for an accounting solution.

☐ Determine what, if any, banking fees should be covered in the budget.

☐ Evaluate and factor in expenses related to credit card processing and / or online event management fees.

☐ If the central alumni association offers an alumni leader conference, how many officers will the Chapter send? Determine the cost per person, considering economies of scale.

☐ Review your Chapter's federal and state tax status, along with the types of revenue it plans to generate, with a local tax professional to determine if income taxes will need to be paid.

☐ If the Chapter is free to do so, determine if it is the right step to convert to a nonprofit, tax-exempt organization at the state and federal levels. If so, build in the costs to complete the process. If already an independent entity recognized by the state and IRS, include anticipated annual filing costs.

☐ Evaluate if the Chapter might benefit from a Remote Chapter Assistant (RCA). If so, determine how much time the Chapter might be able to afford if built into the budget.

☐ Consider if and when a subscription to the SACL Chapter-support infrastructure and instructional guidance is appropriate. Evaluate the most advantageous plan. Possibly request that this service be offered to all Chapters through the alumni association.

☐ Leveraging the **Chapter Budgeting Template** made available as a gift to readers, craft an initial expense build-up to deliver the dream programs, incorporating the costs and plans outlined in the previous steps.

☐ Build a second, more achievable plan for the upcoming year.

☐ Complete the interim annual plans to bridge the two.

☐ Consider the information in the upcoming sections to refine the anticipated costs and develop the revenue plan necessary to meet or exceed the expense demands of each annual plan drafted.

☐ Do not overlook seeking professional guidance from tax and legal specialists where applicable.

Coveted Resources from the Central Alumni Association

Now that the Chapter has a more realistic grasp on several expenses likely to be important in growing alumni involvement, improving operations, and retaining leadership, it is time to build the plan to fund those goals!

The very first step is to determine what financial resources are already available from the central alumni association. Fortunately, incentives are aligned. Just as you are seeking to lead a thriving, active Chapter, it is also in the best interest of the association to have wildly successful Chapters throughout a large alumni network. Accordingly, the central alumni association often provides foundational and ongoing financial support in several ways. The most common include the following:

a. A Chapter liaison
b. Insurance coverage
c. A website platform
d. An annual stipend
e. Specialty and event funding grants
f. Collegiate-branded items
g. An annual leaders conference
h. Supplying occasional speakers, as well as other support

Of the types of support identified here, a couple deliver actual cash. However, as important as it is to capture revenue, it is equally important to minimize the actual cash outlay while not compromising on the goals or quality of operations. The additional methods of support do just that. They deliver the actual products, services, content, efficiencies, or reimbursement that would otherwise have required the Chapter's cash or labor.

To kick off the discussion, there is one item that is commonly offered to Chapters through the central alumni association: name tags. Sometimes these are provided already pre-printed with names, sometimes blank, and sometimes accompanying other support materials such as membership brochures and sign-in sheets. Many alumni associations, such as the American University (AU) Alumni Association, with its thirty-eight communities serving alumni living in all US states and territories, 160 countries, and on all seven continents (including Antarctica every now and then),[1] are prepared to make small items available to Chapters. Like many alumni associations, in addition to name tags, it will send banners, sign-in sheets, and giveaways for events when appropriate.[2]

It is worthy to note that alumni associations offer many other types of Chapter support, such as educational webinars and awards, to name a few. Not to discount those in any way, but this book is hyper-focused only on those products and services that have a direct impact on a Chapter's finances. Accordingly, the following discussions will only highlight such types of support and their relationship to the financial management of a Chapter.

The Chapter Liaison, Your Fairy Godparent

I position the Chapter liaison first and foremost because he or she is the Chapter leader's biggest supporter, advocate, and link to all things the central association has to offer—and often a friend. During my tenure as the Wharton Club of Dallas–Fort Worth President, we would never have become so successful, nor would it have been nearly as rewarding, if Laura Mack had not been such an unparalleled partner throughout the process. In spite of responsibility for more than seventy Chapters, she fought for resources that would enhance our ability to serve the alumni, organized and attended university speaker events each year for us, and always answered our calls—even in the evenings and on weekends.

The Chapter liaison is the voice for the volunteers with the central alumni association. When a few volunteers wish to start a Chapter or a Chapter wishes to advance its effectiveness, the Chapter liaison gets the process started and helps every step of the way. When an event needs to be supported, the liaison finds a way to make it happen.

The process works in reverse as well. When the alumni association wishes to pilot a new program or selects sites for a roadshow introducing a new chancellor, the liaison is who identifies and lobbies for certain Chapters. Their insights into the passion and activity in a certain region help formulate the recommendations. A deep appreciation and close relationship with your Chapter's liaison can most assuredly influence leadership morale and alumni association support.

The University of Kentucky (UK) Alumni Association, established in 1889, now caters to a worldwide alumni population of more than 275,000.[3] It recently conducted a survey of Chapter leadership to better understand the perceived value and importance of different functions and events. When asked to rank alumni club resources in order of importance, the respondents indicated that the staff liaison was the highest value.[4]

I would absolutely suggest getting to know your Chapter liaison personally, not as a simple resource. Take a true interest in him or her, learning what is important professionally and personally. Together, you can make the experience working side by side so much more rewarding—and cost-effective!

Glorious Insurance Coverage

Of the possible resources from the alumni association, this may be the most overlooked. The unexpected can happen at any time, and it is glorious if you and the Chapter are ready. Insurance does not tend to be a topic of interest—or even appreciated—until it is too late. Today, we are going to get ahead of this issue, donning a healthy respect and appropriate gratitude for this foundational gift.

Earlier, we spoke of the importance of general liability and directors and officers liability (D&O) coverage. If the Chapter is on its own with limited capital, these are the ones on which to focus. However, if the alumni association is involved, it is likely to have arranged an insurance policy that may contain more comprehensive coverage than a Chapter can easily afford. In addition to general liability, it may include D&O, commercial crime, commercial auto, and umbrella policies.

Regardless of the policy's custom build, if such an insurance policy is offered, all the Chapter leaders must do is comply with the related university, alumni association, and insurance guidelines and policies. That is the trick—compliance. Just because the liability policy exists does not mean that the situation at hand will qualify for university coverage and support. That being said, insurance coverage is a wonderful gift to the Chapter, and the terms of compliance are rarely unreasonable.

The General Alumni Association (GAA) of the University of North Carolina is one of the oldest university organizations to link former students to their alma mater. It was founded in 1843 and now supports more than 300,000 alumni[5] and ninety Carolina Clubs.[6] It is fitting that they are one such association that maintains a comprehensive commercial package, general liability insurance program that covers alumni association members while performing local Chapter activities. The insurance policy remains effective for any leaders as long as they are active members of the GAA and only if the university's operational policies are upheld.[7]

One such operational policy that must be upheld relates to alcoholic beverages at sanctioned alumni events. Among other requirements, the GAA stipulates that alcoholic beverages may only be served by a hired, qualified third party and that they may not be served "self-service" style, or by any uncontrolled means, or by any volunteer or staff person representing the GAA. Such policies vary somewhat from association to association, but you can bet that adherence to the alcoholic beverage policies will be absolutely required to qualify for coverage under any alumni association insurance policy.[8]

It is worth noting that the GAA expanded coverage to include spouses of qualifying leaders as well. The GAA does acknowledge that this insurance is not intended to replace any leader's personal liability coverage and encourages leaders to consult their own insurance agent.[9] This is good advice.

The University of Tennessee Knoxville (UT Knoxville) Alumni Association is another that provides coverage similar to that above. Alumni leaders and networks are covered under the University of Tennessee (UT) Foundation's general liability policy—as long as events are conducted in compliance with the UT Knoxville Office of Alumni Affairs alcohol policy, among others.[10]

The alumni association does a great job of explaining another important guideline regarding liability for Chapters. Like many other alumni associations, it requires that contracts entered into to provide services to a Chapter must be signed by an authorized signor of the UTFI, not by Chapter leaders. The alumni association states:

> One of the key reasons for this policy is to ensure that our alumni leaders are covered by UTFI policy.... The policy is for your protection as a chapter leader. It allows leaders and chapters to have counsel when being sued in regards to an event or function the chapter is hosting. ... Failing to honor a contract is called a "breach." In the event of a breach of contract, courts can award money damages or force you to abide by the contract's terms. You, personally, do not want the full responsibility by signing the contract. UTFI signing all contracts for chapters will help ensure that, if a breach occurs, the chapters will be covered through the foundation.[11]

The University of Chicago (UChicago) Alumni Association, representing its 150,000 alumni and sixty clubs and communities,[12] offers liability coverage for its Chapter leaders as well. In addition to general liability, it includes automobile liability and D&O insurance. The D&O policy covers

Chapter leadership from claims of negligence or failure by the officer to carry out his duties. This particular policy also covers charges of discrimination or harassment alleged by other volunteers, guests, or any third parties toward an officer.[13]

Insurance coverage is not something to take for granted. As a Chapter leader, be well versed at all times with all terms of such policies, and take extra pains to maintain compliance. In fact, this is so important it would be well worth the Chapter leadership's time to review the insurance and operational policies once a year so there are no questions or gaps in knowledge.

The Foundational Website Platform

The website platform is one of the most consistently valuable elements of support a central alumni association can provide. The website support can range from a simple listing of all Chapters, with the associated contact e-mail addresses, all the way through to a fully functional website encompassing alumni database integration, transactional capabilities, and a communication platform. One size does not fit all. The robustness of the website only needs to meet the demand from the alumni community, which varies significantly by college or university, and by Chapter, for that matter. We will look at three categories of website functionality: a directory-like listing; Chapter-specific informational Web page and website templates; and Chapter-specific, fully functional, interactive sites with transactional capabilities.

Many colleges and universities build their own, proprietary IT solution for the web, while others are becoming more comfortable with outsourcing to third-party vendors. Either way, the support is valuable.

The first category is when the association lists the Chapters along with any communication channels that Chapter might support. A visually effective example of this method is from the University of Connecticut (UCONN) Office of Alumni Relations, serving 255,000 alumni[14] through more than thirty networks and affinity groups.[15] [16] The alumni association cleanly provides a directory-like listing[17] of the Chapters by region with associated linked icons for all that apply of the following: Facebook, Twitter, e-mail, and a calendar of events.

For the second category, many Chapters benefit from a more standard, informational, collegiately branded Web page or website template. All the local leadership needs to do is to keep the pages populated with current text and image content, either directly or by passing the information to the association for updating. This type of web presence tends not to be transactional. The professional and consistent presentation from Chapter to Chapter within the same network, coupled with the domain management and support provided by the central alumni association, are of significant value—and fewer things the Chapter must fund.

There are several approaches to how an alumni association provides an informational, templated web presence for Chapters. We will roughly group them into two categories: a single Web page and a multi-page website. Increases in flexibility and types of content are proportional to amount of effort to maintain current content. The first approach is when a single, branded Web page is offered. The Chapter-specific page may contain very little other than contact information, or it may be more informative.

The University of Arizona Alumni Association (UAAA), with an alumni population of 260,000 former students living throughout the fifty United States and in more than 150 countries engaging through its forty+ Chapters,[18] is one example of a minimal-content Web page. It offers a single Chapter-specific Web page in which only the President and contact information may be listed. Take a look at the YumaCats website to get a better feel for how this can be done. One advantage to the minimal-content approach is that it rarely needs updating.

Virginia Commonwealth University's Alumni Association (VCU Alumni), supporting more than 183,000 alumni through thirty-five+ geographic, academic, shared-interest groups,[19] is another that uses this minimalist approach. The Chapters have access to a single Web page that they may customize with a description and contact information. To the right of the page, a visitor could then navigate easily to any other Chapter's Web page within the network. Visit the VCU Alumni New York City Chapter Web page as an example.

Some associations offer a more informative approach to the single, Chapter-specific Web page containing more sections and types of content, possibly incorporating a welcome message, the list of officers with contact details, a few statistics, upcoming events, maybe past events, photographs, and social media links. The Arizona State University (ASU) Alumni Association makes these types of pages available to each Chapter. The ASU Alumni Club of North Carolina Web page is an excellent example. Alumni are greeted with a local image and a welcome message followed by upcoming and past events, a listing of Chapter leadership and a method to contact them, and immediate access to the volunteer leader tool kit.

Another nice, clean example of the more informative Chapter Web page would be that of Johns Hopkins Alumni Association (JHAA), founded in 1886 and serving over 200,000 in its alumni community.[20] The Hopkins Pittsburgh Chapter's page is an excellent illustration—check out the local alumni breakdown by degree section. Visitors will see some introductory information, learn how to get involved, access leadership contact details, and click through to one of several Chapter social media sites.

The second approach to an informational, templated web presence is that of a Chapter-specific, fully branded website with several tabs or pages. The Texas Exes, the well-known name for the Ex-Students' Association of the University of Texas, offers a more robust website platform to its Chapters. Each Chapter has access to a customizable, full, multi-page website. The Texas Exes Hispanic Alumni Network seems to be making the most of the opportunity. The Hispanic Alumni Network fully embraces the engaging banner image and dedicated Web pages for events, alumni and student profiles, fundraising, the leadership team, scholarships, service projects, and more.

Another school offering a robust, informational, multi-page Chapter website is the Alumni Association of the University of Michigan (AAUM), with an alumni base of 575,000 and association membership of 100,000+ alumni and supporters actively involved in the network of one hundred+ Chapters worldwide.[21] It encourages the Chapters to take full advantage and populate the following content:

- A home page with a welcome message
- An "About" page
- An "Events" page
- A "Scholarships" page
- A leadership page or section with a listing of officers and board members
- A page or section with the bylaws
- A page or section regarding how alumni can get involved
- A page or section with contact information
- A page dedicated to the benefits of membership with the alumni association (provided by the association)[22]

One example of a Chapter that fully embraced access to the association-provided website is the U of M Club of Portland.

The final category is the fully functional, interactive websites, often sourced through a third party. It likely contains several of the following features: a secure login, integration into and synchronization with the university alumni database, photo albums, upcoming events with registration capability, payment processing, a communication platform such a newsletter distribution, an alumni spotlight, a feedback portal, news, links to university resources, a job board, and membership management capability. Due to the high cost of these more complex, interactive sites, it is not uncommon for a central alumni association to limit the rollout to the largest, most active Chapters.

The Wellesley College Alumnae Association (WCAA), founded in 1880 and representing its 35,000 alumnae[23] through more than one hundred clubs, chapters, and contacts around the world,[24] is one such organization that offers the high-end, robust version of a third-party website. A quick look at the Wellesley College Alumnae of Boston site can provide insight into what many such services discussed above might look like, including support for membership dues with database integration and payment processing. The WCAA offers this platform across all Chapters, but it is up to the local Chapters to embrace and populate it.

The existence of website support is by far the most likely to be already known by the Chapter leadership. However, it might be worth a call to inquire if there are plans to enhance or expand whatever is currently available.

The Annual Stipend—Great Seed Money

It is not uncommon for a central alumni association to offer financial support to its Chapters in order to help defray some of the operational costs, especially when Chapters are not authorized to collect membership dues. Some associations offer such support equally across all of its Chapters, while others make it conditional on various factors. In either case, requirements to qualify for a stipend may include maintaining an active membership in the central alumni association (if that exists), completion of requested documentation, maintaining a predetermined activity level, representing a geographic location with a particular density of alumni, or some other criteria.

It is important to note that actual cash stipends vary widely, and regardless of the methods for how support is allocated, it is often balanced out by the activity level of the Chapter and other support from the association provided in the form of services. Smaller universities are likely to have smaller populations of alumni, even in the large cities. So, it would be reasonable that such smaller universities would allocate less to a Chapter than would universities with much larger local populations or activity. Likewise, if an alumni association offers robust services with higher-end tools, the amount offered in the form of a stipend would likely be less than from associations offering less in terms of services and tools.

If a stipend in cash is offered, it tends to be in the range of $250 to $2,000. Make sure you do all you can to qualify for it and take it! Every bit helps. Then use it. A "use-it-or-lose-it" policy may be in effect for a Chapter, in which case it might lose money not used by the end of the fiscal year.

One approach to the annual stipend is supported by sharing a percentage of dues paid to the central alumni association. The University of Hawaii Alumni Association (UHAA), supporting more than 290,000 alumni living in all fifty states and in more than 125 countries,[25] is one such entity. The UHAA collects membership dues and then passes a portion of those dues to the Chapters to assist with operational costs. If the association membership paid is an annual membership, then 30 percent of the payment is delivered to the Chapter indicated by the paying alumna / alumnus. If the membership selected is one of the lifetime options, then a onetime payment of between $25 and $135 is paid to the Chapter based on the type of the lifetime membership.[26]

Another university that provides annual financial support for Chapter activities is the University of Georgia (UGA) Alumni Association, established in 1834 and supporting more than 300,000 alumni worldwide[27] through an alumni network of more than one hundred chapters and affinity groups.[28] The UGA Alumni Association offers up to $450 in annual support based on a federally established tier for the area. This is a more typical level of financial assistance. If UGA alumni Chapters are in need of additional support through the year, they are able to seek it through supplemental annual Chapter funding and grant funding.[29]

One more with a unique twist is that of the University of Florida Alumni Association (UFAA), which serves nearly 370,000 alumni spanning every state and more than one hundred foreign nations through its nearly one hundred Gator Clubs®.[30] The UFAA refers to the annual stipend program as the membership rebate. All active Gator Clubs in good standing are eligible for this rebate, which is allocated on the basis of type of association membership paid by alumni in the region. Rebates range from $2 per recent grad membership to $5 per joint life or annual membership and are available over a total of eight categories.[31]

One last mention is a unique case in which a university has recently shifted to a strong stipend system from a structure in which Chapters collected dues for operational expenses. In doing so, the Florida State University (FSU) Alumni Association has established four funding tiers, ranging from $500 to $5,000 based on the number of friends and alumni in the area, with the upper tier supporting regions with an alumni community of 10,000 or greater.[32]

It can be relevant to mention that, often, the greater the financial support from the alumni association, the greater the documentation and milestones requested in return. Be certain your Chapter is willing to complete and perform the requirements prior to accepting the funding. Better said, ensure your Chapter leadership is prepared to maintain compliance. Do not leave this money on the table.

Research revealed that 59 percent of alumni Chapters receive $500 or less annually from the association, while 7 percent receive between $500 and $1,000, 8 percent benefit from $1,001 to $2,000, and remaining 10 percent receives in excess of $2,000 each year.[33] Typical stipend levels are unlikely to adequately support the needs of a Chapter with dreams of a robust schedule of events. If this is your Chapter's situation, later sections will greatly assist your Chapter in supplementing additional income.

Possible Project or Event Grants for Actual Cash Money

In addition to any other type of Chapter income, some associations offer special funding for specific purposes or events. One such example is the Alumni Association of the University of Michigan (AAUM). On top of the annual minimum stipend of $1,000 per Chapter, some Chapters may qualify for Strategic Priorities Funding (SPF) and possibly Club Membership Campaign Funding. SPF is awarded at the association's discretion for events that promote its brand values and membership in the association. The amount can reach as high as $1,000 per event.

The AAUM's Club Membership Campaign Funding is largely a commission program to encourage Chapters to drive membership in the alumni association.[34] Chapters are rewarded with $5 per local alumnus or alumna who is a member of the AAUM. In a recent new program, Chapters can receive an additional $10 for a total of $15 for every new membership when a special code word is used at the time of joining.[35]

The Arkansas Alumni Association (AAA) Chapters now rely on event funding grants called Chapter Grants for operational funds as of the 2016–2017 academic year. Funds are available on a first-come, first-served basis and max out at $1,000 per Chapter per year. Grants support events that incorporate new member outreach, service to the local community or the University of Arkansas, student scholarship support, or membership in the AAA. There is one additional avenue for special grant funding for AAA Chapters, and that is in support of PIGnics. Chapters hosting a PIGnic are eligible for an additional $300 beyond the $1,000 Chapter Grant limit.[36]

The Brigham Young University (BYU) Alumni Association does not provide direct financial support to its Chapters. However, there is an opportunity to earn money through a program that rewards higher performance. There are two incentive amounts based on meeting basic expectations and hosting a certain number of events across different categories. True Blue Chapters represent the higher performance level and may earn $500 annually, while White Chapters have a slightly lower bar, though not by much, and can earn $250.[37]

With respect to the University of Colorado (CU Boulder) Alumni Association, its alumni Chapters are able to apply for funding based on both the size of Chapter and which pillar of focus (social, professional development, community service, or philanthropy) the event will support. Annual allotments range from $50 to $250 for the smallest Chapter tier and from $250 to $1,000 for the largest tier. Allotments mentioned are per pillar per year and thus can be combined. For example, a tier 3 Chapter may qualify for up to $1,000 dollars for events supporting professional development and up to $500 cumulatively for events supporting philanthropy.[38]

Beyond the pillar / tier approach to allocating funding, there is one more opportunity for a Chapter of the CU Boulder Alumni Association to earn additional money. The recipient of the Chapter of the Year Award wins a cash award of $1,000 to be used for approved purposes within one year from the date of acceptance.[39]

Each alumni association approaches Chapter funding differently, from nothing for Chapters that are to be completely self-sustaining, to creative methods of case-by-case special funding opportunities, to incentive activities that further the association's mission and goals. Be aware of all such opportunities, the operational requirements, and how to best access the funds—even if the strategy is simply to be the first in line!

The Ever-Popular Collegiate Merchandise

In some cases, the Chapter will receive support in the form of branded products. This might include items such as an alumni association banner, coffee mugs or cups, pens, lanyards, bumper or window stickers, balloons, athletic sports schedule cards, pens, license-plate holders, lapel pins, note cards, and T-shirts, to name a few.

Penn State University (PSU) is one of many, many schools that supports programs to deliver branded merchandise to Chapters. In this case, the Penn State Alumni Association offers packages up to three times a year to support

Chapter events, as well as a banner for each new Chapter. It goes even further to organize additional bulk purchases among the Chapters for Penn State shakers, signage, decals, magnets, balloons, pins, ball caps, and other items should there be an interest.[40]

Louisiana State University (LSU) Alumni Association offers free merchandise including name tags, bumper stickers, and sports schedules. Other items can be purchased at cost, such as koozies, pens, and cups, while additional items may be ordered through the Alumni Center Gift Shop at a 10 percent discount. Some items can even be personalized with the Chapter's name at either little or no cost.[41]

While these items are not useful for paying bills, they can significantly decrease your actual cash outlay and boost the professionalism of the attendee's experience. For example, having a nice banner at the entrance to your event is classy and welcoming. The Boise State Alumni Association offers each Chapter in good standing a banner with the local Chapter's name once it completes its first year successfully. Smaller tier Chapters can also qualify for the banner, just after two years of successful operation.[42]

Lanyards and lapel pins are popular giveaways to attendees while further advertising your Chapter and the college or university itself. Playing the devil's advocate on this one for a moment, it is possible that the day of the lapel pin has passed. I recently heard a Chapter leader share that one of her young alumni asked what a lapel pin is, incorrectly pronouncing it "lappel," like "apple" with an *l* and with the accent on the first syllable. We all had a good laugh, largely at ourselves when acknowledging the now obvious. Lapel pins were designed to be worn on the lapel of business suits. With the evolution of business attire from strictly formal professional garb to much more business casual styles, lapels are on their way to extinction. Many millennials do not even own a business suit and thus have little to no exposure to discussing lapels.

T-shirts and coffee mugs make lovely door or raffle prizes . . . maybe even speaker gifts. The quantities gifted by the alumni association rarely lend themselves to being the sole item sold for fundraising, but they do have a perfect place in improving the quality and experience at an event or two.

While straight-up cash is difficult to access, merchandise tends to be much easier. In fact, the central alumni association might just have such items sitting around the office or in a closet waiting to be distributed to a deserving Chapter. Request all that you can!

A Real Gift—The Alumni Leaders Conference

As mentioned in the previous section, not all alumni associations offer an alumni leaders conference (ALC), but if yours does, a high priority should be placed on attending it. You might know this event by any one of many other names such as: Volunteer Leaders Conference, Alumni Leadership Conference, Annual Leadership Symposium, Annual Leaders Colloquium, Club Leadership Weekend, Alumni Volunteer Weekend, or any number of other names. Regardless of the label attached, they all share the same importance to the Chapter leader.

An ALC is exceptionally valuable to the Chapter in several ways. First, it keeps the local leadership current and poised to take advantage of new association-supported programming, tools, and personnel. Second, it further integrates and aligns the local representative with the role, fellow like-minded Chapter leaders, and the alumni association, likely yielding a deeper and longer lasting commitment to the local Chapter. Third, it helps engender the bonds and relationships between Chapter leaders, providing a solid foundation for personal support. Lastly, it more closely aligns your specific Chapter to the central alumni association. Your Chapter will be more likely to come to mind when thinking of programs and beta test groups for new tools. The more attention and higher priority the Chapter leadership places on association programming, the more the association is likely to prioritize your Chapter.

Some alumni leaders conferences are very focused, specifically targeting Chapter leaders, while others on the other end of the spectrum cast a much wider net, including class ambassadors, affinity club leaders, the alumni board of directors, even student leaders, and many others. In any case, the event is not to be missed.

An ALC may run three or four days, combining training with many opportunities to network and have fun. It is not uncommon for an ALC to be scheduled in a way that leverages significant campus events, such as homecoming, a game with a big rival, or another meaningful event that will make attending even more appealing—maybe even advantageous, considering the convenient hotel room block that the alumni association might secure.

From a cost perspective, the alumni association generally provides a reasonable percentage of the meals and often some form of fun or entertainment, while the remaining costs are usually self-funded. As a result, there are typically two types of expenses an attendee might expect: travel costs and registration costs. In most instances, travel costs will be an out-of-pocket expense. However, some ALCs include some type of directed financial relief for hotel, taxis, gasoline, flights, or parking—such as securing a block of hotel rooms at a discounted price.

One typical example is the Alumni Leadership Conference specifically for regional chapters and special interest groups held in Urbana, Illinois, each year by the University of Illinois (UI) Alumni Association. As a frame of reference, the UI Alumni Association serves more than 450,000 alumni through its eighty-five+ Chapters.[43] The UI Alumni Association embraces a holistic approach by placing equal emphasis on celebrating the Chapters, providing training and incorporating networking opportunities. Attendance for the October event leveraging homecoming weekend typically yields thirty to thirty-five volunteer alumni leaders representing approximately twenty domestic Chapters and groups. The UI Alumni Association negotiates favorable rates for a block of rooms and provides meals and thank-you gifts for the club leaders, ranging from Illini memorabilia to football tickets; however, the individuals are still responsible for their own travel costs.[44]

Conversely, I have seen travel grants / scholarships provided by a central alumni association to attending alumni under specified conditions. Ohio University Alumni Association, serving 220,000 alumni through nearly fifty chapters and societies,[45] offers two such travel scholarships. One volunteer—any Chapter leader—from every Chapter is required to attend its Alumni Leaders Conference in May, leveraging the "On The Green Weekend" events. Although one person per Chapter is required, it is not limited to only the one. There is no out-of-pocket cost associated with food or lodging. Attendees are invited to stay on campus in a dorm for both nights, and food during the event is included. With respect to travel, out-of-state volunteer alumni are eligible for one of two $1,000 travel scholarships. The scholarships are not provided in the form of a $1,000 check but rather as reimbursement for applicable expenses up to $1,000 with proper receipts and documentation.[46] Sixty to seventy-five alumni leaders attend each year.[47]

Massachusetts Institute of Technology (MIT) Alumni Association, supporting 135,000+ alumni[48] and more than eighty Chapters around the world, puts on an intense Alumni Leadership Conference each fall, open to any of the 12,000 alumni volunteers of record across all programs. It offers presentations from MIT faculty and nearly fifty best-practice sessions from MIT alumni and staff over a two-and-a-half-day event. They have even developed an app for the conference![49] From a financial support perspective, a travel subsidy is available to the MIT10 community (those who graduated in the past ten years) who would otherwise be unable to attend due to prohibitive travel costs. The subsidy covers 50 percent of transportation expenses up to $200.[50] An amazing 600 volunteers participated in 2016.[51]

Truman State University Alumni Association, serving 62,000 alumni through ten+ chapters and groups,[52] takes another approach to reimbursing travel expenses to its annual Alumni Leaders Conference, scheduled for the afternoon prior to its homecoming weekend each October. It offers tiered travel expense reimbursement up to $350 based on miles travelled. The benefit is extended to all alumni board members and approved Chapter representatives.[53]

One last mention of a university assisting their alumni with travel costs is the Villanova University Alumni Association (VUAA), founded in 1875 and now serving more than 120,000 alumni around the world through eighty-five clubs, groups, and committees.[54] For participation in its Volunteer Leadership Conference, also building on homecoming weekend, the VUAA has a robust reimbursement policy covering practically any mode of transportation to the event up to $500 in airfare. Additionally, for those travelling more than seventy-five miles, it covers one night in the partnering hotel. It also offers largely all of the food for the one-day conference and additional perks such as tickets to the Homecoming Festival and the football game.[55] The audience is broader than just alumni Chapter leaders, and over 150 alumni, staff, and students attended in 2016.[56]

Anyone who has attended just about any ALC will attest that it is absolutely worth the time and costs to participate, even if out of their own pocket. However, as volunteer leaders are already giving of their time (often vacation time) to participate, it would be most appropriate for the Chapter to cover the out-of-pocket costs.

It is highly recommended to find a way to financially support such workshop / conference participation on a regular basis for as many officers as possible. Just be aware of costs to attend and bake them into the annual budget—or at least the wish list. Be creative and look for economies of scale—such as: if the event is within driving distance, the same car can transport several officers. People might even be willing to share a room if a hotel stay is required. If your alumni association offers such a workshop or conference, it is truly advisable to do all financially possible to permit at least one Chapter officer to attend—better yet, two.

Access to Prominent Guest Speakers

With regard to speakers, the central alumni association is often a wonderful source of event speakers. Associations have been known to arrange for prominent administrators, professors, and coaches to visit various Chapters, typically on their off-seasons. These prominent figures tend to draw large crowds of alumni and guests, significantly building the awareness, brand, and participation of local alumni populations. If a Chapter is trying to build a little buffer in its bank account, a well-recognized speaker can draw a sizable audience, yielding a sizable bolus of cash.

Further benefits tend to include the additional marketing the association is likely to launch in promotion of the event, the expenses it will often absorb, and the assistance with planning and coordinating. Should the speaker have recently published a book, there might even be the possibility that books will be provided for attendees. All of this support goes a long way to advance the reputation and quality of your Chapter events.

Wharton Alumni Affairs did an unparalleled job in supporting our Chapter and others by providing speakers. They made an effort—as long as there was significant interest on our side—to produce a prominent professor or administrator once or twice a year. We were fortunate to have had outstanding visits from superstar professors including:

- Jeremy Siegel, PhD, whose economic opinions regularly sought on CNN, CNBC, and other networks, are revered as unilaterally capable of moving the financial markets.
- Stuart Diamond, JD-MBA, our era's most recognized and influential negotiations thought leader and author of best-selling book *Getting More*, now published in twenty-five languages and seventy countries.
- George Day, PhD, one of the few recognized "Legends in Marketing," with more than fifteen books published and countless professional awards.
- Peter Linneman, PhD, the recognized industry mogul who authored the real estate text used in 70 percent of collegiate real estate programs.
- Peter Fader, PhD, one of the foremost highly decorated and published analytical thought leaders in what drives customer shopping and purchasing behaviors and co-founder of Zodiac Analytics.

The opportunity to hear firsthand from legends like these has the impact of drawing out even the most elusive alumni—and offers far grander performances than any local Chapter could sustain without the solid partnership of the central association. Every college and university has its rock stars, figuratively speaking. A strong partnership with the central association can help prioritize your Chapter for an appearance when prominent personalities become available.

The Nebraska Alumni Association (NAA) has developed an exceptionally organized approach for identifying and sourcing ideal speakers through its respective speakers bureaus. The UNL Speakers Bureau is comprised of outstanding academic speakers, while the NAA Speakers Bureau contains former Alumni Masters, alumni award winners, and those featured in the *Nebraska Magazine*. Chapter leaders have access to the lists online and through their Chapter liaison.[57]

Understandably, your central alumni association does not want to be embarrassed in front of the professor or waste his or her time, so we Chapter leaders are expected to help build the excitement and anticipation of the event in an effort to draw a larger crowd. The bigger the crowd, the more successful the event, the happier the guest speaker, and the more likely the association will keep your Chapter on the short-list the next time around.

As the Wharton School is not the most notable in athletics (except for maybe a few exceptions, including Wharton undergraduate Brandon Slay, who won a gold medal in the 2000 Summer Olympics in freestyle wrestling), coaches were never sent as speakers. Conversely, my undergraduate alma mater's alumni association, the Association of Former Students of Texas A&M University, serving more than 417,000 alumni through an amazing 250+ Chapters,[58] puts on an outstanding event in which coaches are the center. Coaches Night is an annual event in Dallas and elsewhere in which a very large crowd of alumni and friends gather to hear the most riveting version of the athletic season's outlook from the head coaches while savoring a huge, Texas-style barbeque.[59] This could not be organized without the support of the central alumni association.

Lastly, I just cannot walk away without mentioning the unique Florida Players Network (FPN) at the University of Florida. The FPN is an organization of former University of Florida football players in which they use their notoriety for the benefit of the university and for the community. The University of Florida Alumni Association (UFAA) is happy to help Chapters arrange for a member of the FPN, as well as other athletic, academic, and administrative personalities, to speak at Chapter meetings and events.[60]

Active, respected coaches, professors, and administrators can be just the right touch of fairy dust to enliven or kick-start a Chapter's annual program.

If your Chapter is fortunate enough to make the tour short-list, be ready to do your part to plan, promote, and execute.

Other Opportunities to Benefit

In addition to each of the above primary areas of support, central alumni associations offer various other benefits that may be of use to a Chapter. Some of the opportunities are more useful if the Chapter is geographically close to the campus, while others are just a little something special that your alumni association dreamed up and made happen.

The use of the alumni center is one such opportunity. Several schools operate a beautiful alumni center, often named in tribute to a prominent charitable alumna / alumnus. Bowling Green State University (BGSU) Alumni Association makes its Mileti Alumni Center available to Chapters for activities, events, and meetings at no cost.[61] The local alumni groups make use of this facility about ten to twelve times each year.[62]

In other instances, alumni centers are available for a price. One such facility is the McNamara Alumni Center at the University of Minnesota. It was a project over twelve years in the making and designed by Internationally renowned architect Antoine Predock of Albuquerque, New Mexico. *Brides* magazine named McNamara one of the Top 50 Places to Get Married in America and was awarded Best High Tech Venue 2015 by UniqueVenues.com. Room rentals range from $200 to $2,400 for the first six hours during the weekdays, with an hourly surcharge for evenings after 8:00 p.m. and weekends outside of Saturday from 10:00 a.m. to 4:00 p.m. For the right events, beautifully architected alumni centers might be well worth the cost.[63]

Keep the Support Flowing

Regardless of what types of support the central alumni association offers or to what degree, thank them! Do so firstly because it is simply polite and secondly because all services discussed truly yield either cash or cost savings, improve the quality of events, and drive increased participation. Finally, thank them because you want them to keep doing it!

If Chapters do not reinforce valuable and beneficial behaviors performed by the association, such behaviors will vanish. It is unreasonable to assume that the central alumni association magically knows what is most valuable to each Chapter—specifically, yours—without feedback. Once something has been cut from a budget, it can be like moving mountains to reinstate it. Do not let that happen to your Chapter. Do not take these gifts of support for granted!

At a bare minimum, take the time to send a thank-you e-mail expressing your appreciation. Better yet, go old school and send a thank-you note signed by as many officers and alumni as possible. If you really want to secure your place in their hearts, send a multi-part gift, such as a modest fruit basket. Items that cannot be missed when being delivered and have sharable elements really create a buzz in the office. Your Chapter liaison is likely overworked, trying to do as much as possible for a larger-than-reasonable group of Chapters. You will likely win mountains of goodwill through such a gesture.

60-Second Takeaway

Both the central alumni association and your Chapter share the same overall incentives and goals: to drive a wildly successful, thriving Chapter(s). Accordingly, it is likely that the central alumni association already has in place one or more means of local Chapter support you can take advantage of. Make certain you reach out to the central alumni association or your Chapter's liaison to inquire about what is available, including insurance coverage, website support, an annual stipend or event grants, discounted branded merchandise, a leaders conference, access to prominent speakers, and more.

If there is nothing officially organized, make a formal request. It is much easier to get branded merchandise over cash, but don't let that stop you from trying! Lastly, don't forget to express your appreciation in some tangible way—often. The central alumni association and specifically your Chapter liaison are your strongest allies. Give the association personnel all of the reasons in the world to want to help you wherever they can.

Make It Happen Checklist

☐ Get to know your Chapter liaison.

☐ Become very familiar with the extent of insurance coverage, paying close attention to gaps and policy compliance requirements. If no insurance coverage exists, look into coverage immediately.

☐ If available, take advantage of existing website and communication support by keeping content current. Then, ask about future improvements and how to qualify for the advanced platform.

☐ Reach out to the central alumni association and inquire if a stipend is available, and if so, understand how to qualify for it, when it can be delivered, and what your Chapter has to do to stay in good standing.

☐ Inquire if there are additional forms of funding available, such as an event grant or special project funding—then make sure you use it.

☐ Follow up with a request regarding what branded merchandise is available to be sent at no cost to the Chapter, making specific item requests if possible.

☐ Learn about any alumni or volunteer leader conference / workshop that might be available to the Chapter leaders. Understand the timing, costs, and expense reimbursement opportunities. Do all possible to arrange for at least one or two leaders to attend.

☐ Request that a well-known professor, administrator, or coach be sent out as a special guest speaker. If one has already been provided, ask for a second—one for each semester. Then, do everything in your Chapter's power to make the event a tremendous success.

☐ Explore what other services or tools the central alumni association might have for the Chapter to support its success, such as access to the alumni center at discounted or no cost.

☐ Take the time to thank the central alumni association personnel for the support they offer that you truly appreciate!

Part II
The Broadest of Opportunities

Chapter Memberships—Great Foundational Income   65

»   Defining Alumni and the Alumni Community   67

»   Chapter-Specific Membership Benefits   70

»   Membership Types à la Carte   71

»   A Dartboard for Pricing Memberships   75

»   When Local Membership Dues Are Prohibited   79

»   60-Second Takeaway   79

»   Make It Happen Checklist   81

Sponsorships Loved Far and Wide   83

»   Cost-Relieving Gifts of Products, Services, or Venues   84

»   A Smorgasbord of Sponsorships   85

»   Sponsor Benefits and Packages   86

»   Danger Zones, Pitfalls, and What Not to Offer   88

»   Sourcing Sponsors   89

»   Weaving a Compelling Story   91

»   Keep Them Coming Back   95

»   60-Second Takeaway   96

»   Make It Happen Checklist   97

Traditional and Not-So-Traditional Fundraising   99

»   Cash Campaigns Plain and Simple   100

»   Merchandise Sale—Come and Get it!   103

»   Auctions Interwoven into Other Events or Solo   105

»   Crowdfunding Is a Crowd Pleaser   108

»   Raffles Can Be Fun but Iffy   111

»   Large-Scale Events: Large Work but Large Money   113

»   The Last Act   115

»   Don't Bite Off More Than You Can Chew   116

»   60-Second Takeaway   116

»   Make It Happen Checklist   118

Mobile Giving Now for Everyone, Big and Very Small 119

» The Modern Twist 120

» How It Works 122

» Cost Considerations 123

» Tips for Success 126

» 60-Second Takeaway 128

» Make It Happen Checklist 129

General Events Are Still the Workhorse 131

» A Sexy Event Subject 133

» A Convenient Date and Time 134

» Determining Attendee Composition 136

» A Venue That Is Right in Every Way 138

» Winning Catering and Beverage Strategies 141

» Enticing Ticketing 145

» Other Elements Not to Overlook 148

» 60-Second Takeaway 149

» Make It Happen Checklist 150

Photo Shoots for Today's Digital World 151

» Headshots—A Must-Have for a Digital Presence 151

» Holiday and Other Themes Spice Up Marketing Efforts 153

» Considerations for Success 154

» Photo Shoot Pricing 155

» Wrapping Up the Loose Ends 156

» 60-Second Takeaway 157

» Make It Happen Checklist 159

Chapter Memberships— Great Foundational Income

The first Chapter-initiated form of income that will be discussed is a membership in your local Chapter. Memberships can be an excellent form of revenue generation, if permitted. Not only do they provide initial income, but memberships are gifts that keep on giving year after year, assuming the Chapter is doing a good job keeping the alumni community engaged. Local Chapter memberships may also be a bit tricky. It is certain that the central alumni association has already established a policy regarding local Chapters collecting membership dues. Accordingly, your Chapter will likely fall into one of the following categories:

a. Local Chapters are free to collect and utilize annual membership dues, while the central alumni association may or may not collect dues at the top level.
b. Only the central alumni association may collect membership dues, while the local Chapters may not.
c. No membership dues are collected by either the central alumni association or the local Chapters.

It may be worth mentioning that the first category represents Chapters that are *empowered* to charge dues. That is not the same as *required* to charge membership dues. Most Chapters in this category simply have the option to do so. Here are some questions your Chapter might want to consider when deciding to or not to charge membership dues:

- Does the Chapter hope to hold larger or more formal programs that may require advance contracts (e.g., space rental or a catering contract)?
- Might the Chapter incur operations expenses, such as insurance or travel for officers to the alumni leaders conference (ALC)?
- How active does the Chapter want to be?
- Will the Chapter wish to host an event or two in which attendance is free, such as a membership appreciation event?
- What benefits is the club prepared to offer for members that pay dues?

Careful consideration of these questions and some other factors will help guide a Chapter to the best answer for itself. An example of the first category is the Troy University Alumni Association, serving a population of 153,000 alumni through seventy-five chapters and groups.[1] In this case, both the alumni association and Chapters are permitted to charge annual dues. A unique twist in this scenario is that the Chapters are also required to pay $5 per Chapter member to the alumni association on an annual basis.[2] This money in turn helps to provide the support through the alumni association back to the Chapters.

Another example of the first category is the Penn State Alumni Association, the largest dues-paying alumni organization in the world, according to the Chapter handbook. Not only do both the Chapters and the alumni association charge dues, but for every new life member of the alumni association recruited by a Chapter, that Chapter receives an additional $50.[3] It is similar to the Troy University Alumni Association approach, only in reverse.

Syracuse University (SU) Alumni Association, serving 254,000 alumni[4] through its eighty+ clubs and groups,[5] is the third example in which Chapters are encouraged to collect dues in support of funding standard operational costs. However, this time, the alumni association does not charge membership dues. The SU Alumni Association makes a special effort to explain that, while the Chapters may charge dues, membership should not be denied for the inability to pay.[6]

Like above, the West Point Association of Graduates (WPAOG), serving more than 50,000 alumni[7] and over 130 regional societies worldwide plus shared interest and class groups,[8] permits its Chapters to charge dues, while the WPAOG itself does not. Graduates of the United States Military Academy are automatically members of the WPAOG at no cost, while membership at the local level may depend on payment of dues as determined by the local Chapter leadership.[9]

It seems that for the Chapters that have access to local membership dues, the alumni association rarely offers additional cash support like stipends or grants. Rather, the locally collected membership dues establish the pool of funds for operations and upfront event deposits.

Alumni associations that have adopted the second category as a model typically operate under some sort of revenue-sharing model in which some portion of alumni association membership dues income is shared with the Chapters through services, a stipend, grants, or some other means.

The University of Iowa Alumni Association (UIAA) illustrates such an example. It charges alumni membership dues to be a part of the central alumni association, while Chapters do not charge local dues. Chapters are financially incented to help drive membership in the UIAA. To partially substitute for lack of dues income, each Chapter will receive funds based on the number of alumni in the area and will have the opportunity to earn up to an additional $240 based on activities of the prior year.[10]

Like the UIAA, the Auburn Alumni Association, in service to nearly 200,000 alumni[11] and managing nearly one hundred chapters and groups,[12] charges dues to be a part of the association, and the Chapters do not. This was not always the case. Previously, Chapters collected dues, but the practice was discontinued in a three-year phased conversion ending in 2011. Now, Chapters participate in the Auburn Club Membership Commissions program, in which the association will pay "commissions" to Chapters that recruit new and returning members to the association. Commissions earned are then exclusively applied to either the Chapter's annual or endowed scholarship fund.[13]

The last category exists when neither the alumni association nor the Chapters are in a position to charge membership dues. Capital to operate the Chapters then falls solely to being earned through margins added to event tickets and other creative methods to be presented in this book.

The University of Tennessee Knoxville (UT Knoxville) Alumni Association operates consistent with the third category, in which neither the Chapter nor the central alumni association charges membership dues. As a result, the Chapters are required to generate all operational income through their programs that strive for a net-neutral outcome.[14]

Other Chapters in this category include those of the Duke Alumni Association (DAA) and Binghamton University Alumni Association. If your Chapter falls into the first category, continue through this section normally. If your Chapter falls into the second or third category, skip on down to the subsection titled *"When Local Membership Dues Are Prohibited."*

Defining Alumni and the Alumni Community

Ideally, your Chapter will have the blessing to capture local membership dues. If so, then the next steps would be to define what qualifies as a member and evaluate what membership structure is most appropriate for your group.

The basic understanding that full graduates of the college or university are considered alumni and should qualify for local membership is clear. Questions begin regarding those that attended but never graduated, people one or two steps removed from the core case, such as a spouse or a child, someone who completed a one- to two-week certification course rather than a full-degree program, parents of an applicant, a visiting professor who did not graduate from the academic institution in question—the list goes on. This will be an important topic to flush out without question among the leadership team in whatever form is most appropriate. The central alumni association may have previously addressed some of these issues. Falling back on its guidance can also supply a "fall-guy" for stickier situations.

In general, many alumni associations support two categories of member-qualifying participants in alumni Chapter activities: alumni and non-alumni supporters. Alumni are typically defined as those having been enrolled in a degree-granting program that crossed some threshold, such as number of hours, whether they graduated with a degree or not. Alumni are produced by the university. Non-alumni supporters can be anyone else, including friends, family, or anyone who simply likes the college or university. The alumni chapter network welcomes these people into the fold, allowing them to be as, or nearly as, connected as full alumni. Together, alumni and non-alumni supporters make up the "alumni community."

The University of Pennsylvania's Office of Alumni Relations (Penn Alumni Relations) offers a definition of alumni and permits the Chapters to charge membership dues. It serves 290,000+ living alumni[15] through more than 120 regional clubs around the world that host more than 800 events annually.[16] According to Penn Alumni Relations, an alumna / alumnus is defined as someone who has attended the University, whether or not he or she has graduated. This definition includes those who took part in certain certificate programs. Thus, the 290,000 living Penn alumni include Penn graduates plus the non-degreed alumni.

From the perspective of Chapter membership and participation, like many alumni associations, Penn Alumni Relations embraces the wider alumni community, including the non-alumni supporters. Further, it offers its Chapters flexibility in how each one wishes to define its own membership:

> Each club is encouraged to reach out to alumni, current parents (of undergraduate students), current students, and friends of the University to recruit club members. As independent organizations, individual clubs are free to define membership as it suits their needs. Two common definitions are:

Mass Membership: Clubs define a member as someone who has registered for club events, or has signed up for the club e-mail or newsletter list, and

Paid Membership: Clubs define a member as someone who pays membership dues. Usually, these clubs charge for events with different price points for members and non-members.[17]

The Louisiana State University (LSU) Alumni Association is another organization that permits Chapters to capture dues and provides guidance on the University's official definition of alumni. Alumni, as defined and supported by the LSU Alumni Association's Articles of Incorporation, includes graduates, former students, and supporters of the University. The association further defines a former student as anyone who has attended LSU for credit. Supporters, also called Alumni-by-Choice (ABC), are those who did not attend LSU but support the University nonetheless.[18]

Referencing the Syracuse University (SU) Alumni Association once more, membership in the association occurs automatically once someone completes sixty credit hours at Syracuse University. However, membership in Chapters is open to far more—the alumni, students, parents, and friends of SU.[19]

The United States Air Force Academy (USAFA) Association of Graduates (AOG), supporting eighty-five Chapters,[20] provides clear and detailed guidance on membership definitions, while leaving the cost of local Chapter dues up to the local leadership. Membership is categorized into four groups: Honorary, Regular, Affiliate, and Special.

- Honorary members are individuals of distinction who are elected unanimously by the Board of Directors because of outstanding and noteworthy service to their community, country, or to the USAFA and are not required to be graduates or former cadets of the USAFA. Any surviving spouse of a deceased member or deceased graduate is automatically an honorary member. The AOG recommends that honorary members do not pay dues.
- Regular members are graduates of the USAFA.
- Affiliate members include any former cadet who was honorably discharged from the USAFA after serving at least until the close of the academic half-year immediately following his or her admission; a spouse, widow, or widower, parent, sibling, or child of a person eligible for regular membership; a parent or sibling of a cadet; a Senator or Member

of Congress; any individual appointed by the USAFA Admissions Office as District Representative, Liaison Officer, Admissions Representative, or by whatever title he or she may be given by that office; and any person who has a member of his or her immediate family on the staff and faculty.

- Special members are cadets from the local area; other cadets who have distinguished themselves by outstanding service to the USAFA and who are in their First Class year at the Academy; and any individual who, by his or her efforts or contributions of time and service, assists the USAFA in fulfilling its purpose. Like the honorary membership, the AOG recommends that special members should not pay dues.[21]

At first glance, defining an alumna / alumnus or a Chapter member probably appeared rudimentary. Leaning in reveals there is more to the conversation than expected. Soon we will discuss membership structures. That, too, seems simple at first blush. When viewed more closely, opportunities begin to emerge surrounding length of memberships, the categorization of types of alumni, and various levels of benefits, to state just a few parameters. Before embarking on that topic, let us start with articulating what value the Chapter has to offer through memberships.

Chapter-Specific Membership Benefits

It is important to note the difference between association-level membership benefits, such as credit card offers or travel clubs, and local-level benefits. Local Chapter benefits will be practical as well as intangible items your group can offer someone at a grassroots level. The focus should be on building the strongest possible list of items that provide significant value to the alumni while generating minimal cost to the Chapter. The following list should jumpstart your Chapter's discussion:

- Member spotlights on the website / in communications / on social media profiling members to the rest of the Chapter
- Chapter-wide professional alerts on behalf of members when they have a significant personal or professional event, such as if they are nominated for an award, just published an article, or received a promotion
- Advanced notice of events, especially ones with limited seating or limited participation including webinars
- Preferred seating at events, such as prime tables at game-watching events

- Access to private receptions or meals with speakers before or after events
- Members-only events
- Discounted or free event tickets
- Free companion tickets
- Discounted or free parking at events
- Member-designated name badges
- Credential-satisfied for Chapter leadership
- Voting rights
- A tax deduction if the Chapter is recognized as tax exempt

The above list is just the tip of the iceberg! Brainstorming with your Chapter's leadership team should precipitate many more ideas. Bear in mind the financial value to the Chapter needs to outweigh the financial benefit being given away within a membership. Second, if the Chapter is designated as tax exempt by the IRS, take time to explore the "*State and Federal Tax Implications*" section later in this text, which addresses under what circumstances membership dues become tax deductible for the alumni.

Membership Types à la Carte

Membership types should be designed to generate income, offer value with incentives to join, and avoid alienating anyone from the alumni community from participating. For example, your Chapter may choose to offer more economically attractive packages to young alumni as well as retired alumni to ensure there are no barriers to their participation. Young alumni represent the future of the Chapter and its leadership, while retired alumni are the keepers of the history and mentors. If your Chapter has a large contingent of active families, maybe a family membership would be appropriate. Regarding the core alumni group, maybe your Chapter wants to offer discounted extended memberships, such as two- or three-year memberships, to drive greater income and secure a longer commitment.

What memberships typically do not take into consideration is the specific degree earned. It very rarely matters, in this type of classification, whether the degree earned was an associate's, bachelor's, master's, doctorate, fellowship, or other level—or if, in the end, no degree was earned at all.

As you consider the different types of memberships introduced below, consider how you might tier the benefits to encourage the alumni behaviors you desire. Also, keep in mind that each one will need a clear definition specific to your Chapter and situation. Here are some ideas:

- **Recent graduate / young alumni membership** – This is a great way to encourage young alumni to get involved with the Chapter while acknowledging and demonstrating appreciation for them. Different definitions of young alumni exist, ranging from one year following graduation, such as in the case of the Truman Alumni Association,[22] to two years, or maybe all graduates under thirty-five years old. Earlier, we touched on the Massachusetts Institute of Technology (MIT) Alumni Association's acronym for this category, MIT10, representing those graduating in the past ten years. The Ole Miss Alumni Association considers young alumni any who have graduated within the past fifteen years.[23] These are alumni association definitions that may or may not be required to filter on down through to the Chapter-level dues plan. It may be worth mentioning that although the term "young alumni" is very popular, some Chapters prefer the term "recent graduate," to be more inclusive of those completing graduate degrees who might not be so young as well as those having attended later in life.

- **Retired alumni membership** – Just as important as engaging the new alumni is retaining the history and experience of the retired alumni. A separate membership level calling out the retirees shows them that the Chapter still values their input and participation. With the enormous baby boomer generation in or moving toward retirement and the silent generation—those prior to the baby boomers—well into retirement, this group should not be overlooked. Geographically speaking, especially in Arizona and Florida, retirees comprise an even greater portion of the local alumni. Many associations promote a special membership for those once they reach their fifty-year graduation anniversary, as well.

- **Standard alumni membership** – This category can be fairly straightforward and typically represents full alumni from the academic institution. The central alumni association may provide a definition of a standard alumna / alumnus for its Chapters. If it does not, the local Chapter will need to determine where they want to draw the line. Just be certain to clearly express the boundaries of alumni so there is no uncertainty. Your Chapter may wish to evaluate some or all of the following topics in which the boundaries of alumni consideration may be vague:

  » Current or retired faculty
  » Non-faculty employees of the college or university

» Executive education programs such as a one-week program designed and offered to employees of a specific company, or possibly a one- or two-week specialty program with open enrollment

» Online degree holders

» Married and unmarried partners of alumni

- **Alumni joint membership** – This is an option to consider for active family alumni populations that might be more palatable than choosing an alumni membership and additional memberships for the significant other. Just be clear regarding what counts as a "joint," such as: Does the couple need to be married? Can they be in a domestic partnership or simply dating?

- **Alumni family membership** – Very similar to the one above, this is another option to consider for active family alumni populations. This membership might include the whole nuclear family, regardless of the number of children of any age. The wrinkle in this one is: Where does the definition of a family stop? A recommendation would be at alumni, spouse, and immediate children under some predetermined age. This may not be the most financially positive approach for Chapters of colleges and universities serving alumni with traditionally larger families. An example is Brigham Young University (BYU), with a predominantly Mormon population having the largest families in America, according to the Pew Research Center.[24]

- **Affinity membership** – This category is valuable if your alumni Chapter represents a particular school within a college or university and your Chapter wishes to show affinity for fellow alumni of other programs. It might also extend to sister international academic institutions with a small alumni population locally. An example of an affinity arrangement would be nursing school alumni and the women-in-business alumni, both in the same city and alumni of the same university, although unlikely to have graduated from each other's programs.

- **Friends of . . . membership** – This might be an option for those Chapters that have high non-alumni supporter participation. Often, family members such as parents or spouses wish to share the experience with the alumni. If they are often present with the alumni, they may wish to enjoy the benefits of membership and participation in the Chapter. As these people are clearly advocates of the program, the Chapter may simply wish to encourage the broader participation and benefit from the added income. Alternatively, this would be counterproductive if the Chapter wishes to remain more exclusive to alumni only.

A personal example would be an affinity between the Wharton Club of Dallas–Fort Worth and the Wharton School's sister programs at INSEAD in France or the London Business School. We chose to name this affinity with others, including family members and those who have taken a one- or two-week executive course, and group them into a membership called Friends of Wharton.

- **Premium membership** – A premium membership would offer all of the benefits of a standard membership plus additional special perks, such as more prominence on the website, enhanced recognition, a gift from the Chapter, or access to special events exclusively for premium members. This category is an option for those who value special privileges or are especially enthusiastic about supporting the Chapter and school. It might be named a Gold Membership or some name tied to the school or mascot.

- **Multi-year memberships** – Often, people are attracted to multi-year options due to comparatively reduced cost and the decreased administrative hassle of renewing each year. These memberships can be very beneficial for the Chapter by providing more cash up front. If someone is willing to pay in advance, the Chapter should help him or her do it. Who knows if that alumna / alumnus will still be living locally a year or two from now, or if he or she will have the same feelings about prioritizing dues to the Chapter at that time? Combining that with the time value of money concept, in which a dollar today is worth more than that same dollar tomorrow, multi-year memberships can be rather valuable.

- **Lifetime membership** – If you are considering a lifetime membership, talk it out with your team. The upside is that a significant payment is made up front. The primary downside relates to the many years following, in which no income is generated from that member, yet they will likely be benefiting from member discounts and special pricing. You might also be betting that alumna / alumnus might not actually be around to be a paying member for the long term. If you choose to implement lifetime memberships, the Chapter will need to think like a farmer whose entire annual income is paid out following the harvest and must last all year—only your Chapter will need it to stretch over several years. This can be a great option for very fiscally responsible Chapters.

It may be worth mentioning that in no way is this section suggesting that all of the above options be implemented simultaneously. Rather, this is a more of an à la carte menu of options for consideration in what the Chapter might use as the foundation for a lively discussion driving toward a solution that best fits the Chapter's constituents.

A Dartboard for Pricing Memberships

Using the same categories presented above as illustrative, some considerations and price ranges will be offered as a frame of reference. All pricing presented is assumed to be an annual rate unless otherwise stated.

- **Recent grad / young alumni membership** – It is recommended that this membership be fairly low priced or complimentary. Very few people walk away from a free membership. In reviewing a number of young alumni memberships for various universities, it is common to offer a 30–50 percent discount on the standard membership. Typical range for this membership would be $0 to $35. From another perspective, placing a $0 price on something may signify it has little value. It has been my experience that a floor of $10 is affordable yet high enough for there to be some level of value associated with it.
- **Retired alumni membership** – Again, this group should be encouraged to participate; however, they are largely on a fixed income. The Chapter might consider a low annual rate ranging from $15 to $25.
- **Standard alumni membership** – There are no special considerations here. The standard alumni membership should be meaningful but not cost prohibitive. A typical range is from $30 to $75.
- **Alumni joint membership** – As this is a two-for-one deal, a reasonable range would be something about $5 to $10 less than twice the standard alumni membership.
- **Alumni family membership** – This could represent two, three, or more people. Based on our earlier example, a reasonable range would be between $65 and $125.
- **Affinity membership** – Of the options so far, this group is the furthest removed from actual alumni, so a higher price is justified. However,

that person is likely already paying dues elsewhere. Consider pricing the membership just above a standard alumni membership, from $45 to $80.

- **Friend of . . . membership** – This membership takes it even further outside the circle than the affinity membership. Price this membership as a bit of a premium around $55 to $90. An example of this category could be the Alumni By Choice (ABC) group listed by the Louisiana State University (LSU) Alumni Association, as noted earlier in this section.

- **Premium membership** – This one is intentionally a deluxe standard alumni membership and should be priced accordingly. The Chapter might consider pricing this one in the range of $75 to $100.

- **Multi-year memberships** – Assuming this is for the largest group of members—alumni—these should be priced just below what someone would spend if they paid for the standard alumni membership each year. For example, a two-year membership should cost just under twice the price of a one-year standard alumni membership.

- **Lifetime memberships** – If selling this one, your Chapter is seeking the money up front and / or possibly betting on the chance that alumna / alumnus might not be locally active for the foreseeable future. This one should be a bit higher, in the couple-hundred-dollar range.

If all of these membership types were to be adopted by a Chapter, a membership structure with pricing might look similar to the following:

Membership Type	Example Pricing
Recent Grad / Young Alumni	$10
Retired Alumni	$15
1-Year Premium Alumni	$100
1-Year Standard Alumni	$45
2-Year Standard Alumni	$85
3-Year Standard Alumni	$120
Lifetime	$500
Alumni Joint	$85
Alumni Family	$100
Affinity	$45
Friend of . . .	$65

The categories above are examples of how a Chapter might approach memberships. They are not recommended to be used as a complete list. Mix and match the concepts—such as creating a lifetime joint membership—then choose what is most appropriate for your Chapter.

More often than you might expect, I have heard complaints from alumni after receiving a request for becoming a member or a membership renewal. The problem generally stems from the invitation itself—rather than the concept—and the absence of a value proposition or gratitude. What instantly jumps to mind is the Chapter's poor job of either providing value or effectively communicating and / or demonstrating the benefits of membership. If so, you are already armed with strategies to counter these issues.

If not, there is another possibility since there are two sides to the value equation: what people receive and what they pay. The resistance could be less about what the Chapter is offering for or communicating about the membership and more about the actual amount of the cash outlay relative to those benefits. Sometimes, it can take a mountain of intangible value to justify spending hard-earned money. One way or another, alumni need to feel the value.

Focusing on the extremely financially motivated alumni, one approach to countering opposition to the cost is presenting an irrefutable incentive to join the Chapter during event registration. To illustrate this point, let's make two assumptions: a standard, annual alumni membership is $40, and the desired member price for an event is $20. We already touched on steering people towards purchasing a membership based on the differential between the non-member and member prices. Thus, the non-member price should be in the ballpark of $30 or $35.

Taking this a step further, the Chapter could also offer a third ticket that represents a combination of event registration with a membership. Consider pricing the bundle measurably less than the addition of the two, while not being too much more than the price of a non-member ticket. This is a delicate balance. You are trying to make it difficult, almost illogical, for a non-member to choose anything other than the membership option. Let's continue to put numbers to this example laced with an intangible benefit to spice it up:

Anywhere Alumni Club of
Fictitious State University's Speaker Event

- $20 member ticket – includes event registration plus access to a private, members-only reception with the speaker following the talk.

- $30 non-member ticket – includes event registration.
- $45 annual alumni membership + event registration – includes annual membership, plus event registration, plus access to the private, members-only reception with the speaker ($60 value).

You may be concerned that your Chapter is missing out on the additional $15. I would suggest the contrary, based on the fact that this attendee has not previously been compelled to become a member despite all of the wonderful incentives that may have been offered. After the sparkly benefits have been dangled and the emotional heartstrings have been pulled, the last-ditch effort to convert the alumni community should be rooted in a strategically financial incentive—and registration is where you make that play.

Your Chapter will also need to decide if the memberships will be rolling, meaning they will expire in twelve months (or twenty-four or thirty-six months) from the date of purchase. The alternative is to pin the membership to a specific twelve months, such as the calendar year, starting in January, or the administrative year, likely starting in July. The advantage to the fixed year is that the Chapter only needs to focus on membership renewal at one time a year (and it will be easier for alumni to remember when a renewal comes due). The downside is that the Chapter may now need to consider prorating memberships throughout the year as alumni sign up or possibly face unhappy constituents.

If the Chapter chooses a rolling year from the time a membership is activated, money will be coming in all throughout the year from satisfied alumni. The flip side of this situation is that as the money trickles in, the Chapter will not know exactly how much money it will have available to fund the programs that year.

One more option to consider revolves around membership renewals. The Chapter may wish to adopt an automatic renewal option in which alumni could opt in or out at the time of establishing a membership or anytime thereafter. Membership renewal pricing could be set as equivalent to the prior year or at a slight discount rewarding those who chose to opt in. The Chapter might also choose to prompt other members just prior to expiration with a slight discount to renew early.

These programs are easiest to administer if the Chapter is using some version of software that has the ability to automatically renew, invoice, or at least alert alumni approaching their membership expirations. Efforts to encourage renewing a membership rather than waiting on the alumni to remember are largely rewarded. It is positive for both sides. More alumni typically renew, generating more income for the Chapter, and the alumni are pleased because they did not have to take responsibility to manage their own membership account.

Two last notes before moving on relate to managing multiple names related to a joint or family membership and tax implications. It might get tricky associating more than one name to a single paid membership. It is advantageous to have an electronic system to manage whatever method is chosen. Some payment-processing vendors might even offer some of the necessary functionality. Second, and related to taxes, if the Chapter is a 501(c)(3)-recognized entity, membership dues may be tax deductible under certain circumstances. For example, if the benefits are small and largely intangible, then most dues under $75 are likely to be deductible. More information about this topic can be found in the much later section *"State and Federal Tax Implications: 501(c)(3) vs. 501(c)(7) and Tax Deductible Donations."*

When Local Membership Dues Are Prohibited

If the Chapter falls into the second category, in which the central alumni association collects membership dues while the Chapter cannot, then it is reasonable to expect that the association will share some of the proceeds with the local Chapters (possibly as described in the previous section, *"Coveted Resources from the Central Alumni Association: An Annual Stipend—Great Seed Money"*). If it does not, then the next sections of this guide may be all the more valuable.

Chapters falling into the third category, in which both alumni association and Chapter participation are expressly automatic rights of college or university enrollment or affinity in which no dues will ever be collected, could find themselves in a similar situation to many in the second category. If so, the recommendation would be to move on and focus on alternative and approved methods of income.

It is important that if the local Chapter is prevented from collecting membership dues by central alumni association or college / university policy, the policy should be respected. There are several other income-generating options to embrace.

60-Second Takeaway

If local Chapters are free to collect membership dues, it opens the door to dependable, recurring income. Be certain to spend some time exploring the following concepts as they best apply to your Chapter: appropriate definition of a member, benefits of membership, various membership types, pricing strategies, and characterization of membership administration. The next considerations include automatic and / or prompted renewal strategies based on goals, culture, and ability to administer. On the other hand, if policies exist that expressly prohibit local Chapters from collecting any form of membership dues, they should be respected. No fear; there are several other methods of revenue generation that may be acceptable to adopt.

SOCIETY FOR ALUMNI CLUB LEADERSHIP

DRIVING THRIVING NETWORKS

If you find the material in *FULLY FUNDED* valuable, consider providing a book to each of your volunteer alumni club and affinity group leaders. The practical guidance, checklists and free accompanying resources will generate mountains of positive benefit – not to mention the amazing goodwill!

We offer discounts by the case. Order through SACL or CASE, or after Sept. 5th, also through your university book store.

It also makes a great alumni leaders conference take-away!

Make It Happen Checklist

☐ Inquire with the central alumni association regarding what policies might exist related to local Chapters collecting membership dues.

☐ If Chapters are free to collect dues:

» Become clear on the official definition of alumni as stated by the alumni association.

» Assess the make-up of the population likely to pay membership dues and develop clear definitions for each membership type.

» Build an appropriate membership structure and apply pricing to each type.

» Define the membership year.

» Determine what method the Chapter will embrace to manage memberships. Will there be an associated cost?

» Determine if an automatic and / or prompted renewal strategy could be implemented and initiate it if possible.

» Provide proper documentation upon payment of dues.

☐ If Chapters are restricted from collecting dues, yet dues are collected by the central alumni association, inquire about receiving some version of revenue-sharing or incentive-based financial support.

☐ If both Chapters and the central alumni association are restricted from collecting dues, respect the policies and move on to other avenues of revenue generation.

Sponsorships Loved Far and Wide

Sponsorships are magical! They can be of any size, can span any length of time, and can be associated with a variety of categories. Sponsorships can be at the Chapter level, spanning a year, or they can simply be event specific. Sponsorships are both income if in the form of cash *and* cost relief if in the form of products, services, or venue space.

University alumni associations each have their policies regarding sponsorships. Of those that permit them, some Chapters are free to accept sponsorships directly, while some are able to do so only by way of the alumni association. An example of the latter is offered by VCU Alumni. Chapters of VCU Alumni are closely affiliated subordinate groups unable to accept direct sponsorships; however, VCU Alumni established a mechanism by which the Chapters can directly benefit as follows:

> All contributions, sponsorships, program revenue, and fees should be made payable to VCU Alumni with the memo line indicating which constituency group [Chapter] and what funds were used for. These funds will be attributed to the individual constituent organizations within the financial system and restricted for their authorized use.[1]

Not all universities support soliciting sponsorships or donations to the Chapter; however, for those that do, I highly recommend that Chapters do not take it for granted. Such support can be a game changer when it comes to the quality of Chapter events. The Georgia State University Alumni Association (GSUAA) encourages sponsorships and states:

> Clubs are encouraged to solicit and secure sponsorships whenever possible, be they for the club's general operations or specific events. It fattens clubs' accounts, increases industry awareness and adds prestige.[2]

If the Chapter plans on pursuing sponsorships, it would be wise to establish a dedicated leadership role to take the lead. There is enough to strategize, plan, develop, and execute that it would truly be too much in addition to another role.

We will explore the primary benefits of sponsorships, list various types, brainstorm potential benefits to sponsors, identify danger zones to avoid, discuss sources of sponsors, review an example of a compelling Chapter overview, and learn how to keep sponsors once they have committed to the first one.

Cost-Relieving Gifts of Products, Services, or Venues

Sponsors, also occasionally referred to as underwriters, may provide direct cash payment, or they may provide needed products or services to the Chapter. Direct payment is simple to grasp, so let us spend a few moments understanding the budgetary benefits of an in-kind arrangement. An in-kind donation or gift is when, instead of giving money to buy needed goods and services, the goods and services themselves are given. The Chapter benefits just as much from a sponsor that is willing to provide goods or services for which a Chapter would have otherwise had to pay, such as a venue or even legal guidance, as it does from direct cash—and possibly more so (see later section "*State and Federal Tax Implications*" for more information on this concept).

For example, a local sports bar and restaurant might be an excellent sponsorship target for game-watching parties. The sports bar might be willing to dedicate a part of the space for your Chapter and agree to play the games on the largest screens. It might also be willing to throw in free appetizers during the game or a gift card as a door prize. This is an ideal win-win situation. The Chapter scores a consistent, supportive venue with ideal AV equipment and food—all at no cost, while in return the sports bar gets free promotion to the entire local alumni population and the reliable opportunity to sell more beverages and meals.

There is one more exceptionally important benefit to this particular scenario illustrated above—all of the selling and serving of alcohol is done directly between the sports bar and individual alumni. The Chapter must know to stay very clear of purchasing, selling, or serving alcohol in any way, shape, or form—in order to comply with the vast majority of insurance policies. It is likely that the alumni association has an alcohol policy and possibly insurance with guidelines established, of which your Chapter leaders should be well aware.

The University of Georgia (UGA) Alumni Association is an advocate of in-kind sponsorships. They have this to say about them:

Chapters can have local businesses, companies and/or individuals help offset costs for a chapter event. Local companies may want to provide door prizes, event supplies, or a monetary gift. In return for providing these gifts or services, they can receive gift recognition from the UGA Foundation. Sponsorships are great ways to further fund chapter events and the university! Chapter event sponsors can be recognized on event marketing materials, as part of the event program, and on social media pages.[3]

While some alumni Chapters are permitted to accept sponsorships directly either in-kind or in the form of cash, not all can—especially when the Chapter is not a separate entity but rather tightly tied to the alumni association from a legal standpoint. Don't give up; associations like the UGA Alumni Association and the Johns Hopkins Alumni Association (JHAA) have identified a way to make it work to the benefit of the Chapter. The JHAA has found that if an alumna / alumnus wishes to financially support the Chapter or an event directly, it is preferable if they actually purchase the event food or parking and then donate that product or service to the Chapter for the event. The alumni association is then able to provide a gift-in-kind donation letter in return for tax purposes.[4]

In short, either a direct cash sponsorship that qualifies as revenue or a sponsorship of products / services / venues offsets a cost the Chapter would have had to cover.

A Smorgasbord of Sponsorships

As mentioned in the opening of this section, sponsorships can be of any size, can span any length of time, and can be associated with a variety of categories. We will start by exploring categories of sponsorship.

A person or business may sponsor the entire Chapter in general, or it may sponsor only a specific event. An example of sponsoring the Chapter itself would leverage the sports bar from the earlier example. In this case, the restaurant continues to offer benefits throughout the season, week after week, game after game. This routine support could very well be classified and acknowledged as a Chapter sponsorship.

Chapter sponsors may be service-related as well, such as a marketing sponsor, or any entity that wishes to keep its name in front of the alumni throughout the year. An example of a service-related sponsor might be a website provider. It was noted earlier that 9 percent of Chapter websites are donated by a member or a sponsor.

An event sponsorship might look more like the following example. The Wharton School is well known for its focus on commercial real estate. The Wharton Club of Chicago hosts an event in which a prominent alumna and CEO of a large real estate company is the honored speaker. Naturally, parties interested in being associated with this industry at this level would be ideal event sponsors. Examples might include other real estate companies and corporations that provide services to real estate companies, such as banks or architecture firms.

Event sponsorships can be further dissected. They may be applied to the entire event, or they might be specific to only a part of the event, a service, or a function. For example, your event may have a specific valet parking sponsor, a welcome reception sponsor, and a photo booth sponsor. This approach allows sponsors to experience some exclusivity at a more agreeable price.

Regarding the length of time, event sponsorships are clearly situational and have a specific start and end to the relationship. Chapter sponsorships are typically for one year—be it the calendar year or the administrative year (that more closely follows the academic year). It is not unusual to negotiate effective dates of two or more years, should circumstances be appropriate. This is akin to a multi-year Chapter membership for alumni.

Sponsorships are magical, shape-morphing pots of gold. Feel free to be creative with the scope, length of time, niche, or combinations thereof to identify good opportunities for both your Chapter and the sponsor.

Sponsor Benefits and Packages

Next, we will visualize and discuss sponsorships from the perspective of a series with graduating value. As your goal is to generate revenue, offering various benefit levels for sponsorships has been known to drive candidates to commit greater dollars to the Chapter. For explanation purposes, we will simply use the concept of a standard series of bronze, silver, and gold levels and apply them specifically to full Chapter sponsorships (rather than events).

Identify what your Chapter has to offer sponsors (ideally, low- or no-out-of-pocket-cost items) and build those benefits into increasingly attractive packages. Since sponsors primarily want recognition and access to the alumni population, those elements should be the cornerstones of your packages.

A bronze sponsor may get their logo on the Chapter's Web page, and that is it. A gold sponsor might have the logo on the sponsorship page and, at each event: 1) verbal recognition by the President, 2) a certain number of tickets to attend, and 3) the opportunity to display its marketing materials. The silver sponsor would experience something in the middle.

A Chapter may choose to limit the number of sponsorships available at a certain level to enhance exclusivity. I recommend waiting to add any such limitations until the sponsorship program is well underway—unless an irresistible offer is made. Initially, do not incorporate too many parameters. Make it as easy as possible for a sponsor to get to a yes decision. If the program is well executed and becomes a thriving success, take it anywhere you wish to go from there!

The Binghamton University Alumni Association is a real supporter of sponsorships, stating that they enhance engagement activity and the ability to reach more alumni. The association has designed two event sponsorship packages for Chapters as follows:

Level 1: $500

» Name/logo recognition on postcard/e-mail invites to the event (2 or 3 e-mail invites for each event)*

» Name/logo recognition on event follow-up e-mail

» Name/logo on display at the check-in table

» Company pamphlets or other literature present at the check-in table

» Name/logo listed on the Alumni Association's regional event/ affinity group sponsor web page for as long as the event appears

» One representative from the sponsoring company may attend the event at no cost

Level 2: $1,000 – All items under Level 1 plus the following:

» Name/company tagged as a sponsor on chapter/affinity group's Facebook Page as events are promoted (2 time minimum for each event)*

» Name/logo recognition in event coverage in Alumni Connect e-newsletter

» Name/company recognition during event remarks as a sponsor

» Two representatives from the sponsoring company may attend the event at no cost

» Promotional e-mail sent out on behalf of sponsor to all event attendees after event

*Sponsors will be included in all promotion leading up to an event upon being confirmed and receiving their sponsorship payment.[5]

Sponsorship packages like the ones above offer real value to both parties. It is not difficult to design appealing packages since most sponsors simply want recognition and access to the alumni.

Danger Zones, Pitfalls, and What Not to Offer

Many colleges and universities have marketing agreements with particular product and services companies, including food and beverages companies. It is imperative that the Chapter not accept a sponsor that may be in conflict with one already contractually seated with the university. The central alumni association will be able to identify a conflict, so work closely with them through the process. For example, the Georgia State University Alumni Association (GSUAA) expressly outlines such types of sponsors to avoid:

> Clubs may not solicit the following types of companies, due to exclusivity contracts: financial institutions; mortgage; hospitals; auto & home insurance; credit card; and vehicles.[6]

Also, it is important to understand that sponsorships are rarely acceptable when they represent tobacco products, alcoholic beverages, or gambling. Even if a Chapter is generally permitted to seek sponsorships for events, permissions may not extend into these three areas. The Nebraska Alumni Association (NAA) is one of many schools to adopt this perspective, stating quite succinctly that

> sponsors and promotions that include tobacco products, alcoholic beverages and gambling are not permitted.[7]

Your Chapter's best bet is simply to avoid the dangerous three altogether. If the opportunity is so great that your Chapter cannot bear to walk away, reach out to your alumni association. It will be able to confirm any such restrictions—or provide the green light.

Next, be mindful not to violate the Taxpayer Relief Act of 1997, which states that use of the sponsor's name or logo as part of a sponsored event is acceptable as long as there is no other substantial return benefit. Attention to this issue varies from alumni association to alumni association, so check with your Chapter liaison. Absent that, it is prudent to err on the side of caution. In general, avoid:

- Comparative language (such as "the best . . .")
- Any mention of pricing or other indications of savings or value
- A personal or Chapter endorsement
- Inducements to purchase or use products / services

It is best to simply introduce the sponsor and publicly thank them while abstaining from any color commentary. The University of Florida Alumni Association (UFAA) strongly agrees with the above approach. It warns its Chapters not to venture too close to what the IRS would consider advertising. It uses examples like "the restaurant where Gators eat" or "the official Gator restaurant" as phrases to avoid. If the Chapter is a 501(c)(3)-tax-exempt organization, ramifications of violating this regulation include the disqualification of the payment as a charitable contribution for the contributor and reclassification of the money as taxable unrelated business income for the Chapter and / or alumni association.[8]

Lastly, it is essential that Chapter leaders understand that contact details for their alumni are confidential information. It would be absolutely shocking if the central alumni association had not already established an iron-clad policy regarding confidentiality and safeguarding of such alumni information. Accordingly, a Chapter should never agree to offer alumni contact details to a sponsor, including e-mail addresses, home addresses, phone numbers, etc. An example would be if the sponsor requested the event registration list. A prudent response would be to decline the request. Rather, sponsors should be given full access to make personal connections at events, facilitating the direct, manual collection of the desired contact details from the alumni themselves.

Although sponsors can be a vital component of a Chapter's financial strategy, just be aware of the potential danger zones when soliciting and executing sponsorships.

Sourcing Sponsors

Alumni make the most sympathetic and easiest-to-identify sponsorship candidates—especially for Chapter-wide sponsorships. Start by mining your own local alumni database in search of self-employed and small-business leaders. These people tend to truly appreciate the relationships and connections available to them through the alumni network.

Next, focus on the alumni in leadership with larger companies, as they tend to have deeper pockets. The Harvard Business School (HBS) Club of

Dallas has mastered the steps of enticing local alumni to become Chapter sponsors. It has a list as long as your arm of those who have stepped up year after year. It has become a point of pride and prestige to be an HBS Club of Dallas sponsor. The club offers a simple Gold package for $250 with free admission to club lunches as well as a Platinum option for $500, incorporating the additional benefit of free admission to club breakfasts. Approximately 22 percent of the local membership base opts for the sponsorship packages over the standard membership.[9]

The third step in Chapter-wide sponsor hunting is to seek out service providers beyond your alumni pool that would benefit from access to your alumni. Hypothetically, the Stanford Club of Washington might reach out to retailers of high-end outdoor-sports equipment as sponsors. In fact, the product or service provider might actually sponsor an entire event that helps highlight their solutions.

In 2015, Tesla used this strategy by reaching out to alumni Chapters of targeted schools across the country. They offered to host a driving experience in which alumni could each log time in one of the newly launched cars. Tesla hosted the events at their facilities with non-alcoholic beverages and hors d'oeuvres available while alumni waiting their turn could network amongst themselves and sales personnel while learning about the safety and performance features of the cars. The driving experiences were interesting, and alumni in each city seemed to enjoy knowing the inside story.

In another example in which the alumni Chapter represents a prominent school of hotel and restaurant management, sponsors might be any company focused on the hospitality industry. You might target local boutique recruiting firms, specialty food service providers, or maybe a specific hotel company with a headquarters in your region. All would be very interested in access to your Chapter's overall population.

For the fourth step, target event sponsors by identifying events throughout the year with a specific focus. Make a list of businesses that would consider the attendee population of that specific focus to be of value. For example, maybe your Chapter is hosting an event in which a panel of speakers will discuss the best ways to get accepted into your alma mater and the application process itself. Targeted event sponsors might be SAT preparation businesses and those wishing to equip new students in new living quarters, such as backpack and luggage retailers.

If sponsorship is or becomes a priority for your Chapter, it is often more successful under the charge of a dedicated leadership role, such as the Vice

President of Sponsorship. Then start strategically attacking the challenge, beginning with your local alumni in small businesses, followed by those in companies with deeper pockets. Next, approach third parties with a broad appreciation for the uniqueness of your total population and conclude with organizations that have subject matter alignment with your specific event topics.

Weaving a Compelling Story

Your Chapter must present a viable value proposition in return for sponsorship to secure a commitment. Sometimes, the value is as simple as feeling good about supporting the local Chapter in which they participate. Often, and especially if there are more decision makers involved other than just alumni, the sponsorship must yield a measurable business benefit.

One way we tackled this through the Wharton Club of Dallas–Fort Worth was to take inventory of our population. We built a summary describing our membership in terms of size, industry breakdown, job functions, corporate seniority, and geographic distribution. We then compiled information regarding past activities, speakers, events, and charitable projects, pairing them with participation counts. Lastly, we elegantly packaged sponsorship plans for the upcoming year. From that information, we could tailor a pitch to just about any prospective sponsor. Not only did that data help entice potential sponsors, but it was also the ammunition needed to sell the sponsorship up the chain of command in the potentially sponsoring organization. Although it was generated six years ago, it is effective and still requested today. The opening of the twelve-page document is shared below.

The Wharton School

The Wharton School at the University of Pennsylvania was established as the world's first collegiate business school in 1881 and is part of the Ivy League family of renowned academic institutions. It has the largest and one of the most published business school faculty with more than 250 standing and associate instructors and has been recognized as the number-one ranked business school countless times by publications including *Business Week* and the *Financial Times*. Graduates have completed at least one of five programs: undergraduate, standard MBA, executive MBA, doctorate, or the fellows program. The 86,000 alumni span 146 countries around the globe and interact through the network of seventy-eight alumni clubs—and are leaders in almost every industry.

Wharton Club of Dallas–Fort Worth

The Wharton Club of Dallas–Fort Worth ("Club"), a federally and state-recognized 501(c)(3) nonprofit, tax-exempt organization, has a longstanding history of strength. It began as a simple association in the early seventies and was formally incorporated in 1981. Today, there are more than 1,000 alumni located in the DFW metroplex.

The Club's leadership consists of seven officers, twelve directors at large on the Board, and our General Counsel—all of whom serve on a volunteer basis. The alumni themselves represent decision makers almost exclusively, with more than 83 percent at the director level or above and 68 percent at the Vice President level or higher.

From an industry perspective, our alumni cross numerous sectors. However, the most dominant by far is the financial sector, spanning banking, private equity, venture capital, hedge funds, investment management, and more, representing over 30 percent of our alumni's focus, followed by consulting at approximately 15 percent. Real estate totals 8 percent, right ahead of energy (including oil and gas) at 6 percent. The remaining 47 percent support more than 40 different industries.

The Club maintains a local website and communicates through weekly e-newsletters, our local LinkedIn Group, a Facebook Page, and direct mailings. We offer our members a robust schedule of programs to meet their various professional and personal interests as well as their schedules. The Club hosts approximately four formal Club-wide, Club-sponsored events in the fall and another four in the spring, complemented by happy hours, University sponsored webinars, and special on-location trips and events. Additionally, the Club hosts an exceptionally popular annual gala heavily attended every January by alumni and guests as a kick-off to the year's spring schedule. As an introduction to the Club's programs, the robust 2011 spring line-up is still evolving; however, the following represents the schedule as it has evolved thus far:

January

» Jan 12 – Wharton Health Care / Alumni Happy Hour at the 2011 J.P. Morgan Healthcare Conference (San Francisco)

» Jan 25 – Quarterly Wharton Webinar Series: Nation Branding: Applications for Israel with Wharton's William Stewart Woodside Professor and Professor of Marketing David Reibstein

» Jan 25 – Wharton Health Care Alumni Association Webinar: High Growth Medical Device Markets – How do later entries gain a toe-hold?

» Jan 29 – Annual Wharton Membership Gala – An Evening to Remember (Foundation Room, Dallas)

February

» Feb 2 – Limited Lunch with Wharton's own real estate mogul, Professor Peter Linneman (Dallas) – SPONSORED BY ORIX

» Feb 4 – The Future of the NFL as a Business with Ken Shropshire, Faculty Director, Wharton Sports Business Initiative (WSBI) and Derrick Heggans, Managing Director, WSBI and former NFL attorney (Old Red Museum, Dallas) – SPONSORED BY WSBI

» Feb 9 – Getting More: How to Negotiate to Achieve Your Goals in the Real World with World Renown Wharton Professor of Legal Studies, Adjunct Professor of Law, Stuart Diamond (Cooper Guest Lodge, Dallas) – SPONSORED BY EZforex. com

» Feb 25–27 – Wharton Alumni Vail Ski Weekend hosted by Rob Katz W'88, CEO of Vail Resorts and sponsored by the Wharton Club of Colorado (Vail)

» Feb 26 – Wharton Le Cordon Bleu Culinary Experience (Dallas)

March

» Mar 9 – Evening with Darren Rodgers, President and CEO of Blue Cross Blue Shield of Texas (BCBS Offices, Richardson) – SPONSORED BY BLUE CROSS BLUE SHIELD

» Mar 24 – Quarterly Wharton Webinar Series: Getting More: How to Negotiate to Achieve Your Goals in the Real World with Stuart Diamond, Practice Professor of Legal Studies, Adjunct Professor of Law

» Mar 26 – Wharton Ladies Tea (Stacie's Home, Dallas)

April

» Apr – An Evening with Tiffany's (Northpark, Dallas) – SPONSORED BY TIFFANY & CO.

» Apr 27 to May 10 – Himalayan Leadership Trek to Mount Everest with Wharton Professors Michael Useem and Edwin Bernbaum sponsored by Geographic Expeditions (Mount Everest)

May

» May 3 – Quarterly Wharton Webinar Series: The Lessons and Legacy of Napster with Peter Fader, Frances and Pei-Yuan Chia, Professor; Professor of Marketing; Co-Director, Wharton Interactive Media Initiative

» May 13–15 – Wharton Alumni Reunion Weekend (Philadelphia)

June

» June 26–30 – The Normandy Leadership Experience: Critical Lessons for Today's Leaders (France)

Other events in planning and yet to set a date include the Wharton Legal Lunch (sponsorship in process), Wharton CEO Lunch, the Wharton CFO Lunch, and others.[10]

Notice the inclusion of a broad swath of programs for the year, including ones we were directly managing as well as some that were designed by the alumni association supporting the entire network. This provides a better idea for the level of activity and the affinity for the university. Not including such information may be shortchanging the true value of your Chapter. Be careful not to suggest sponsors would have exposure to attendees of the wider programming, however.

This overall introduction sets the stage for why someone should be interested in our local alumni base. It demonstrates organization, relevance, quality, and opportunity. This summary is followed by several sponsorship packages increasing in value and financial commitment and finally closed by an application indicating a fixed expiration in December. In this case, it was an effective strategy, generating a sense of urgency on the part of the sponsor. Since we were presenting this packet in January and it expired at the year end, the more time wasted on the front end was simply the sponsor's loss.

In order to generate the sponsorship packages, the Chapter leadership team should consider conducting a brainstorming session. This is not the only way to establish credibility with a potential sponsor, but it is highly effective. Assuming sponsorships are approved by the alumni association and your Chapter does not have access to the database of local alumni, reach to assess what might be available. Analyze and develop your own Chapter profile blended with possible sponsorship packages and see how far it might take you. Reach out to me via any of my or SACL's social media platforms if you would like the rest of this document.

Keep Them Coming Back

Selling sponsorships is not enough for a sustainable program. The Chapter must then deliver to ensure sponsorship renewal. The sponsor must feel that the Chapter fulfilled its entire side of the proposition. First, do not over promise. That is a surefire way to lose a sponsor and damage a relationship.

Second, do everything in your power to demonstrate appreciation for sponsors, including introducing its representatives to alumni and acknowledging the support publicly at gatherings, in newsletters, and on social media. Most certainly, ensure that all commitments made in the sponsorship agreement on the side of the Chapter are visibly upheld.

Third—this may seem a bit old school, but it yields mountains of goodwill—send a thank-you note to the individual responsible for establishing the sponsorship and to the company. Depending on the size of the organization, address the letter to the appropriate recipient: the marketing manager, charitable giving manager, the CEO, or possibly the individual's boss. This tiny step goes a long way to secure a positive experience for the sponsor.

Fourth, on an annual basis, review the sponsorship program and evolve the packages to improve the benefits and keep pace with technology. There will likely be many modifications after the first year, once the Chapter has a little experience under its belt. Additionally, as technology advances, so are the likely desires of sponsors. For example, social media may continue to offer expansion opportunities over time.

Lastly, be prepared with the paperwork to renew the sponsorships in plenty of time before they expire. This is especially important if they expire at the end of the calendar year. With the holiday chaos, the uptick in the use of vacation days, and year-end sales targets during December, be prepared.

Landing a new sponsor is to be celebrated. From that point, the sponsorship is yours to lose. That loss can especially sting when there are alumni relationships tangled within. It is not difficult to build and maintain a healthy, happy long-term relationship with the sponsor, but that relationship does need tending. Do not take it for granted when the paperwork is signed; rather, make it last.

60-Second Takeaway

Sponsorships are amazing sources of income and cost elimination for a Chapter in the forms of cash and in-kind contributions, respectively. They can be designed to fit almost any situation (function, length of time, specific events, tiered categories, and more) and are options available to many Chapters. The local alumni base is an excellent source of sponsors, followed by businesses that find the alumni population attractive continuously or during a topically relevant event. Be mindful of the pitfalls: do not compete with alumni association sponsors, be aware of blatantly "advertising," and never share alumni contact details with sponsors.

A professional yet brief profile of the college or university, as well as the local Chapter, followed by various sponsorship opportunities and an application / contract is an excellent place to start when building a sponsorship packet. However, landing a sponsor is not enough. Ensure that the Chapter fulfils its commitment to the sponsor, going above and beyond to build the relationship for the long term, while not violating laws. Evolve the sponsorship packages annually, demonstrate gratitude to relevant people, and be prepared to renew them in plenty of time. Once your Chapter lands a sponsor, it is then yours to lose. Don't let that happen.

Make It Happen Checklist

- ☐ When embarking on sponsorships, confirm association approval and establish a dedicated sponsorship role for the Chapter, such as the Vice President of Sponsorship.
- ☐ Review budgeting goals and sponsorship needs.
- ☐ Identify the university and alumni association's contracted sponsors and exclusion criteria.
- ☐ Brainstorm a list of benefits the Chapter has the capacity to offer sponsors. Seek a wish list from prospective sponsors to expand and round out the list.
- ☐ Build a structure for sponsorships most appropriate for the Chapter, including the types of sponsorships, sponsorship levels, benefits, timeframes, and pricing.
- ☐ Access whatever data is possible to analyze and build a compelling college / university and Chapter profile, using the example as a guide.
- ☐ Thread it together with the sponsorship packages to generate an enticing sponsorship packet for distribution to targets.
- ☐ Identify potential sponsors from within the alumni pool, first targeting small-business owners, followed by those employed in large companies with deep pockets.
- ☐ Identify third-party organizations to which the Chapter population as a whole is enticing, followed by those to whom specific Chapter event topics may be of special interest.
- ☐ Stay mindful not to violate any university policies and / or state and federal laws regarding sponsors / sponsorships.
- ☐ Close as many sponsorships as possible in accordance with all guidelines.
- ☐ Report and celebrate the new and / or ongoing sponsorships with the Chapter.
- ☐ Ensure that the Chapter's commitments are upheld and that the sponsors are abundantly pleased with the opportunities made available to them.
- ☐ Demonstrate appreciation often, publicly, and thank sponsors in writing.
- ☐ Evaluate and update the sponsorship packages at least annually.
- ☐ Be prepared to seek sponsorship renewals in plenty of time prior to expiration, especially if it aligns with the end of December.
- ☐ Have fun with your fellow alumni and the sponsors!

Traditional and Not-So-Traditional Fundraising

Like sponsorships, traditional fundraising is a wonderful income-generating opportunity that has been practiced for ages—and will be for ages to come. It can take place in the form of a simple campaign for cash donations, small programs in which items are sold at an inflated price, various types of auctions, or even large-scale events, such as golf tournaments, to name a few.

It is amazing how willing alumni can be to donate to their Chapter and / or university—and how often the opportunity is missed. I spoke with one alumna from Colorado State University who mentioned how much she was looking forward to a local alumni dinner coordinated by the alumni association. Expecting the dinner was a fundraising opportunity, she arrived armed with a checkbook. Much to her surprise, no one requested any donations at any time throughout the dinner. Disappointed, she went home without having made a contribution. The takeaway is that all that was needed was an ask for the donation. One might say that she could have offered a check before leaving, and that is certainly true. But she didn't, and that is an important point. She had wanted her money to have been needed. Fulfilling a need is far more rewarding than simply throwing money at someone or something. If your Chapter intends to raise funds, presenting a need and asking for the funds to solve it is a strikingly simple yet remarkably effective formula.

A volunteer alumni leader of Northwestern University's Kellogg Network DFW shared a similar story, only with a very different outcome. The leadership was reaching out to local alumni who had not yet been active with the Chapter, hoping to inspire new participation in Chapter activities. Near the end of one conversation, the alumnus contacted thanked the Chapter leader for reaching out and asked if there was anything that he could do in the meantime. It was a long shot, but the leader asked for a sizable donation, and the alumnus happily obliged. This is another great example of a generous donation that would have been missed if the alumnus simply had not been asked. Establishing a formal fundraiser, like the ones discussed below, can be just the ticket, giving your alumni the opportunity to write that check or send that mobile contribution that they are already poised and ready to execute.

One more note before looking into specifics. Fundraising, regardless of the method, tends to be far more effective if there is a stated purpose, especially one to which people can relate. Simply raising funds in general is a steeper hill to climb. Your Chapter might find it more effective if it were to choose a focus for the raise, such as scholarships or a student-recruiting effort. Operational expenses are fair game as well; just identify the specific need, such as insurance or administrative help. In this case, the theme of the fundraising might be "to keep the lights on."

Also, just as you would when running a membership campaign, make sure the Chapter leadership does an effective job of demonstrating what the impact of meeting the funding goals would be, how it makes a difference, and, if applicable, why it is directly beneficial to the alumni or their community. When it comes to scholarships, it might be a pretty easy sell. For operational expenses, the Chapter might highlight how not having the insurance coverage would affect the type of events the Chapter could host, such as being able to offer a particular picnic or having alcoholic beverages at events. If the need is for administrative assistance, then share how not having it would impact Chapter functions, such as how there might be fewer communications or how one or two Chapter officers would have to step down because they do not have the time for the administrative parts of the job. The takeaway here is that your Chapter needs a purpose for the raise, and that purpose needs to resonate with the alumni—both the potential benefit(s) and / or the repercussions for not achieving it.

Embarking on fundraising can be an involved effort. It is recommended, should a Chapter wish to take this path forward, that it does so with a local leader specifically dedicated to fundraising. Depending on the complexity of the type of fundraising, additional volunteers may need to be recruited as well. This function will most certainly be a bit much for other leaders to tack onto their existing responsibilities.

Throughout this section, we will touch on time-tested favorites, but with a more modern twist, as well as newer, technology-enabled methods including crowdfunding.

Cash Campaigns Plain and Simple

The fastest and easiest of the fundraising methods involves a basic campaign simply asking for money. This can be a one-on-one ask, a series of one-on-one asks, or a more organized event appealing to a broader group of alumni. The Brigham Young University (BYU) Alumni Association acknowledges that Chapters need operating capital and mentions seeking individual cash donations from local alumni, among other alternatives to help cover Chapter expenses. The BYU Alumni Association also acknowledges the volunteer's time and effort necessary to raise funds, encouraging larger requests less often by stating:

> Occasionally alumni appreciate an event that has no costs involved. It is better to make big amounts of money at one time than nickels and dimes at every activity.[1]

Sometimes, a one-on-one conversation is all that is needed. A Chapter leader may reach out to a generous individual with an affinity for the university and state the need. Maybe one or maybe a couple of these conversations covers it. In cases like these, just be careful not to dip into the same well too often, or you might find it runs dry.

If the fundraiser is to be a more organized event, the Chapter may choose to launch the campaign at the home of one of the alumni, during which Chapter officers talk about the upcoming plans and the expected costs. You will have an interested and captive audience, as most attendees will be there expecting to make a donation. Those not interested will be unlikely to show.

It helps to provide specific amounts for which to write the checks. Amounts may represent expected costs for services or might represent specific donation levels. For example, the Chapter might indicate that they are looking for two donors to split the annual cost of directors and officers insurance, or several donors to pick up one to three months of remote administrative assistance. Another category might be covering a flight for an officer to attend the annual alumni leaders conference. For each proposed item, a specific amount should be assigned just as if it was an item in a retail store with a price tag.

Another option is to offer pre-determined donation levels. The Chapter might offer a Bronze partnership for $100, Silver for $250, Gold for $500, Platinum for $1,000, and Diamond for $2,500. The Chapter might wish to identify this type of contribution differently than a sponsorship, or each contributor could be recognized accordingly as a sponsor. This example is similar to how the Harvard Business School (HBS) Club of Dallas approaches raising funds for the club, as discussed earlier; only there, it applied the concept of levels to individual sponsorships (see *Sponsorships Loved Far and Wide: Sourcing Sponsors*).

Assuming the event will be in person, where the donors will be present, needs can be announced through either a live-auction-like format, in which someone shouts out a request and confirms takers before moving to the next line item, or a more private format, in which a list of needs is distributed and attendees respond privately. If the chosen approach is the live-auction format, then take a close look a subsection not much further called *"Auctions Interwoven into Other Events or Solo"* for more tips.

Traditionally, this type of event would close with the grateful collection of hand-written checks. That was then. The use of checks has been in decline for the past fifteen years, with electronic forms of payment taking the lead. Today, electronic payments continue to take market share, but, most specifically, it is the use of mobile technology that will soon be the dominant force—mobile initiation of standard electronic payments as well as direct mobile transfers. Take a look at some of the statistics:

- Use of checks is dropping fast. The Federal Reserve reports that check payments have been dropping steadily for over a decade. Specifically, check payments have been decreasing an average 6.6 percent per year from 2000 to 2012.[2]

- While check usage drops, electronic payment rise. According to the most recent Federal Reserve study, debit card, credit card, and ACH payments grew 7.1 percent, 8.0 percent, and 4.9 percent, respectively, while payments by check continued to fall, but by 4.4 percent this time, from 2013 to 2015.[3]

- Mobile banking is becoming the norm. According to research, 43 percent of all mobile phone owners and 53 percent of smartphone owners with a bank account had used mobile banking in the twelve months prior to the survey, and both groups are growing.[4]

- Mobile payments are on the rise. Data suggests that 24 percent of all mobile phone users and 28 percent of smartphone users made a mobile payment in the twelve months prior to the survey.[5]

- More than half of the millennials are already transferring money via digital channels,[6] while more than half also state that they never use checks.[7] In fact, one in five millennials has never even written a check.

- Nearly 70 percent of millennials with a smartphone embrace mobile banking, while a third make mobile payments. Even when it comes to baby boomers, roughly a third with smartphones use mobile banking and a fifth embrace mobile payment.[8]

For these fundraising events to be the most successful, especially ones in which the money is to be transferred in the very near term, Chapters and central alumni associations should seriously consider embracing new methods of payments such as mobile giving, including online and text payments and donations. More can be learned about this topic in the next section, *"Mobile Giving Now for Everyone, Big and Very Small."*

There will be a subset of alumni who would be willing to help further the cause or meet the need but will not be available to attend your event. Reasons might include travelling for work, illness, too far to drive from where they live, or can't find a sitter. Accordingly, the Chapter would be wise to follow up with an electronic communication that states the purpose and offers one more chance to donate. In addition to an address to which a physical check could be mailed, a link to making an online donation would prove fruitful. It is a good time to stop soliciting. Too many requests for money can be detrimental and a real turnoff to the alumni pool. Your leadership team does not want to be known for constantly having its hand out rather than leading great, engaging events. An event like this should occur no more than once a year as an annual drive.

If your Chapter might be catering to a particularly young group, possibly the entire campaign might be managed electronically with no brick-and-mortar event at all. The Chapter can choose what is most effective for its alumni and cause.

Advantages of a simple cash fundraiser are that it can be conducted with minimal fanfare and is often quickly executed, funds are immediately deposited, and there is little follow-up other than thanking the donors, reporting the results to the Chapter, and a little paperwork. The primary downside is that asking for cash can sometimes be awkward and, if not executed well, could turn off some alumni from Chapter participation.

Merchandise Sale—Come and Get it!

Another approach to fundraising is to sell particular sought-after collegiate branded merchandise. Typical items tend to be things like T-shirts, baby onesies, and license-plate holders. The Chapter might even have T-shirts made specifically for the raise with a local theme. Since the cost of such items is low, it is easy to add a reasonable margin for the Chapter and still keep the overall price reasonable enough for many alumni to participate.

The University of Georgia (UGA) Alumni Association supports the ability of Chapters to sell merchandise in a special way. For their top-tier Chapters, known as Arch Chapters, the UGA Alumni Association not only will create a special logo for the Chapter but will go as far as designing and / or approving special Chapter designs that can then be applied to the collegiate merchandise. This adds a unique twist of exclusivity to the merchandise sale in that these are items that can only be purchased through the Chapter—and they represent local pride.[9]

The University of Florida Alumni Association (UFAA) has arranged an interesting and profitable approach to merchandise sales. A Chapter is paid either a flat fee or a percentage of the sales to allow an authorized, licensed vendor to set up a display of branded merchandise for sale at the Chapter function.[10] This idea is intriguing. The Chapter benefits from the income yet is not tangled in ordering, shipping, or distribution particulars.

Several alumni associations have arranged for Chapters to purchase items from the university store at a discount. Ex-Students' Association of the University of Texas (Texas Exes) negotiated an outstanding deal to offer Chapters 25 percent off when the purchase is for fundraising.[11] Another more typical example is that of the West Point Association of Graduates (WPAOG). It has arranged for the Chapters to receive a 10 percent discount on items purchased through the WPAOG Gift Shop.[12]

There may be an additional cost buried in this one, however. It may be possible that the Chapter would be required to collect sales tax on items sold for fundraising, or file for a sales tax license if it conducts this activity more than once a year. If the payments are moving through the alumni association on behalf of the Chapter, it may negate such issues. Check with your Chapter liaison as well as a local tax professional for further guidance.

The upside of this approach is that many alumni are likely to participate, and the Chapter successfully disseminates branded merchandise, raising awareness of the college and the Chapter. Challenges include the small, incremental nature of each donation, the potential sales and incomes taxes, and the distribution of merchandise to alumni. The items can be mailed, but that adds to the cost. Items can be brought to an event for distribution, but you will likely need to do that repeatedly to whittle down the supply, and your Chapter will probably still have to ship some.

Selling collegiate merchandise as a fundraiser is rather popular and heavily practiced across the country; so many Chapters have conquered the challenges with pleasing results.

Auctions Interwoven into Other Events or Solo

Fundraising auctions deserve special attention. They can be run as the primary method of fundraising, often during a dinner or lunch, or they can be integrated into other events, such as during the awards ceremony of the Chapter's golf tournament. The most popular version of an auction for alumni Chapter fundraising is the silent auction.

Silent auctions are auctions in which bids are written on a sheet of paper in front of the item or description of the item, with each additional bidder offering more than the one on the line before. At the predetermined end of the auction, the highest listed bidder listed on the paper wins. As long as there is at least one bidder, the item sells, and revenue is generated.

A silent auction can be conducted without disturbing speakers or cocktail hour conversation, and they reportedly attract greater participation by women. Items that are best valued when seen up close are excellent candidates for silent auctions. Purdue Alumni Association offers a few tips for running a silent auction:

> » Display the item and provide a list for people to bid against each other.
> » A minimum bid should be provided. For example: Purdue Pete – $25.00.
> » The bidding list should include name, phone number, and bid amount.
> » A five-minute warning should be offered for bids to close.
> » Club officer should collect sheets with bids when indicated.
> » Announce the winners.
> » Have the treasurer or appointee ready to accept monies from winners.[13]

There is a creative twist to maximize the proceeds for silent auctions that you must know. If the item's contributor can produce more than one of the offering, then the extras can be sold to the next highest bidders at their bid price. This is easiest to do when the offering is a service from which many people can benefit simultaneously, such as ballroom dancing lessons. However, the tactic can be utilized whenever multiples of any item or service can be made available. Silent auctions have been going on for decades with a great deal of success. They may be worth exploring for your Chapter.

Another type of auction is a live auction, which is hosted by an auctioneer in real time and is held before an audience of bidders, such as a room of alumni seated around dinner tables. The goods are described and listed, then an auctioneer solicits bids, or offers, for each item. Bidders simultaneously vie to lock in their bids, accomplished when the auctioneer acknowledges the bidder and the bid verbally. Immediately thereafter, the auctioneer solicits a higher bid and bidder. This goes on until there is only one bidder still competing. The highest bidder wins the auction. This approach tends to feed on the excitement of the competition. In general, live auctions usually bring in bids close to or in excess of the item's market value, while silent auctions bring in only about half their market value.

Bowling Green State University (BGSU) Alumni Association supports silent and live auctions as a method of fundraising for its Chapters. It makes a few suggestions for live auctions as follows:

- A professional auctioneer is not required to successfully host an event.
- Display the items, their value, and the minimum before the auction begins.
- Know each item. The background information / story can be influential in raising the price.
- Use a warning system when closing bids, such as, "Going once, twice, sold, to . . ." to give others time to jump in at the last minute.
- Have an officer write down the item, the winner's name, and the winning bid during the auction.
- Have an officer, ideally the treasurer, ready to accept payment as soon as possible without being intrusive.[14]

One especially fun auction item made available from the BGSU Alumni Association is the opportunity to be a hockey coach for a game. If there is one thing to know about BGSU alumni, it is that they love their hockey! This is an immensely popular item, causing a frenzied competition. The winner gets right up in the action. He or she sits among the players in the box alongside the rink during the game and participates in the locker room pep talks.[15]

A third type of auction has a more modern, digital twist; it is an online auction. Items are described and visually displayed via photographs or video online, using some charitable auction hosting site. These auctions may be active for a couple of days to a couple of weeks. This is a great way to make your auction accessible to alumni in all time zones and without interrupting personal or business commitments. Additionally, fewer volunteers are necessary to manage the event. The Chapter would only need someone to set up the auctions and then a person or two to ship the winnings.

From a budgeting standpoint, and assuming all auction items are donated, the in-person auction (silent and live) costs are mainly associated with hosting the event, such as the venue and catering, while the online auction will cost in terms of a portion of the proceeds going to the auction website.

Auction items for any style auction are typically donated by alumni, local businesses, and the Chapter's alma mater. Examples of auction items include:

- Bottles of wine
- Sports memorabilia
- Artwork
- An iPad or other tablet
- High-end headphones
- Jewelry
- Gift baskets
- Fruit-of-the month service
- Catering
- Wine tastings
- Concert tickets
- Tickets to the theatre, opera, symphony, or ballet
- Vacations
- Rounds of golf
- Photography services
- Personal or business coaching services
- Lunch or dinner with a celebrity or prominent alumna / alumnus
- Tutoring services
- Landscaping packages
- Flower delivery for specified time
- Private yoga lessons or a personal trainer
- Music lessons
- Cooking lessons
- Ballroom dancing lessons
- Game tickets
- Tossing the coin at a game
- Coach for a day
- Signed football, basketball, or other piece of equipment
- Sports or fitness equipment

The items are typically donated to the event with all proceeds going to the Chapter. If winners paid more than the fair market value of the items won, then additional information might need to be collected for tax purposes based on the tax structure of the Chapter and possibly alumni association. The association will likely be able to guide your Chapter on the matter. If not, seek a local tax professional to weigh in, preferably *before* the auction so you are ready if and when the situation arises.

Advantages of auctions—silent, live, and online—include that significant money can be raised, that they are truly interactive experiences for the alumni, and that auctions can be integrated into other fundraising events. Such events do require time to source and prepare items / services / experiences to be actioned, in addition to the time and resources to plan and execute an elegant dinner with entertainment or whatever the rest of the event entails.

Crowdfunding Is a Crowd Pleaser

Crowdfunding is the practice of funding a project or need by raising money from a large number of people, and it is nearly always executed over the Internet using social media and often in small bites. Of the types of crowdfunding (donation, rewards, equity, and debt), donation-based and rewards-based crowdfunding are most applicable to alumni Chapters.

Donation-based describes when individuals contribute to a project without expecting a return on their contribution. Donation-based crowdfunding generated $2.85 billion worldwide in 2015[16] and has been growing at an incredible rate . . . and millennials make up roughly a third of those contributing to cause-based crowdfunding sites.[17]

Rewards-based crowdfunding offers goods or services in return for a financial contribution. Its success largely stems from its appeal to supporters who wish to get something tangible from their pledge. An alumni Chapter selling T-shirts to raise money for an overnight bus trip to an on-campus baseball game and tailgate would be a very practical example of a rewards-based campaign.

In comparison with traditional promotional activities, crowdfunding can facilitate greater awareness among a larger number of potential donors. It also empowers alumni to tell their own stories, which can greatly impact their network of friends and family members. Since crowdfunding campaigns are highly shareable, it's easy to spread the word and raise funds.

Crowdfunding is highly collaborative, and collaboration is a third hallmark of the new digital economy. With the right crowdfunding platform and ample promotion, a crowdfunding campaign has the potential to raise quite a lot of money in a very short period of time. Further, people love to come together under one common cause. It gives them a sense of purpose and empowers them to openly support something they care about. Crowdfunding also has the advantage of being free of geographic limitations or time zone constraints. The message continues to proliferate, and donations can filter in twenty-four hours a day, seven days a week.

According to the Pew Research Center, 22 percent of Americans have participated in a crowdsourced fundraising project,[18] and of those, 32 percent have contributed to a project for a school.[19] On average, contributions are small. Only 17 percent of crowdfunders have contributed more than $100 to a cause, while 62 percent gave $50 or less. On the upside, they do tend to give more than once. At least 87 percent have contributed to up to five projects. To be on the conservative side, assume average contributions will be between $25 and $50.[20]

When evaluating overall demographics, 30 percent of those between the ages of eighteen and twenty-nine and 27 percent of those between thirty and forty-nine are crowdfunders. Participation drops significantly after that, with 18 percent of crowdfunders between the ages of fifty and sixty-four and 8 percent over the age of sixty-five. This approach is much more appealing to millennials, followed by Gen Xers. Crowdfunding is also most prevalent among college graduates and those with incomes exceeding $75,000.[21]

From an organization's perspective, any Chapter can leverage crowdfunding—assuming it is acceptable to the alumni association. A Chapter does *not* have to be a 501(c)(3)-designated entity or even a nonprofit to participate, but it is a plus when the donation is tax deductible. The Chapter does need a compelling cause, however.

An example that might best utilize the benefits of crowdfunding, and the expanded reach, could be that of establishing an endowed scholarship in the name of a recently passed alumna / alumnus who achieved great recognition in their profession or for charitable works. For example, Michael Graves, one of the most famous US designers of his generation and a pioneer of architectural postmodernism, passed away March 12, 2015. He was born in Indianapolis, Indiana, and had offices in both Princeton, New Jersey, and New York City, New York. He earned his bachelor of science degree in architecture from the University of Cincinnati and continued his studies at the Harvard Graduate School of Design.[22]

His life could be honored by establishing an endowed scholarship in his name by an alumni Chapter of either the University of Cincinnati or Harvard University from any of the three cities of importance to him. In this scenario, let us assume that the University of Cincinnati alumni in New York City decide to do just that. They announce the launching of a fund to establish an endowed scholarship for students from New York City wishing to pursue a degree in architecture at the University of Cincinnati. Since Mr. Graves was so widely known from Indianapolis to the East Coast and around the world, an online channel to raise funds is likely to be very effective. Crowdfunding would be the perfect vehicle.

To launch such a campaign, the Chapter would then need to establish an account with an appropriate crowdfunding website. Pay close attention to the details, as some sites have specific requirements and parameters, such as that the campaign cannot exceed sixty days. Also, watch for the payment terms. Often, a site will charge approximately 5 percent for their services in addition to passing through the 3 percent for credit card processing.[23] There are sites that will charge a lower fee for more personal causes. The landscape is constantly changing, so do your diligence.

Once the account has been established, your Chapter can start reaching out via e-mail and social media to the local alumni and other groups that would have an interest in your cause. The wider the net cast, the better. In general, the most common amount pledged is $25,[24] so it might take some time. Here are a few statistics provided by @Pay:

- Campaigns that reach 30% of their crowdfunding goal within the first week are substantially more likely to reach 100% of their goal by the end.
- 17% of crowdfunding donations are made on mobile devices.
- For every increase in Facebook friends (10, 100, 1000), the probability of a crowdfunding campaign's success increases drastically (from 9% to 20%, to 40%, respectively). The more Facebook friends an organization has, the more likely that organization's crowdfunding page will be to be funded.
- There's an average of a 35% increase in giving when there's a crowdfunding thermometer.[25]

One alumni association that encourages its Chapters to take full advantage of crowdfunding is the University of Tennessee Knoxville (UT Knoxville) Alumni Association. Chapters are welcome to use a custom crowdfunding platform called *VOLstarter*[26] for raising scholarships. It is available to any Chapter, any time, and the alumni association will gladly assist a Chapter through the process.[27]

Another progressive example comes from the University of Missouri–St. Louis (UMSL) Alumni Association, supporting nearly 94,000 alumni across the globe[28] through its nine chapters, networks, and groups.[29] It offers a platform, known as Crowdfund.umsl.edu, designed to empower the UMSL community to raise the funds they need for the projects, events, and organizations. Since the launch of the program in 2015, just over $100,000 has been raised through nearly 1,250 gifts.[30] Although available to alumni within university-recognized organizations for fundraising, it is currently restricted to raising money that ultimately is used for the university. For example, it is perfectly acceptable to raise funds for a scholarship, since that money will be eventually be paid to the university. However, it would not be an approved use to raise money to provide school supplies for local underprivileged children or to cover travel costs for Chapter officers to attend the alumni leaders conference.

One brave group of alumni has dared to venture into these new waters to launch a scholarship campaign—and came out on top! The UMSL Business Marketing Advisory Board is an alumni group comprised of over thirty executives. Its goal was to establish a new scholarship fund for students studying marketing within the College of Business Administration, with an immediate objective of funding five $1,000 scholarships. Donation options included $15, $35, $50, $100, $500 and $1,000. The fund was oversubscribed, generating $5,313 in thirty-five days from thirty-five donors. A closer look at the distribution of donors revealed one $2,000 donor. If we consider that one an outlier and focus on the remaining contributions, the average donation was $97, with nearly half of the donors pledging at the $100 level.[31]

Crowdfunding is a viable, growing electronic vehicle that has found its place in the landscape of fundraising. It is extremely attractive to millennials and younger contributors due to its collaborative nature, its unmistakable fusion with social media, and the ability to make even the smallest donation count. Even those with shallow pockets have an opportunity to participate in a meaningful way. Crowdfunding's success is also based on it boundless existence—accessible by anyone, anywhere, anytime. The approach continues to grow in acceptance not only with younger contributors but with all demographics. There are few if any downsides, but a word of caution would be to carry out your due diligence so that your Chapter does not hemorrhage a disproportionate share of the donations in fees to the crowdfunding site. Also, this option may not reach its full potential if your Chapter does not have an active social media presence or if your primary population has yet to embrace online giving or payments. Having a social media champion that can really stoke the campaign's digital fires can make all the difference.

Raffles Can Be Fun but Iffy

A raffle is defined as a game in which people purchase tickets for the chance to win a prize, generally through a drawing. This can be great fun and more enjoyable than door prizes for attendees simply due to the fact that, by purchasing a ticket for the prize, the alumna / alumnus has already indicated that they want whatever the prize might be. Great raffle prizes for alumni events are game tickets, signed university sports memorabilia, and other things trending, in short supply, or difficult to access.

The difference between a raffle and a door prize is the requirement to pay to participate in the raffle. Alumni could also increase their chances of winning a raffle by purchasing more tickets. Door prizes operate differently. All participants are entered into the drawing simply by having attended the event, and each person has an equal chance to win.

I recently attended a fundraiser in which fifteen to twenty high-end, luxury purses were elegantly displayed, each with its own colorful tissue-paper-lined bowl in front. Attendees were given the opportunity to purchase as many tickets as they desired—encouraged by volume discounts. They could then place tickets in the fish bowls corresponding to the purse(s) they most wanted. At the end of the evening, as the ladies and gents held their breaths, the Charity President went down the line, extracting a single ticket from each fish bowl. Over and over, the lucky winner was revealed, followed by a gasp and applause from the crowd. The raffle raised significant money for the charity and was an experience enjoyed by all—especially the many winners!

It is common for alumni associations to list raffles as suggested fundraisers. The University of Iowa Alumni Association, for one, promotes a 50 / 50 raffle in which raffle tickets are sold with the proceeds split evenly between the winner and the Chapter.[32] The 50 / 50 raffle is one of the easiest fundraisers to administer, so it is not surprising that it is so popular.

However, raffles should also be approached with some caution, as should their sister, lotteries. Technically, raffles and lotteries qualify as "games of chance" in charitable gaming. Most states require a license for gaming and only permit a certain number of events per year, typically about two. In those states, and without the license, a raffle is illegal. In the State of Texas, the qualifying nonprofit must be at least three years old and have a gaming license and cannot offer cash as a prize. The latter eliminates 50 / 50 raffles altogether in Texas.[33]

The laws vary from state to state, so it is important that a Chapter consult with the central alumni association and legal counsel before hosting a raffle. The University of Minnesota Alumni Association supports raffles and auctions as revenue sources but does remind the Chapter to check with local and state laws.[34] In response to the legal and fiscal complexities, some alumni associations simply ban raffles and lotteries altogether, like the Syracuse University (SU) Alumni Association. The SU Alumni Association clearly states in their handbook that raffles, and, for that matter, any type of gambling activities, are not allowed to be hosted by the Chapters.[35]

Other alumni associations take a hybrid approach by keeping Chapters on a short leash and limiting winning items to those under a specific price. The University of Florida Alumni Association (UFAA) is one that puts specific parameters in place. Interestingly, the guidelines established technically alter the experience from being a raffle to a door prize by removing the requirement to purchase a ticket. In the State of Florida, Chapters may operate such a contest, but only if no one had to purchase anything special to do so and "No Purchase Necessary" is disclosed. For example, as attendees are checking in for the event, a Florida Chapter volunteer might tell each person about the chance to win the special prize. The volunteer would be clear that although a donation of $10 would be appreciated, no purchase is necessary to be included in the drawing.

For out-of-state Chapters, the UFAA permits raffles, but only under certain conditions. All material for such drawings must disclose:

» The rules governing the conduct and operation of the drawing.
» The full name of the organization and its principal place of business.
» The source of the funds used to award cash prizes or to purchase prizes.
» The date, hour, and place where the winner will be chosen and the prizes will be awarded, unless the brochures, advertisements, notices, tickets, or entry blanks are not offered to the public more than 3 days prior to the drawing.
» That no purchase or contribution is necessary.[36]

Raffles, if approved by the alumni association and administered within the boundaries of the state law, can be effective and fun ways to raise Chapter funds. Just do not execute one without the proper due diligence.

Large-Scale Events: Large Work but Large Money

Some larger, more organized Chapters have ventured into the big-fundraising-event arena. They have hosted events such as golf tournaments, tennis tournaments, and community foot and bike races from 5K on up in distance with a great deal of success. These events tend to yield thousands of dollars in profit and significantly raise awareness of the Chapter. However, they require a large team, tremendous planning and preparation, a significant outlay of cash prior to receiving the donations, and time to build up into a smooth, financially successful endeavor. If done poorly, they can do more damage than good. They are often dependent on the weather as well.

One such Chapter event that has overcome the challenges and has consistently flourished as a result of a large-scale fundraising event takes place in horse country. For over fifteen years, the University of Kentucky (UK) Fayette

County Alumni Club has partnered with the City of Lexington in the fall to host a **Par-3 Golf Championship** featuring eighteen holes of stroke-play competition. All proceeds benefit the Chapter's scholarship fund.[37]

The event is well run, with men's and women's champions crowned in each of four divisions. Participants pay $60 to play, and sponsors are invited to participate as a Leaderboard and / or a Hole in One Sponsor. Following this day of ultimate alumni fellowship, the Chapter raised approximately $15,000 for the 2016 scholarship fund. The total scholarship goal was $20,000 to award twenty scholarships, and the golf tournament satisfies the lion's share of the fund-raising needs. The remainder will be supplemented through additional fundraising programs.

As if the Fayette County Chapter is not already doing a tremendous service for young matriculates and for its alma mater, this year it is in the process of further expanding the program to include an alumni mentor for each scholarship recipient. The mentor will stay close to the student throughout the duration of his or her time at the university, and hopefully beyond. The intentions are to build an incredibly strong relationship between the student and mentor, to provide an unbiased sounding board in times of uncertainty, and to instill the value and natural progression from student life to alumni Chapter involvement.[38]

The New Orleans Ole Miss Club of the University of Mississippi (Ole Miss) Alumni Association recently took on the tall task of establishing a tennis tournament to raise scholarship money. The doubles tournament, called the **New Orleans SEC Tennis Tournament**, takes place in May, and 2016 marked its third year. Although run by the New Orleans Ole Miss Club, alumni and friends of all SEC universities are invited to participate. In fact, the other schools are not only invited but will walk away with proceeds proportional to the number of participants representing their university. What a great deal for other local alumni Chapters! Proceeds received from Ole Miss alumni and friends will benefit the New Orleans Ole Miss Club Scholarship Endowment.

A very reasonable fee of $52.50 per doubles team includes visor, towel, breakfast, lunch, snacks, and cold beverages. Additionally, sponsorships are available in $100, $250, $500, and $1,000 increments with graduating benefits and privileges.[39] Unlike the University of Kentucky (UK) Fayette County Alumni Club discussed above with more than a decade of practice and promotion under its belt, the New Orleans Ole Miss Club's tournament is still in its early formation years. It recently logged approximately thirty players and was able to contribute about $1,000 to its scholarship. The real money will be in sponsorships for such an event, and the sponsorships will come with increased exposure. The volunteer leadership team has shared some of the trying times in establishing a large event like this. For them, choosing the right date has been one such challenge. They found that competing with Mother's Day and Memorial Day weekends in May left them with few options, only to land on a weekend that had a competing local tennis tournament. The club is committed to growing the event and making a significant contribution to scholarships, so it will persevere—as it should!

You may recall the earlier example of when the Kellogg Network DFW launched its big event to support Big Brothers Big Sisters. That event took several years to get traction and is incredibly successful today. The **New Orleans SEC Tennis Tournament** has that same potential if the club leadership can maintain focus and effectively evolve from year to year, building on it successes and learning from its failures. The club has a great concept with a share-the-wealth attitude, supporting an important cause—scholarships. Make it happen, New Orleans Ole Miss Club!

This guide does not spend much more time on this approach, as few Chapters have the resources—personnel or financial—to pull it off successfully. Additionally, the concepts related to fundraising, sponsorships, event pricing, and more are already covered throughout this book. A deeper dive into this type of event is more of a discussion on how to execute the event rather than any additional commentary on financial impact.

For those brave souls who embark on these large-scale events, hats off to you; we cheer for your success! This topic will be thoroughly dissected in a future book discussing Chapter event best practices.

The Last Act

Once the fundraiser is all said and done, properly take the last steps to make the event truly successful by setting the stage for the next one. Be certain to circle back around with all participants who made the fundraiser what it was by sharing the results and sincere gratitude for their contributions to that end. Such behavior is the professional touch that solidifies in each participant the pleasure to have been a part and the willingness to do so again.

The results should further be shared with the broader alumni population with a qualifying statement for how the fundraiser performed according to goals and reiterating what the Chapter plans to do with the money. In addition to being good form, such transparency helps to gain the confidence of the alumni and will pay dividends when your Chapter runs another similar event.

Don't Bite Off More Than You Can Chew

The entire point of fundraising is to support a healthier, more active Chapter. So, be very careful not to embark on such a big effort that the preparations strain the budget or, worse yet, the Chapter leadership. If the Chapter volunteers become overtaxed and disenfranchised, the Chapter is worse off than when it had a positive vibe but could only offer a few events per year.

The best ways to avoid overtaxing the leadership team are, first, to choose one of the easier approaches to fundraising. Second, pull together a large committee, and divide up the work into bite-size pieces. Third, organize regular meetings often. Lots of tiny deadlines keep things moving and help minimize a big crunch at the end. Fourth, it can be a very smart move to solicit third-party assistance when possible. Lastly, make certain that everyone who had a part in the success of the evening is acknowledged publicly.

Successful Chapters exhibit a few similarities. One of those is unquestionably continuity in leadership. On an ongoing basis, the Chapter leaders and other volunteers must feel that they are appreciated, that they have a sense of the Chapter's purpose and their part in it, and that it is fun. Events tend to operate more smoothly when the leadership team has experience. The better an event can be managed and the more fun it can be for the volunteers, the more likely they will put their names in the hat once again the next year. That continuity is so important, so don't burn them out. Adequate funding never hurts, either! Be certain not to let visions of grandeur negatively impact the unity of the leadership.

60-Second Takeaway

Fundraising has been a lifelong friend to Chapters, associations, and universities. If fundraising is to be carried out by your Chapter, it is recommended to have an officer dedicated to the function. Typical fundraisers for alumni Chapters include cash campaigns, merchandise sales, auctions, crowdfunding, raffles, and large-scale events such as golf tournaments—each with their own pros and cons.

Fundraising, regardless of the method, tends to be far more effective if there is a stated purpose, especially one to which people can relate. It also helps to isolate specific needs, functions, or amounts when asking for contributions.

One additional consideration is expanding the channels by which alumni and friends may contribute beyond that of the traditional check by embracing mobile payment options and other online or digital methods.

The Chapter will need to carefully determine what resources—both personnel and upfront cash—it has to dedicate to the fundraiser before choosing an approach. Keep the effort within reason, and safeguard the time and mental state of the Chapter's leadership. Don't forget to have fun!

Make It Happen Checklist

☐ Determine the alumni association's stance on fundraising, the parameters, and the tools available to the Chapter in support of such an event.

☐ Establish a dedicated leadership role, such as the Vice President of Fundraising, supported by a Fundraising Committee.

☐ Determine for what specific purposes the money is needed and how much will be necessary.

☐ Evaluate the currently available resources, including personnel and upfront cash.

☐ Determine what approach is best for your Chapter—a cash campaign, merchandise sale, an auction (silent, live, or online), crowdfunding, raffles, a large-scale event, or a combination.

☐ Consider expanding the means by which the Chapter can accept contributions, including mobile and text payments.

☐ Reach out to a local tax professional to confirm your expectations regarding what might or might not be taxable income and implications.

☐ Build a budget to expose all expected costs, and define an income goal that allows the Chapter to meet its needs after expenses have been paid.

☐ Plan and promote the event in a big way, using all appropriate channels within reason and budget—and start early.

☐ Keep all parties, including the broader alumni base, aware of the campaign's progress. Use a thermometer approach if at all possible.

☐ Report and celebrate the results with the Chapter and all participants that contributed to the outcome, including partners like the auction contributors.

☐ Publicly thank all volunteers, vendors, and partners that made it happen.

☐ Have fun, and build connections every step of the way! That is what alumni leadership is all about.

☐ Plant the seeds about the next event in the minds of your now-experienced volunteer team to start the recruiting process.

Mobile Giving Now for Everyone, Big and Very Small

In the age of social media and the use of our mobile phones for just about any function or service that can be digitized, donating by phone seems natural. The American Red Cross put mobile giving through text-to-give donations in the spotlight in 2010 when it and other agencies raised over $43 million for Haiti relief efforts through text giving, $10 at a time.[1]

Mobile giving is basically making contributions to an organization using a phone or tablet. It may involve directly texting a donation, or it may take another form in which text messages and e-mails utilize the Internet to facilitate the donation through web and mobile pages. This channel has significantly evolved over just the past five years already.

Mobile giving's roots are in the first donation Web pages established on an organization's standard website. Initially, sites were designed to be engaged on a desktop or laptop with a full-sized monitor screen. As the world became more mobile-centric, these websites proved ineffective when accessed on a smartphone. Over time, as websites became more responsive to mobile devices, giving channels evolved as well. The rise of texting further enabled yet another avenue for the faster, easier movement of money.

At its onset, the text-to-give channel was only available to the very large, 501(c)(3)-designated nonprofits, in which charges passed through the cell phone carriers. When a keyword was texted to the short five-digit code, a predetermined, specified charge (usually $5 or $10) would appear on the mobile phone holder's monthly cell phone bill. The carrier would then pass the donations through to the charity in a lump sum on a monthly basis approximately 60 to 120 days following the donation. Donating to a cause utilizing text giving became almost effortless.

This system was not available to all organizations, however. First, the organization had to be an IRS-designated 501(c)(3) entity, and even then, it could not simply sign up for the text-to-give service. Before being permitted to accept such donations, the nonprofit would undergo strict governance, operational, and financial vetting by the gatekeeper—the Mobile Giving Foundation. The requirements for approval were set in such a way that only the largest and most mature charities could pass. Those that benefit from such a program include the March of Dimes, Lighthouse for the Blind, National Wildlife Federation, National Center for Missing and Exploited Children, UNICEF, and the Smithsonian Institute, to name a few.[2]

Even today, a minimum of $500,000 in revenue is still just one of the steep requirements to work with phone carriers. Approval was just the start. Then, the costs to establish the channel were prohibitive to almost anyone but the largest charities. The short five-digit code alone costs approximately $3,000. This method was anything but available to alumni Chapters.

The Modern Twist

The good news is that, today, the world of mobile giving leveraging texting has changed dramatically. First, it is no longer exclusive to designated 501(c)(3) charities or even other nonprofits. Any organization can activate this channel. Now, it is really just another mechanism through which to move money, much like websites, e-mails, and other social media.

Second, no longer is a contract necessary with a cell phone service provider, nor is the donation limited to a preset $5 or $10. Now, donations are made directly using any credit card of choice and for nearly any amount.

Third, the need for short codes has been eliminated altogether, and so has the high price to secure one. A standard phone number is all that is required today—and it is often provided at no additional charge through the mobile-giving software vendor.

Regardless of which service / software provider an organization engages to enable mobile giving through texts, the process is fairly straightforward. Once applicable accounts are established, the provider secures a dedicated phone number on behalf of the Chapter. Occasionally, the Chapter might even be able to choose a number from a list and often at no charge. That is pretty much it on the Chapter's side, other than getting the word out.

The donor simply sends a text containing the amount to be donated to the dedicated phone number. If it is the first time a donation has been sent from that phone, the donor will be directed to enter the credit card information and relevant details. From that point on, the credit card may be stored linked with the donor's cell phone number, enabling incredibly efficient future donations. The second time the donor sends a donation, the process will skip the credit card entry, only requiring a simple confirmation. Should a donor get interrupted while completing the credit card information or fail to click the confirmation, most vendors launch a polite reminder one or more times.

Although the mechanism by which the money is transferred has changed so much that it hardly resembles its predecessor, the benefits of enabling contributions through mobile giving, and especially by text, are just as strong as ever. Such platforms have several important advantages, including:

- Leveraging heavily used communication channels already very familiar to alumni.
- Donations can be captured in the moment, such as during a commercial at a basketball-game-watching party or when a moving story has concluded and the ask is made.

Further, as the alumni populations continue to age, millennials and future generations begin to mature in their careers, becoming better positioned to be donors. Engaging them through channels with which they are most comfortable will significantly improve the outcome of any campaign to raise funds.

Overall, 91 percent of Americans now own a smartphone. Mobile giving has increased 205 percent over the past year, while overall giving grew only 4 percent. The average size of a single donation via text is $107.[3] Looking deeper into the next donating generation, it might be fascinating to learn that according to the **Millennial Impact Report** by research group Achieve, 84 percent of millennials made a charitable donation in 2014, and 70 percent spent at least an hour volunteering.[4] Blackbaud's **Next Generation of American Giving** report revealed that, on average, millennials give an annual gift of $481 to each of 3.3 charities.[5] They are most likely to contribute to local causes and engage in impulse giving, such as a few dollars for the Salvation Army Red Kettle. The former is where the alumni Chapter becomes a prime recipient. Prioritizing a giving channel attractive to such a large, sharing group of potential donors is simply common sense.

In general, mobile giving, including texting, is an important channel in today's movement of money. No longer will fundraisers be dependent on collecting checks. Today, if alumni Chapters are to garner the payments and contributions they seek and need, they will have to meet the alumni where they are by expanding the methods of payments accepted. Having a mobile payment option or texting number available can significantly improve the number of contributions. Consider offering an easily accessible mobile giving page or a text-giving phone number at a simple cash-campaign event or at an auction to collect the final payments. It can be used to collect sponsorships or membership dues on the spot. In addition to improving the ease by which transactions can be made, the barriers of time can be eliminated, enabling alumni to make immediate contributions.

How It Works

Mobile giving via text is incredibly simple. Regardless of which mobile-giving software vendor is chosen, they all work largely in the same way. First, Catherine, a hypothetical alumna from Fictitious State University, wants to support the Chapter President and Treasurer attending the Alumni Leaders Conference. So she sends a text with the amount of the donation—or, at this point, technically it is just a pledge until it is processed—to her alumni Chapter's unique ten-digit phone number distributed by the Chapter. The amount of the pledge is entered into the body of the text without any additional words or symbols. If $25 is intended to be donated, then Catherine types only the number 25, not $25. The unique phone number is typically provided with your local area code and generated by the mobile giving software vendor at no additional charge.

If this is the first time Catherine is making a donation, she receives a thank-you followed by a link to provide her credit card information. Once that is complete, she is asked to confirm the pledge prior to processing the donation. An e-mail receipt is immediately generated and sent bearing the name of the Chapter and relevant details, which is especially convenient if the gift is tax deductible.

The next time Catherine texts money to the Chapter, she will get to skip the credit card entry step for an even faster experience. After clicking *send*, she will receive the same thank-you, but this time, she will bypass the payment details and immediately see the confirmation question. Today's software recognizes Catherine's phone number and pairs it up with her credit card already on file.

Some mobile giving software vendors are so savvy that if your mobile number is anywhere in its system, regardless of what cause to which you had previously donated, it immediately jumps to the confirmation step. In other words, if you previously made a text donation to the Girl Scouts of the USA and then to your Chapter the following week, assuming they both use the same mobile giving software vendor, you would not need to enter your credit card in twice. Obviously, this is not as requirement but rather a convenience feature. A donor could change the credit card on which the payment will be made at any time.

One more very important feature of any mobile giving software vendor is the follow-up. As you can see in the example above, it takes three steps to complete the first donation—the initial pledge, entering the credit card details, and confirming the donation. This is different from texting-to-give's predecessor via the cell phone service provider. In the earlier situation, once the donor hit *send* the first time, it was finished. No extra step to enter a credit card was necessary because no credit card was required.

Now that the credit card step has been interjected, it is possible that a donor, such as Catherine, does not immediately complete the payment details step, and the pledge fails to convert into a donation. This scenario already has a name—donor abandonment. It is most likely that the donor became distracted or simply forgot to circle back around to completing the transaction. Most software vendors have addressed the issue in one way or another, generally by sending follow-up reminders . . . one or several times. In fact, a vendor's specific success in minimizing donor abandonment is an official metric often touted as a sales benefit.

Although this overall process description is largely consistent across vendors, each one will offer slight variations in the flow, such as the ability to direct the donation into a specific bucket or a step to populate the leaderboard with the names of contributors. Just ask; the vendors will be more than happy to share what makes them special.

Cost Considerations

Before anyone runs off demanding that their Chapter establish a mobile giving campaign, there still are some important considerations and costs to understand. Mobile giving requires the use of credit cards. In order to receive funds processed through credit cards, a Chapter will need to have the proper accounts that combine in some way to provide the following three components:

- Mobile giving software with a text-to-give service.
- A payment gateway that allows credit card information to be sent across the Internet through to the credit card processors.
- A merchant account, which is a special bank account that enables your Chapter to accept credit and debit card payments online. A standard bank account only allows the owner to accept cash, checks (all types), and wire transfers—not credit cards.

The later section titled "*Collecting and Handling the Money*" goes into greater depth regarding the banking practices of a Chapter. For now, this section will focus on the details around only the mobile giving software, its costs, and what may or may not be included.

Software providers offering mobile text-giving platforms support event-specific giving, ongoing campaigns, or both. Event-specific programs are characterized by operating a text-donation campaign during a single event (often in which the event is thirty days or less).

A hypothetical example of an event-specific program could be if, during an Army–Navy football game, the US Naval Academy (USNA) alumni and the US Military Academy (aka West Point) alumni in the South plan to gather at a neutral sports bar to cheer on their teams. Knowing this event will be well attended, both alumni groups set up the appropriate accounts to run text-giving campaigns so that, in addition to the athletic competition, they will run a charitable competition in parallel.

The game is on, drinks and appetizers are flowing, and the Navy scores! Cheering, the USNA Chapter President jumps up and enthusiastically encourages fellow alumni to celebrate by supporting the Chapter's charity of the year, Carry the Load.[6] Everyone is invited to text $10, $25, $50, or $100 to the specified phone number. The Army scores! The West Point Chapter President leaps up and challenges her alumni to out-donate the USNA grads! The West Point alumni are raising money for Allies in Service in this scenario. The request is repeated each time either team makes a touchdown, completes a pass, drives yardage, or whatever comes to mind. When the teams go for two, maybe the ask is prorated. The competitive spirit really drives the numbers, so a contest is the perfect way to go. There is a game winner and a charity winner. Before the night is over, both Chapters have accumulated a healthy sum for their charities.

From a cost perspective, when embarking on an event-specific campaign, the Chapter is likely to be charged a single set-up fee with additional transactional fees in the form of a fixed fee per transaction and / or a percentage of the transaction. The pricing structure will vary by vendor and depend on how much of the process (gateway, processing, and merchant account) might be rolled into the service.

On the other hand, if the Chapter intends to solicit text contributions a couple or more times a year, it may be more useful to consider an ongoing solution. One upside to this approach is that the dedicated text donation phone number can be saved by alumni in their phones and accessed easily throughout the year. In an ongoing scenario, the Chapter would be charged an annual or a monthly fee plus a fixed fee per transaction and a percentage of each transaction. See the table below for an over-simplified fee comparison.

Event-Specific Campaign Fees	Ongoing Campaign Fees
One-Time Set-Up Fee and Percent of Transaction and / or Fixed Fee per Transaction	Monthly Fee or Annual Fee and Percent of Transaction and / or Fixed Fee per Transaction

It is very important to understand that the fees above may be all encompassing or in addition to fees for the parts of the process not bundled in. Fees might also be tiered based on the total sum raised over the specified window of time. The tiered packages may be advantageous if the Chapter intends to raise significant sums of money. Once the costs are flushed out and vetted, all the Chapter needs to do is make an educated guess as to whether the expected contributions will outweigh the costs.

Although the information above may sound daunting at first, do not be alarmed. It is possible to establish a texting channel with a vendor that incorporates the mobile payments option in less than ten minutes—inclusive of the gateway and merchant accounts. It even deposits the money directly in the Chapter's primary checking account automatically. I will admit that understanding the details of these concepts was initially challenging for me. I had a lot to learn about the hidden processes to fully grasp the inflection points in the benefits and fee structures. However, that works to your benefit. While conducting research for this book, I analyzed many companies and options in an ocean of providers. Many do not want the business of small players such as alumni Chapters, and their fees ensure they will not have any. I did identify a couple of companies that very much appreciate groups like Chapters and offer attractive pricing. I was even successful in having the fee structures reduced even further and restructured so that Chapters pay less overall set-up and fixed fees. If interested, contact me directly for today's quickest, most economical path to receiving text payments at Stacie@SACLeadership.com. The results of my research are not published here since this space is rapidly evolving. Rather, it will be a topic I will follow and adjust my recommendations as they evolve.

Tips for Success

It is worth taking a few moments to punctuate specifics that help ensure a successful text-to-give experience for all involved, including: choosing a cause, making it very easy to execute the gift, documenting the vendor accounts, and closing the loop by sharing the results with the alumni.

Much like many other fundraising campaigns, text-to-give efforts tend to be far more successful if centered on a specific cause. Funding scholarships to the Chapter's alma mater, a charitable donation to another group, coats for homeless children this winter, or even a specific operational expense such as D&O insurance for the Chapter are all examples of causes. The cause does not need to remain constant; rather, it can change from time to time or event to event. It just needs to be focused in the moment. Simply asking for money to support the Chapter is a bit too broad and is unlikely to garner the emotional alignment necessary to motivate enough donors to participate.

In sticking with the military theme for the moment, a practical example of executing a mobile-giving program in support of an immediate need could be offered by United States Air Force Academy (USAFA) Association of Graduates (AOG). Each year, cadet teams and clubs participate in trips throughout the United States, such as playing in an away game or competing in a competition. In many cases, these trips provide an opportunity for the local Chapter to assist with food, lodging, or inclusion in the related Chapter events, such as a pre- or post-game party.[7] The cadet trips offer a contained, well-defined and immediate need that could easily benefit from a mobile-giving campaign. The Chapter leadership could simply ask for specific contributions during a game-watching party or a Chapter lunch. Alternatively, the leadership could send out an e-mail or a text with the Chapter's text-giving phone number and the request. Remember, if the Chapter has ongoing access to the same phone number and the Chapter member has previously used it to give, then the current ask could be fulfilled as easy as hitting *send* and *confirm* in less than twenty seconds. What could be easier? When embracing mobile giving for the right needs, your Chapter might be pleasantly surprised at how quickly and easily a funding goal can be reached.

Make it as easy as possible for someone to make a donation. Provide a one-page instruction sheet with exactly what number to dial, what to do, and when to do it. Use screen shots of the actual software, provide the proper phone number to use, and explain the syntax of what to enter in the body of the text. Also, explain the difference between a pledge and the donated gift. Make sure alumni are aware that the credit card details need to be entered and the pledge confirmed before it converts into an actual donation. These instructions should be made available via all standard communication channels used by the Chapter. Making payments by text is fairly common practice these days. In-depth instructions are not necessary, but it always helps to have a cheat sheet!

Something easy to overlook is vendor documentation. Especially as leadership tends to turn over from time to time, ensure that the account details are recorded some place accessible for years to come. Specifics to document include:

- The vendor itself
- Account number
- Online-access user IDs, passwords, and security question answers
- Vendor contact name, phone number, and e-mail address
- Your Chapter contact on record
- Terms of the contract or arrangement, such as expiration date

The current and next Chapter leadership teams will be most grateful for the organization and forethought!

Finally, be certain to celebrate the results and success of the campaign with the Chapter. People love to know the outcome of a campaign and how much they contributed to its success. Alumni enjoy the connection they share. They enjoy being part of a winning team. Reporting the results is an important way to bring closure to an event, further the awareness of the effort, and pay proper respect to contributors along the way. The last thing your Chapter wants after a successful text campaign is a constituency that feels resentful because you took the time to ask for something but cannot be bothered to acknowledge the donors after you got what you wanted from them.

Involvement in an alumni Chapter is largely emotional. It is not a requirement; there are plenty of other ways to fill one's time. People engage in the Chapter because it makes them feel good to be around others like them, to be a part of something bigger, to give back to something that gave so much to them. Remember that always. Each time they make a contribution or step up to volunteer, they are doing it for emotional reasons. Do not be remiss in circling back to them and validating that desire. Be grateful, and inspire that gratefulness in others.

Your leadership will want this to be a good experience for the present and for the future. Celebrating statistics like the number of contributions, the average contribution, and the total amount raised are a good place to start, but do not stop there. Be certain to translate it in to something more meaningful. If your cause was to raise money for scholarships, convert the total into the number of scholarships your Chapter can grant. Maybe your Chapter was raising money to buy winter coats for homeless children. Be sure to let the alumni know how many children will now have a warm coat this winter thanks to them.

The idea that an individual Chapter could possibly afford a mobile text-to-give campaign is a very recent phenomenon. As the technology and pricing that make this option reasonable has only been in existence of late, there are very few examples to share with you. Be among the early adopters to embrace this channel, and report the experience back to us.

60-Second Takeaway

Mobile giving and text donations have come a very long way in only a few short years. Gone are the days in which only large 501(c)(3) charities could participate. Gone also are pre-set donation limits of $5 or $10 dollars, the need for cell phone provider partnerships, and expensive short codes. Today, any organization—nonprofit or otherwise—can facilitate credit card gifts on a single-event or ongoing basis through a variety of channels, including texting.

Pricing is not difficult to master, but it can be tricky at first blush, consisting of possible cascading charges from the mobile-giving software provider plus the credit-card-processing gateway plus the merchant bank account. Although many providers cater to larger organizations, there are a few vendors that have been singled out as offering more reasonable packages for groups such as alumni Chapters. There is no doubt that a successful income strategy for any Chapter moving forward will need to consider mobile giving and payment channels.

Make It Happen Checklist

☐ Define a specific goal or cause around which to build a mobile-giving, text-based campaign, such as raising a specific amount for scholarships.

☐ Determine if the Chapter wishes to run an event-specific campaign or maintain an ongoing channel for multiple opportunities to leverage text donations.

☐ Vet the costs associated with preferred vendors, referencing the websites and / or talking with them directly to confirm current features, pricing, and related fees.

☐ Reach out to me if you become overwhelmed.

☐ Confirm the expected donations minus the costs will yield enough income to justify the campaign.

☐ Select a vendor and set up the necessary chain of accounts (combination of software provider, gateway, and merchant account as dictated by the software provider).

☐ Document all vendor account information, including account numbers, passwords, vendor contact, and the Chapter contact on file with vendor.

☐ Prepare a short document to explain the process on the alumni side so that both the Chapter leadership and the donating alumni are fully informed.

☐ Promote the text-donation campaign and phone number on the Chapter's website and through all standard communications methods—especially at events.

☐ Execute a wildly successful campaign, and have fun!

☐ Report and celebrate the results with the Chapter.

General Events
Are Still the Workhorse

General events are the heart and soul of alumni fellowship. Coordinated events are what alumni want and expect, so it is logical to consider such events as possible avenues to generate revenue to in turn further benefit the Chapter's alumni. Regardless of how active or inactive a Chapter might be, it is likely that it gets together at least a couple of times a year. Here is a short-list of some typical alumni events:

- Alma mater game watching
- Local speaker event
- University-sponsored speaker event
- Happy hour
- Local sports game with families
- Panel of speakers on a topic
- Investment deal flow events
- Welcoming young alumni and others new to the area
- Seminars
- Holiday parties
- Family picnic or barbeque at park or theme park
- Fundraiser for Chapter's favorite charity
- University fundraiser
- Tailgating
- Student send-off party
- Admissions reception
- Networking event
- Notable university dates, such as a Founder's Day
- Community service projects
- Bus trips to campus / games
- Museum or theatre outings
- Scholarship awards party
- Continued education event
- Wine tasting
- Small group dinner event
- Annual meeting
- Career-advancement events

Although not exhaustive, this list demonstrates that there are many flavors of events a Chapter might host. These could take place in the morning, afternoon, or evening, as well as during the week or on weekends. It may not be surprising to learn that nearly 70 percent of alumni Chapters gather to watch football games, and 43 percent do so for basketball games. Networking is also at the top of the list for 53 percent of Chapters, followed by some sort of outdoor activity like picnics, hiking, and float trips at 33 percent. About a third of Chapters conduct volunteer events, with the same number attending professional sporting events together. Moving down the list, 22 percent of Chapters engage in cultural events, and 19 percent in school-spirit events, while 15 percent host a formal dinner or dance. Surprisingly, only 13 percent of Chapters coordinate professional development activities. At the lower end of the list, group movie watching shows up for 6 percent of Chapters, and 5 percent take part in sports leagues like flag football.[1]

Not all of the above are ideal for revenue generation, but most are. From a fiscal perspective and at a minimum, the Chapter should strive to operate net-neutral events. In other words, most events should at least generate enough income to pay for themselves. This is a typical approach for many Chapters, especially if the Chapter can tap into multiple streams of revenue. If other methods generate the bulk of the operational capital or if it is adequately supplied by the association, then all the Chapter needs to do is break even from event to event.

For example, the Tulane Alumni Association (TAA) encourages its Chapters to approach events with a net-neutral strategy. The TAA Club Coordinators offer their experience and historical data to help plan and price events to achieve the desired outcome. Even if attendance was not as expected, causing a net loss for the event, the TAA is supportive and encouraging—especially in regard to newly established Chapters—specifically stating:

> Don't be discouraged [Chapter leaders] if your event does not break even due to unforeseen costs or a poor turnout for an event. If a club president has a good idea for an event and is willing to volunteer to make it happen, the TAA and the Office of Alumni Relations will try to help.[2]

That being said, there is another way to look at general events other than with a net-neutral perspective; rather, each event itself could manifest as a meaningful revenue-generating opportunity. If that is the desired outcome, a successful strategy benefits from a well-vetted subject, speaker(s), venue, catering, pricing, promotion, and creative compounding of opportunities. The University of Minnesota Alumni Association acknowledges that additional financial support to fund Chapter events and activities is sometimes needed. In addition to supporting sponsorships, raffles, and auctions, it suggests leveraging event fees where pricing "should include a surcharge above the cost of the event."[3]

The remaining text in this section will assume that a Chapter does intend to generate a profit, however small, when hosting an event. Planning successful events is a significant topic worthy of its own dedicated book. Here we will focus on only the most critical highlights directly influencing the financial success of the event. Don't be surprised if the sequel to this book might very well be a much more in-depth look at event ideas, planning, and execution.

A Sexy Event Subject

Assuming that revenue generation is one of the primary goals of hosting an event, the Chapter will want as many people attending it as possible. Accordingly, the subject should be unique and interesting to a broad spectrum of people. For example, many of your Chapter's alumni might seek to write a book. Budding authors span those wishing to launch a professional platform from which to be recognized; active hobbyists, such as historians or fly fisherman; those wanting to share deep, meaningful personal experiences, like caring for a loved one during hospice; and creative types who write poems or short stories. Taking into account the above, "Getting Your Book Published" might be a great topic catering to a large population of alumni.

Maybe your university has a real strength in political science and it is an election year. Everyone in our country is impacted by a presidential election—alumni and all of their friends and family. A great revenue-generating event might be hosting an event in which professors from the campus and / or qualified local alumni share their thoughts on the election, including how it is being viewed by other countries and possible impacts to personal and business finance—as objectively as possible. Another idea might be to host a post-election event discussing likely changes expected to things such as taxes and policies based on the state of the Congress, the House of Representatives, and the Federal Reserve.

A note of caution for 501(c)(3)-designated entities should be emphasized here related to the example above. To maintain compliance with IRS regulations, a Chapter that has 501(c)(3) status is absolutely prohibited from directly or indirectly participating in, or intervening in, any political campaign on behalf of (or in opposition to) any candidate for elective public office. Violating this prohibition may result in denial or revocation of tax-exempt status and the imposition of certain excise taxes. However, any of the above activities would not be prohibited if they were done in a non-partisan manner.[4]

Once a topic is finalized, the speaker or panel of speakers should be chosen, keeping in mind the likely draw each one will have on attendees. Taking it one step further, the Chapter might also wish to consider the number and quality of attendees each speaker will specifically recruit as a result of his or her own network or size of the local office.

Maybe the event is a trip to see a local musical. A great lead for this outing might be local alumni with a background in theatre who could frame the context for period and explain the story line. Maybe the speaker is actually the director of the theatre, who provides an account of history and the little-known background secrets. Every event bears the possibility of a subject matter expert. Find him or her.

Returning to our "Getting Your Book Published" example, one such speaker would be someone in a recognized position in a local author's club, meet-up group, or creative writing class. Other possible speakers might be a local publisher, a literary attorney, or someone who has successfully published a book—ideally, prominent alumni where possible. If chosen well, these speakers not only entice many to attend the event but also have a large sphere of connections to access in support of your panel and your alumni afterward.

The Wharton Club of Dallas–Fort Worth did actually host such an event at one time, and it was a huge success. Panelists included a nationally recognized media attorney, a CEO of a self-publishing company, an executive from a royalty-based publisher, and a local TV personality who had become a best-selling author.

At the time, the event was a bit of a gamble since it was the first time trying such an approach. Luckily, it was well attended—in fact, it sold out. Each panelist brought several books to distribute as door prizes throughout the program. Many happy alumni left as winners that night, prizes in hand. The evening was exceptionally interactive, with a plethora of questions and answers volleying back and forth up until the very end. The venue actually had to push us out the door, as nearly half of the attendees stayed afterward to pepper the panelists with more questions. We closed the place down that night!

This story goes to show just how rewarding an event can be for everyone involved—alumni, Chapter leadership, and panelists—especially if the leadership thinks a little creatively about a unique yet broadly appealing subject.

A Convenient Date and Time

Be very careful to select a date and time wisely. Review the calendar closely with a watchful eye toward anything that may conflict with attendance for that event. Such things include holidays, personal- and business-tax submission deadlines, local and major sporting events such as the Final Four Championship, religious holidays that apply to your alumni population, elections, school holidays such as spring break, and other university events, to get the list started.

As club President for the Wharton Club of Dallas–Fort Worth, I made a serious error in scheduling a speaker one year. The speaker—who was a prominent Jewish businessman—and I were scheduling his talk without proper calendars in front of us. We started to mentally scroll through dates something like this: "How about the third Tuesday in April? No? OK, how does the second Tuesday look? Not good, either? Hmm. OK, let's switch over to Thursdays. How about the third Thursday? It is open? Fantastic! Let's book it."

Well, when the week of the event rolled around, I started to receive some seriously disgruntled e-mails and voice messages from would-be attendees. We had locked the speaker in—a Jewish speaker, I remind you—for the most important day of Passover. He and I then knew why that date had been open on his calendar. Neither of us caught it at the time of scheduling, and the speaker was equally as disappointed by the oversight. By then, it was too late to cancel the venue, so we went forward with the talk. As expected, the turnout was low. After the onslaught of nasty grams and low participation, I learned my lesson quickly!

Regarding the timing of the event, a Chapter has several options. Of those, the most popular are a breakfast that starts at about 7:30 in the morning, a lunch inside the 11:30 to 1:30 time window, an evening event after working hours, or during the weekend, usually on Saturday. The best times really depend on the type of event, the Chapter's alumni pool make-up, its geographic distribution, and the types of occupations alumni are most likely to have, as well as other factors. The goal is to choose the best time that ensures the greatest possible turnout.

Sometimes, the event itself dictates the time. If it is a fundraising dinner, that narrows the options considerably. Events related to a football or basketball game are scheduled for your Chapter. Happy hours and wine tastings are typically at the end of the day. Anything that involves the entire family, such as a picnic, makes a better weekend event. Other types of events are purely up to the Chapter.

Speaker events, for example, are completely open to the Chapter's preferences during the week. They can effectively be hosted during any of the three popular time slots—breakfast, lunch, or dinner. Unless the speaker is paired with a holiday event, weekends are not the best time for them.

If your alma mater is a conservatory, be mindful of typical times the alumni would be performing or formally practicing. Should your Chapter be the Chicago Booth Alumni Club of the San Francisco Bay Area, the business school alumni of the University of Chicago with a strong finance program, then breakfast events might be a terrible idea. With the stock market opening at 9:30 a.m. EST, that would mean many West coast alumni would start their day at 6:30 in the morning. It is not likely that many would be drawn to a 5:00 a.m. breakfast event, nor could they attend if the breakfast were held any later. An understanding of your alumni population will fuel better choices.

Choosing well-vetted dates and times can go a long way in ensuring an excellent turnout, but it is not a guarantee. The final step will be trial and error. After a couple events, your Chapter will gain a much better feel for what time of what day is most convenient for your alumni.

Determining Attendee Composition

The topic of who should be invited and / or attracted to the event will likely spark an interesting dialog within the leadership team. A balance will need to be struck between alumni-exclusive events and open-door events. Your Chapter might already have a "come one, come all" attitude, and, if so, then this is a nonissue and you can skip to the next section. If your Chapter prefers some exclusivity, then there will a bit more discourse around the topic.

One such example is that of the US service academies. Alumni of the United States Air Force Academy Association of Graduates (OAG) value their association with each other greatly and celebrate it whenever possible—as they should. If they are to expand access to a particular event, it is very likely to only be to the alumni of the other service academies. That may or may not be the position your Chapter takes when planning events. For the sake of argument, I will propose that your Chapter does enjoy a degree of exclusivity. In this case, only a couple of events might be sacrificed to revenue generation in which a broader attendance base of non-alumni paying higher fees can be attractive.

It is also possible that the popularity of the speaker may dictate the approach, or at least factor in. Should the speaker be broadly recognized and maybe even have cost the Chapter to speak, then producing a large crowd may become of high importance. Your Chapter may have had to guarantee a certain-sized audience, or it simply may take that many people to generate the income desired by the Chapter.

In some cities, the pool of alumni for a particular college or university can be very small. The city may be very far from the epicenter of the university; the university may not graduate a large enough number of alumni, or it may be too young to have created a critical mass outside of the neighboring states; or some other reason. The pool of alumni may be too small to support any regular programming—thus making it difficult to draw great speakers or run any events with the intention of funding anything, even a modest charitable cause.

This was one reason we founded the Dallas Business Club (DBC). The now twenty-five+ members of the DBC are alumni Chapters themselves, only specifically of MBA programs. All alumni of a member Chapter are encouraged to participate in DBC programs. The DBC hosts a full slate of original programming compounded by shared events from member Chapters. For individual alumni, the established structure offers expanded access to outstanding and fun events across the metroplex and the ability to build a broader social and professional network. For Chapters, it reduces the burden to produce overly robust annual programs and provides access to a much larger pool of participants when desired. For example, alumni of Emory University's Goizueta Business School number just a hair north of 200 people across all of Dallas–Fort Worth. However, as a member of the DBC, they can attract a great speaker and guarantee a reasonable-sized audience because participation may be open to all members of the DBC.

Other cities also have formal alumni Chapter consortiums or alignments that can broaden exposure and participation. The DBC was actually patterned after similar organizations in New York, Seattle, and Denver. Several cities are also fortunate to have super-alumni organizations (SAOs) based on athletic conferences, like the SEC Alumni and Fans of Boston. They represent the New England alumni Chapters of the fourteen universities that make up the Southeastern Conference. Each school organizes its own area alumni events, while they often organize joint events to celebrate the unity and camaraderie that makes the Southeastern Conference the self-proclaimed "best collegiate conference in America."[5] The SEC Universities include the University of Alabama, University of Arkansas, Auburn University, University of Florida, University of Georgia, University of Kentucky, Louisiana State University, University of Mississippi, Mississippi State University, Texas A&M University, University of Missouri, University of South Carolina, University of Tennessee, and Vanderbilt University.

The Big Ten Alumni of Atlanta is yet another of many such organizations. It supports local alumni clubs by offering Atlanta-area alumni opportunities to meet in social, professional, and civic settings. To that end, they schedule a variety of events during the year with the goal of offering activities that will appeal to the broadest possible cross-section of alumni. Universities of the Big

Ten Conference include the University of Nebraska, Northwestern University, Michigan State University, Purdue University, University of Illinois, University of Michigan, Penn State University, University of Minnesota, University of Wisconsin, Ohio State, University of Iowa, Rutgers University, University of Maryland, and Indiana University.

The first step is for your Chapter to definitively agree on who is going to be invited to the party—will it only be alumni and their close circle, or will it be broader, focusing more on the revenue-generation aspect of this one event? If a wide net is to be cast, consider sister-school alumni groups and seek out SAOs in your area. You might take it even further to establish one if nothing currently exists. For more on this topic, read the section *"Promotion for Maximum Impact: Physical and Digital Third-Party Channels—Secret Weapons"* found later in this book.

A Venue That Is Right in Every Way

Venue selection may seem trivial; however, it is anything but. There are many considerations that can significantly influence attendance for this event and ones that follow. The Binghamton University Alumni Association certainly agrees. It states that

> the ability to choose an appealing and appropriate venue can single-handedly ensure either success or failure.[6]

First, the venue selected must meet the requirements set forth by the alumni association's guidelines for venues and conduct. The American University (AU) Alumni Association's policy states that

> no alumni-sponsored activities should be held in facilities that restrict entrance on the basis of sex, race, or religion. [7]

Some examples of venues to avoid would include country clubs in which women or other groups may not be welcome, are excluded from membership, or are denied voting privileges. Some restaurants with themes or environments that may be demeaning or uncomfortable to some alumni should also be avoided, such as Hooters. Choosing a venue in which any alumni may feel uncomfortable, even mildly, is poor judgment and can have a detrimental impact on attendance, as well as on the reputation of the Chapter, its leadership, and the university.

Next, the appropriate-sized venue must be identified. Ideally, there should be very few open seats during the event. A venue that is too small limits the possible revenue that could be generated. A venue that is too large, with many open seats or space, leaves attendees feeling like it was poorly attended.

The location is also key—it needs to be fairly easy to access at whatever time the event will take place. The Chapter would not want to choose a venue next to a major sporting arena on the night of a home game, for example. If the event will be in the evening, then rush hour traffic needs to be taken into consideration, as even those in close proximity to the event might see the traffic as too onerous to be worth it. In general, the trendier the venue, the better. People enjoy visiting popular places that they might not yet have had a chance to visit.

It is always a win if the venue ties well to the subject or topic of the evening. If the event is a game-watching party, then a sports bar or similar is ideal. If alumni are gathering to hear about the business of artisanal, organic food, then it would be advisable to hold the event on location at an appropriate restaurant and include samples and maybe a tour. An event focusing on the economy could be hosted at the local Federal Reserve Bank.

If food that requires a plate is offered, then table space is important—especially if utensils are necessary. That table space can manifest in the form of full tables at which the attendees eat during the talk, or it may simply look like an area at the back of the room or an adjacent room with sufficient cocktail tables for eating prior to being seated for the main event. If alcohol is available, ensure that a third party, not the Chapter, has sold and served it to the attendees, due to liability issues. These space considerations are all very important in selecting the best venue.

Regarding catering, most of the issues are related to food itself; however, there is one important tie to the venue that significantly impacts venue selection. The Chapter will often want to secure its own caterer for better cost and quality control. Many venues, especially hotels and ones with an existing relationship to a food venue, may insist on using their caterers. Such circumstances may not be deal killers; just know and evaluate your Chapter's options.

What about the audio / visual equipment (A/V) needs? It will be important to understand what the format of the event will be, such as a speaker at a podium leveraging a PowerPoint presentation or an emcee roaming around while talking and engaging the audience. An ideal venue will have the appropriate equipment and acoustics and will permit the Chapter to choose the supplier of its choice. A/V is always an expensive line item. Chapters will be charged for every little request. Do your best to keep this cost under control—and venue selection plays a big role.

One more consideration is how the venue will insist upon payment. It may require a healthy upfront deposit, possibly well in advance, to secure the space. Through the eyes of the Chapter leadership, it is always better to pay as little upfront as possible before the Chapter has had the chance to sell tickets, collect registration fees, secure sponsorships, or receive contributions. A good venue will work with the Chapter on terms that are more palatable.

The last issue related to the venue is parking. Venues with perceived difficult parking—expensive, dangerous, or far away—tend to be a detractor. If possible, choose a location with excellent, well-lit parking very close to the entrance, or have the cost of a valet covered in some way. Valet parking is an excellent sponsorship opportunity, as discussed in an earlier section.

Do not forget that if the event is being held near campus, the alumni center itself may be an option to consider. Just be mindful of rental and service costs, just like any other venue. The University of Illinois (UI) Alumni Association's Alice Campbell Alumni Center is one such center available to alumni as well as to the general public. It is a beautiful facility able to accommodate up to 250 people banquet style or 500 when configured in reception style. Costs for alumni to rent room space at the Alice Campbell Alumni Center range from $100 to $550 during the week and are a bit higher on weekends. Additional services are available à la carte.[8] If a Chapter event is revenue generating and near campus, the use of the alumni center may be worth the cost.

There is one additional, especially unique scenario that is well worth mentioning. Very few alumni Chapters occupy their own building or facility—in fact, those that do can be counted on one hand. One of these is the Yale Club of New York City, the only physical Yale Club in the world.[9] The Association of Yale Alumni (AYA) serves 165,000 alumni globally through its network of 180 clubs.[10]

In New York, the breathtaking clubhouse spares no expense and includes a full-service hotel with nearly 140 rooms, some of which are capable of sleeping up to six; a state-of-the-art spa and athletic center with weight training, squash courts, exercise equipment, a plunge pool, saunas, steam rooms, and a massage studio; four dining options to suit your mood; a full library, home to more than 39,000 volumes in the collection; a rooftop terrace; and a comfortable lounge complete with a fireplace. The Yale Club of New York City has 11,000 members and hosts more than 300 events per year, from lectures to parties.[11]

Interestingly, membership is not geographically bound and is open to all Yale University graduates, as well as graduates of the University of Virginia, Dartmouth College, and the DKE fraternity.[12] This is an unparalleled venue opportunity for those with access.

With any venue, there are important costs to consider. Understand if a deposit will be required and what the refund policy might be. Also, ask about what guaranteed minimums might apply. Costs such as catering, A/V, furniture, and parking may be additional and tied to the venue. Learn what degrees of freedom might exist and where third parties may be contracted. Build all of these into the budget.

Winning Catering and Beverage Strategies

Should your event contain a food and beverage component, do not take it lightly. The food must be good or great, and drinks must be enjoyable while not subjecting the Chapter to unnecessary liability.

Beginning with the food, it should be as applicable to the event and the audience as the venue will be. In fact, food might be the epicenter of the event itself. Maybe your Chapter is hosting a crawfish boil, like the Houston Chapter of the Southern University Alumni Federation, one of forty+ alumni Chapters[13, 14] representing more than 100,000 alumni.[15] The annual **Alumni Crawfish Boil and Fish Fry Fundraiser** attracts over 500 people from Houston and the surrounding areas.[16] Just maybe, your Chapter might be the Cape Fear Chapter of the Campbell University Alumni Association, one of fourteen Chapters[17] serving 49,000 alumni,[18] hosting a more intimate BBQ on the beach for about forty alumni and friends.[19] Possibly your Chapter is the Washington, DC, Chapter of the University of Utah Alumni Association (UUAA), one of approximately thirty Chapters serving 270,000 alumni through nearly 300 events a year.[20] The DC Alumni Chapter hosts an old-fashioned hamburgers-and-hotdogs picnic at Lake Accotink in honor of the state's Pioneer Day.[21] Ensure that the food is of great quality—they are coming for the camaraderie, and they are coming for the food that they are feeding to their families!

If the event is more professional in nature, such as a speaker event or a panel discussion, the food offerings are more likely to be along the lines of hors d'oeuvres. Even happy hours are likely to—and should—have appetizers available. Here are a few tips to keep your attendees happy and coming back to the next event.

Make certain the food offering is broad enough that all alumni will be able to enjoy something to eat. For example, ensure that there are several good options for vegetarians. In addition, be aware that the vegetarian / vegan options must not be cooked together or on the same grill with meat. Ensure that the caterer / restaurant is aware and can certify this fact to alumni. The Seattle Chapter of the Virginia Tech Alumni Association, one of more than one hundred Chapters[22] serving over 250,000 alumni in one hundred+ countries,[23] understands this culinary need. It runs a **Summer Picnic and Student Send-Off** that advertises veggie burgers in addition to hamburgers and other items on the menu.[24]

Depending on the make-up of your local alumni population, you may want to consider including a few kosher items as options. If so, also keep in mind the proper storing, serving, and handling of kosher food, along with extra utensils to maintain appropriate food separation all the way through.

Support healthy eating choices in addition to the barbeque and chips, such as fruit, salads, and chicken. Having a low-calorie ranch-dressing fountain for dipping raw veggies can be fun for children and adults alike. Berries and / or angel food cake make lighter dessert options to add to the cobblers and cookies. The San Francisco Bay Area Chapter of the US Naval Academy Alumni Association gets this right! It held its **Army / Navy Game Party** in Palo Alto, and in addition to standard fare, it offered smoked pulled chicken and fresh mixed fruit for those seeking healthier options.[25]

Many people have serious food allergies these days. One way to prepare for this is to allow comments regarding food sensitivities at the time of registration. This will help provide a heads-up when working with the caterer or restaurant. You may choose to avoid food with peanuts and tree nuts just in case, such as cookies or brownies with walnuts or peanut-butter-and-jelly sandwiches for the kids.

It is always good practice to label each food item with a name card containing as much information about the food and ingredients as possible. Mark the cards with any special classifications, such as vegetarian, vegan, kosher, gluten-free, contains nuts, sugar-free, or any other relevant category. If the event includes a plated dinner, substitute the name cards with a menu card listing all the same information.

Look at each time someone mentions a food request or concern as a gift. They are helping you to avert either an unpleasant experience or possibly a serious medical emergency.

Regarding the beverages, it is hard to go wrong with water, iced tea, lemonade, sodas, and maybe even coffee at just about any event that you can host—depending on the type of event. It gets a little trickier when alcohol is involved. Alcohol is by no means a stranger to alumni events, and it is possibly even a primary staple at some, like game watching.

Most alumni associations maintain an active policy regarding alcoholic beverages at alumni events, but even if one does not exist, it is prudent to follow a few basic tips to minimize potential issues and liability. The Florida State University (FSU) Alumni Association frames it best with the following procedures:

Alcoholic Beverages May Only Be Served:

» in a manner that is consistent with all local, state and federal laws and regulations
» by a hired, qualified third-party alcohol server
» as a part of an event that includes food service and non-alcoholic beverages

Alcoholic Beverages May <u>Not</u> Be Served:

» in a manner that promotes the service of the alcoholic beverages as "free" or "without cost"
» "self-service" style or by any other uncontrolled means
» at programs designed to attract current or prospective students who may be under 21 years old
» by any volunteer or staff person representing the FSU Alumni Association.[26]

Many universities take a very similar approach to the presence of alcohol at events. The above is a nice summary of what you might see explained by your alumni association as well. It is prudent to seek out this policy and make certain your Chapter's leadership team is aware and onboard.

There are a few points about the above not to miss. It is really, really important that the Chapter is not in a position to have either purchased, sold, or served the alcohol for / to the alumni. The act of purchasing, selling, or distributing (serving) the alcohol is what defines who is liable for any fallout. To be specific, the Chapter should avoid the following when actively adopting strategies to minimize liability:

- Including the cost of an alcoholic beverage in the cost of an event registration (selling alcohol).
- Selling drink tickets at the event on behalf of the venue (selling alcohol).
- Picking up the tab for the alcoholic drinks at a happy hour (purchasing alcohol).
- Passing out the drinks at an event at the home of an alumna / alumnus (distributing alcohol).
- Having a serve-yourself beer keg at an event (uncontrolled distribution).
- Offering the first round of drinks on the Chapter for a happy hour (purchasing alcohol).

Don't look at this discussion as a killjoy. Rather, know these are the pitfalls to directly avoid. You certainly would not want your wonderful, revenue-generating event to cost the Chapter significant issues with liability, nor put the Chapter's active status in jeopardy.

Now that your Chapter leadership is further enlightened, you are ready to embrace alcoholic beverages in a safe and enjoyable manner. Make sure a licensed third party is selling and serving the alcoholic drinks. This works seamlessly for happy hours where the bar or restaurant is taking the money and serving the drinks. At other events, include a cash bar where a licensed third party is staffing the bar.

If you do not want a cash bar, a sponsor may be responsible for the alcoholic drinks. For example, a reception sponsor could pay for and have the proper service staff onsite to distribute the drinks. In fact, sometimes an alcoholic beverage company wishes to be your event sponsor. If the alumni association approves, then the beverage company could provide the alcohol as long as it also provides the licensed service staff to serve and monitor consumption. Maybe the local craft brewery wants to provide an in-kind sponsorship and distribution of its seasonal beer at an event. These circumstances are typically acceptable.

Lastly, be cognizant of the likelihood of underaged attendees, such as students, applicants, and family. While some events are less likely to involve children or young adults under twenty-one, such as an alumni speaker dinner, others will, such as a family picnic. Be mindful of the attendee composition when making your decision to include alcoholic beverages, and ensure that the appropriate safeguards are in place.

When properly managed, alcoholic beverages can be an acceptable and enjoyable addition to an event. Tulane University even has a vendor agreement in place that provides for the exclusive use of particular brands of alcohol, thus obviously approving the use of alcoholic beverages at functions. At all University events where alcoholic beverages have been approved and which maintain compliance with the University's alcohol policy, organizers must serve only liquors or beers from the approved brand list.[27]

Clearly, there is a time and place for the inclusion of alcoholic beverages; just stay aware and smart about the circumstances. The planning and management of the food and beverage portion of an event can be fun, but it must be taken seriously—especially when it is such an important factor in the overall experience and a heavy determinant for future event attendance.

Enticing Ticketing

Now that an outstanding panel of well-connected, prominent speakers has been assembled, followed by the selection of an ideal venue for the perfect time and date, we will focus on the next topic—ticketing. As this event is not only a wonderful opportunity to gather for fun and fellowship but specifically designed to generate important capital necessary to fund the Chapter's operations, ticket options and prices are important.

The Chapter may wish to separate the attendees into categories based on their relationship to the Chapter and / or price elasticity. Some possible ticket categories presented in increasing values are:

- **Young alumni** – Often, young alumni are considered to be heavily laden with debt. These are the Chapter leaders and supporters of the future, so they should be encouraged to come at a very low cost—something from $5.00 to break even per person. The Chapter will not make money with this approach. However, if the ticketing practices drive young alumni away from participating, there will not be much of a Chapter to support in the future.
- **Members** (if your Chapter / central alumni association supports memberships) – This should be a fairly low-costing ticket yet established to provide a reasonable margin. If memberships are not appropriate for your Chapter, then the category might simply be Alumni.
- **Chapter affiliate members** – Affiliates can be defined as loosely or broadly as the Chapter wishes. This ticket simply represents something between core alumni and unrelated guests. The ticket prices for this category might be equivalent to or slightly higher than those of the members / alumni. Of the categories presented here, this one would be the first one to eliminate if the Chapter prefers a simplified approach.

- **Guests** – A guest ticket should be the highest ticket price of them all.

If the event is a family event in which food is a major component, such as the upcoming **New England Clambake** hosted by Chicago Chapter of the University of Rhode Island (URI) Alumni Association, one of seventy-five Chapters serving 123,000 alumni,[28] then maybe you would like to divide tickets by age group. Consider this approach:

- **Adults** – These folks are likely to eat the most.
- **Children from eight to thirteen** – Reduced price tickets could make sense for this group, as they do not eat nearly as much.
- **Children seven and under** – These little guys eat close to nothing, so they might be welcome for free.

The age classifications make this type of event more affordable for families and are in line with approximate consumption and thus cost. The specific age brackets are simply examples. There is no reason you could not create a ticket structure that combines appreciation for members with age group breakouts. Determine what is best for your Chapter and what will achieve the income target without alienating potential attendees. The ticket categories presented above are not the only options for consideration; however, they should provide a reasonable foundation to start a conversation and build the best structure for your Chapter's events.

In addition to the tiered-ticket types themselves, timing can advantageously play into pricing. The Chapter may offer early-bird pricing until a certain time, followed by a window of time in which standard ticket pricing applies, expiring a day or so prior to the event. From that point on, attendees could purchase tickets at the door, where the tickets always cost the most.

The Texas Christian University (TCU) Alumni Association, with 88,000 alumni[29] and ten+ Chapters,[30] is an advocate of higher at-the-door pricing to encourage early RSVPs at certain events.[31] It is a good idea to alert alumni to the fact that there will be a price difference at the door in the promotions. A surprise at check-in will likely cause frustration and disenchantment while doing nothing to have encouraged early registrations. Higher onsite pricing only drives earlier registrations if people are aware of the difference.

When it comes to determining the actual amounts to charge for each ticket, you might try backing into it. Start with determining what the event will cost (C_{TOTAL}), fixed costs, plus the variable costs based on the estimated attendance.

Then, establish what profit level the Chapter desires (Profit). The total of the costs plus the desired profit is equal to the target revenue (R_{TOTAL}), or, otherwise stated, it is the minimum that the Chapter should intend to earn at the event.

$$C_{TOTAL} + Profit = R_{TOTAL}$$

Now that you have a feel for what income (R_{TOTAL}) the event will need to generate, next determine how that will happen. Add up any anticipated revenue from sources other than tickets (R_{OTHER}), such as sponsorships. If you subtract the other revenue from the target revenue, that leaves the amount the tickets will need to produce, the target ticket revenue (R_{TICKET}).

$$R_{TOTAL} - R_{OTHER} = R_{TICKET}$$

From here, using some basic modeling scenarios around the average ticket price (T_{AVE}), the Chapter can determine how to price the tickets. In our example, we developed four types of tickets over three time periods. A rough starting point might be determined by taking the target ticket revenue and dividing by the number of expected attendees.

$$T_{AVE} = R_{TICKET} / \text{Expected Attendance}$$

The result is a rough approximation for the middle of the ticket-pricing chart. In our example, it might become the regular members / alumni price. From there, increase it a bit for the affiliates and then again for the guests ticket prices. Reduce the regular members / alumni price to set the young alumni ticket.

	Early Bird Pricing	Regular Pricing	At-the-Door Pricing
Young Alumni Members	$(T_{AVE} -) -$	$T_{AVE} -$	$(T_{AVE} +) -$
Regular Members / Alumni	$(T_{AVE} -)$	T_{AVE}	$(T_{AVE} +)$
Affiliate Members	$(T_{AVE} -) +$	$T_{AVE} +$	$(T_{AVE} +) +$
Guests	$(T_{AVE} -) ++$	$T_{AVE} ++$	$(T_{AVE} +) ++$

At this point, drop the full series of regular ticket prices by some appropriate number or percent to yield approximate early-bird pricing while then bumping the regular prices by an appropriate amount to generate a guide for the at-the-door ticket pricing. Running the numbers forward under a few scenarios will help refine the prices. This is a crude, high-level example, but hopefully it communicates the general concepts and will provide some assistance for your own pricing.

The final step in preparation is the promotion. As this is so important to producing a successful revenue-generating event, it will be addressed in its own section called "*Promotion for Maximum Impact*" later in the text.

Other Elements Not to Overlook

The list above covers the majority of important issues and costs for many types of events; however, there are a few additional line items that should be recognized before saving and closing the budgeting file, such as entertainment, transportation, and insurance.

The event may warrant some sort of entertainment. We have actually hired a petting zoo to be a part of a family picnic, with great satisfaction! Other types of entertainment include music in the form of a DJ or possibly a live band, face painters, clowns, a photo booth, or anything else that may appropriately liven up the program.

If the event is a road trip to a game or a casino night out, or if it is a dinner theatre on a train, there may be transportation costs to consider. The Chapter may wish to charter a bus for the drive. Coordinated transportation might even be appropriate if the group is travelling to a local professional sporting event in which the stadium is not so close. Some alumni associations may have specific requirements regarding transportation companies, such as the Villanova University Alumni Association (VUAA). It requires a signed transportation rider prior to rendering services. The rider is a contract with the transportation company that lists university requirements, including driver requirements, licenses and permits, insurance requirements, and indemnification.

Lastly, as touched on early in this book, insurance may be an appropriate extra expense. Obviously, Chapters that do not have any coverage will most certainly want to establish either an annual policy or a contract for a steady stream of special event liability policies. Even if the Chapter is covered by an alumni association or university policy, the event may fall outside the covered conditions. Examples include events in public places like parks or beaches, events on a boat, or events in someone's personal home. If so, it may be prudent to pick up a special event liability policy.

These three items, though not exhaustive, are additional important factors in designing a successful event and anticipating the total costs.

60-Second Takeaway

General events are the heart and soul of alumni fellowship. Coordinated events are what alumni want and expect. So it is logical to consider such events as possible avenues to generate meaningful income to in turn further the Chapter's operations on behalf of the alumni. Driving successful, revenue-generating events follows a formula: choose an interesting, broadly appealing topic or subject; select a well-recognized speaker(s) with a large network; agree on the make-up of the audience; lock in an ideal date and time; identify an appropriately themed, sized, located, and laid-out venue with a simple parking solution; prioritize the quality of the catering, being mindful of dietary needs; evaluate the appropriate inclusion of alcoholic beverages; determine additional costs, such as entertainment, transportation, and insurance; price it strategically; and promote it well.

It is important that the Chapter build a solid budget going into any event so that pricing is established in a way to meet the Chapter's goals. Know the refund policies, and gather certificates of insurance. If this approach is taken each time the Chapter seeks to generate income on an event, it will have ample funds for whatever the goal, be it funding scholarships, supporting operations, or whatever else the Chapter can dream of doing.

Make It Happen Checklist

☐ Determine that the Chapter wishes to use a specific event (or maybe events in general) as a channel for generating meaningful revenue.

☐ Identify a broadly appealing subject that is a unique opportunity— something that will draw the interest of a broad swath of alumni and possibly family and friends as well.

☐ Identify a well-known speaker(s) with a large, local network. Choose alumni where possible.

☐ Pick a date and time not likely to conflict with official holidays, largely observed religious holidays, state or federally significant dates, typical vacation weeks, major or local sporting events, or large-scale events of the Chapter's alma mater.

☐ Determine what the make-up will be of the event attendees—alumni only or a broad invitation.

☐ Select a venue of appropriate theme, location, size, and layout with a favorable parking solution.

☐ Identify catering options that align with the event and that take into consideration the dietary needs and restrictions of the alumni population.

☐ If alcoholic beverages are to be included, be mindful of maximizing safety and minimizing liability.

☐ Determine any additional costs, such as entertainment and transportation.

☐ Purchase special event liability if necessary.

☐ Consider incorporating one or more other methods of generating revenue / fundraising into the event, such as sponsorships, if appropriate.

☐ Build a comprehensive budget for all costs the event is likely to incur.

☐ Gather vendor insurance certificates.

☐ Determine the different ticket types, valid windows of time for the pricing tiers, and actual prices.

☐ Promote the event early and often through direct communication, social media, and, if appropriate, third-party channels. (See the *"Promotion for Maximum Impact"* section for more on this subject.)

☐ Execute an amazing event, and have fun!

Photo Shoots for Today's Digital World

Photo shoots are a very special type of event that deserve to be called out on their own merit, as social media continues to evolve as a major communication channel in both private and professional circles. Photographs are not only important personally as a mechanism to immortalize memories, but they are downright imperative for professional pursuits today. Our digital world demands quality visual content. Accordingly, photography offers a great opportunity to generate Chapter income while offering practical and immediate value to the alumni.

A photo shoot event staged by your Chapter will require a compelling theme. A couple of promising examples include professional press photos and holiday themes. Before jumping into this specialized event, it would be prudent to confirm the alumni interest. That can easily be done via a poll or survey. Once confirmation is received, it is safe to move forward.

Headshots—A Must-Have for a Digital Presence

Never more than today, when we are all visually inundated with data and messaging, are quality professional photographs more important. Any and all people with a profession should have a presence with a photograph online through any of the many digital venues, including:

- On his or her own personally branded website
- Communication portals such as Facebook, Basecamp, and others that enable individual comments
- Business materials highlighting the team and / or management, including a pitch deck
- Websites of for-profit and not-for-profit organizations listing advisors, directors, and other leadership
- Group directories
- Blogs, vlogs, and articles
- As part of "About the Author" or "About the Artist"
- Bios used anywhere, including at speaking engagements and in webinars
- Most certainly on LinkedIn

- Possibly even on the alumni Chapter website and other communication channels

In spite of such an overwhelming demand for properly crafted headshots, it is exceedingly common for people to use old, dated pictures, post pictures made using a mobile phone in poor lighting, forget to update pictures over time, or, worse yet, neglect to post any photo at all. In today's digital economy, such behavior can have a measurably detrimental impact on desired results. Old images have tells, including the hairstyles, clothing, and accessories of the time during which they were taken. Alumni intending to position themselves as go-to authorities on a current subject will have a difficult time doing so if the pictures tell a different story. Worse yet, if the client is expecting a person in his thirties to show up, and someone a decade older appears, it is hard to turn that look of surprise into a positive. An old picture misrepresents who someone is and reflects poorly on that person's attention to detail and timely perspective on any subject.

This is a great opportunity to organize professional photography in which the alumni could have several photos taken to cover each need and look, such as the formal businessperson or the relaxed professional. A popular approach to headshots today is the casual, entrepreneurial look with a living-the-dream expression. A great photographer is able to capture the true essence of someone—what makes them unique. The trick here is to identify that great photographer. If you can find the right artist, it can make all the difference in the world.

When it comes to scheduling, photo shoots are very different from other events in which the alumni congregate for the event at the same time. Conversely, the photographer will need to spend a certain amount of time with each person in each change of clothes—one at a time. As such, the photographer will likely suggest a method of scheduling that may end up looking like many ten- to twenty-minute time slots spanning several hours during the day and into the evening. Your Chapter may consider booking time slots based on the number of clothing changes desired. For the alumni, they are in and out fairly quickly. However, for the Chapter volunteers and the photographer, it will be a long stretch.

To position your alumni for the best results, do not schedule the shoot the week following a big celebratory event such as Memorial Day weekend, the Super Bowl, or New Year's Eve. Alumni will need to be well rested and hydrated for days prior to the photo shoot to look their best. Keeping that in mind, photo shoots are best scheduled for late summer or early fall. Alumni will have the best color to their skin and will likely be the thinnest of the year. Never schedule pictures for January or February if it can be avoided, as this tends to be the time when most people will have put on maximum weight and illnesses are rampant. This photograph will be immortalized in time for who knows how long, and who knows when the next one will be taken. Help the alumni make it count! Having a hair and make-up person on site is also a great idea.

Not all of the responsibility is left to the Chapter to produce great images that will dazzle; rather, it is shared with the alumni. As another display of gratitude for purchasing the book, a list of **Head Shot Dos and Don'ts** is available to assist in producing the best results. The guidelines address choosing clothing, colors, preparatory grooming, make-up (yep, both men and women), and more.

If handled well, this can become an annual event—or even once every two or three years—that is much anticipated by alumni. The event has the potential to become one actually relied upon by alumni. One reason people do not have photos taken very often is largely due to the time it takes to identify a photographer in whom they have confidence, schedule an appointment, and then participate in the shoot itself. Cost is also a part, but it is secondary to confidence in the results and inconvenience.

As such, alumni are a bit elastic when it comes to price. If the Chapter can go through the effort to organize and coordinate a very reputable photographer and convenient staging, alumni are likely to take advantage of the opportunity even if the sticker price is moderate to high (although I recommend the moderate range to attract as many as possible). If the photographer is willing to work with your Chapter, the event could yield reasonable income.

The Chapter may further wish to promote this as a great opportunity for all of the executives, managers, or employees of a company to get an updated photograph for the website, social media, or other corporate materials. Although current headshots are the core need across the alumni, there are other themes and opportunities that the Chapter may wish to exploit.

Holiday and Other Themes Spice Up Marketing Efforts

The United States celebrates several fun and engaging holidays throughout the year that provide excellent fodder for themed events. Let's start with Christmas. Children's pictures with Santa Claus are and will continue to be a huge hit for generations to come. Additionally, Christmas / holiday cards are now a typical vehicle for disseminating current images of the family as a whole or just individual children—and don't forget the beloved family pets! Your Chapter could offer a few different religious themes to be more inclusive.

Other applicable holidays include Easter with Easter bunny pictures. The Fourth of July, Veteran's Day, and Memorial Day make excellent opportunities to offer patriotic family photos, possibly as part of a larger family picnic event. Such a theme would be especially opportunistic for alumni of the US service academies.

Valentine's Day offers a romantic opportunity for couples to capture the moment in time. A quick stop for a surprise portrait photo while on the way to the Valentine's dinner could really impress one's significant other.

Considerations for Success

In order to host a wildly successful, revenue-generating photo shoot, there are some important considerations, including an excellent yet altruistic photographer with support, an ideal location, and a dependable scheduling tool. Focus on convenience, quality, and value when making each decision.

Starting with the photographer, his or her skills and equipment will need to be substantial so the photos can be taken efficiently and will be pleasing to the recipients. Further, this seasoned photographer must be willing to offer services at a substantial discount to provide an adequate profit margin. The most ideal candidate would be a professional photographer within the Chapter's local alumni pool, where the exposure would be sufficient for payment. Good luck finding that unicorn! For all others, the promise of repeat business ("volume" of work), as well as the exposure, might help achieve more favorable pricing.

If at all possible, it is recommended that the photographer also have an assistant. The assistant would prep the next person / family in line, adjust how the clothing hangs on the subjects, fix rogue and out-of-place hair, and attend to other details so the photographer keeps snapping pictures as efficiently as possible.

The final element associated with the right photographer is the "deliverable." Either the final product could be entirely digital, for which the alumni will receive links to edited pictures at some point following the event, or there might be a printer onsite, enabling alumni to walk away with photographs in hand. The best approach is entirely dependent on the theme and the intended uses of the photographs.

Next, the location is critical to a successful event. The location should be as easily accessible as possible for a quick in-and-out experience. It should also be meaningfully related to the photo shoot theme. Should the theme be patriotic, then possibly the local military museum or VFW might offer an appropriate backdrop.

The location should also be sizable enough to accommodate different motifs. If the theme is family holiday pictures, then a venue that might allow for a couple of staged areas inside and outside would be advantageous. For example, one staged area could have a Christmas tree while another is more influenced by Hanukkah, and a third could be an outside theme with trees and the beautiful leaves of autumn.

Should the photos be professional, then the motif options could be a vague office backdrop or a standard solid background. A warehouse or workshop-like theme is more typical of a more casual, hands-on-operational, entrepreneurial look.

Once all of the plans are in order, a dependable system for scheduling the alumni is paramount. Scheduling could take place through a single person or an electronic system. Either way, it would need to be welcoming, easy to engage, and simple to reengage when making changes. Should finding the time and availability to manage the scheduling be difficult, it could be well managed by SACL's Remote Chapter Assistant (RCA)—always a resource to perform the Chapter's back office processes.

Photo Shoot Pricing

There are a couple of ways that the Chapter may wish to approach pricing for the photo shoot and that are tied to the relationship with the photographer. One scenario is that the photographer might not charge for the photo shoot; rather, the alumni pay for the digital images ordered thereafter. If so, then the Chapter might simply require the alumni to purchase a ticket to the event or what amounts to a sitting fee. Keep in mind that the tickets should account for some specific number of poses / motifs.

From a scheduling perspective, charging for the appointment / sitting does wonders for reliability. Those who have committed actual money tend to be far more dependable. They actually show up, and, if they are delayed, they are more likely to alert the scheduling team in advance.

In another scenario, the photographer gives a portion of his or her earnings back to the Chapter. In this case, maybe the registration pricing is a bit lower since the revenue would be compensated by the photographer's donation. This can be a bit uncertain if it is the first year organizing the event, not knowing what the resulting orders might be. However, if the price to play is low enough, maybe the increase in participants is worth it.

With respect to the types of charges to the alumni, one approach is to divide the ticket types as follows:

- **Individual sitting** – This is where a single person will sit for the photograph. There might be additional individual options for multiple motifs or wardrobe changes. This should be the least expensive ticket.
- **Family sitting** – This is where a full family of two or more will sit for the photograph. The family tickets should cost a slight bit more because it takes more time to position the subjects and adjust the lighting for more than one person. There might be additional family options for multiple motifs or wardrobe changes.
- **Corporate packages** – These packages would contain specified numbers of individual and group photographs. An example would be a package in which five executives each has an individual, professional photograph taken, and then a group photo is taken as well. Variations could include number of participants, number of wardrobe changes, number of group shots, etc. This would obviously be the most expensive ticket.

This approach could also be combined with member vs. non-member enticements.

A photo shoot, if repeated on a predictable basis, could become a dependable source of income. Further, the online presence of your alumni base will be significantly expanded and elevated—indirectly enhancing the image of the alumni and your Chapter.

Wrapping Up the Loose Ends

This is another type of activity that could benefit from sponsorships. Alumni with businesses in marketing, advertising, consulting, social media, camera equipment, and coaching are just a few functions / industries that could very easily benefit from exposure under these circumstances. A sponsor that could provide just the right facility could be rather valuable. Think creatively about how to maximize both the take for the Chapter as well as the value for the alumni.

As touched on earlier, a photo shoot event is likely to be a fairly long day for organizers and volunteers—assuming it is popular. Be sure to have an ample list of volunteers that can swap in throughout the day. Some thought will need to be put into who is to be contacted for last-minute schedule changes and how that process will be communicated to participants. It cannot be a temporary someone. The contact e-mail, phone number, or other method of reaching event schedulers will need to be accessible and available onsite throughout the event. You will also want to have clear, written instructions to pass from one to another. Keep a stash of snacks and drinks available for volunteers and the photographer's team. Hungry, thirsty people are not happy people. Depending on how long it will take, your Chapter might want to order lunch in for the team. Either a lunch break should be scheduled into the program for the day, or people should eat on a rotating schedule.

Build a full and complete budget for the event, including any rental fees and small items we discussed. Promotion should also be factored in. Read through the later section *"Promotion for Maximum Impact"* for more on determining the audience and applicable promotional methods.

While the photo shoot is in progress, take behind-the-scenes pictures to use in publicizing the event. These pictures are great for posting on social media throughout the event to build more interest. They will also be useful in developing the event summary for use with the local alumni, for the Chapter liaison, and possibly for the alumni association magazine or website. This will set the stage and help build interest for the next one.

We live in a digital era where we are constantly being presented with visual media, to the point that it is expected. Photos are necessary to stay relevant professionally. This is where the alumni Chapter can step in, offering a truly needed service in a mutually beneficial way.

60-Second Takeaway

Today, our visual, digital presence is critical to both our professional and personal lives, yet many people lack the time to have a proper photograph taken, opting for outdated images or, worse, none at all. This is a great opportunity for the alumni Chapter to offer a real benefit to its alumni. Photo shoots are an unrestricted, fun approach to generating Chapter revenue while providing immediate value to the alumni. More popular themes include professional and holiday-centric photos for print and online use. The Chapter reaps the most benefit if the photo shoot is well received and can grow through repeated occurrences.

The Chapter should focus on convenience, quality, and value. The photographer should be experienced and efficient; the location should be convenient and appropriately sized, with indoor and outdoor staging as necessary; and the scheduling system must be simple and accessible. Revenue models vary, with one option being to charge the alumni a bit more to participate, while another is a donation from the photographer back to the Chapter of a pre-determined percentage of orders.

Photo shoots generate compounding benefits, including raising funds for the Chapter, providing an important service for a broad swath of the alumni, and indirectly enhancing the online image of the Chapter.

Make It Happen Checklist

- ☐ Survey the Chapter to determine if there is interest in a photo shoot. If so, narrow down the types to be most valuable.
- ☐ Identify the photographer with the best fit for the Chapter's needs, including equipment, availability, support staff, skill level, image distribution, and pricing. Ideally, this would be an alumna / alumnus.
- ☐ Negotiate payment with the photographer.
- ☐ Identify the best location for the shoot, taking into consideration theme, weather, ease of access, staging, and size of venue.
- ☐ Establish a scheduling system that is easy to use and modify.
- ☐ Seek sponsorships and other forms of income to support the event and revenue goals.
- ☐ Build a budget capturing all costs, including deposits and rental fees, as well as anticipated revenue sources.
- ☐ Determine ticket pricing for different options or packages, such as individuals, families, and corporate groups.
- ☐ Brainstorm and prepare the appropriate staging for each applicable motif.
- ☐ Effectively promote the photo shoot to all constituents.
- ☐ Adequately staff the photo-shoot day, and prepare clear written instructions to be passed to the next volunteers when they arrive.
- ☐ Be prepared with snacks and drinks.
- ☐ Maintain an accessible person dedicated to managing the schedule the day of the event to handle real-time changes.
- ☐ Capture behind-the-scenes pictures for real-time social media posting, as well as summary reporting for the Chapter and the association.
- ☐ Share the behind-the-scenes pictures and some of the final professional shots with the alumni.
- ☐ Above all else, have fun!

Part III
New Horizons for 501(c)(3) Chapters

Giving Days Are Sweeping the Country   163

»   Advantages and Compounding Funds Up for Grabs   163

»   Important Guidelines for Chapter Leaders   166

»   Other Giving-Day Scenarios   167

»   Flawless Campaign Execution   168

»   60-Second Takeaway   170

»   Make It Happen Checklist   171

Matching Gifts—Big Money Left on the Table   173

»   Typical Exclusion Criteria   174

»   Executing a Campaign   176

»   60-Second Takeaway   177

»   Make It Happen Checklist   179

Volunteer Grants Are Easy Money for Chapter Leaders   181

»   Grant Allocation Methods   182

»   The Process and Typical Exclusions: Pay Close Attention   185

»   Landing the Grant   187

»   60-Second Takeaway   189

»   Make It Happen Checklist   190

Giving Days Are Sweeping the Country

Regional giving days, sometimes called community giving days, are wonderful opportunities for Chapters to receive *more* than was actually donated; however, *only* Chapters that qualify as 501(c)(3)-recognized charities and are in good standing with the IRS may participate. All others should simply skip this section and move to *"PART IV: Operational Essentials."*

A regional giving day is a powerful, time-limited, online fundraising competition that unites a community around local causes. It is typically hosted by the area's community foundation over a twenty-four-hour period using a single online donation platform in which donations can be directed to specific, registered charities. More than fifty regions across the country are now actively hosting a giving day, such as the Connecticut Community Foundation, which raised $1.2 million for the 215 local charities on May 3, 2016,[1] or the North Texas Giving Day, which raised an astonishing $37 million for 2,518 nonprofits on September 22, 2016.[2] Since its inception, the eighteen-hour North Texas Giving Day has raised more than $155 million for local charities and is the largest in the nation.[3]

The first regional giving days were launched in 2009 by a couple of forward-thinking organizations. In addition to the Communities Foundation of Texas, the Minnesota Community Foundation and the Pittsburgh Community Foundation also top the list as early adopters. Seattle Foundation's GiveBIG campaign brought the program to the Northwest in 2011 and has become one of the country's most successful campaigns, raising $78 million to date. The 2016 campaign inspired nearly 45,000 donors to make almost 90,000 gifts to 1,600 nonprofits, yielding a 30 percent growth in contributions over the prior year.[4, 5]

Regional giving days are powerful; they provide interesting new opportunities for alumni chapters with several upsides.

Advantages and Compounding Funds Up for Grabs

In addition to the publicity provided by the sponsoring community foundations, there are several uniquely beneficial reasons for taking part in one. There are a few extra-special benefits of leveraging a regional giving day beyond that of traditional fundraising that should not go overlooked, including:

- The possibility of winning prize money
- The availability of matching funds and proportional bonuses
- The lack of geographic donor limitations
- The lack of requirements on who can donate
- The possibly of being a small player in a newly organized regional giving day

Chapters may receive more than was actually donated as a result of possible giving-day incentives. Participating nonprofits may win monetary prizes coordinated by the hosting organization throughout the day, and / or they might receive a direct or proportional match based on contributions. Prize categories vary significantly; however, typical prizes are for highest total giving, most unique donors, most donors from a geographic area, and largest increase over last year, among others.

Each prize type can further be segmented into categories, such as small, medium, or large nonprofits, or into time slots, such as during a specific hour. Prizes can be of significant value to a Chapter and tend to range from as small as $250 to as much as $10,000 or more. In May of 2016, the BIG Day of Giving in California yielded $93,000 in additional prizes for sixty-five of its 568 participating nonprofits.[6]

Chapters also have the chance to capture a proportional bonus or a direct match to what was contributed. A direct match refers to a whole-number ratio between the donation amount and the match amount (e.g., $1 match for every $1 raised). A proportional bonus means a distribution of bonus money based on each nonprofit's percentage of total giving-day funds. In this example of a proportional bonus, on giving day, your Chapter receives $9,000 in donations while the entire giving day raised $3 million. Since $9,000 is 0.3 percent of $3 million, that is your Chapter's proportion. If the bonus pool were $500,000, your Chapter would then also receive 0.3 percent of the $500,000, or $1,500. Your Chapter's total would be $9,000 + $1,500 = $10,500.

These matching and proportional bonus scenarios may be coordinated by the host organization, such as in the example above. They may also be organized and executed within the community of local alumni. For example, a particular alumna / alumnus may announce that she or he will match whatever money is directed to the Chapter through giving day. From the Chapter's viewpoint, it would be advantageous to solicit such matching donors and promote the challenge. The existence of a matching donation is highly motivational to other donors. Further, the more money that moves through the giving-day platform, the greater the take of the organizer's match and proportional bonuses for the Chapter.

Further, there are no limitations on donor geography. Donors may participate from anywhere in the world. The only geographic limitation that applies is related to the Chapter and with which regionally specific giving day it may register. For example, an alumna might live in Atlanta, Georgia, but her consulting work takes her to Seattle, Washington, every week. While there, she participates in the activities offered by her alumni association's local Seattle Chapter. In this case, she might be inclined to make a donation on Seattle's GiveBIG Day to the Chapter even though she does not actually live in Seattle.

Not only are donations accepted from anywhere, but there are no requirements about how a donor is affiliated with the Chapter. In typical Chapter fundraising activities, the Chapter is likely to reach out largely to local alumni. In a giving-day scenario, anyone can be encouraged to donate to the Chapter, including parents of students, friends that owe you one, businesses, service providers seeking the Chapter's favor—the list goes on.

Lastly, participation in a giving day can especially work in your favor if your Chapter happens to be in a region that is new to hosting a giving day. In this situation, there are likely to be fewer participants with whom to compete against for prizes or matches. In the following year or two, there may be less competition for awards based on most improved as well.

We should revisit the hypothetical example provided within the earlier subsection on crowdfunding. You may recall that the University of Cincinnati Alumni Association's (UCAA) New York Network desires to establish an endowed scholarship fund in memory of a prominent alumnus, Michael Graves. Because Mr. Graves was known and loved around the world, a campaign that could leverage the unrestricted reach of the Internet across the globe and without hindrance of time zones would be advantageous. Additionally, since Mr. Graves and his design business were well connected through existing social media channels, each fundraising channel that could take advantage of the established network would be ideal. These were reasons that a crowdfunding campaign was so very appropriate.

However, if we now interject one more assumption such that the UC Alumni New York Network is a 501(c)(3)-recognized entity, then the doors to also benefiting from participation in a regional giving day swing wide open. The local alumni Chapter could then take part in the Give Local NYC regional giving day to support this scholarship. By funneling the funds through a regional giving day, the scholarship fund becomes further eligible for prizes and matching bonuses, both of which help to maximize the scholarship's total income.

Important Guidelines for Chapter Leaders

Although rules and guidelines may vary from giving day to giving day, there are a few standard guidelines of which a Chapter should be aware. First, the Chapter will need to be a nonprofit organization recognized and in good standing with both the state and the IRS. The text discusses this topic in much more detail in the later section on tax implications. For now, just keep this in mind.

The Chapter will also need to be prepared well in advance of giving day, four to six months, to comply with the schedule and deadlines. Often, participants are required to complete a profile in addition to other registration activities by specific dates in order to be included.

The giving-day sponsor usually establishes a minimum and maximum donation, typically $25 and $25,000, respectively. All donations must be made online, on the specific day, and according to the rules.

Donations may not be used to pay for anything that might be perceived as a material benefit to the donor, including dinner tickets, membership fees, golf fees, admission tickets, raffle tickets, event tickets, sponsorships, or other gifts. This is very important. The donations must be free and clear of anything in return—tangible or intangible. The donations must be considered unrestricted gifts to the Chapter. Accordingly, the donations are then 100 percent tax deductible. A donor may, however, express the desire that a gift be used for a specific program or project in the notes field of some giving-day forms. It is then the responsibility of the Chapter to follow through with that instruction.

Although this last one is not an official guideline, it is an important one if the giving day is to be successful. Unlike how open people may be to donations to the general fund for Junior Achievement, alumni are less compelled to make a general donation to the Chapter. To counter that behavior, the Chapter leadership should identify specific needs that are broadly compelling. I often refer to scholarships throughout this text as an easy example. In fact, this same argument was made in the opening statements of the section "*Traditional and Not-So-Traditional Fundraising.*" The same principles apply whether the ask is being done through a more traditional fundraiser, via crowdfunding, or through a giving day.

Other Giving-Day Scenarios

There are a couple of other giving-day scenarios, such as Giving Tuesday and organization-specific giving days, worth discussing.

Giving Tuesday, often written as #GivingTuesday and referred to as the National Giving Day although it is a global phenomenon, refers to the Tuesday after Thanksgiving Day. Established in 2012, it is an international day of giving at the beginning of the holiday season, encouraging people to take the individual initiative to support their favorite charities. It was started to bring focus to the charitable season in the wake of the highly commercialized Black Friday and Cyber Monday. In 2016 alone, 700,000 people contributed $116,700,000 in seventy-one countries through an average donation of $107.[7]

If a Chapter is a registered 501(c)(3) and can identify a specific giving initiative, like funding a scholarship to your alma mater or maybe a science, technology, engineering, and math (STEM) initiative, it can also take advantage of Giving Tuesday.

Before getting too excited about Giving Tuesday, know that it does not work in the same way as a regional giving day. They are the same in that the motivations are positive, the goals are to raise funds for charities, and they happen on a specified day. This is where they start to differ. Regional giving days are specific events with a known responsible party that provides a common platform through which donations are made to one or more specific charities. On the other hand, Giving Tuesday is in and of itself a holiday without corporate sponsorship or a unified platform. Just as Halloween is a holiday in which it is up to the individual to purchase a costume and distribute the candy, so is Giving Tuesday. It is a recognized day for each of us individually to go to the websites of the charities we wish to support and make a donation.

Although there are no costs to choreograph Giving Tuesday, there is little else other than the marketing benefit of attempting to leverage the day itself. There is no central portal for donations. All donations must be managed and handled by the Chapter itself. Also, unlike a regional diving day, there are no prearranged prizes or matches. Basically, the Chapter would have to plan, execute, and operate the entire day's giving activity on its own, only benefiting from the broad and well-recognized marketing campaign related to Giving Tuesday.

Giving Tuesday is a holiday that the Chapter can leverage to encourage donations. Just understand that it requires a bit more effort and is self-administered.

With respect to organization-specific giving days, some colleges and universities run their own giving day. In 2015, Columbia University raised $12.8 million in its fourth annual Columbia Giving Day,[8] then topped that by raising an outstanding $14.6 million through 14,269 gifts in 2016.[9] As a thank-you, the university generated a short video that embodied the gratitude of the school, its faculty, and students, which can be watched on YouTube.[10] Nice job, Columbia community! Columbia typically holds its annual giving day in October.

Another university that has successfully executed an annual giving day is Purdue University. The University raised $13.7 million in its 2015 Purdue Day of Giving, held in late April.[11] Purdue went on to break its own record, raising a mind-blowing $18.3 million through 12,872 donations during the 2016 campaign.[12] As has now become the tradition, the University has issued a thank-you video to the community on YouTube.[13] Way to go, Purdue supporters!

Although very successful and worthy of praise, these are university-level programs and do not filter down to the bank accounts of the alumni Chapters. They do, however, support the Chapter's alma mater, a mission that all Chapters share within the network. As such, supporting them with the Chapter's best performance is unquestionably the right thing to do—and your Chapter might even win recognition for a large total contribution from a geography / region. Just don't factor in any such revenue on your local books.

Flawless Campaign Execution

If your Chapter qualifies and is interested in pursuing a giving-day campaign, it would be among the pioneers! Like text-to-give mobile campaigns, regional giving days are a more recent phenomenon to sweep the alumni Chapter landscape. As such, I have only encountered a small handful of early adopters in the alumni Chapter community that have ventured into this arena.

Supporting a giving-day campaign can be very exciting! The costs are so very low, and the upside can be so very beautiful. From a cost perspective, the only expenses are associated with the promotional campaign. There are no venue, food, entertainment, or parking costs. This is a virtual donation event; rarely is there even a cost to register. The only costs beyond promotion I could possibly see factoring in are ones in which the Chapter was not a 501(c)(3) and decided to become one prior to the regional giving day. Even so, those costs would be allocated to general and administrative rather than the event. You will want to heavily promote this event, so build a robust plan with a timeline and costs to guarantee that your Chapter is ready.

First, the leadership should determine if the Chapter is located within the boundaries of any regional giving day. This can be done by simple online searches, reaching out to the local community foundation and checking the **List of Community Giving Days** provided as a gift to readers. The list compiles many regional giving days across the United States, sponsoring community foundations, and recent dates available. Reference the appendix titled "*Free SACL Tools and Resources Available for Readers*" for instructions on how to access it. Should an applicable regional giving day exist, then review the date and registration deadlines. If the deadline to participate has not expired, your Chapter is in business. Otherwise, there will be plenty of time to prepare for next year's event.

The Chapter leadership would need to establish buy-in for the concept and likely establish a dedicated leadership position. This role is more of a Director or Chairperson position that would report to the VP of Fundraising or similar. Together, the team should determine the very compelling stated purpose(s) for the fundraising goal.

Review the prize categories, and understand the matching and proportional bonus opportunities. Strategize how your Chapter can make the most of the benefits, including layering on an internal matching challenge wagered by alumni or their companies. Seek a donor or two that would be willing to match giving-day donations to sweeten the deal.

Make certain to register and complete all identified milestones on time. The rest of the campaign is simply promotion—and lots of it. Read the later section "*Promotion for Maximum Impact*" to gather ideas on how your Chapter might best benefit. Since this is a virtual fundraiser, it is ripe for social media. Through the promotions, be certain to direct your alumni to the giving-day portal with step-by-step instructions for how to funnel the contribution to the Chapter. In addition to your Chapter promotions, the organizer of the regional giving day will have a robust promotional plan as well, with many opportunities to involve registered charities. Do what you can to qualify for the online, TV, and radio slots. Be ready and armed with the Chapter's succinct, compelling need for the money and the amazing benefits it will afford the local community at a moment's notice. The fruits of your planning and execution will all become visible on the big day.

Since this is a one-day-only opportunity, be strategic about reminding the group before and during the giving day. Also, keep the Chapter apprised of progress and any prizes won. If you successfully identified a matching donor, keep the match front and center in the minds of your alumni. Encourage the matching donor to taunt and inspire further donations throughout the day on social media and e-mail. Go out with one last push in the last couple of hours of the event.

When it is all said and done, celebrate the win and report the victory—whatever it may be. In addition to the dollars received that day, your Chapter will forever be a pioneer by embracing regional giving days as a source of income. As always, take time to thank the alumni community, the donors, and the volunteers that carried your Chapter into a new era.

60-Second Takeaway

Regional giving days are wonderful opportunities to raise money; however, *only* Chapters that qualify as 501(c)(3)-designated entities and are in good standing with the IRS are qualified to participate. Chapters may receive more than was donated as a result of giving-day incentives, including monetary prizes, direct matches, and proportional bonuses based on contributions. Such matches may be orchestrated by the community foundation and also internally by the local alumni community. There are special benefits of leveraging a regional giving day, including no limitations on donor geography and no limitations on affiliation with the alumni Chapter. Further, if the giving day has been recently established, it can be advantageous relative to incentives to be among only a few early "competitors."

There are very few costs associated with a regional giving-day campaign other than promotional. Should there be an applicable regional giving day for the Chapter, make the most of it. Be prepared, promote the event extensively, and celebrate the victory. As always, thank the donors and volunteers that made it happen. Chapters may also choose to leverage Giving Tuesday, although it is a much more self-administered process; in any case, always support your alma mater's college or university giving day.

Make It Happen Checklist

☐ Confirm the Chapter's good standing with the state and federal governments relative to its nonprofit, tax-exempt status.

☐ Evaluate any and all regional giving day opportunities, referencing the **List of Community Giving Days**, the Internet, and the local community foundation to determine if your Chapter resides within the boundaries of an established regional giving day. If so, proceed.

☐ Review the actual regional giving-day date and the registration deadlines for time still left to participate. If not, your Chapter has a jump on the next year.

☐ Check with the alumni association for any reasons the Chapter might not be encouraged to pursue such a funding opportunity.

☐ Establish a dedicated leadership position on the team.

☐ Identify a compelling cause or causes for which the Chapter will request support.

☐ Review and understand the prize-matching and bonus money opportunities. Develop a strategy to maximize the benefit.

☐ Reach out to the local alumni community, and identify one or two donors willing to fully or partially match giving-day donations.

☐ Prepare a FAQ sheet that can be shared with alumni and other potential donors. Be sure to include details about the prizes and the match as enticements.

☐ Begin promoting the giving-day event through all channels available to the Chapter. Promote often, and provide links to the donation page—especially the day before and day of.

☐ Embrace e-mail and social media during the event, including progress and any prizes won. Encourage the matching donor to participate in the enticements and taunts.

☐ Report the results back to the Chapter with excitement and fanfare, highlighting any bonus money received.

☐ Have fun, and celebrate the win!

☐ Thank as many of the actual donors as possible via the most meaningful channel—phone call, e-mail, handwritten card, or text—especially if you want them to ever donate again.

☐ Follow up with a Giving Tuesday campaign, if appropriate.

☐ Should the Chapter's alma mater also run its own higher education giving day, throw the Chapter's support wholeheartedly behind it as well.

Matching Gifts—
Big Money Left on the Table

Nearly $10 billion in corporate matching donations are left on the table annually, according to Causecast[1] and the PIF Foundation.[2] A matching gift, or matching donation, is a charitable monetary gift made to a nonprofit, tax-exempt organization by a third-party donor (such as an employer) in response to an original donor first making a monetary gift to that organization. In our situation, the organization is the Chapter, and the original donor is an alumna or alumnus.

This is an excellent form of income yet so often overlooked. Companies from big to small and everything in between match gifts. According to Double the Donation, 65 percent of Fortune 500 companies match donations from their employees,[3] while the Conference Board and CECP's **Giving in Numbers Report 2016** determined that nearly 50 percent of companies offer a year-round matching-gifts program, while only 7 percent of employees take advantage of it.[4] There is a good chance that a few of those companies employ your Chapter officers.

Once such leader in matching gifts is the GE Foundation, which has operated a matching-gifts program since 1954. In 2015, it matched $43.5 million for a cumulative total of more than $1.2 billion since inception. They even match gifts for their retirees and surviving spouses of retirees (under certain conditions).[5] That is beyond impressive!

Matching gifts are typically offered in a ratio of one dollar matched for every dollar contributed by the employee; however, matches may take the form of a fractional ratio to multiples of the donation itself. ExxonMobil is one company on the top of the most charitable list with a three-to-one ratio.[6] That is, if an alumna working for ExxonMobil contributes $100 to a qualifying Chapter, ExxonMobil makes a donation of $300.

In addition to the match ratio, companies may also have an approved donation range with which they will match. Minimums often fall around $25, where maximums vary significantly from about $1,000 to $35,000. Soros Fund Management blows all others out of the water with a three-to-one match ratio and an unparalleled upper limit of $300,000 per year per employee. They even match partner gifts at a multiple of two to one.[7] Matching gifts can be game changers to Chapters that qualify and make the most out of promoting the opportunity.

There is one special requirement to call out, and that is the deadline to submit matching donation requests. Each employer can set its own deadlines within its own programs. Deadlines are typically based on the calendar or are in relation to when the initial donation was made. It is advisable to make the alumni aware of such a parameter when executing a push for matching gifts.

The general process is very simple. Alumni make contributions to the Chapter. If the employer operates a matching-gifts program, then the alumna / alumnus should complete and submit the short paper or online form as directed by the company to facilitate the match. The employer will then contact the Chapter to verify the employee's donation. Upon positive confirmation, the matching gift is dispersed.

In order for a Chapter to cleanly benefit from this method, the Chapter should be recognized as a 501(c)(3) tax-exempt entity by the IRS. Some Chapters are not independent organizations but rather are structured at the federal level as groups or subordinates of a central alumni association. If your Chapter falls under the subordinate structure, seek guidance from the central alumni association as well as local counsel before embarking on a matching-gifts campaign, as the Chapter may not be eligible. Referencing the GE Foundation once again, it states the relevant eligibility criteria to include the following:

>> Recognized by and registered with the United States I.R.S. as a 501(c)(3) charitable organization; or . . .

>> Accredited Public or Nonprofit Colleges and Universities in the U.S. to which contributions are tax deductible under the Internal Revenue Code of the United States.[8]

If your Chapter is established as its own independent charitable entity, a matching-gift option might very well be available to you. Even so, it would still be prudent to start by confirming this with a local, knowledgeable professional before moving forward.

Typical Exclusion Criteria

Under the assumption that the Chapter is in the clear, the next step would be to identify what alumni contributions qualify for the match. For example, unrestricted cash donations are the most perfect form of donation that is most likely to be matched. However, many other types of contributions do not qualify. Since each company has different criteria, it is difficult to draw absolute lines in the sand. This list below, however, is derived from analyzing many programs and distilled down to only the ones that most apply to alumni Chapters.

- Typically, all donations to a fraternal organization are ineligible—that is, any college or university fraternity or sorority, including their alumni Chapters.
- Donations in which benefits can be inferred or implied, such as sponsorships or game tickets, may not apply. For example, payment made for football tickets through the Chapter is not an appropriate source for a matching gift.
- Contributions of anything other than cash or stock are unlikely to qualify. Donations of time, goods, or property to the Chapter fall into this category.
- Pledges of cash or stock almost universally do not qualify. It must already have been contributed, not just pledged, to apply.
- Contributions made outside of a specified window of time will become ineligible.
- Occasionally, money donated through a giving-day portal or in any other indirect way to the Chapter may not qualify.

Each company will have its own set of acceptance and exclusion criteria for both the Chapter itself and the type of donation. It falls to the alumni to seek the existence of a matching-gifts program and vet acceptance criteria. For example, a few of Bank of America's relevant rules include the following:

> » Eligible U.S. Charitable Organizations: Charitable organizations in the United States must be tax-exempt under section 501(c)(3) of the Internal Revenue Code and not be classified as a private foundation or certain types of supporting organizations.
> » We do not match charitable gifts that provide benefits directly to employees or their families, such as trips, tours, internships, tuition, event tickets, parking privileges, club dues, products and services, or discounts on products or services.[9]

In short, Bank of America, which matches full- and part-time employee gifts, specifically requires the recipient of the matching gift to be recognized as a 501(c)(3)-tax-exempt organization and precludes membership dues. The Apple Matching Gifts Program goes as far as restricting "dues to or volunteering with alumni or similar groups."[10]

Although some payments or contributions to a Chapter will not qualify with all employers of all alumni, there remains significant opportunity through which to reap matching gifts. The preceding text highlighted what will *not* qualify. It may be helpful to touch once again on what *will* apply. Assuming alumni groups themselves are not excluded, alumni may successfully seek matching gifts for any cash donation between $25 and some company-specific upper limit to a 501(c)(3)-recognized alumni Chapter for which they do not receive anything in return. Earlier examples of text-to-give contributions are likely to qualify if over $25, as would the proceeds of cash campaigns and possibly some membership dues and sponsorships depending on the terms.

Executing a Campaign

Again, under the assumption that the Chapter is in the clear and has identified qualifying contribution types that are likely to be acceptable to the majority of employers, there are two more preparation steps in the process, followed by launching the awareness campaign among the local alumni.

The vast majority of college and university departments responsible for donor development have a widget or a link on the website that accesses a database of employers that operate matching-gifts programs. It would be most ideal to locate the link to that page for use in your Chapter's materials. For example, the link to determine if a company matches gifts to Yale University can be found at Giving.Yale.edu/ways-to-give/matching-gifts. Similarly, Auburn University alumni may search the database at this link: MatchingGifts.com/auburn.

Next, it would be advisable to generate a one-page document explaining the very simple process from the perspective of the alumni. Include an explanation of why seeking matching gifts is a great idea, how easy it is to request a matching gift from an employer, and a reminder to identify any deadlines that might apply. Do not forget to provide details for whom employers should contact to verify the employee's contribution. This effort will undoubtedly increase the actual number of people who will take action.

All that is left is to promote the program. If a website is available, post the matching-gift ask there, followed by engaging all of the Chapter's standard communication channels to disseminate the information. See the section *"Promotion for Maximum Impact"* to delve further into the marketing aspect of the process.

The most likely alumni to take immediate advantage of the campaign would likely be those who have already made the initial qualifying contributions.

Leveraging the example of qualifying contributions above, a likely scenario would be someone who has contributed to the annual scholarship fund. Thus, special emphasis should be directed at those already satisfying one or more of the qualifying contribution types. An e-mail communication reaching out to all parties that have already contributed to the annual scholarship fund, encouraging them to submit a matching-gifts request to their employer, is an excellent start.

If the Chapter takes advantage of outsourced administrative assistance, it could take that short-list of contributors, identify employers, and check for matching-gifts programs. This takes one step off the alumni, refines the short-list, and ensures a higher probability of success.

If the contribution to the Chapter was made via a check in both names of a married couple, it may be possible to seek a matching gift from the spouse's employer as well. Sometimes, employers even offer partner matching gifts, such as Soros Fund Management mentioned above. Make your Chapter's alumni aware of these facts.

While a matching-gifts campaign is in effect, it is advisable to keep the Chapter up to date with its progress. Status updates provide an excuse to further build awareness of the program while maintaining enthusiasm. Keeping the alumni in the loop is also a sign of respect—for them and for the contribution they are making.

As always, publicly thank those making contributions and the matching-gift employers as well. Generate a feeling of pleasure and satisfaction for having made the donation and gone the extra mile. This can be done through thank-you videos (very popular!), posts on social media, the website, the newsletter, the phone, or hand-written thank-you notes.

60-Second Takeaway

In this case, a matching gift is a monetary gift made to a qualifying tax-exempt, 501(c)(3)-recognized alumni Chapter by an employer in response to an initial gift made by an alumna / alumnus. This form of income is hugely overlooked, as nearly $10 billion in matching donations are left on the table each year; yet it requires so little from the Chapter and even the alumni to secure. Matching-gift parameters include match ratios for each dollar of the original contribution, minimum and maximum match amounts, and deadlines.

Each employer has a unique program with its own rules and inclusion / exclusion criteria; however, there are some commonalities that apply to alumni clubs. Pledges, contributions other than cash or stock, donations in which something of value is received, and indirect contributions typically do not qualify for matching gifts. The most free and clear qualifying contributions are cash donations between $25 and some company-specific upper limit from which the donor does not receive anything in return. The biggest effort on the part of the Chapter is promoting the matching-gifts campaign. Report progress to the Chapter regularly, and thank the donors and gifting employers as publicly as possible.

Make It Happen Checklist

☐ Confirm the Chapter's organizational structure and federal tax-exemption designation as a qualifying 501(c)(3) and that it is in good standing with the IRS.

☐ If qualified to receive matching gifts, identify examples of contributions that an employer would likely match, such as donations to a scholarship fund.

☐ Generate a brief, one-page document explaining the process from the perspective of the donating alumni, being certain to include the contact details of whom at the Chapter should be contacted by the employer to confirm the original donation.

☐ Post the program details, and promote the campaign through all of the Chapter's standard channels.

☐ If the Chapter uses administrative support, request that the assistant conduct a first pass through the list of those already having made a likely qualifying contribution to confirm or deny the availability of a matching-gifts program.

☐ Else, reach out to that list, and ask that they seek a matching donation from their employer if such a program exists.

☐ Further, suggest to the same group that they identify if the employers of alumni spouses have such a program or maybe even a spouse matching-gift arrangement as well.

☐ Promote the program to the entire alumni base to encourage support.

☐ Keep the Chapter updated as to the progress—fueling awareness and momentum.

☐ Thank the alumni and companies making the matching gifts as publicly as possible, including but not limited to a thank-you graphic or similar on the website, a thank-you video posted on the website and YouTube, a thank-you news release, a shout-out in the newsletter, or an actual thank-you note to the company.

☐ Celebrate one more win for the Chapter and its alumni!

Volunteer Grants Are
Easy Money for Chapter Leaders

Even more free money for 501(c)(3)-recognized Chapters! Not only are cash donations matched, but many companies also offer additional grants to organizations for which employees regularly volunteer actual time. These programs, called Volunteer Grants, Volunteer Awards, or Doing for Dollars, are another part of corporate or employee giving programs just like matching gifts.

A volunteer grant is a monetary gift awarded to a charity in which an employee volunteers a meaningful amount of time. It essentially converts time into money in an effort to encourage volunteerism. In all cases, although the grant is requested by the employee and based on the employee's volunteer hours, the payment is made directly to the nonprofit. Research suggests that 32 percent of companies offer volunteer grant programs, but only 5 percent of employees take advantage of them.[1]

There is a "use-it-or-lose-it" approach to these programs. The money allocated to an employee for volunteer grants in any given year does not roll over to the next year if unused. It is simply lost forever with no way to get it back. Don't let hard-earned volunteer grant money get withheld from your Chapter!

The question may arise about why a company would offer employee-giving programs such as volunteer grants. The reason is both financially and socially motivated. When a company not only encourages local volunteerism from their employees but offers a monetary grant as an additional inducement, it's going to get recognized in the community. Most nonprofits publicly thank their donors and volunteers through marketing materials like annual reports, social media posts, and news-media outlets. Thank-you videos are on the rise, as could be seen even in giving-day campaigns. Having a company's name in a thank-you campaign shows the community how invested the company is in its wellbeing and success, making the company exponentially more likely to experience increased customer loyalty.[2]

The **Giving in Numbers 2016** report re-confirmed the linkage between corporate giving and the customer response. The report separated companies into two buckets: those that increased total giving by 10 percent or more vs. all other companies. It then compared financial performance. The average revenue growth rate for all other companies during that time was

-2.3 percent, compared to 8.3 percent for companies that increased total giving as described. On a pre-tax basis, those rates are -0.3 percent and 2.6 percent, respectively.[3] The takeaway is that companies actively giving back to the community grow faster than companies that do not. As a result, 65 percent of Fortune 500 companies now offer matching-gifts programs while 40 percent offer volunteer grant programs.[4]

Further, Deloitte's **2016 Impact Survey** indicates that volunteer experience may play a big role in building leadership skills considered to be must-haves for successful leaders. Findings from the survey—which was targeted at individuals who either directly influence hiring or indirectly influence the person making the hiring decision—also support the idea that including volunteering experience on a résumé may make job candidates significantly more attractive to employers. Findings also revealed that nearly two thirds of Gen Y employees (largely millennials) surveyed prefer companies that let them volunteer skills, and millennials who frequently participate in workplace volunteer activities are more likely to be proud, loyal, and satisfied employees.[5]

Grant Allocation Methods

Although there is no hard rule for how grant money is allocated, there are two typical approaches. The first is based on a particular dollar amount per hour volunteered. From the information I have collated, the typical amount ranges from as low as $8 per hour to the high end of $25 per hour, with many companies settling in at about $15 hourly. Most often, employers establish a minimum number of hours volunteered to qualify for any payout, such as ten or twenty hours. Very rarely is a minimum not required.

Microsoft is one company that offers an hourly match for volunteerism—and has eliminated all minimums. It offers a 1:1 match on donations and provides a grant of $25 per hour volunteered to the qualifying charity. Every qualifying dollar donated and hour volunteered is eligible for match, up to $15,000 combined per calendar year for each US employee. That makes Microsoft's program exceptionally generous, with no minimum hours and one of the highest volunteer rates per hour. It should be no surprise, then, that in 2016, Microsoft employees raised a record-breaking $142 million for nearly 18,900 nonprofits and schools across the globe with participation rates of 74 percent, an all-time high. Since 1983, at the program's inception, employees have donated 3.65 million volunteer hours to nonprofits.[6]

In the second and more popular approach, a company sets a fixed-grant amount based on an employee having volunteered a certain number of hours for the same charity. In this case, there is always a block of volunteer hours that must be satisfied, typically ten, twenty, twenty-five, or fifty hours at a time. Employees may be able to apply for a grant more than once per year if they meet the volunteer requirements again.

Regardless of which method is used to compensate the nonprofit for volunteer time, companies typically set annual maximums per employee and per nonprofit. Roughly, maximum grant money earned per employee per year ranges from $250 to $4,000. Total maximum grants from a company to a single nonprofit tend to range from $750 to $25,000, with $25,000 being a lovely extreme. The maximum combined grant limit doled out to a nonprofit becomes relevant when many employees working at the same company also volunteer for a popular charity, and even more so when spouse and domestic partners are included in the volunteer grant program. Unless the majority of the Chapter leadership all works for the same employer, this is unlikely to be an issue.

How each company operates its volunteer grant program can be very different. Chapter leaders and committee members should check into the specifics of any grant programs their companies may offer. Below are a couple examples of some generous, socially conscious company programs.

The Verizon Volunteer Grant Program provides opportunities for employees who volunteer fifty or more hours in a current calendar year with eligible nonprofit organizations to request a $750 grant from the Verizon Foundation on behalf of that organization. A second $750 grant may also be earned and requested for a second qualifying organization in the same year. A single nonprofit may receive up to a combined total of $25,000 per year through this program.[7]

Pfizer offers a volunteering incentive but using a slightly different approach. Pfizer employees and legacy Pfizer retirees may request one $1,000 grant for one organization each year. The employee must volunteer at least six hours per month for at least six months before requesting a grant—thus, a minimum of thirty-six hours but within a specific distribution of time. The maximum amount an eligible organization may receive from the Pfizer Foundation Volunteer Program in any given year is $5,000.[8]

The Kimberly-Clark Foundation will recognize the volunteer efforts of employees and their spouses or domestic partners by making $500 grants to the charitable organizations to which they volunteer at least thirty hours. Each employee can request one $500 grant per year. Each spouse or domestic partner can request an additional $500 grant per year. Each organization can receive a maximum of ten grants totaling $5,000 per calendar year.[9]

When a PricewaterhouseCoopers (PwC) partner or staff member volunteers twenty-five hours of personal time to a qualifying nonprofit organization, the Foundation will donate $375 to that organization. The annual limit is four grants for a total of $1,500 per employee. In an inventive twist to expand its Dollars for Doers program, PwC will award $125 directly to an employee who successfully refers a colleague to apply for a volunteer grant. The company will honor up to four referral awards per employee per year.

Overall, the money available through volunteer grants tends to be less than money available through matching-gifts programs; however, it is typically additive to a matching-gifts program. Annual volunteer grant award maximums per employee and annual matching fund maximums per employee are generally independent of each other. There are exceptions, like Microsoft's program mentioned earlier, in which volunteer grants and matching gifts may have a combined annual limit for a particular organization. The details for how a company operates its programs will be made available to any requesting employee when asked.

As an example, suppose the Fayette County UK Alumni Club's fundraising committee volunteer fifty-two hours assisting the Chapter in preparation for the **Par-3 Golf Championship** mentioned much earlier in the book. Also, suppose that that volunteer worked for Bank of America Merrill Lynch, which has a volunteer grant program in which a volunteer that donates fifty hours of time to an eligible charity may qualify for an award of $250 to that charity. If the volunteer contributed more than one hundred hours of time, the award would be raised to $500.[10]

In our example, the fundraising committee volunteer would be eligible to trigger a gift of $250 to the Chapter for doing nothing more than what she is already doing out of the goodness of her heart and loyalty to her alma mater. If that same example scenario occurred, only this time the fundraising volunteer worked for Microsoft rather than Bank of America Merrill Lynch, then that volunteer would be able to qualify for a $1,300 grant for the Chapter—enough to fund one more scholarship with a little left over.

Volunteer grants are free money every way you look at it. The Chapter leader is already dedicating the volunteer time, so if the grant is not requested, it simply slips away and is lost to the world forever. Think of the volunteer grant money like flexible spending account (FSA) money. The unused employee giving money (matching gifts and volunteer grants) made available for you through your company will not be allocated to another employee, it will not be allocated to another deserving group, and it will not be carried over to next year. Every year, the maximum amount possible per employee is earmarked for you (and maybe your spouse / domestic partner as well). Use it or lose it.

The Process and Typical Exclusions: Pay Close Attention

Within company employee-giving programs, organizations that are eligible for volunteer grants may be as broad as those that qualify for matching gifts, but more likely they will be a more restrictive sub-set. Volunteer grant organizational eligibility criteria often start as comprehensive as most US-based 501(c)(3) organizations, US public and private schools, and US-accredited colleges and universities. There are a few fairly consistent exclusions to most programs that restrict profit-making organizations; political, labor, and fraternal organizations; and any organization that illegally discriminates in its constitution or practice against persons or groups from being eligible. Additionally, there are a couple of other items adopted by a few volunteer incentive programs that may be relevant to Chapter leadership:

- Hours must be volunteered on employee's personal time to qualify.
- Organizations that the employee founded may not be eligible.

The last bullet most pertains to Chapter leaders that founded the Chapter. Newly formed Chapters are more likely to have founders still in leadership. Please note that the restriction only applies to the founder him or herself when applying for a volunteer grant, not other Chapter leaders.

Some companies may have further honed their own program to best meet the needs of the company's goals and those of the communities in which it operates. In particular, their volunteer grant programs will be designed to be selective of specific charitable causes in line with particular business needs or the corporate mission. Do not use the company's matching-gifts guidelines as a rule of thumb for volunteer grant criteria. It is important to note that just because your company matches a gift to your Chapter does not guarantee that it will consider the Chapter a qualifying organization for volunteer grants, or vice versa.

An example from ExxonMobil's Volunteer Incentive Program Guidelines lists the following under the "Ineligible Organizations" header:

> Limited constituency and other organizations with a non-charitable focus, such as sororities, fraternities, alumni associations, business leagues, foreign language & social clubs, and veteran's groups.[11]

In this instance, Chapter volunteerism would not qualify for a volunteer grant, as was confirmed when I spoke with two different customer service representatives while pleading a case for a couple one-off scenarios.

In addition to your Chapter needing to qualify as an eligible entity, the actual volunteer activities need to as well. Qualifying volunteer activities include the giving of hands-on or skills-based time without a monetary benefit going to the volunteer, such as tutoring, mentoring, providing management consults on strategic planning or financial management, preparing for and hosting fundraising events, building homes, and cleaning a trail. Time spent in Chapter leadership meetings (full officer or board meetings) is likely to qualify; however, do not be surprised if such qualifying time is capped at ten to twelve hours a year. Committee meeting time dedicated to planning for a specific event does not often fall under that same definition of leadership meeting and is, therefore, qualifying and unlikely to be capped.

Again, there is no absolute list of volunteer time activity inclusions and exclusions referenced for all programs. However, presented here are a few exclusions that have been noted and are most applicable to Chapter operations and activities:

- Time spent during fundraising activities such as garage sales, lemonade stands, bake sales, one-off or single charity events (such as auctions, galas, balls, etc.) might not be eligible unless the employees / alumni are part of the planning committee.
- Similarly, all time spent running / walking in "-athons," such as marathons, walkathons, 5K Family Fun Runs, etc., might not be eligible unless the employees / alumni are part of the committee that planned the "-athon" or similar event.
- The time spent commuting to a volunteer project is not qualifying time unless the driving is the volunteer activity, such as driving to pick up retired alumni to attend an event or delivering meals to veterans.
- Sometimes, hours spent volunteering during a corporately organized volunteer event do not qualify, while other times, they do.

With so much variation regarding Chapter and volunteering-activity eligibility, it is important to review the program guidelines very closely. Even when it appears by all measures that a Chapter and the employees / alumni volunteer hours are eligible, there is still no guarantee. Nearly all volunteer grant programs clearly state that applications are subject to a final review and approval, thus granting the company the right to refuse any application. Although true, I would not look at that as simply a way to deny payment. The company established the program to encourage volunteerism, so it is likely to find ways it can publicly benefit by incorporating your generosity into its numbers.

As expected, there are deadlines within which the volunteer hours may have been performed and deadlines for when grants must be requested. There is also a deadline for which the Chapter must verify the hours contributed to the Chapter. The method by which this happens again varies. A company representative may reach out to the Chapter contact via phone or e-mail, or an automatically generated e-mail may be sent from the company upon application submission. Confirmation on the side of the Chapter may be done over the phone or via a reply e-mail, or the Chapter contact may be instructed to login to the company's system to perform the verification. Either way, the process does require action on the part of the Chapter.

When considering the Chapter budget, these deadlines are also relevant since grant awards may be distributed on a specific schedule, such as monthly, quarterly, or annually—and possibly in the year following the one in which the volunteering was performed. Be sure to guide your Chapter leadership in what to look for when reviewing their company's employee giving policies.

Landing the Grant

As this income is based on a significant number of hours provided by a volunteer in service to the Chapter, the people most likely to qualify for the grants will be the Chapter's leadership team, extending from the board through the committee volunteers. Accordingly, there is no real benefit to a Chapter-wide promotional program. Extracting the maximum possible benefit can be done simply within the leadership, but not without a plan.

If the Chapter solicits remote administrative support, it may be useful to have him or her perform a small bit of research on the subject prior to your leadership team meeting. Since you will already know for what company each volunteer works, the remote administrator could research the volunteer grant programs at each. What you might not know is for what company the spouses or domestic partners work. That information could be requested in advance of the meeting and added to the research, or it could be left up to each volunteer to track down.

The subject of volunteer grant opportunities can be addressed at a standard meeting of the leadership, or a special meeting may be called. It is beholden on the Chapter President or leader bringing the opportunity to light to effectively impress upon the others the value of the benefit and the exceptionally limited nature of who can qualify for one. Encourage the leadership to inquire about volunteer grant programs (however they may be referenced—Doing for Dollars, Dollars for Doers, Volunteer Awards, Volunteer Incentives, etc.) with employers. Be certain to explain the important parameters relevant to exploring all possibilities including:

- **Chapter leader eligibility** – Inquire about a grant program with the Chapter leader's employer, or employer at the time of retirement. If one exists, identify all possible eligible participants (full-time and part-time employees, spouses and domestic partners, retirees, board members, others). Is the Chapter leader eligible? Are any others in the family eligible?
- **Chapter leader eligibility through spouse or domestic partner** – Inquire about a grant program with the employer of the Chapter leader's spouse or domestic partner, or employer at the time of retirement. If a grant program exists, identify all possible eligible participants (full-time and part-time employees, spouses and domestic partners, retirees, board members, others). Is the Chapter leader eligible for this program?
- **Chapter leader couple eligibility** – If both members of a couple are volunteering in service of the Chapter, then evaluate the first two bullets from both perspectives, Chapter leader 1's perspective and then Chapter leader 2's. The yield might be as high as two separate grants from each of two companies.
- **Chapter eligibility** – Understand the nonprofit inclusion and exclusion criteria to determine if the Chapter is eligible for a grant as an organization.
- **Volunteer time eligibility** – Review and understand what activities performed for the charity are eligible and qualifying hours.
- **Payout** – Understand what money may be available to the Chapter, including how it is paid (hourly, blocks of hours), what the maximum might be, and the payout structure.
- **Deadlines** – Identify the deadlines for performing the volunteer hours, for requesting the grant, for the Chapter's confirmation of the hours submitted, and for receiving the funds.
- **Limits** – If several eligible Chapter leaders and / or eligible extended family will be tapping into the same employer, determine if organizational maximum annual limits will impact payout.

If the above reveals that one or more Chapter volunteers will be eligible for volunteer grants, then a process will need to be developed by which the volunteer hours, accompanied by a description of time, dates (possibly), and activities performed, can be verified. Initially, the process might be as brute-force as each qualifying volunteer maintaining a log that the Chapter President reviews and approves from time to time. The Chapter should maintain and store volunteer time records for those applying for grants in a format and location readily available when the employer seeks confirmation from the Chapter.

Next, since the entire purpose of this exercise is to take advantage of money available to support the Chapter, it would be time to build in any such expected grants into the budget, noting the deadlines and payout schedule.

As several people within your Chapter's leadership will be spending many hours over the year in volunteer service to the Chapter, it is possible that there is a magical pile of volunteer grant money just waiting to be claimed! If the Chapter does receive a volunteer grant, keep the Chapter updated, and do all that the Chapter can to thank the company as publicly as possible—on the website, through a video, on social media, in the newsletter, in a press release, and / or in a thank-you note. The more public, the better, and the easier it is to share or to reference, the better.

60-Second Takeaway

A volunteer grant is "free" money awarded by an employer to an eligible, recognized 501(c)(3) charity to which an employee volunteers a meaningful amount of time as defined by the employer. Companies do this for the visibility, increasing customer loyalty and ultimately revenue. Internally, the results are happier, more satisfied and loyal employees.

Volunteer grants are distributed two ways: by the hour volunteered or in fixed amounts for specified blocks of hours volunteered. Companies typically establish minimum hour requirements, maximum annual payouts per employee and per nonprofit, and deadlines for grant requests. Not all charities will qualify. Not all time spent in service to a qualifying Chapter will count as eligible volunteer time, and unclaimed money does not carry over to the next year. Be certain your Chapter volunteers know about these grants and how to pre-screen for eligibility. There may be expansion opportunities through a spouse's / domestic partner's company. Volunteer grants provide valuable funds for no additional work or cost on behalf of the Chapter leadership. Do not let them slip away unclaimed.

Make It Happen Checklist

☐ Confirm the Chapter's organizational structure and federal-tax-exemption designation as a qualifying 501(c)(3) and that it is in good standing with the IRS. If there is an uncertainty, confer with your alumni association.

☐ If generally qualified to receive volunteer grants, identify those in Chapter leadership who provide volunteer time to the Chapter, and assemble them (not to include the general members who simply attend events).

☐ Explain the ins and outs of volunteer grants, and impress upon the volunteers how the benefits from work the leaders are already doing in performing their standard duties can be magnified.

☐ Request that all leaders inquire with their employers regarding the existence of a volunteer grant program, and pre-screen the policy for the following:

» Qualifying participants: Is the leader eligible through his or her own employer? Is the leader eligible for the significant other's employer program?

» Organization inclusion and exclusion criteria: Is the Chapter eligible?

» Volunteer activity inclusion and exclusion criteria: What time volunteering for the Chapter is eligible?

» Deadlines.

» Payout opportunity.

» Repeat from each perspective if both within a couple volunteer in service to the Chapter.

☐ Provide each volunteer with the Chapter point of contact (name, phone number, and e-mail address) for employers to call when validating volunteer hours.

☐ Establish a process by which hours will be tracked for volunteers intending on requesting volunteer grants.

☐ Ensure Chapter volunteers confirm volunteer hours with leadership and Chapter point of contact prior to requesting a volunteer grant.

☐ Ask qualifying leaders to apply for the grants.

☐ Revise the budget to account for expected grants based on anticipated payout schedules.

☐ Respond quickly to corporate inquiries to validate volunteer time submitted on applications.

☐ Keep the Chapter updated as to grants received.

☐ Thank the company making the volunteer grant as publicly as possible, including but not limited to a thank-you graphic or similar on the website; a thank-you video posted on website and YouTube; a thank-you posted on each social media channel; a thank-you news release; a shout-out in the newsletter; and / or an actual thank-you note to the company.

☐ Celebrate any grants received!

Part IV
Operational Essentials

Promotion for Maximum Impact   195

» Know Your Target Audience   196

» Websites Remain the Anchor   201

» Surprise! E-mail Is Still King   204

» Social Media Is Not Optional   210

» Text Messaging, Not Just Twitter   221

» Don't Ignore Print Media Just Yet   225

» Phone Calls Still Have Their Place   230

» Physical and Digital Third-Party Channels—Secret Weapons   231

» Blogs, TV, Radio, and Other Alternatives   237

» Best Strategies by Generation   238

» Ensure They Show Up   242

» Integrated Campaigns Are Most Effective   244

» 60-Second Takeaway   250

» Make It Happen Checklist   251

Collecting and Handling the Money   253

» A Checking Account—The Most Basic Requirement   256

» Valid Business Documentation   258

» Credit Card Payments 101   263

» Payment-Processing Options   264

» 60-Second Takeaway   267

» Make It Happen Checklist   268

State and Federal Tax Implications   269

» 501(c)(3) vs. 501(c)(7) and Tax Deductible Donations   271

» When to Pay Income Tax   277

» A Closer Look at Tax-Free Purchases   279

» Total Annual Receipts and Income Thresholds   282

» 60-Second Takeaway   284

» Make It Happen Checklist   286

Promotion for Maximum Impact

Once the Chapter chooses to launch an income generating activity, be it a symposium, an auction or a matching-gifts campaign, the key to success is promotion! It comes as no surprise that the number-one talk requested from this book has been related to effective, strategic promotion, specifically by generation. When polled, 78 percent of alumni Chapters shared the most significant challenge faced by a long shot is event attendance.[1] The Georgia State University (GSU) Alumni Association may say it best:

> The most dynamic program or event will fail without strategic publicity. Any event, no matter how well planned, will fail if the right people do not know about it. Efforts to secure great speakers and sponsorships are wasted without audience participation.[2]

The best communication strategies are targeted, compelling, and comprehensive—yet not too numerous nor wordy. They are also aligned with resource allocation and available budget.

The next subsections will walk through thoughtful discussions on the target audience, multiple channels for consideration in today's environment, and how to apply the concepts. Not all channels or communication vehicles will be discussed. The ones presented here are those that made the short-list based on maximum reach, minimal cost, and minimal effort necessary for Chapter adoption.

Before taking the promotional deep dive, two last pearls of wisdom will be offered here, mainly because they apply across the board yet there does not seem to be the right place to interject them. No matter what channels your Chapter elects to use, all of them share the commonality of containing actual text. Be ever so careful not to launch un-proofed material out across the vast population of recipients—no matter how rushed you might be. Spelling mistakes, cut-and paste errors, and much more can compromise the effectiveness of the communication and the professional image of the Chapter—even of the university. Always seek a fresh set of discerning eyes, maybe even two if possible, before locking the content in as final. The author cannot objectively proof his or her own work. As the author, you read what you *intend* to read, not what is actually in front of you.

A little trick I often implement is to perform a copy and paste of the material from whatever program into Microsoft Word and change the font and the color. Microsoft tends to catch the majority of grammatical, structural, and formatting issues up front. The color and font changes help you see it as new text for a fresher read.

Lastly, as the Texas State Alumni Association reminds us:

> All log-in information for other chapter social media outlets, such as Twitter and Instagram, should be shared with the Association in the event of leadership changes within the chapter.[3]

For a variety of reasons, you should consider keeping the alumni association not only in the loop regarding your communication channels but as an administrative part of such. Far too often, Chapters hit rough patches when the passionate leader is no longer available to drive the enthusiasm and activity. It is equally common that the communication channel's administrative access has not been documented, yielding difficulty when turning over leadership. Maintaining active administrative rights for an alumni association representative will help minimize these problems and others.

Know Your Target Audience

Targeting the audience can be done from several different vantage points. We will start with age since the Chapter will serve a very broad range. Although one can segment age groups into many bite-sized brackets, it is generally accepted to separate the population most relevant to alumni leadership into three buckets:

- Millennials, born 1977 to 1995 (roughly those in their twenties and thirties)
- Generation Xers (Gen Xers), born 1965 to 1977 (generally those in their forties)
- Baby boomers, born 1946 to 1964 (those in their fifties and sixties more or less)[4]

The birth year brackets are not absolute, yet they do not vary widely, either. Each generation thinks, absorbs information, and engages differently.

The most successful promotional strategies will take this into account and approach each group in the manner it best accepts information.

The generation prior to the baby boomers is called the Silent Generation. This group tends to be strong rule followers, and, percentage-wise, they are likely to be among the highest alumni association members. Several are also likely to be in alumni Chapter leadership. However, as a portion of the whole alumni population, they represent a much smaller group of those likely to be active in Chapter events and in many ways are similar to the baby boomers. As a result, they are not a specific focus of this generational breakdown and analysis. Do not mistake this rationale to mean that they are not exceptionally important mentors, teachers, and givers to the cause; otherwise, you would be very wrong.

Before we explore differences, let us point out similarities. Everyone across the generations enjoys images and e-mail. A picture says a thousand words, so allow the picture to it. Use images where possible, but without cluttering communications. We will delve into e-mail a bit more in a moment. Well, that about does it for similarities, other than the universal love for and dedication to their alma mater.

Indulge me for one last caveat. Although the information presented below offers generalities about each generation, it does not specifically describe every person within that age demographic. They are generalities, not absolutes; nor are the generalities intended to offend anyone. Now let's explore some of defining characteristics of each generation.

Millennials have grown up during the rise of the Internet, two serious crashes of the stock market, terrorism on our own soil with the attack on the twin towers of the World Trade Center in New York, and graphic exposure to international natural disasters, including the earthquake in Haiti. They are on track for being the most educated generation thus far. However, they entered the workforce at a difficult time, during the nation's deepest recession in decades, and they have experienced more challenges than others in finding employment. At eighteen to thirty-three years old, 78 percent of male Gen Xers were employed compared to 68 percent of male millennials. And the same can be seen for women of the same age. While employment for women has been increasing, 69 percent of female Gen Xers were employed compared to 63 percent of millennial women. Further, they are twice as likely as their grandparents to be single and thus going it alone.[5]

Half of millennials (50 percent) now describe themselves as political independents, 29 percent say they are not affiliated with any religion, and they tend to vote heavily Democratic. Millennials are the most racially diverse generation in American history, with 43 percent being non-white. They are also the generation with the lowest trust of people in general, with only 19 percent agreeing with the statement "Generally speaking, would you say that most people can be trusted . . . ?" compared with 31 percent for Gen Xers and 40 percent for baby boomers. Millennials are more upbeat than older adults about America's future, with 49 percent of millennials saying the country's best years are ahead.[6]

Millennials, more than other groups, seek the approval and cohesiveness of their peers. Approximately 70 percent indicate they are more excited about something when their friends are in agreement, compared to 48 percent of the rest of the population. About 68 percent millennials state that they do not make important decisions without discussing them with people they trust. That is 16 percent higher than reported by non-millennials.[7] They are highly technically savvy and are constantly connected to communication channels using their mobile phones. According to Adestra, 92 percent of millennials own and use a smartphone, and 84 percent own and use a laptop—the highest for both categories of those surveyed.[8]

As we learned earlier in the "*Mobile Giving Now for Everyone, Big and Very Small*" section, millennials are a generous generation. Nearly 85 percent contribute to charitable efforts, and they do so via impulse giving or to local causes. Alumni Chapters qualify as a local cause.

Now for Generation X. Their thoughts and attitudes were formed as a result of experiencing the AIDS epidemic, the hostage crisis with Iran followed by the Iran-Contra hearings, the crash of Space Shuttle Challenger, and the falling of the Berlin Wall. Although they comprise only about 25 percent of the adult US population, Gen X has the highest income of the three brackets and will have the highest spending power when they reach age seventy of any generation to date. The Gen Xers represent 29 percent of net worth and 31 percent of total income.[9] In addition to making the most income, they are also big savers, with their children's college education, becoming financially independent, buying a home, minimizing taxes, providing an estate for their heirs, and starting a business as top priorities, different than other generations.[10]

Gen Xers are smaller in number than either the millennials or the baby boomers, and they typically have less of a unique identity than the other two. This group is incredibly independent and practical. They like to work things out for themselves and love family, freedom, and technology. In general, they fall right in the middle statistically between the millennials and baby boomers on almost any survey topic.

In spite of those somewhat mundane statistics, Yahoo concluded a study that suggests that Gen Xers are actually the most influential generation. It reports that 25 percent of Gen Xers have started their own companies, and 31 percent consider themselves entrepreneurial. In fact, a look at start-up company founders revealed that an exceedingly high percentage were Gen Xers—55 percent, compared to 29 percent that were baby boomers and 17 percent that were millennials.[11]

Gen Xers are also heavily overloaded with work and family responsibilities. About 75 percent of Gen Xers are financially assisting elderly parents,[12] while 52 percent are also financially supporting adult children (millennials).[13] It is not surprising that more than half fantasize about having a day or night to do nothing at all![14]

Gen Xers are avid online users, consumers of digital content, and technology adopters. About 82 percent of Gen Xers are multi-platform users, and 84 percent own a smartphone.[15] Approximately 77 percent of Gen Xers use social media,[16] and they are the largest consumers of digital video of all age groups, with 79 percent downloading or streaming online video at least once a month.[17] This group is tech savvy, has a high income, and carries significant influence and responsibility.

Our third big age demographic is the baby boomers, those whose generation was defined by the boom in US births following World War II. Attitudes of the baby boomers were shaped as they experienced the Vietnam War—either serving or protesting—Woodstock, McCarthyism and the Red Scare, the Civil Rights Movement, and the space race. Baby boomers number approximately seventy-five million people in the United States and were the largest living generation until recently, when millennials inched past them.[18] They are confident, independent, and self-reliant. Baby boomers are also extremely hardworking and motivated by position, perks, and prestige, defining themselves by their professional accomplishments. They are goal-oriented, competitive, clever, and resourceful, and they strive to win.[19]

Baby boomers are a very patriotic generation, with 75 percent self-proclaimed patriots compared with only half of millennials.[20] They are also more religious than the other two groups, with 61 percent considering themselves religious. When it comes to God, they are even more connected, with 93 percent believing in God. This is the same non-believer number for Gen Xers, while the number of non-believing millennials is almost double at 11 percent.[21] The baby boomers are a trusting generation, more so than any other group, even their elders. About 40 percent feel most people can be trusted.[22] More than any other group, baby boomers significantly value staying connected with friends, surprisingly followed by millennials and then Gen Xers in last place.[23]

While they are not the largest generation of earners today, they are very significant to the economy and charities. Baby boomers have 70 percent of America's disposable income, and they will inherit $15 trillion over the next twenty years.[24] This group also generates some $4.6 trillion in economic activity in products and services.[25]

Boomers will also be the most important group to charitable fundraisers. According to Merrill Lynch, baby boomers are set to give $8 trillion to charity over the next two decades in the form of money and volunteer hours, and giving by retirees will account for half of all giving by 2025.[26] When those that are retired were asked how they sought to fill their everyday leisure time, 56 percent responded with friends and social connections, 47 percent reported personal learning, and 41 percent stated that they wanted to give back.[27] This bodes well for participation in alumni Chapters!

Don't count the baby boomers out of the workforce yet, as they are not going quietly into the night. Nearly 40 percent don't plan to retire until sixty-six or older, with 10 percent never planning to retire. Their driven nature makes it more difficult than other generations to gear down. Baby boomers seem to maintain a similar percentage of their generation in the workforce, as do millennials and Gen Xers—31 percent, 33 percent, and 32 percent, respectively.[28]

From a technology standpoint, boomers are contenders as well. About 65 percent of baby boomers own and use smartphones, 64 percent own and use laptop computers, and 47 percent even use a tablet.[29] Nearly 80 percent check e-mail before they leave for work in the morning, and 86 percent report checking e-mail randomly throughout the day. Further, 91 percent report using one or more social media sites.[30] Keep all of this in mind as your Chapter designs and promotes events to baby boomers.

Another way to segment your audience is based on relationship to the Chapter's alma mater. For example, you may look at the populations as alumni, family of alumni, friends of alumni, related alumni, and all others. In an earlier section of the book, "*General Events: Attendee Composition,*" we looked at planning events as either alumni-exclusive or open door. Since the topic has been addressed already, we will not go into depth here. That being said, the choice of audience exclusivity or inclusion will affect your promotional strategy and the channels the Chapter engages. The broader the target audience, the more channels the Chapter is likely to engage to effectively reach them.

There are other ways to segment your program audience, such as according to professional life stage: recent graduates, those with young families, and retirees, for example. Conveniently, these categories align nicely with age group segmentation. Recent graduates are most likely to be millennials. Those with young families will span older millennials through Gen Xers, and retirees will most likely be in the baby boomer demographic and beyond.

You may also wish to look at targeting your desired audience by industry or function. On one hand, this approach is excellent if your event has an industry or functional focus, such as the example in the *"Preface"* in which a retired airline industry CEO was speaking. Those in the airline industry may be specific targets for promotions. One the other hand, if your Chapter is intending to host as large of an audience as possible to support revenue generation, then choosing a tight definition of the intended audience may be less productive. The right balance will be different for each Chapter and for each event. Your officers will need to weigh the pros and cons of the various promotional options available to you.

As we close this subsection, I hope it provided a few pearls of wisdom that can help as you apply the concepts to your Chapter's events and promotions. From here, we will explore a series of short-listed promotional channels for consideration.

Websites Remain the Anchor

Of all communication tools, the website is still the most central, comprehensive, and expected source for Chapter insights. Since most consumers of information today tend to be exceedingly limited in amount of content that will be tolerated, other highly utilized methods of outreach must remain very brief and utilize the website for the full story. Just over 50 percent of alumni Chapters report having a dedicated website. Of those, 25 percent update it weekly, with another 33 percent updating it at least once a month. Nearly all shared that no more than three people have access to do so, however, with half of them restricting access to a single person.[31]

If a Chapter has a unique website, it will be the primary address at which alumni expect to find complete information about Chapter activities. If a Chapter-specific website does not exist or the website is actually a Web page bearing only Chapter contact information, then either the local Chapter's Facebook account will be the trusty go-to resource (more about Facebook later), or the association's central alumni events calendar will be. One of these three will likely serve as the anchor-posting location, the single location to find the full, up-to-date story.

The anchor post, likely on the Chapter website itself, will serve as the epicenter for communication and possibly for RSVP and payment transactions. Accordingly, all other mobile marketing channels and campaigns, including e-mail, are recommended to link back to it. In this digital mobile age, the website will be most effective if it is mobile responsive. Keep in mind that according to Litmus Software, Inc., 45 percent of people have unsubscribed from e-mails because it or the website did not display or work well on their smartphones.[32] Thus, the website content should be as mobile-friendly as possible.

Chapters are unlikely to have much control over this issue, so hopefully the alumni association is staying on top of these trends and has the support from the university to keep up. Regardless of website responsiveness, all the Chapter can do is the best with the technology at hand. The next paragraphs will focus on the content and structure for your program's anchor post—the first step in any promotional campaign.

Generate a catchy title, and make the post informative and comprehensive yet as brief as possible. All three generations have indicated that the most ideal length for content is about 300 words.[33] Although that statistic is really more directed toward original content rather than event postings, there is a takeaway for all of us. Three hundred words should be ample space to introduce the program, present speaker bios, and cover any special circumstances. Use effective images and / or video links to provide visual and audio enhancements to the posting. Details about the program should include:

- **Event / program title** – To the point and maybe a little fun or punchy.
- **Date with the day spelled out** – To support rapid absorption of the information, e.g., Tuesday, May 23, 2017.
- **Time with time zone** – Especially when posting on the association's calendar but also on your Chapter's, since many people travel. Depending on their phone's travel settings, events may appear at different times on the smartphone and can lead to some confusion. A reference to the time zone is all that is needed for confirmation.
- **Venue with room or area specified**.
- **Location address** – (With nearest cross streets) written in a way that navigation apps can identify.
- **Link to a map**.

- **Food and drink summary** – Reference made to what food and drink will be available so alumni know whether to eat beforehand, bring food, or bring money for food.
- **Dress code** – Self-explanatory.
- **Parking instructions** – Be kind, and note special street closings, parking preferences, valet options, and any costs.
- **Registration costs and instructions on how to pay** – Including either the quick payment buttons embedded in the post or links to the payment page.
- **Registration close** – Be certain to note when the online registration will close and what to do once that happens, such as payments taken at the door. Include a reference to maximum attendance should there be a possibility that capacity could be reached, causing people to be turned away.
- **Refund policy** – It is perfectly acceptable if your Chapter does not wish to offer refunds, especially when numbers had to be provided to vendors in advance. Do know that if all sales are final, it will have an effect of delaying registrations as alumni wait to confirm that they will be available. Whether refunds will be made or not, make the policy for that event known in writing to minimize conflict.
- **Tax deductibility** – Include any notes regarding the full- or partial-tax deductibility of the event price if applicable.
- **Inclement weather plan** – Such as "rain or shine" or possibly a time by which the event might be called off if bad weather looks like it will persist. Include not only the immediate action but where it has moved to or when it will be rescheduled, along with how the Chapter will handle tickets. It is possible that refunds are in order when an event is postponed. Make all such details clear.
- **Contact** – Include a person's name, e-mail address, and mobile phone number—so those needing to make a change to the reservation last minute or calling to say they will be late with the Chapter banner due to traffic can reach the right person. The contact might be an officer or other volunteer of the Chapter, or it may be the Chapter's administrative assistant.
- **Social sharing buttons and links** – Do not forget these! Remember the statistics from above: nearly 50 percent of people get more excited about things their friends are also excited about, while with millennials that number reaches 70 percent. Make it as easy as possible for their fellow alumni friends to get interested.

- **Other communication channels** – Be certain to make readily available the way to access or opt-in to all communication channels, such as links to the Chapter Facebook account or how to receive text updates.

Not all of the information above is likely to be required, which is a good thing since it has to come together in 300 words or fewer! Do remember that this anchor post will be the one place to disseminate all relevant information about the event or program. If changes occur, make a note of them here with special emphasis, possibly using color or asterisks and / or placing the new information at the beginning of the text.

If experience is any indicator, the Chapter might not have all of the above information available at the same time the program becomes a certainty. For example, maybe your Chapter plans a baseball-watching party for the season opener. The date, time, and opposing team are likely to be known, but the venue might still be in flux. Do not delay posting the event on the website. Simply post it with all information known under the sub-heading "SAVE THE DATE," and mention there is more information to come.

Finally, it is advisable to use a medium to medium-large text size, especially if the website is not responsive. Millennials will most often be reading the information on their phones, where resizing is as easy as pinch or zoom. Although some baby boomers will be doing the same, many will choose to view the website from a laptop or desktop computer, where resizing is not always easy or even an option. Larger text is more baby boomer friendly and inviting. Keep that in mind if you are hoping to attract baby boomers to the event.

Other communication channels employed should reference or link back to the anchor post for the full story. The anchor post serves as mission control regarding general information and facilitation of required interactions—be it registration to attend, payment for a ticket, identification of someone to contact with questions, and / or the social sharing of the event. Make sure establishing this anchor post is the first order of action once an event concept is confirmed.

Surprise! E-mail Is Still King

Who would have guessed e-mail as a communication channel would still be relevant after industry titans declared it was going the way of the buffalo years ago? In 2010, Sheryl Sandberg, COO of Facebook and best-selling author of *Lean In*, famously said: "If you want to know what people like us will do tomorrow, you look at what teenagers are doing today. E-mail—I can't imagine life without it—is probably going away." That same year, Facebook CEO Mark Zuckerberg also declared e-mail dead. "We don't think that a modern messaging system is going to be e-mail," he said at the launch of Facebook's messenger app.[34]

Against the odds, e-mail is still the most preferred relevant communication channel by far for how all age groups want to receive information, ranging from 68 percent to 78 percent, with Gen Xers in the lead—but not by much.[35] Not only is e-mail welcome, but Americans love to multitask with e-mail all day. They check e-mail while watching TV or a movie (69 percent), in bed (57 percent), and on vacation (79 percent).[36]

Even the future of e-mail looks bright. About 77 percent of millennials surveyed have an e-mail address because "it's a part of everyday life."[37] Almost half (44 percent) report that checking e-mail is the first thing they do in the morning, before even getting out of bed, while 34 percent of baby boomers prefer to have coffee first and *then* get into their e-mail.[38] Additionally, 82 percent of millennials and a surprising 86 percent of baby boomers check e-mail "at random, all day long."[39] This is excellent news because e-mail communications are so very budget friendly.

But beware! Some 68 percent of millennials to baby boomers will delete e-mails if they do not look good on a mobile phone, as was further revealed by Adestra's **2016 Consumer Adoption & Usage Study**.[40] It is becoming critical that not only websites are mobile responsive but e-mails must be as well . . . and the world is getting it. Responsive e-mail designs have increased to 50 percent in June 2016.[41] Hopefully, your Chapter's alma mater is among those that have adopted the new formatting.

At this point, there should be no dispute regarding the criticality of embracing e-mail as a primary communication channel, especially responsive designed e-mails. Equally important are the tools for disseminating the e-mail messages. E-mails, including e-newsletters, are distributed in several ways:

- Through the alumni association directly to constituents.
- By the local Chapter through an alumni association-sponsored tool (website feature, LISTSERV, or other).
- By the local Chapter through its own mechanism, using personal e-mail accounts or an e-mail distribution vendor.

These distribution methods are not mutually exclusive. A Chapter may have access to only one or any combination of the three. Be strategic and make the most of what is available and approved by the alumni association. Not only did we already learn that e-mail is overwhelmingly preferred by alumni, but Chapters have gotten the message. Just over 70 percent of Chapters use e-newsletters in some form to notify the alumni community of upcoming events.[42]

Many alumni associations will send a specified number of formal e-mails per year to the local alumni on the Chapter's behalf. This is to ensure consistency of branding and to maintain data privacy. If this is the only mechanism by which approved e-mail messages may be disseminated, then it is also to control the frequency, avoiding over-communication to and frustration on the part of the alumni. Overall, about 60 percent of those surveyed reported getting too many promotional e-mail communications.[43] It is important not to alienate your alumni due to over-communication.

Formal, association-initiated e-mails may take the form of an electronic newsletter or specific e-mails regarding your event pushed to your local population. The Fresno State Alumni Association (FSAA), supporting 233,000 alumni through nearly thirty alumni chapters, clubs, and networks, is one of many associations that distributes a well-organized and professional e-newsletter. It launched a whole new content strategy for its electronic newsletter in June of 2015. The FSAA implemented a new story-telling / sharing content strategy, along with a new minimalistic design that focused less on branding of the newsletter itself and more on the content. It is distributed monthly through e-mail to approximately 85,000 recipients. The content strategy and results won the District 7 CASE (Council for Advancement and Support of Education) Bronze Award.[44]

Benefits of university-managed e-mail include the credibility associated with a formal communication, the wider swath of alumni who could be accessed, including parents of students, and possible access to more up-to-date e-mail addresses. To properly utilize this service, the Chapter will need to plan programs well in advance by months in order to produce the complete content and particulars in time for such a circulation (remember these are limited in number). I have seen submission deadlines range from one to six months prior to the event. Work with the alumni association to establish a regular system for submitting content, if one does not exist already.

The second distribution method, Chapter-initiated e-mails with support of the central alumni association, assumes Chapters are granted access to two things: an alumni database, a LISTSERV, or similar, and an e-mail distribution vehicle. Although Chapter leaders in this situation often do not have access to the individual e-mail addresses, they have access to the use of them in more of an automated bundle, for the most part. Chapters in this situation have much more control over when communications go out, who receives them, and how far in advance details must be solidified. Chapters can also more easily send urgent announcements to the broad recipient list, such as a last-minute change in venue.

It's important that the Chapter use that access prudently; otherwise, it may risk distributing too many communications, causing recipients to unsubscribe—and the alumni association to reconsider such open access. Additionally, the professionalism of the Chapter is at risk. I might suggest that only one person remain in charge of designing e-mail communications, preferably one who is clear regarding the alumni association's guidelines and has a background in marketing or communications.

I have witnessed firsthand the lack of consistency regarding content, formatting, layout, use of imagery, and other issues when several people have their hands in the project—all with the best intentions of helping. Unfortunately, the result is sloppy. Text sizes may vary, as might font and font treatments such as bolding, underlining, and italicizing. The location of the event address or contact details may migrate throughout the content from message to message. Embedded images may be significantly differently sized to be too small or, on the contrary, crowd the text. These issues—unlikely to register with good-hearted volunteers lacking marketing / communications training—make it less likely that alumni will easily find the information they seek in the short time they will allocate to scanning the message.

If the Chapter approaches e-mail communications prudently and with the respect the communication function deserves, having the freedom to communicate at will can be exceptionally powerful—especially when interlacing local flair. From the alumni perspective, such communications can be far more meaningful as well. You may recall the increased affinity for the university referenced in the "*Preface*" when local volunteers are driving alumni activities. It does not take a big leap to understand how that increased affinity applies to local events and programs when the local leaders are directly behind the preparations and promotions.

The third e-mail distribution mechanism describes when the Chapter must build its own list and establish a vehicle by which to properly send communications. According to a recent survey, 54 percent of alumni Chapters maintain an e-mail newsletter list independently from the association, and 55 percent share that they send e-mails from personal addresses.[45] Yikes! Let me be clear—do not distribute Chapter newsletters from personal e-mail addresses. It is exceedingly important to use a commercial e-mail distribution vendor, of which several are free or low cost. There are two primary reasons for this: one relates to spam filters, and the other is ease of unsubscribing. If large volumes of e-mails or e-mails with many people in the To, Copy, or BCC fields are sent from personal or work e-mail addresses, filtering algorithms may identify the messages as spam and either quarantine them or block them altogether. Worse yet, the server from which your e-mails originated could very likely be blacklisted. Try explaining that to your boss! The use of mail distribution providers circumvents those issues.

The latter issue relates to the ability for someone to unsubscribe himself or herself from your Chapter's communications. A Chapter leader sending a personal e-mail does not have an automated method for removal of a specified e-mail address or the assurance that it stays removed. If alumni would reply requesting to be removed, the originator would have to comply manually— every time—and ensure that alumni did not accidently get added back on when the next e-mail list were pulled. E-mail distribution vendors provide the functionality to easily unsubscribe and can uphold the integrity of the request going forward. If people cannot easily find an opt-out or unsubscribe link, they may simply block it altogether or report it as spam.

If your Chapter absolutely must send a personal e-mail to alumni, do so only when communicating with a small group of alumni on a very specific topic. Also, be certain to respect alumni privacy by placing the e-mail addresses in the BCC field.

The Stanford Alumni Association (SAA) does a nice job of leveraging e-mail to perform or provide almost all of the options above. The SAA sends two e-mail-based communications on a monthly basis. *The Loop* is sent to all alumni, while *Stanford Where You Live* is regionally focused and distributed to eleven specific regions with the largest concentration of alumni. With seven days' notice, the SAA will also send a custom e-mail to those in a particular geographic area.

Additionally, SAA Chapters are empowered to communicate directly with their alumni base. Through the online membership module, Chapters are able to connect with all local alumni or selected subsets. Some Stanford alumni Chapters even draft and distribute their own newsletters for a more personal touch. Obviously, with so much potential communication, all parties must be cognizant and respectful of avoiding overuse. It is clear that the SAA has truly embraced e-mail as a primary communication channel, and, one might add, very effectively, as it reports to have current and valid e-mail addresses for nearly 70 percent of its alumni and parents of current undergraduate students.[46]

The Florida State University (FSU) Alumni Association takes a different approach, encouraging its Chapters to embrace a third-party e-mail distribution tool. In addition to the FSU Alumni Association's eBlasts, sent university-wide, it specifically calls out the use of Constant Contact and MailChimp as services predominantly used by its Chapters for direct Chapter communication.[47] FSU Chapters are not the only ones utilizing these providers. In a nation-wide survey of alumni Chapters representing nearly one hundred colleges and universities, 28 percent use MailChimp, and another 18 percent use Constant Contact.[48]

Assuming a Chapter has control over e-mail, here are a few guidelines for developing effective e-mails in today's digital climate.

- **The name in the From field** – Should be recognizable to the alumni, ideally the Chapter's name or something equally credible. For example, every e-mail distributed by the US Naval Academy Alumni Association of North Texas to its alumni reads that it is very clearly from the US Naval Academy Alumni Association of North Texas, not a specific person.
- **Subject line** – Make it short yet informative. Start with your alma mater's name or some approved abbreviation followed by references to the most important topics within the message. Referring back to the example with the US Naval Academy Alumni Association of North Texas, the subject line of every e-mail sent by them starts with "USNAAA NTX:" and is followed by a brief reference to topics covered.
- **Content** – The content should contain the event or program name and date. If there is a keynote speaker, include the name and relevance of that person. Should this be an annual event, reference the success it was last year and maybe how many people attended. Do include a registration deadline, if there is one. Other than that, a link to the anchor post for more information should do the trick.
- **Formatting** – Like best practices for the website, it is advisable to use a medium to medium-large text size in your Chapter's e-mails. "E-mail that is too small to read and interact with" ranks as the third biggest turnoff.[49] Make content as quickly absorbable as possible. Avoid long paragraphs

of text. Instead, use bulleted or blocked text that breaks up the content, leaving a fair bit of white space. This will help alumni scroll through the information quickly and be able to pull out what is immediately relevant to them. Include a link to the anchor posting for further details. This will also help to maintain a brief communication.

- **Social sharing** – Do not overlook the inclusion of social sharing buttons or links in the e-mail for the same reasons they are added to the website.

More and more these days, e-mails are initially scanned rather than read, often with the intention of reading them later. According to Adestra, the adoption of this "inbox triaging" practice starts at 44 percent of baby boomers and grows all the way up to an astonishingly high 81 percent of millennials.[50] Your Chapter's e-mail message better look darn good and interact well on the smartphone!

It will be important not to send too many e-mails, just as the alumni associations will most assuredly espouse. As stated earlier, six out of ten Adestra's respondents feel they get too much e-mail already,[51] and 44 percent of the respondents to the Relevancy Group's **Exploring the Benefits of Real-Time Email** report stated the number-one biggest turn-off regarding e-mail is receiving too many.[52] The moral of the story is to be prudent with appropriately valuable and timely information.

Keeping in mind the popularity of e-mail, the increasing need to absorb e-mail content quickly on a mobile phone, and the catastrophic implications of executing any of this poorly, e-mail messaging should be supported by a thoughtful strategy and a plan—for the long run.

Social Media Is Not Optional

According to Pew Research, 76 percent of people with a college or graduate degree and 70 percent of those with at least some college education use social media.[53] Great news! Alumni are people with a college education. Thus, we are very likely to find alumni on social media.

From a generational perspective, social media usage spans all ages, but, as expected, the younger age groups dominate. Millennials are heavy users at 90 percent. More than a third (35 percent) of all baby boomers have also embraced social media, an impressive surge from only 2 percent ten years earlier and tripling in the last five years.[54] According to Statista, since 2010, the US population with a social media profile has grown a steady 8.4 percent annually to reach 78 percent in 2016.[55]

All those statistics seem to indicate that alumni associations and Chapters should be rushing to establish and build their social media empires. However, that data actually just tells us that people of all ages are increasingly embracing social media. It does not tell us the preferences for its use. A deeper dive into the analysis reveals that social media is mainly preferred for personal communication. Surprisingly, people surveyed stated that social media was not even in their top five preferred methods for non-personal communication.[56] The one exception to that was millennials, who ranked it second-most preferred (after e-mail, as discussed earlier).[57] Alumni Chapters seem to fall into a special category all unto themselves, somewhere in between personal and non-personal communication.

That being said, social media is growing in preference with younger generations and will likely become more of a preferred channel as it matures. You may also recall the earlier statement regarding how important the opinions of others are in decision making for millennials. Social media facilitates the ability of millennials to see how much others like something. Additionally, Chapters lacking a dedicated website have already overwhelmingly chosen social media as the next best communication channel. As a result, social media makes my list as a top Chapter promotion tool.

The realm of what is lumped together as social media encompasses many different companies and tools. In order to identify a reasonable social media strategy that does not necessitate an overwhelming commitment to execute, I will distill the options down to the absolute most effective ones with the broadest reach according to current research. Thus, the rest of this section will focus on Facebook and LinkedIn—both highly recommended. Text-related tools have specifically been selected for a closer look in the next subsection.

You may feel that other great tools are being overlooked—and you may be correct. However, we are not running a NYSE-listed growth company in the retail space supported by paid employees with stock options. We are time-squeezed, charitable volunteers managing an alumni Chapter supported by a time-squeezed alumni Chapter liaison. Data supports that Facebook and LinkedIn are the most developed, they have the broadest reach into alumni populations, and they yield the biggest result for the effort. If you still wish to pursue additional social media channels for promotion and awareness, it certainly cannot hurt.

Beginning with Facebook, it absolutely eclipses all other social media activity. Approximately 1.86 billion people worldwide use the site *monthly*, with 94 percent of that activity through mobile devices. If we focus in on *daily* users, we find that 1.23 billion people access Facebook globally every day. Approximately 15 percent of those daily users, 185 million people, do so from the United States.[58] That astonishingly represents more than half of the entire population of 325 million people in the United States—checking their Facebook *daily*.[59] And 79 million Americans report checking in several times a day![60]

Pew Research Center's report **Mobile Messaging and Social Media 2015** supports the outrageous Facebook usage. It found that 72 percent of US online adults (over the age of eighteen) use Facebook. The research reveals an enormous chasm between Facebook usage and the next runner-up, Pinterest, with a penetration of 31 percent of online adults.[61]

Let us look at the statistics as they relate to the total number of social media visits in the United States. In August of 2016, 42.4 percent of all US social media site visits were on Facebook. Again, there is an enormous gap between first place, Facebook, and second place, YouTube, which took 24.3 percent of site visit market share.[62] A further breakdown reveals that as high as 82 percent of millennials, 79 percent of Gen Xers, and approximately half of baby boomers are users. The same report also suggested that users are largely evenly distributed across education levels, income, and population densities.[63]

One last way to examine Facebook usage would be a breakdown of total users in the United States by age distribution. ComScore found that millennials represent 37 percent of users over eighteen, another 37 percent are Gen Xers, and 26 percent are over fifty-five.[64] Any way you slice the data, Facebook is the social media 800-pound gorilla.

Facebook is not only the biggest network; it is arguably the most versatile one, too. Your Chapter can use it to share photos, videos, important alumni company updates, and more. Additionally, Facebook can be more low maintenance than other social networks. Whether you post several updates a day, a few a week, or only a couple a month, it won't make much of a difference in terms of what your alumni will think of you or the Chapter—especially as frequency of content engagement is controlled by the user. Different from push communications, Facebook is more of a pull, in which your alumni choose how often they wish to be informed of updates on Facebook.

It is probably no coincidence that alumni associations and Chapters across the United States have chosen to adopt Facebook in droves in addition or as an alternative to maintaining a current and informative website. Alumni Chapters report that an overwhelming 90 percent use Facebook, while 60 percent specifically use Facebook for notifying the alumni community of upcoming events.[65] If the Chapter is using Facebook in place of a website, then much of the information presented in the earlier subsection *"Websites Remain the Anchor"* applies here. Facebook then becomes the location of the anchor post. The list of data points to be included most certainly applies.

If the Chapter Facebook account is additive to the Chapter's website, then it is recommended to make simultaneous posts initially, only taking a more abbreviated approach on Facebook linking back to the website anchor post for more information, such as presented in the *"Surprise! E-mail Is Still King"* subsection.

Although I am treating both Facebook and the website as equal substitutes in these paragraphs, it is important to recognize there is a very big difference. Website information is constant—again, like an anchor. Each time someone clicks to the event posting, it will be there front and center. Facebook, on the other hand, rapidly changes with time. Notes and updates posted on Facebook are current until someone else posts anything at all. As minutes pass, more and more posts supersede yours, and it gets pushed further and further down. This is one reason that important information will need adequate support from the Chapter leadership and volunteers to keep it top of mind.

In general, keep posts short, relevant, and regular. Encourage the alumni to "like" events, comment on posts, and share them with fellow alumni. If your alumni are at all behaviorally similar to the general public, then they will have ample time to support Facebook activity within the fifty minutes each day they devote to it and other Facebook products, including Instagram.[66]

Facebook is truly social—so take advantage of it. Make regular contributions to the Page or Group as it gets closer to the program, providing small updates, launching additional tidbits of information out to the followers, and maybe even reporting on RSVP progress—especially if the count is high. If your event is designed to raise scholarship funds, post historical facts about past recipients and where they are now, incorporating pictures from the last event or of the recipient.

Maybe the program announced is a matching-gifts program. Make regular posts regarding the matching-gifts programs of local employers, one at a time. Keep the alumni apprised of the matching-gift goals and progress toward them. Publicly thank all alumni and employer pairs that make a matching gift happen—being careful not to include the amount of the gift.

If the revenue-generating program is an end-of-the-year membership renewal drive, use Facebook to post reminders. Spread out the details across several posts, and address any early renewal discounts, tax implications, and benefits of membership. Share membership growth statistics. Ask alumni to post positive personal or professional happenings as a result of engaging with the Chapter and fellow alumni, similar to the story about Evan Shelan and Robert Crandall presented in the *"Preface."*

Maybe your Chapter is hosting a photo shoot. Facebook is perfect for sharing a steady stream of images of what to do and what not to do leading up to the event. Remind alumni of grooming tips in time to get them done, such as noting there is time to lose weight a couple months in advance, getting hair colored and trimmed at least a week prior, alerting them to specific clothes to bring in time to be dry cleaned, reminding them of the often-overlooked eyebrow manicure, and many more tips.

Facebook provides an excellent and interactive communication vehicle between the Chapter and its alumni. If it is the sole oracle of Chapter information, ensure that the posting is complete though not excessive. Then, regardless of its primary or additive status, take advantage of all the social benefits that the Chapter can by encouraging as many related posts, shares, likes, and interactions as possible. Maintain the energy by keeping the conversation alive and fresh.

Unlike website postings and e-mail communications, in which professional consistency is best executed by a single, trained volunteer, Facebook activity is most effective when many alumni are engaged and participating. With 72 percent of US online adults with at least some college education having a presence on Facebook,[67] it should not be difficult to access or engage your Chapter's alumni pool. Facebook could be one of your Chapter's greatest promotional tools.

The Association of Yale Alumni (AYA) leaves the decision of whether to specifically establish a Facebook Group or Page up to the Chapters. Groups make it easy to connect with specific sets of people, like family, teammates, or coworkers. They offer places to bilaterally share updates, photos, and documents. A member can message other Group members. The administrators have the option of setting the group as either a "private" or "public" Group. A Chapter might want a public Group when newly established and in growth mode or if they simply want to be all inclusive. Conversely, a private Group might be desired when the Chapter wants to facilitate communication only between alumni, for instance. Only current members of the Group can see content of the Group, including stories and what other members post. Closed Groups do require an additional step—authentication by the Group administrator.

Regarding Pages, they were designed more for businesses, brands, and organizations to unilaterally communicate with customers by posting stories and hosting events, much like a website behaves when visited but not exactly. The broader community receives the Chapter updates via news feeds if that someone has "liked" the Page. Everyone can see everything posted on a Facebook Page at any time. There is no privacy option when using the Page.[68]

The Emory Alumni Association (EAA) serves 141,000 alumni through its sixty chapters and affinity groups around the world[69]—it is also a Facebook fan. Chapters are encouraged to open and actively maintain a Facebook account, more specifically a Facebook Group with an "open" privacy setting rather than a Page. The guidelines recommend naming the new Group using the city name followed by "Chapter of Emory Alumni." The EAA will even assist the Chapter in designing and formatting a Group cover photo for the account.

The EAA further brings to light the use of the "Ask Questions" feature of Facebook Groups. "Ask Questions" acts as a polling tool in which the Chapter can assess preferences of the local alumni population. A Chapter might ask what events the local alumni prefers, which professors or coaches as speakers might generate the most interest, or even what is the most liked venue for an event. This tool works well when Facebook is an active channel for the alumni.

As one last mention from the EAA: it notes how important it is to welcome new Facebook Group members. One of the Chapter officers, possibly the person responsible for communications or membership, should take on the responsibility to welcome each new member openly on Facebook. The text does not need to be long; rather, something short and sweet, such as, "Welcome to our chapter, Ariane!"[70] is plenty. Should you know something more about Ariane and want to make a more personal message, feel free to do so.

Also a fan of Facebook Groups over Pages is the Arkansas Tech University Alumni Association, serving 40,000+ alumni and nine regional, academic, and affinity chapters.[71] Its naming formula specifies the name starts with "Arkansas Tech" followed by the Chapter name. It also echoes the prudent words of the Texas State Alumni Association earlier in the section when it emphasizes that a staff member of the alumni association be provided administrative privileges for the Facebook account.[72] That way, the alumni association can step in and provide assistance if needed, as well as pick up the management of the Group should a Chapter begin to struggle. Keeping an alumni association representative as part of those with admin rights is good advice across the board for all social media accounts. This is so important that it is worth recounting.

Marquette University Alumni Association (MUAA) not only encourages the use of Facebook for its Chapters but also suggests the use of Chapter event-specific Facebook advertisements as another extension of the social media tool's promotional functionality. It encourages the ability to easily tailor ads promoting alumni events to specific regions or audiences within the alumni community with help from the MUAA.[73]

In all of the excitement around Facebook as a go-to promotional channel, Penn Alumni Relations shares a word of caution regarding event registration confusion. It reports that:

> If you have a Facebook Page or Group for your club, you can and should post details about your events there. However, some clubs have realized that people will RSVP to an event via the Facebook event RSVP system and not via the club.[74]

With that note in mind, it would be wise to make it very clear where alumni and guests are to register for events. Specifically state that registration is on Facebook, or repeatedly provide the link with instructions to register on the website.

After Facebook, LinkedIn is one of the most heavily used social networking platforms. It is the largest professional networking site available today and is an excellent fit when one of the primary reasons alumni prioritize interacting with each other is the potential for professional opportunity—clients, partnerships, employees, contractors, or advancement. Alumni can host their own super-charged version of an online resume, espousing their job progression, accomplishments, recommendations, education, volunteer activities, publications, awards, notable skills, and more.

LinkedIn touts a network of over 467 million registered users worldwide in over 200 countries, growing at a rate of two new members per second. Approximately 133 million of those members are living in the United States.[75] Not long ago, it was believed that LinkedIn catered more toward the mid to older demographics, much like the erroneous rumors associated with e-mail and Facebook. LinkedIn reports that there are over 40 million students and recent graduate members on its platform, representing its fastest-growing demographic.[76] About 25 percent of all US Internet users over eighteen use LinkedIn, while the percentage of online adults with a college education that have a profile on LinkedIn has climbed to 46 percent.[77] This is excellent news relative to identifying ideal promotional channels for college and university alumni communication.

A breakdown of LinkedIn users reveals that 38 percent are millennials, 39 percent are Gen Xers, and 23 percent are age fifty-five and older.[78] The breakdown is strikingly similar to that of Facebook users, only of a smaller pie. LinkedIn users are also engaged. About 52 percent of US LinkedIn users (69 million) confess to accessing the site at least every week, while 22 percent (29 million) are *daily* users, a 69 percent increase over the seven months prior to April 2015.[79] Many alumni Chapters have also figured out the benefits of LinkedIn, as 27 percent of Chapters are users. Interestingly, however, the Chapters labeled as highly active with over thirty events per year are even greater users of LinkedIn, with 27 percent responding affirmatively.[80]

Chapters can establish a LinkedIn Company Page with information about the Chapter. However, of LinkedIn's services and tools, the greatest benefit to an alumni Chapter is the ability to create its own LinkedIn Group at no charge. LinkedIn Groups provide a place for professionals with similar interests to share content, find answers, post and view jobs, make business contacts, and establish themselves as industry experts.[81] The LinkedIn Group may be set up as open to all those wanting to join, or entry into the Group may be subject to the Group manager's approval should the Chapter wish to restrict participation.

Like Facebook, LinkedIn Groups:

- Are an excellent way to share information and host open discussions with the entire pool of members.
- Use a person's image of his or her choosing as that person's icon.
- Allow Group members to indicate that they like posts or comments.
- Can limit viewing discussions to only those included in the Group.
- Facilitate alumni from out of the area who regularly travel to your city for work or other purposes getting connected since the virtual Group itself has no geographical boundaries.

Unlike Facebook, information posted here is more professionally oriented. LinkedIn has established itself as the single go-to site for professional connections and background research heavily accessed by recruiters and other professionals. Alumni would not post about the tailgate they went to over the weekend or share what they had for lunch at this great, new restaurant they recommend; nor would they complain about the terrible coaching decisions that contributed to losing the baseball game championship. Personal banter is avoided, even inside a restricted Group.

LinkedIn posts should consist of alumni event announcements; the congratulatory sharing of professional accomplishments such as promotions and publications; posting job openings alumni want to make available to other alumni; any discussions alumni want to post for open comments, such as soliciting ideas and volunteers for the Chapter fundraiser; school ranking announcements; and similar topics. Alumni should be encouraged to comment, like the programs, and invite other alumni and Chapter members to join the Group. Any topic that could appropriately be posted on LinkedIn could very easily be posted on Facebook. However, not all Facebook-worthy content should be posted on LinkedIn.

One bonus feature of LinkedIn is its ability to identify alumni in your vicinity. With so many professionals actively consulting LinkedIn on a regular basis, it tends to be one of the most reliable sources of up-to-date alumni employment and geography information. Therefore, it is an excellent way to track down those in the area. Using the advanced search capabilities available to even the basic membership holders, your Chapter can locate all self-identified alumni within a specified radius. The smallest radius is fifty miles, which is more than sufficient when considering the limitations on how far people will likely travel for alumni events.

Once you have identified local alumni, they can be electronically invited to join your Chapter's LinkedIn Group. If this approach is adopted, you are strongly urged not to use any canned invite language. Use the established templates in LinkedIn, but take a few moments to customize the wording to reference your alma mater and the local Chapter. In my experience, very few invitations to link or join a Group are ignored or declined when personalized.

Invitations can be sent individually, or they may be processed in a batch (also called being pre-approved). The latter option is ideal if your Chapter already has e-mail addresses for its alumni. LinkedIn allows names and e-mail addresses to be uploaded from a CSV file and invitations to be sent from there. The only catch is that the LinkedIn profile and Chapter e-mail addresses will need to match for the invitations to be extended. For example, if the e-mail address the Chapter has for Bob Smith is bob.smith@company.com, and the address associated with his LinkedIn account is bsmith@personalemail.com, then a batched invitation / pre-approval will not make its way through to Bob. In spite of this technical hurdle, the batch process is absolutely highly recommended and will get the Group started quicker. Just know that it is not a perfect system.

LinkedIn offers an advantage to Chapters in that professionals are more likely to maintain a more updated LinkedIn profile than the college or university alumni database account. Thus, it is possible that implementing and maintaining a Chapter LinkedIn Group may cast a wider net, reaching alumni not necessarily accessible through the university-supplied tools or on Facebook.

A LinkedIn post includes a title, an image, text content, and opportunities to include links. The title should be brief and informative. One approach is to convey the event or program, a date, and maybe an urgent call to action, such as "SMU vs. Navy Game, Nov. 26 – 8 Tickets Left" or "Young Alumni Happy Hour, July 17 – NEW LOCATION."

The image can be of whatever is appropriate. Images can communicate so much, so take advantage of the opportunity. A picture of a past event, a networking graphic, a football action shot—any of these can instantly convey the topic. There are some size restrictions, so keep the image file light. If you cannot think of an image, an idea would be to upload the alumni association logo if your Chapter has permission to use it; at least it is quickly identifiable.

Regarding the content, LinkedIn provides quite a bit of space for material. It is possible that the Chapter uses a LinkedIn post to contain the full event information—technically, there is room. If your Chapter does not actively use a website page or even Facebook, this would be the next best place to establish the anchor post with all details. However, if an alternative anchor posting location is available, I would recommend posting the highlights on LinkedIn and linking back to the anchor post for more information. Again, this is due to the highly likely scenario that alumni are reading the post on a mobile device, coupled with the short attention span for content review.

Lastly, LinkedIn, like Facebook, offers the ability to share the content on other platforms. Alumni may comment on a post and then share it with others on LinkedIn or Twitter. This is a great way for the alumni to help promote an event, show support (especially valuable for millennials viewing), and encourage others to get involved. Further, the person posting the event, adding a comment, or sharing the material reaps two secondary benefits in the LinkedIn community.

The first is simply being recognized as a leader within the Group and among the professional landscape. Stepping up with a show of support or being a part of making something great for others is a wonderful way to develop positive presence. As LinkedIn's process is blind to title or position, all participants are equally empowered to take the center stage. Alumni do not need to be high ranking in a company to be viewed as leaders on LinkedIn.

Second, each time alumni interact on LinkedIn, it raises that person's internal activity score, for lack of a better description. Internal algorithms are necessary to assist LinkedIn in parsing out the most relevant information to promote throughout the network. One way it does that is by tracking how active someone is within the LinkedIn community. The rough assumption is that someone highly engaged and continually interacting with other members is likely to be important within their community. Although details of the algorithms are not made public, it is a good bet that sharing posts externally to Twitter is likely to provide an added boost to the score. In short, openly supporting the Chapter on LinkedIn and promoting Chapter programs can actually improve the professional standing and reach of alumni on LinkedIn as a whole. Promoting Chapter programs on LinkedIn is a win-win. The Chapter benefits from the added awareness and support, while the contributors making that happen grow in online stature.

Villanova University Alumni Association offers a few tips to make the LinkedIn Group inviting to all. It suggests using the Chapter's branded logo provided by the alumni association and generating a Group description such as:

Official account of the [Org Name] of the Villanova University Alumni Association. Villanova alumni, parents, students and friends are welcome and encouraged to follow.[82]

The Binghamton University Alumni Association makes a very interesting point when describing the posts on Facebook and LinkedIn, among other social media outlets, as authentic communication. They acknowledge the natural flow and address how far to go to manage the content as follows:

Social media aren't simply extensions of e-newsletters; they are forums for conversation. Don't be shy about asking a question in order to get our alumni talking about something. Please be prompt in responding to comments and questions from your followers or group members.

As the saying goes, be ready for anything. Social media, when executed well, are populated by authentic conversations. In an ideal world, all the content on your social media pages reflect favorably on the University. In the real world, that is simply not attainable. According to best practices, comments should not be deleted, unless they are profane, obscene, illegal, reasonably objectionable or are otherwise not appropriate for the group. Audience members disengage if they sense that social media are heavily censored. Please offer commentary on behalf of the chapter or affinity group, but resist the natural temptation to respond in kind to negative comments because that will only escalate conflicts. If someone makes a comment that is violent or threatening in nature, please alert the Alumni Relations office immediately and report it to the site's administrator.[83]

A social media presence through Facebook and LinkedIn is exceptionally valuable for all concerned. It is clear that the target audience for alumni Chapter programs is aware of and heavily engages in social media. Further, there is no cost to implement either of these accounts. Facebook has incredible penetration across all types of alumni and supporters and, thus, unparalleled reach. LinkedIn offers geographical insights in the presence of local alumni unlike anything else, and it enables the alumni to personally and professionally benefit from active participation.

Based on the penetration and benefits afforded by both forms of social media, I feel that additional social media channels are unnecessary to get the word out. Unnecessary does not mean not beneficial. It is hard to argue against the fact that each new channel will engage a small subset of the alumni community beyond that of the others. However, the additional penetration is not likely to significantly benefit the Chapter more than already achieved, especially compared to the added cost in time and effort. The Wisconsin Alumni Association (WAA) mentions keeping volunteer bandwidth in mind, reminding us that it is better not to use social media than it is to use it badly.[84]

The high adoption, interactive nature, and prioritization of Facebook and LinkedIn, combined within the target populations across all relevant age groups, make them the recommended channels of choice for alumni Chapter promotional activity. With certainty, using social media as a communication channel to promote program participation is a must—today and very likely for some time to come.

Text Messaging, Not Just Twitter

Americans indicated that they prefer non-personal communication to be delivered through texts just over social media, 19 percent vs. 17 percent respectively, officially placing texting in their top five choices.[85] As one might assume, the younger demographics trended higher for the preference, but don't count baby boomers out when it comes to embracing texting. According to Deloitte's annual media research, 66 percent of baby boomers use text messaging to stay in touch.[86] Adestra confirms the finding by reporting that 57 percent of baby boomers said their primary method of communicating with friends is through texting.[87] So, they have adopted the channel for personal communication. It's just not their *preference* for non-personal information.

The text communication space is cluttered with several players, including chat apps like Facebook Messenger, WeChat, and Twitter, to name a few, and a litany of SMS group-text messaging tools. After evaluating many options, I choose to hone in on Twitter, a bit of a crossover with social media and a more standard group-text messaging tool, for best fit with alumni Chapter promotional communications.

Twitter is a well-recognized social networking application. With Twitter, you can share text updates up to 140 characters in length, along with videos, images, links, polls, and more. It is in the top ten social networking sites worldwide,[88] with 317 million users active monthly worldwide, including sixty-seven million in the United States.[89] About 23 percent of all online adults in the United States use Twitter, just slightly less than that of LinkedIn. Interestingly, the 23 percent mirrors usage in the prior year, indicating lack of overall growth.[90]

It also appears that more educated people are more likely to use Twitter than otherwise, as Pew Research Center reports that 27 percent of online adults with a college education are users compared to only 19 percent of those with a high school education or less.[91] Thus, alumni are more likely users than non-alumni. Again, according to the Pew Research Center, only 15 percent of online adults living in rural communities are users, compared to 30 percent online adults living in urban settings. This information suggests that urban Chapters are more likely to find Twitter effective.

Twitter users are highly engaged, with 59 percent of reporting that they use it at least weekly, including the 38 percent who are daily users.[92] When evaluating market share of all social media visits, Twitter captures 5 percent.[93] Age demographics are not significantly different than those of Facebook and LinkedIn, but they do skew a bit younger. About 40 percent of users are millennials, 37 percent are Gen Xers, and 23 percent are baby boomers.[94]

Twitter is an established social media version of a texting application. On the upside, people are familiar with it, it has a social aspect to it (making it especially convenient for promotion), alumni are among the more likely users, and it may capture a bit more of the younger demographic than other methods discussed. Other considerations include that it seems to be stalling out in its growth, and it may be a bit more difficult to contain Chapter content to within a specified group. Research indicates that 30 percent of alumni Chapters currently use Twitter. When honing in on the behavior of highly active Chapters, we find that Twitter usage more than doubles to 62 percent of Chapters.[95]

Tufts University Alumni Association (TUAA) serves more than 100,000 alumni through seventy+ regional Chapters and has a few tips for using Twitter. The TUAA feels that Twitter is a good way for new Chapter members to become acquainted with the group, while the leadership learns more about the members. They may be right when suggesting that you can learn more about a person through their tweets regarding their personality and interests than by reviewing someone's Facebook Page.[96]

When it comes to strategies for use, the TUAA recommends retweeting interesting topics to the group, adopting hashtags (#)—especially for event planning, since tweets with hashtags receive twice the engagement than those without—and engaging in tweetups, where tweeters get together in person to meet each other. They suggest sharing links to the Chapter's other social media platforms, such as Facebook or LinkedIn, regularly sharing quality content, and integrating pictures of past events.[97] The more pictures, the better!

The Iowa State University Alumni Association (ISUAA) makes a few recommendations regarding the naming of Twitter accounts. It suggests using a formula that starts with the city name followed by referencing its mascot. The formula for ISU would look like "@CITYCyclones," since Twitter handles must begin with the "@" symbol.[98] A good example is the @PhoenixCyclones page.

Not all alumni associations approve the establishment of a Twitter account for an individual Chapter; VCU Alumni is one example. It will provide a Chapter-specific Facebook account but specifically discourages the use of Twitter other than through the alumni association's master Twitter account.

> Constituent organizations are discouraged from creating their own Twitter, Instagram or Pinterest accounts as communication tools. Constituent organizations, however, are encouraged to disseminate information through these platforms by using the VCU Alumni accounts.[99]

Prior to opening a Twitter or any other communication channel account, make certain your Chapter is in line with the central alumni association's policies and guidelines.

A completely different way to deliver text messages is to utilize a group text-messaging tool. Tens of thousands of businesses, community groups, educational institutions, and faith-based organizations already use group texting as a way to communicate with large groups of people simultaneously. It is simple and effective. A shocking 94 percent of group text messages are opened and read within three minutes of receipt.[100] Group texting software is easy to use and can be accessed from any Internet-connected device. Further, it uses SMS technology and therefore works on 2G as well as 3G and 4G mobile networks. That ensures that people with older-model cellphones can receive messages in addition to those with smartphones.

The way your group text-messaging tool is populated by mobile phone numbers is a combination of uploading and opting in. A Chapter is able to upload a spreadsheet of mobile phone numbers into the tool, often after being asked to confirm that the Chapter has the permission of the mobile phone number holders to do so. Second, an invitation can be sent out or posted, and alumni may opt in. Such tools can facilitate the addition of such numbers without passing the mobile numbers through to the Chapter. In this way, a group text-messaging tool offers some anonymity while still benefiting from the communications.

In my assessment, a Chapter promotional campaign should consider including a text channel option. Twitter is by far the most adopted by alumni Chapters; it feeds the social sharing needs of a good communication tool, and it facilitates easy communication for all to see. The cons for this one are that growth and adoption are stalling, in spite of the slight resurgence instigated by President Donald Trump's use of the platform, and, of these two options, it has a more limited reach into the alumni base. Twitter's purpose would be more for hype. It would be most advantageous if there were an active millennial component of the Chapter that could not be easily reached via Facebook.

A group text-messaging tool has the ability to connect to those with 2G and 3G phones, enabling access to nearly 100 percent of your local alumni. The cons include the effort to entice alumni to opt in and share their cell phone numbers, even if they will remain shrouded from Chapter access; it generally lacks facilitated sharing, and it is less designed to communicate back to the group. The group texting tool's purpose would be more focused on sending fewer, specific alerts and messages that you know will be read within minutes of delivery.

If you can only implement one, I suggest the group messaging tool. My reasoning is that the SMS approach has the ability to reach more people, it is as close to a guarantee as one can get that the message will be read in minutes, and, if the Chapter already has a Facebook account, many of the social media benefits are already covered there. If you have the bandwidth and desire, do not let this stop you from also engaging Twitter.

Both social media channels and text messaging channels offer an additional benefit over the formal alumni databases, and that is the inclusion of others beyond actual graduates and beyond the geographic perimeter. The alumni association database and the membership records for the Chapter contain contact information specific to alumni only, making alumni the only accessible communication recipients. Facebook, LinkedIn, Twitter, and a group text-messaging tool allow parents, spouses, children, professors, and others to opt into communications, significantly increasing the awareness of—and, thus, participation in—Chapter programs.

Don't Ignore Print Media Just Yet

Digital communication has not killed physical channels for promotional purposes, nor has it even come close. About 48 percent of American adults reported that they preferred non-personal communication to come through the postal mail.[101] You may be as surprised as I was to learn that the postal mail preference presented in a linear increase from 29 percent for millennials through 68 percent for baby boomers.[102] Nearly a third of millennials still want snail mail communication! Possibly its scarcity these days is what makes it stand out. Just over 20 percent of alumni Chapters report sending postal mail to alert their community regarding events,[103] but maybe it should be higher. We will contain our discussion of print media options to postal mail pieces like flyers, newsletters, and invitations, as well as alumni magazines.

There are some practical upsides to distributing a physical communication. First, postal mail is tangible. It must be removed from the mailbox, and it will be seen during the sorting process. If it is a postcard, the information has already been absorbed that quickly—awareness is accomplished! Second, and especially when sent to someone's residence, it is "received" by more than a single recipient at that address. A spouse is much more likely to learn about an event when the invitation comes to the door than if the only communication was electronic and directed at the alumna / alumnus.

Postal mail—aka snail mail—is probably not the answer for everything, namely because it is expensive relative to many free digital options. Such pieces also require much more time—full content must be finalized, and they need to be designed, printed, and mailed. In light of the cost and time, maybe mailings are reserved for the largest-scale events in which your Chapter is targeting equal representation across all generations, such as the annual fundraiser or the annual holiday gathering. Another approach might consider sending the mailers only to the demographic groups most receptive to print mail.

Several alumni associations make a limited number of mailings available to the Chapters in some capacity. If your association does, it may be worth taking the greatest advantage of the service. The University of Iowa Alumni Association (UIAA), for one, offers this option for Chapters. It does require some planning, as it will take six weeks from the time the copy is submitted until a mailer appears in your alumni's mailboxes.[104]

Texas Christian University's (TCU) Alumni Association will design, print, and mail two approved invitations / announcements per Chapter per year for Chapters in the initial stages of formation and for chartered Chapters. This service requires a two-month lead time but covers all costs for qualifying Chapters.[105]

The General Alumni Association (GAA) for the University of North Carolina varies the service by activity level of its Chapters. Bell Tower Clubs, the mid-tier Chapters, may benefit from the design and printing of mailings once a year, while the most active Chapters have unlimited access. In both situations, the Chapter is required to pay the postage,[106] which probably tempers potential abuse of the unlimited assistance and printing.

In addition, or as an alternative to the full-service approach to designing, printing, and mailing a specified number of mailings, some universities will support the Chapters in preparing and sending their own mailers. This is done through providing pre-printed mailing labels or a PDF version of the labels. There is still some oversight, usually contained to requiring approval of the mailer itself and limited by the number of address label sets provided during the year. Even a PDF file has limited use since people are constantly moving in and out of the geography.

In combination to the age demographics discussed earlier, I would also suggest that gender has an impact on our alumni community and pushes us toward certain postal mail announcements. For example, the Wharton School, like many business schools, was and continues to be male dominated even today. In spite of Wharton admitting more women than any other US business school, the MBA Class of 2016 is represented by only 43 percent women.[107] So you might imagine how male dominated the alumni activities of business schools can be when factoring in that the alumni population represents over five decades of past graduates.

Recall my earlier story of the annual membership gala that the Wharton Club of Dallas–Fort Worth hosts as a membership appreciation event each January / February (found in the subsection *"Stepping Up the Game"*). All paid members are invited and encouraged to bring their significant other. Traditionally, the Chapter has chosen to print and mail an invitation based on two primary considerations: age and gender. We most certainly did not want to miss out on participation from our most experienced, wise, and mentoring alumni, a group that has typically embraced electronic communication less than other age groups. Second, we knew that in our male-dominated, older populations, we might be missing out because the spouse was not informed. In the earlier generations, either both parties maintained the social calendar or the wife did so on behalf of the family. Although this was an alumni event, it was still a holiday party and thus a social event.

Our hypothesis was that if we only sent electronic invites for the event, then we would miss many older alumni altogether. Accordingly, each year, in addition to the announcement and reminders sent through electronic newsletters, we also mailed invitations and experienced a lovely turnout.

In 2016, the Chapter took the opportunity to test this theory, as times may have progressed past our original biases. The announcement, invitation, and reminders for the party were sent exclusively via e-mail newsletters that the Chapter had full autonomy to send at will. Attendance was significantly lower than in previous years. As an exhaustive analysis of attendance motivators was not undertaken, it is difficult to attribute the change to any one thing. Possibly the date or the venue or another factor swayed attendance as well. That being said, it is likely that eliminating the snail mail invitation was a contributing factor in the lower attendance based on the demographics of the actual attendees.

Data from one episode is not conclusive, but two years would be more telling. The same approach, that of only sending electronic announcements of the gala, was repeated in 2017. However, in this case, we had the added benefit of one young graduate who took it upon herself to stage a social media blitz, enticing fellow alumni to participate. The number of baby boomers in attendance could be counted on two hands, and of those, not one had a significant other alongside. On the other hand, the number of young alumni was much higher than seen previously. Again, this was not a controlled study. The venue changed from year to year, as did other factors. Nevertheless, I do feel comfortable drawing a couple of loose inferences. First, eliminating the postal mail invitation did likely impact the attendance of baby boomers and some Gen Xers in 2016. It also might have had a compounding effect that played out in 2017. Second, the social media campaign waged by the recent graduate is very likely what yielded the large millennial turnout. Armed with this information, just wait to see how we tackle 2018!

One consideration that was glossed over in the annual membership gala example above was cost. A paper invitation must be designed, printed, and mailed. It is likely that someone among the alumni would volunteer the time to design the invite. It is also possible that maybe someone in the alumni pool might be in the printing business, though that is less probable. Printing costs can be minimized by purchasing the materials and printing on a home printer rather than having formal invitations made—depending on the quantity. Maybe an employer might approve the printing of a reasonable number of them at the office as well.

With respect to postage, the least expensive item to mail is a postcard. A drawback to postcards is the tendency for them to get lost in the mail because they are smaller in size than typical mail and much thinner, never making it to the homes of the alumni. Either way, a postcard or an invitation / envelope pair, it will require postage—there is no avoiding that. If the alumni association is covering your postage, you are in great shape. Otherwise, we are adding a line item to the budget.

Should the Chapter be recognized as a tax-exempt nonprofit, *and* should it send mail each year in batches of 200 pieces or more, it might be able to qualify for special postage rates. There are costs associated with applying for the nonprofit mailing rates in the range of $175, compliance requirements that must be met on an annual basis, and time required to process the request. Regardless, if your Chapter is large and active and wants to cover postal mailings, it may be worth evaluating. If you choose to go down that path, the USPS has a "calculator" to help determine what the nonprofit rates would be for your piece.

There is one more consideration related to a snail mail campaign, and that is the availability of a trustworthy database of valid mailing addresses. That might be the least controllable aspect of all. To provide a little perspective about how dynamic physical addresses can be, the General Alumni Association (GAA) of the University of North Carolina reports that it makes an average of 150 address updates a day![108]

In my earlier annual membership gala example, we were confident we had a high-quality address database since we periodically did a total database scrub. The exercise gives us an opportunity to reach out to our alumni—especially the ones we don't see very often—and it keeps the data up to date. If the address data is poor or uncertain, that alone may steer your Chapter away from incorporating a postal mail component into your promotional efforts.

Up until this point, we have been looking at the decision to embrace postal mail in general—and especially at the Chapter's cost—as a binary, when in fact it is not. The Chapter is not limited to either a yes or no answer. Rather, the answer might be "some." Mailings could be sent more often, but only to a subset of the alumni population, specifically those who most value postal mailings. Assuming the address lists could be generated in a way that isolates alumni graduating before a specific year, this strategy would work. Not only would that yield significant cost savings, but it would demonstrate an effective understanding of the market. For those readers that are analytical types, you might also wish to factor in an adjustment for alumni whose initial graduation from your alma mater was with a master's or doctorate degree—should the data be available.

In the end, the cost of a mailing is very important and should not be minimized. Circling back to the purpose of this book, which is to help adequately fund the Chapter, the cost of promotion combined with other expenses to execute the program should not exceed the income generated. If the total cost of the mailing will be absorbed by the association, be strategic about when, but do it! Take advantage of *all* postal mail opportunities it will support. Beyond that, evaluate the likely increased benefit to your Chapter's event by incorporating a postal mail piece. Weigh the demographics, the size of the recipient population, and the quality of the address database against the costs, including design, printing, and postage. The result will guide your decision.

Before we move on from evaluating the effectiveness of postal mail, it might be a good time to touch on leveraging the alumni magazine. In the same research study that showed postal mail was favored by 48 percent of respondents, 31 percent of US adults also shared that they also prefer print media communications such as magazines.[109] This suggests that the alumni magazine is still a relevant tool for an awareness campaign. The preference ranges from millennials on the low end at 22 percent up to 42 percent for baby boomers.[110] Although there is no direct cost to the Chapter to leverage the alumni magazine, its value as a promotional vehicle warrants acknowledgment in this text.

The Arizona State University (ASU) Alumni Association publishes the *ASU Magazine* quarterly, which is a bit of a well-read anomaly in today's times. It reaches approximately 340,000 readers, the largest circulation of any publication produced by the university. Recently, in an online survey of alumni, respondents specifically listed the magazine as one of their primary sources of information about ASU.[111]

It is most certainly worth reaching out to the alumni association to understand how frequently and on what cycle are magazines distributed and when content must be submitted to be included. This method bears no cost to the Chapter yet adds the opportunity to reach a subpopulation not effectively captured by digital channels.

Phone Calls Still Have Their Place

This is about as far down the preference list as we will go. Phone calls registered as a communication channel of choice for non-personal information, according to 16 percent of adult Americans.[112] That may sound like a fairly low number, but not necessarily when you consider it fell just one percentage point below social media. You might want to sit down for this, but millennials lead the pack, with 21 percent listing phone calls as a preference. The age group preference responses for phone calls decline somewhat linearly down to the baby boomers at 9 percent.[113] In spite of that, 62 percent of baby boomers have and use a landline, compared to 22 percent of millennials.[114]

Phone calls can be especially effective if the need is urgent, if the Chapter is in the early stages of establishment, and when reviving a floundering Chapter. The urgency might be around a last-minute change in venue, or it might just be a countermeasure attempting to improve turnout when registrations look too low too close to the event. If the Chapter is a fledgling group, then a personal phone call to engage alumni might be necessary as the leadership strives to generate interest and build relationships.

An extensive review of alumni association guidance materials and interviews revealed that many alumni associations promote and encourage the use of phone calls to establish a more personal connection with alumni. Among a full range of alumni association-supported marketing efforts, including the website, e-mail blasts, Facebook, and Twitter posts, and the UD magazine *Messenger*, the University of Delaware (UD) Office of Development and Alumni Relations is a supporter of phone calls. It will go as far as assisting the Chapters in actually making calls to help boost attendance for larger events.[115]

We implemented a calling campaign twice at the Wharton Club of Dallas–Fort Worth with positive outcomes. However, the time required to recruit, organize, and manage the callers, in addition to the time to actually make the calls, was burdensome. Referencing the annual gala once more, we used the phone-tree approach to support class-specific gatherings before the big event. Since the gala was one of the most heavily attended events all year and its purpose spanned serving the entire alumni base, we came up with the great idea to encourage each class, or a group of classes, to get together prior to the gala for a pre-party happy hour. Several classes did in fact gather together, and participants thoroughly enjoyed it.

Today, if we were to embark on a similar program, we might still establish a lead contact per class but then incorporate other less expensive and laborious methods to unify the groups first. We may or may not tack on a phone-tree strategy at the tail end, depending on initial results and enthusiasm of the volunteers.

The St. Bonaventure University Alumni Association, founded in 1888 and now serving more than 28,000 alumni and thirty+ regional Chapters[116] that collectively host seventy events per year,[117] offers a unique service associated with phone calls. In addition to encouraging the personal touch through live telephone calls, the alumni relations department has the ability to provide robocall reminders before Chapter events and does so regularly.[118]

Phone calls are launched not only on the front end to promote an event but also on the back end as a follow-up. For example, maybe after a fundraiser, your leadership team wants to personally thank donors for their time and contributions. Each leader might also take that moment to suggest the possibility of a matching gift from the donor's employer. In this instance, a phone call can further the relationship between the two alumni, enhance the donor's affinity with its alma mater, and drive closer to the fundraising goal.

As long as the Chapter leaders have unlimited calling plans or the calls are local, there are no financial costs to budget for this communication channel. The only cost is time. Although millennials value electronic relationships as much as they do in-person ones, Gen Xers and baby boomers still tip the scales in favor of live interaction.

Phone calls do have a place in Chapter communications; however, that place is getting crowded with the rise of more efficient and accepted channels. The results of the age group preferences related to phone calls was really shocking, so keep that in mind if your Chapter is considering a phone-tree campaign to support your program—beforehand or afterward.

Physical and Digital Third-Party Channels— Secret Weapons

Although there may be appropriate uses when targeting only your alumni base, third-party channels are most applicable when hosting an event for which the intended audience extends past the realm of your alumni and their families. An example of the former includes if your Chapter is in early formation or revival phase; you may need to consider using these wider-net approaches just to find your alumni. Otherwise, it is unlikely that a Chapter program such as matching gifts, volunteer grants, or regional giving days would be promoted to those outside the alumni population and maybe one degree beyond.

A Chapter will want to advertise broadly when hosting a fundraiser for a specific cause, such as backpacks and school supplies for underprivileged children in your city, or if your Chapter is hosting a speaker event in which the speaker is exceptionally well known and a large audience is desired. Maybe the speaker is a corporate executive of a large company, or a best-selling author, or maybe even a famous actor. Such events are excellent opportunities to host a memorable event, provide an audience pleasing to the speaker, and generate some real income.

Third-party channels include other organizations of real people as well as digital options. Third-party organizations as defined here are any organized groups, commercial or other, through which a Chapter or individual might promote an event. Organizations are grouped into other alumni-related, business and professional associations, and personal. Examples of alumni-related organizations are:

- Other alumni groups serving the Chapter's alma mater, such as the local school of medicine alumni Chapter, the local Chapter of an affinity group, or the local parents' alumni Chapter (assuming that is a separate organization)
- Super-alumni organizations (SAOs), the joint athletic conference group in the area, such as alumni from the Pac-12 Conference universities
- Formal alumni Chapter consortiums, such as the Dallas Business Club (DBC)
- A one-off partnership with another alumni Chapter, such as two alumni Chapters watching a game in which their alma maters are playing against each other or Chapters representing the alma mater for each degree earned by a speaker

The first bullet references the various groups associated with the Chapter's alma mater. The Duke Alumni Association (DAA), founded in 1858[119] and supporting 165,000 alumni[120] through ninety-five+ groups around the world,[121] is a great example of a university with many organized groups throughout the alumni population. In addition to a full network of regional Chapters, the DAA supports affinity and academic Chapters. The affinity network includes the following identity, professional, and special interest groups:[122]

- Duke Black Alumni
- Duke University Hispanic / Latino Alumni Association
- Duke Entertainment Media Arts Network (DEMAN)
- Duke LGBTQ Network
- Duke Muslim Alumni Association
- Duke Presbyterian Campus Ministry Alumni
- Duke Global Entrepreneurship Network (DukeGEN)
- Duke Network for International Affairs (DukeNIA)
- Duke Real Estate Group of DC
- Duke Band Alumni Association
- Duke Global Health
- Duke Women's Forum

Of those affinity groups, the Duke Women's Forum is so strong that it has colonized Chapters of its own, fifteen or more of them. Beyond the affinity groups, Duke Alumni hosts academic groups based on schools:[123]

- Duke Divinity School
- The Fuqua School of Business
- Nicholas School of the Environment
- Pratt School of Engineering
- Stanford School of Public Policy
- School of Law
- School of Medicine
- School of Nursing
- The Graduate School

With so many organized groups, it should be incredibly easy for Duke alumni Chapters to solicit the connections to draw a sizable crowd in just about any location.

In the case of the University of Colorado Boulder (CU Boulder) Alumni Association, it also has multiple constituent groups. In addition to the geographic regional alumni Chapters, there are nine currently active affinity groups.[124] They include the:

- Air Force ROTC Detachment 105 Alumni
- American Indian Alumni Association
- CU Boulder Black Alumni Association
- CU Boulder Latino Alumni Association
- CU Boulder Veterans Alumni Club
- Directors Club
- CU Boulder Gay, Lesbian, Bisexual and Transgender (LGBT) Alumni Association
- Silver Buffalo Alumni Band
- President's Leadership Class Alumni Club

These groups represent a much broader swath of organized alumni with whom to partner.

As an example of embracing the second and fourth groupings, SAOs and one-off alumni Chapter partnerships, the Marquette University Alumni Association (MUAA) leverages game-watching events as one of their primary alumni activities, thanks to its participation in the BIG EAST Conference that allows their men's and women's basketball games to be nationally televised. The MUAA encourages the Chapters to partner with the rival team's local alumni Chapter to heighten enthusiasm, engagement, and participation.[125] As demonstrated in the *"Mobile Giving Now for Everyone, Big and Very Small"* section, such a scenario can yield an excellent outcome for raising charitable and scholarship funds.

The third grouping mentions formal alumni consortiums such as the DBC, an organization of more than twenty-five+ local MBA alumni Chapters. As mentioned in an earlier subsection, *"General Events Are Still the Workhorse: Determining Attendee Composition,"* the DBC was patterned after organizations in other cities such including Seattle, New York, and Denver. The Denver Business Series, for example, is a consortium of twenty-four MBA alumni Chapters. There are other types of consortiums as well, like the Ivy League and Ivy+ alumni Chapter consortiums. Examples of those are the Ivy League Alumni Club of Palm Beach, Florida and the Colorado Ivy+ Women.

Do a little research in your region and determine if there are any SAOs or alumni consortiums for which your Chapter qualifies. If so, consider participating in them. If not, this may be an opportunity to establish one if you are so inclined. From the northeast, Dartmouth College Office of Alumni Relations is a fan of nearly all of the above, stating:

Alumni Relations encourages all clubs and groups to collaborate with one another and with other Dartmouth alumni organizations, with similar alumni organizations at other colleges and universities (particularly Ivy+ schools), and with community organizations.[126]

Communicating with local alumni leaders of other colleges and universities is not a new concept; it is just a good one. In fact, 71 percent of alumni Chapters report that they do so, and 22 percent do so regularly.[127]

That wraps up the first category, so we will move on to category two, business and professional organizations. Businesses, shops, stores, and professional organizations make excellent partners and promotional vehicles if they are aligned with the program in question and the values of the Chapter. Examples include:

- Local businesses supporting an event, such as a golf equipment store when the event is a golf tournament
- A one-off partnership with a local industry organization focused on the subject of the talk, such as the local Chapter of the American Marketing Association when the university is sending a prominent marketing professor to your Chapter

Finally, personal organizations are our third category. These are other groups in which your Chapter leadership might be involved, including community boards, professional organizations, churches, charitable groups, and parent groups, to name a few. If your Chapter is a part of the Notre Dame Alumni Association, serving 135,000 alumni through 270 clubs,[128] and you attend a Catholic church, then it might be very appropriate to share certain Chapter events with the congregation. Each Chapter leader is capable of sharing the event announcement with multiple other networks.

These in-person, third-party partnerships can provide unparalleled opportunity to promote your event to a large audience. You may recall from an earlier conversation that open-door events drive revenue faster through the sale of higher-priced, non-member tickets while also helping to further offset prices for alumni and members. Embracing these expansion groups—including the various alumni organizations, businesses, and professional organizations, as well as those from personal networks—has the ability to do just that.

Beyond the flesh-and-bone-coordinated organizations, third-party digital channels add yet another dimension to your Chapter's promotional strategy.

There are many event posting websites that are either free or require only a nominal cost. There might be particularly popular web locations in your community for local activity. The ever-popular Craigslist might be an example of a no-cost option, while Meetup.com is designed specifically for bringing people together through actual events. These are only two of many, many options of which your Chapter might take advantage.

The Syracuse University (SU) Alumni Association is one association that supports Chapter Meetup.com accounts, among others.[129] Locals will also find that Chapters including the Texas Exes Rocky Mountain Chapter[130] (University of Texas) and the Colorado Duke University Alumni Chapter[131] are users of the site as well.

Popular third-party blogs can also be leveraged, as the Marquette University Alumni Association (MUAA) knows. It recommends reaching out to the most popular Marquette basketball blogs, CrackedSidewalks and MUScoop, as digital, third-party channels to reach alumni for big game-watching events.[132]

Once physical and digital third-party channels are identified, the next step is to determine what information each needs when promoting the event. I would suggest that your Chapter maintain the integrity of a single, primary on-line source for all information, the anchor post. Each partnering organization should provide an abbreviated promotional summary that links back to the anchor post—rather than repeat the anchor information. This is recommended to establish a clear understanding of where to seek last-minute updates.

For example, should the weather turn so sour that the event must be relocated indoors, postponed, or cancelled altogether, it would be exceptionally difficult in an already chaotic situation to identify all channels with primary information feeds and to ensure they have been updated. In this bad weather example, the event leadership would update the anchor post with changes and simply distribute an alert to all partnering third parties stating something like:

> URGENT WEATHER DELAY. Very Special Event with the Local Alumni Club of Fictitious State University. Click for more information.

Updating a single anchor post of which all parties are aware is most ideal and much more manageable for the alumni and the guests.

If your Chapter does seek to involve a large contingent of the non-alumni community or is just wanting to cast a wide net, then leveraging third-party channels is most certainly the way to go. This is another channel that is easy on the budget with little to no associated costs. Carefully consider your event subject, determine what partnerships would be most aligned with your event, and begin disseminating information as early as possible. Lastly, send brief, periodic reminders to each of those channels for distribution as appropriate.

Blogs, TV, Radio, and Other Alternatives

The options listed above are by no means the only promotional channels available to Chapters, just the most effective ones. For example, Chapters may be empowered to launch their own Chapter blog that is a discussion or informational website consisting of discrete, often informal, diary-style text entries on various topics. Penn State Alumni Association, for one, encourages Chapters to consider developing a blog of their own to support Chapter communications.[133]

Other Chapters may be permitted to seek TV or radio publicity in support of an event. They may be encouraged to generate a press release, such as the Chapters of the University of Kentucky (UK) Alumni Association haven been. The association even provides these helpful guidelines for writing press releases:

1. Respect deadlines for all press releases.
2. Give the most important information at the beginning and limit copy to 1 page in length.
3. Include the 5 W's: Who is participating? What will they be doing? When and Where will it happen? Why are they doing the activity, and Why is the community interested?
4. Be brief. Use short paragraphs and short sentences.
5. Date the release, and include a contact name and phone number.
6. Send or deliver the press release to the editor, unless otherwise specified.[134]

If used appropriately, the media can be a real friend to the Chapter. Once a press release has been sent to the media, they might very well contact your Chapter for more information. It is possible that the media could catch wind of something your Chapter might be doing—even without your prompting—and contact you all on their own. The Alumni Association of the University of Michigan (AAUM) has this to say about Chapters and the media:

> Strong relations with the media are important for raising the Association's profile and reputation. Club leaders should generally feel free to respond to requests from the media regarding their club's

activities, but please notify the Association's regional relations team as soon as possible of the contact.[135]

Journalists can be tricky, but they can be great friends to a Chapter as well. It takes a few press releases to get their attention, so just start pushing them out there. Per the request of the AAUM above, keep the alumni association in the loop regarding encounters with the media—planned or otherwise.

The Ole Miss Alumni Association has a similar position regarding leveraging the media; however, it also shares the importance of restricting any news releases or comments to the media to information relative to club activities and events only.[136] It turns out that 8 percent of alumni Chapters in a national study report using the local media to announce events. If your Chapter is interested in reaching out to local media, take note of the alumni association's position, as not all associations encourage contact with the media.[137]

Blogs, television, radio, and newspaper outlets are great ways to get the message out about your events, and they bear no costs to the Chapter. Prepare a good press release, and unleash it on your media targets. Lastly, keep the alumni association in the loop at all times.

Best Strategies by Generation

Overall, the three primary age groups have a number of distinctive characteristics that make promoting events and programs to each unique. They want to receive information differently; they process information differently; and they make decisions differently. Here are a few guidelines to help improve the effectiveness of your promotions to each age demographic. As a reminder:

- Millennials were born 1977 to 1995 (roughly those in their twenties and thirties).
- Generation Xers (Gen Xers) were born 1965 to 1977 (generally those in their forties).
- Baby boomers were born 1946 to 1964 (those in their fifties and sixties, more or less).

If millennials are a target—either solely or as part of the overall audience—one of the most important parts of effectively communicating with them is enabling sharing. Adopt marketing channels that incorporate the ability to easily share the content with others. You may recall that millennials tend to like things more when their peer group likes it. Sending announcements via social media with sharing features already embedded enables them to like something faster.

Understanding the influence of peers on this group can provide strategic insight as to how your Chapter can entice large numbers of millennials to participate in a program. Announcing high pre-registration numbers before an event, for example, could influence more millennials to join in. This is where the social media channels become especially useful: they facilitate easy sharing.

Millennials have a fairly low trust of people in general. Thus, it will be important to reinforce the trustworthiness of the Chapter. Make certain only to communicate program details of which the Chapter is absolutely certain. This will minimize the number of changes that have to be announced. Do your best to ensure transparency. Share accurate numbers—registrations, donations, etc.—throughout the process, and always report final results. This goes for all things, especially fundraising. Keep the alumni community continually updated, and stay true to the use of funds.

Furthermore, millennials have a short tolerance for too much content. Also, know that they will be viewing any electronic communication on their smartphones, as 93 percent of all US millennials are.[138] Make announcements short and sweet with links to more. This way, they are likely to get the core of your announcement in the few seconds allocated to each "record" as they quickly scan e-mail and texts before getting out of bed in the morning. A responsive format for electronic communications will go a very long way in saving the message from instant exile to the cyber trash can and maybe even get it read.

In addition, millennials care a lot about securing a job now and finding the next one. If the Chapter's event will offer significant opportunities to network, make that known. Find ways to facilitate networking, such as making sure name badges offer not only the name but also the company and function. Announce sponsoring companies so those interested can plan to connect with them. Consider interjecting a short speed-networking session during the first ten or fifteen minutes before launching into the event. Use the Chapter's online and social media presence to circulate internship and job opportunities. Find creative ways to weave networking into events, and get the word out prior to the event.

Lastly, if your event is a fundraiser of any sort, make absolutely certain there are multiple opportunities to contribute using mobile giving strategies. Millennials do not carry cash, and they certainly do not carry checkbooks. At a minimum, the ability to swipe or type in credit cards is a must. Better yet, establish a text-giving channel, and provide the number everywhere in the announcements and at the event. Then, provide several opportunities to give small amounts throughout the event. Millennials are a charitable group, and they especially like to give often in small bites. Help them to do so.

If your Chapter is targeting Gen Xers, there are a couple things to know about them. First, if you also plan to target millennials and baby boomers for your program, then by default much of what you will already be planning will cover the Gen Xers. It is a simple truth for the small generation sandwiched between the two larger groups on either end; Gen Xers are the transition from one to the other.

Gen Xers are as tech savvy as millennials, though they tend to hang on to an appreciation of postal mail, a bit more like baby boomers. They are more independent than millennials, and, although they are avid users of Facebook and other social media, the sharing nature of their digital behavior is more informative than influential. Gen Xers share because something is interesting rather than as a necessary tool to facilitate knowing their friend's preferences and intentions.

Since Gen Xers tend to be heavily entrepreneurial and comprise the largest group of company founders, topics and events related to funding, small-business challenges, and preparing a company for a lucrative exit might be most attractive to them. They also care deeply about elder-care issues and financial management in preparation for retirement. If specifically targeting Gen Xers, these are important topics to consider. Further, this group dreams of a night with no responsibility. Casual, fun events where, rather getting dressed up, they can just relax with friends and a drink can be especially enticing to this group. Think casual date night. Play up these aspects in the promotions.

Gen Xers do tend to be especially health conscious and focused on preventative measures. Should your Chapter's event be a walk or run, this is your target group! Such healthy events are attractive as family-togetherness activities and an opportunity to demonstrate a commitment to being healthy in front of the children. Do all you can to ensure your message is reaching and appealing to Gen Xers.

When your target is baby boomers, know that your alumni will likely be among the 65 percent that have a smartphone, while also realizing that the other 35 percent do not. Because standard mobile communications will fail to connect with a third of your Chapter's baby boomers, consider an SMS text message campaign. We already know baby boomers are text savvy based on their preference to use texts for personal communication and that SMS messages reach both smartphones and older phones that operate on 2G, 3G, and 4G networks.

Baby boomers are also very receptive to postal mail—nearly 70 percent![139] Although they are tech savvy, there is most certainly a sub-group that will be missed if all communications are digital. If the Chapter has a large baby boomer population, it may be advisable to incorporate postal mail in your campaign. It might also be worth submitting an article about the upcoming event / program to the alumni association for inclusion in the printed alumni magazine, since postal mail and print media such as the alumni magazine rank second and third for most preferred communication channels by baby boomers.[140]

If the baby boomer population is small, you may choose to reach out via phone. Although this group least preferred phone calls, according to research, they do report a significantly higher likelihood of owning and using their land-lines in addition to mobile phones. In my experience, I have found phone calls especially effective for alumni-based communications.

Baby boomers and retirees have also expressed a strong desire to connect and stay connected with friends, significantly more so than any other generation. Setting aside special seating for these groups—maybe even by years or a bracket of years if the population is large—could go a long way in attracting these alumni. It may also be advantageous to make a list of attendees available at check-in. This would allow participants to seek out old friends that they might otherwise miss.

Earlier, we learned that baby boomers and retirees have and plan to contribute large sums of money to charity in the coming years. They are not necessarily more charitable than others; however, realistically, they are just in the stage of life when their priorities have shifted to giving back as a primary focus. Make an extra effort to build targeted promotions honing in on this group when your Chapter's event is a fundraiser of any kind. Baby boomers want to make a difference; they want to contribute. Allow them to do so.

From a topical standpoint, baby boomers will resonate more than others with patriotic events such as a Memorial Day picnic or a military speaker. Know that they might very well be working and not yet retired. And don't make the mistake of thinking this group will be footloose and fancy free, with all of the time in the world on their hands. In fact, even of those that are retired, most will have an incredibly busy schedule packed with family and volunteer activity tucked in around travel. Gone are the days of sipping iced tea on the front porch during a retirement that started in someone's mid to late fifties.

If there will be ample seating and / or a quieter element of the program, let that be known. Baby boomers will appreciate opportunities to sit throughout the evening more than other groups. They also do not enjoy loud venues or activities nearly as much as millennials will. Age-related hearing loss is called presbycusis. It can start as early as eighteen years old[141] or younger, by some accounts, and not until our thirties or forties[142] by others. To put it in perspective, think about the high-frequency ringtones teenagers like to use on their phone so adults can't tell they are getting a call or a text. Gen Xers are experiencing this to some degree, but not as much as baby boomers. Should the event be a holiday party where the layout of the event is less obvious, take a moment to touch on the great seating and pleasing acoustics. (This is also an important venue selection consideration.) Tie this in with reserving a special area for their graduation class(es).

Lastly, this group is more likely to read e-mails on a computer than the others—and computer monitors do not zoom as easily as tablets and phones. Ensure that all of your promotions use a medium to medium-large font for easy reading. Although this is especially appreciated by baby boomers, reasonable font size is not a detractor for any age group. It is a good idea to keep that in mind for communications across the board.

Although the groups are distinctive in many ways, there are also some commonalities across the board regarding promotional strategies. First, everyone understands that the website is mission control (if your Chapter has one). That is the first place to post events, programs, supporting materials, and anything else associated with the program. Second, use e-mail as your primary method of communication with all parties—it is still the most flexible, most cost effective, and most accepted method of outreach for everyone. If you can do nothing more, this is a reasonable place from which to operate.

Ensure They Show Up

Congratulations are in order when your Chapter successfully sells a large number of tickets to an event! But before you clink the champagne flutes, selling the tickets is not enough. People must actually attend; otherwise, your Chapter could face the negative impacts of no-shows and disappointing requests for reimbursement. This is bad for several reasons.

First is the obvious loss of ticket revenue. Second is the visibly low showing at the event, such as empty seats or golf teams short of a foursome. Low turnout can affect morale and impact future events. Third is the increased time and expense of processing refunds. If refunds are by check, they must be processed and delivered. Hopefully, it could be done electronically, mildly speeding up the process. If refunds are by credit card, there might be fairly high fees for doing so beyond the cost of the ticket. Either way, checks or credit cards, it is time and effort required by your Chapter or the alumni association that would best be spent doing something to move the Chapter forward instead.

Most of the time, Chapters open ticket sales / registration within a few weeks of the event. Other times, there is a significant gap between when the payment was made and the event itself. In these instances, enthusiasm for what is to come will begin to diminish as time goes on. Therefore, continually creating excitement and intrigue is essential. To do that, start by filtering your contact lists for each channel you plan to utilize by only those already attending the event. Then, develop a communication series that regularly reminds and excites these attendees about your event. Keep the communications brief and focused on a single topic. Be certain the announcements contain useful and relevant content rather than simply reminding them of the event.

An example involves a tennis tournament. A great way to keep people engaged would be to arrange and announce a guest appearance by a top-tier tennis player. Suggest that people should have their cameras ready for a selfie with the pro. Repeat the announcements periodically with new information. This tactic will keep interest and enthusiasm from waning over time. It never hurts to prearrange some excited responses over social media to liven up the conversation.

If your event is a sell-out and you want to ensure that there are few, if any, open seats on the day of the event, maintain a waitlist. This is more critical when there is considerable time between when tickets were purchased and when the event takes place. Life happens, and, more than likely, someone who intended to go to the event will be unable. That attendee may have to go on a business trip, a family member may become ill or injured and need attention, or a conflicting event may spring up that takes precedence. Whatever the circumstance, it is virtually guaranteed that not everyone who registered will be able to attend.

It is not uncommon for some events to state "no refunds" due to commitments required by vendors. However, if the unusable ticket can be easily re-sold through the use of a waitlist, the Chapter may reconsider such a policy. One Chapter that wishes to remain unidentified attempted to facilitate reselling tickets that would go unused by connecting the sellers and the buyers. At first blush, it seemed to help the alumni, while not incurring fees or extra work. However, in reality, it was unpleasant because the registration list was no longer in sync with the people checking in. If the Chapter embraces reselling tickets to those on a waitlist, it should assume control of the entire process—fees and all.

If your Chapter adopts the waiting list approach, it is important to communicate with those on the waitlist just as frequently as you would others. By the very nature of being on a waitlist, their plans are uncertain and in flux. That is not a comfortable position for most. Silence breeds curiosity and concern, yielding a barrage of frequent inquiries. In order to maintain a content waitlist– for their sake and yours—be as transparent as possible. Regular updates specifically regarding waitlist activity are essential.

A successful promotional strategy not only drives the desired awareness and ticket sales but also includes the follow-through of ensuring actual attendance is as expected. Only once the event starts is the revenue generated locked in for the Chapter.

Integrated Campaigns Are Most Effective

Obviously, there are countless opportunities to promote your Chapter's program, and your volunteers can run themselves into the ground trying to utilize them all. The smartest move is to use a strategic, integrated approach that casts the widest net for the minimum cost and effort. Before we jump into an example, it is a good time to review and note a few tips and tricks, regardless of communication channels embraced:

- Be concise and to the point.
- Have someone else proofread material before you send it out.
- Your tone and language should be respectful, polite, and professional at all times—as well as fun.
- Adhere to the alumni association's branding guidelines.
- Be mindful and strategic regarding frequency.
- Use links, pictures, and videos in electronic communications where possible. The University of Chicago (UChicago) Alumni Association reminds us that links can get rather long, so consider using a link-shortening service such as Bitly.com.[143]
- On social media and other channels for which the Chapter has an account, include someone from the central alumni association with administrative rights.
- Enable alumni to share posts with others and across platforms.
- To maintain compliance with 501(c)(3) guidelines, do not discuss politics or candidates.

Each program for each Chapter will be different. The promotional effort to make each one a success is equally as different. That being said, I am going to walk through what a grand integrated campaign could look like for a hypothetical example. In order to sketch out an ideal campaign for this discussion, a few assumptions will be made. The event in need of promotion will be a tennis tournament to raise money for local scholarships. In order to raise the most money, the Chapter will open participation up to those beyond the alumni, encouraging anyone and everyone to attend. We will also assume that the Chapter has done everything exceptionally well up to this point, including appointing a Vice President of Fundraising and a few appropriate chairpersons. The local country club, with its ideal tennis facility, has been secured for the best possible date, as have several sponsors. Multiple competition categories have been established to allow for many winners. All that is left is promoting the event to attract the most people.

First, as the concept of the event / program is being vetted, design the promotional strategy. Take into account the event, target audience, channel access, costs, and resources to execute. Since budgeting for promotions must be built into the overall event budget, this process should be complete prior to the decision to move forward with the event . . . and most certainly before placing the Chapter or association at risk by securing a date and venue without a vetted, thorough plan.

Second, once the event is confirmed, establish the anchor post to which all other communication channels will point. Do this at the very onset of securing the date for the tennis tournament, hopefully at least six months prior to the tournament. Post the date and all known information (even if the only thing known is the date). The anchor post should be the first of the Chapter's website, the Chapter's Facebook Page, or the alumni association's network-wide calendar—in that order, based on what is available. Generate only one fully informative anchor post.

Third, prepare your communication plan with the alumni association. Establish the schedule of association-sponsored communications, including the association website, newsletters, targeted e-mails, the alumni magazine, and any print-related materials your Chapter wishes to request—time will be the challenge. Ensure that all necessary information has been assembled to support timely and effective distribution. All such communications should encompass the most important details and hooks, while linking back to the anchor post for more information.

As tennis is popular across the ages, and we are looking to raise scholarship funds, a postal mail piece should be a part of the campaign. This will be an effective complement to the direct, digital channels by expanding the reach to families, older baby boomers, and retirees. As several alumni associations will support one or two mailings per year, start there before carrying the cost by the Chapter.

Fourth, engage social media. Post a save-the-date, or make a brief announcement on the Chapter's Facebook account (if it has not already been done because it is the anchor post) and LinkedIn Group that links back to the anchor post for more details—these are both recommended. This is where you will touch all three age groups, while simultaneously enabling your millennials and families to start sharing the tournament among themselves and beyond the inner circle of the alumni population.

Fifth, if the Chapter can disseminate its own communications, keep reading; otherwise, skip to the next paragraph. Remember, e-mail is king. Such an event would warrant its own dedicated communication; however, it may also be the headliner for a more comprehensive Chapter-wide e-mail newsletter. The e-mail should be enticing and contain the most relevant information, but maintain a balance with brevity, lest you lose the attention of many readers. Reference the recommended e-mail set-up and content presented earlier for specifics. Simply use a link back to the anchor post for more information.

Sixth, engage a texting strategy. As we discussed earlier, Twitter would be the best, established social texting option. However, I would suggest embracing a no-charge SMS group texting tool regardless of whether you engage Twitter. Then, announce the event with something short and to the point like:

> The Local Alumni Club of Fictitious State University announces date for the 2016 Tennis Tournament – June 14. Registration details coming soon.

If possible, include a link to the anchor page. The text communication will be read by everyone from millennials to baby boomers in less than five minutes, even if they carry old-style flip phones!

Seventh, wake up Siri and Ok Google, and get to work! Design a phone-tree-distribution plan based on the number of volunteers available to assist and a script of information to be shared. Group call lists by class year, and try to align the volunteer's class year with the class(es) they are assigned for best results. If a person is not going to attend the event, the volunteer might be instructed to let him or her know how to contribute to the scholarship fund in another way. Your leadership team might even use this opportunity to poll the alumni while on the phone. If so, keep the questions very few in number, maybe no more than three.

Eighth, expand physical third-party promotion by reaching out to local alumni networks, such as the other Chapters and affinity groups from your alma mater and those that represent your university's athletic conference. It may even be possible to set up a few internal challenges between different groups to heighten the engagement—university alumni vs. other university alumni, or university alumni vs. the business school alumni. Get creative, and leverage as many relationships as possible, all the while heightening engagement.

Ninth, mobilize your flesh-and-blood, physical third parties in the form of local businesses and companies. The hosting country club would be my first stop since it has a stake in the game, and this is excellent publicity for them. Next, reach out to organizations that have either tennis teams or provide tennis lessons and stores / companies that sell tennis equipment. Some of these might also be sponsors of the event; if so, all the better. Local high schools, community colleges, the YMCAs and YWCAs, and private instructors are also good places to begin. Then, explore opportunities with big sporting equipment chains like Dick's Sporting Goods, Academy Sports + Outdoors, Nike, and REI, to get the list started. For this scenario, it might even be fruitful to leave flyers at local gyms, especially those with tennis facilities. Let your creativity fly. Stores for runners typically sell a full range of shoes, so don't overlook them! Keep going . . . What about health and medical offices, such as chiropractors, massage companies, sports medicine practices, and orthopedic surgeons! Even food and nutrition suppliers are fair game, like smoothie shops, healthy food grocers and restaurants, and protein bar and hydration companies.

Tenth, focus on more third-party promotion, but now concentrate on professional organizations that might have an interest. With respect to the tennis tournament, of the United States Tennis Association, Women's Tennis Association, or the Intercollegiate Tennis Association, among others, one or more is bound to have a presence in the region and would want to be associated with the tournament.

Eleventh, make the most of digital third-party options. Get the word out to related bloggers. Post the tournament on free event websites like Craigslist.com and Meetup.com.

Twelfth, engage your Chapter leadership and their networks. Each leader can disseminate the information to their other volunteer groups, professional organizations, work friends, customers, religious groups, community boards, sports clubs, animal rescue networks, and parent groups (such as soccer team parents or PTA groups). There are very likely many tennis players among those clusters of people!

The Penn State Alumni Association, like many alumni associations, is an avid supporter of multi-dimensional promotional strategies. It suggests that using multiple forms of communication when sharing messages typically leads to greater success. It further recommends that Chapters test and try different options to see what works best for their groups.[144]

Thirteenth is all about the media! Write a great, succinct, compelling press release, and scatter it around the TV stations, newspapers, and radio stations. Use your connections to find just the right reporters and journalists who would be interested in your story.

The first thirteen steps are in an effort to announce and establish awareness of the event. Make certain someone is on top of overall promotion—each channel and frequency of communication from initiation onward. As time draws closer, frequency can increase, but not too much.

Fourteenth, update the anchor post as soon as any new information is confirmed, such as a new sponsor. Keep that up to date at all times. Announcements for approaching deadlines are acceptable and helpful. In our case, the tennis tournament has a discounted early registration fee. It would be acceptable to remind people two weeks prior, one week prior, and two days prior. Depending on the method of communication, it may be possible to use a last-minute reminder the morning of the deadline. If you do choose a day-of-deadline e-mail, then make certain it goes out very early in the morning to catch the still-in-bed e-mail screeners. Then, space out communication again until the next major deadline.

Ensure each round of communications offers something new—don't just recycle the same text. New information would include prominent attendees who have agreed to attend (and endorse the use of their names), new sponsors, the addition of a prize category, current registration levels, deadlines, and when the event gets close to approaching capacity.

I typically like to send out information the day before the event as a reminder; however, I suggest using a guise to do so rather than a direct reminder. A great example would be a notice about parking in light of the large turnout or a special update about what to do if weather is uncooperative. Consider closing with a note about accepting registrations at the door. This will give the green light to the person who was on the fence about participating but might show up at last minute. These snippets of important information are appreciated, not seen as nagging, and serve as a general reminder. Unless the event is sold out, these notes should be sent out to the entire audience, not just those that have registered. I have found that there are always people who planned to get around to registering but never did. These last-minute notices drive them to action.

Fifteenth, keep those registered engaged and those on the waitlist informed. Remember that having sold the tickets or received the registrations is not enough. People must actually attend the event.

Throughout the process, the promotions should alert everyone that match pairing will be done by class year groups; reassure millennials that they will have outstanding networking opportunities; expound on the Gen Xer's love of healthy activities in a relaxed environment that can be done as a family; and remind baby boomers what a great chance this will be to reconnect with their classmates in a wonderful environment to sit and talk while they have an opportunity to contribute to a worthy cause such as scholarships. Make sure your Chapter delivers on all promises.

Finally, the last car on the promotional train becomes relevant on the day of the event itself. Take countless photos; post, text, and tweet throughout the event. Start during the set-up for the "behind-the-scenes" sneak-peek. Keep it up throughout the day. Definitely post all the way through the awards—showering as much recognition on others as possible, including the players, sponsors, winners, and volunteers. These actions may drive some immediate attendance, but what they really do is set the stage for a much greater event the following year.

What is outlined above depicts a carefully orchestrated example in which nearly all channels and considerations presented could be wrapped into a single master promotional strategy. In our example of a tennis tournament in which we wanted as many people as possible to attend to raise money for scholarships, the above is a solid and comprehensive approach to promotions—if you had an army of volunteers! Real Chapters do not.

Use the above as a best-case scenario, and peel away what does not apply to your Chapter or event; then continue peeling off what is unrealistic with the volunteer team available. It is important to step back and realize that engaging each additional channel spreads an already stretched volunteer pool thinner. An effective promotional strategy will take into account not only the audience(s) and channels but the resources available to effective execute. An overly ambitious strategy that is poorly executed may do more harm than good. It is highly recommended to design an effective strategy and then scale back, if necessary, to what can be reasonably performed by the volunteer(s) in charge.

The Grand Canyon University (GCU) Office of Alumni Relations, serving 117,000+ alumni through its three organized Chapters,[145] could not agree more! It recognizes that even the most enthusiastic Chapter leader may get tired of being in charge all the time and encourages leaders not to get burned out. They suggest cutting back or further delegating to reliable Chapter members if the work becomes arduous.[146] This applies to all Chapter leaders across all Chapter functions. There is no question regarding the critical importance of a well-designed and executed promotional strategy. Just don't promote your Chapter out of its leaders and volunteers.

60-Second Takeaway

The key to revenue generation is promotion! The best communication strategies are targeted, compelling, and comprehensive—yet not too numerous nor wordy. Know your target audience, understanding them by age demographic: millennials, Generation Xers, and baby boomers, among other perspectives. Next, consider the most popular primary promotional channels based on your audience, including websites, e-mail, social media, text messaging, postal mail, print media, phone calls, third-party avenues, and the press. The most effective campaigns consider the event, the segmented audience, available channels, and special efforts to minimize no-shows when designing the optimal strategy.

Although not all of the promotional channels are electronic, many are. In today's world, effectiveness of digital communication is highly dependent on responsive formatting. Chapters are unlikely to have much control over this issue, so, hopefully, the alumni association is staying on top of these trends and has the support from the university to keep up.

A few pearls of communication wisdom include: plan ahead; be polite, respectful, and concise; follow the association's guidelines; have the content proofread; use lots of pictures, images, and videos; provide admin access for all accounts to the alumni association; be mindful of frequency; avoid politics; enable the sharing of everything; and have fun! Finally, the best results emerge when the execution plan is scaled not to exceed the volunteer's capacity.

Make It Happen Checklist

- ☐ Choose your revenue-generating activity / event / program.
- ☐ Establish a specific Chapter leader responsible for communications and promotions to ensure appropriate strategy, design, content, integration, and frequency.
- ☐ Determine the ideal audience to attract. Consider alumni only vs. all-comers. Also, consider age demographic for positioning.
- ☐ Have all text proofread prior to distributing.
- ☐ Establish an anchor post for the event that is comprehensive, usually on the Chapter website or Facebook Page, otherwise on the alumni association's website.
- ☐ Coordinate the event and communication plan with the alumni association, including a channel strategy (network-wide calendar, e-mail, newsletters, alumni magazine, postal mail) and timeline for both content and distribution.
- ☐ Highly leverage e-mail communications, either single-subject or newsletter-like distributions. Be brief, and embed links to the anchor post.
- ☐ Engage social media through both Facebook (if not already the anchor post) and LinkedIn. Announce the event with flair, yet briefly, with links back to the anchor post. Use pictures from the previous event where possible.
- ☐ Engage a text channel. Consider an SMS messaging tool and / or Twitter.
- ☐ Assess the benefit of a printed mailer / invitation through the association or your Chapter.
- ☐ Determine if a phone call campaign is appropriate.
- ☐ Determine if reaching out to the related alumni community, other alumni Chapters of your alma mater, alumni club consortiums, and SAOs is appropriate.
- ☐ Determine if partnering with professional organizations related to the topic is appropriate.
- ☐ Engage third-party businesses aligned with the subject or target audience.
- ☐ Encourage Chapter leadership to promote the event throughout their personal network, including community boards, parent groups, and professional groups.
- ☐ If appropriate, distribute a press release, and engage the local media.
- ☐ Once the ideal promotional strategy is outlined, scale it back not to exceed volunteer capacity.

☐ Following initial communications announcing the event, be especially mindful of follow-on communication frequency. Ensure each wave contains new information while getting briefer along the way and always linking back to the anchor post.

☐ Strategically increase communication frequency approaching deadlines, truthfully emphasizing discounts or limited availability.

☐ For millennials, keep communications especially brief, enable sharing, emphasize networking opportunities, and engender trust by only communicating information of which your Chapter is absolutely certain—and hope your communication tools are responsive!

☐ For Gen Xers, emphasize casual evenings without responsibility, events with healthy activities for the whole family, and topics related to managing small businesses, navigating elder care, or minimizing taxes.

☐ For baby boomers and beyond, use a larger font, and consider a postal mail piece and an SMS tool. Know that patriotic events, those making reconnecting with friends possible, and those in which it is easier to hear and have lots of seating will be most attractive.

☐ Keep those who have registered engaged all the way until the event to minimize no-shows.

☐ If the program sells out, consider establishing a waitlist to further minimize no-shows. Maintain regular communication with that group to control excessive inquiries.

☐ Once the event starts, breathe a sigh of relief—but continue taking pics and posting fun moments throughout the day.

☐ Kick back, and enjoy the fruits of a promotional campaign well executed!

☐ Remember to have fun! Scale back if it is no longer fun.

☐ Promote the results of the program / event back to the Chapter.

☐ Thank the participants and volunteers profusely.

Collecting and Handling the Money

This book has presented items and services that improve the activity and operations of an alumni Chapter. We have also explored several methods of generating the income necessary to afford those items and services. Now it is time to look at issues and pathways associated with moving the money from the alumni and donors into the Chapter's control (or the association's control on behalf of the Chapter).

The degree to which a Chapter has input or authority over how "its" money is accumulated or used varies widely from alumni association to alumni association. Financial freedom—or burdensome financial management, from another perspective—seems to fall into a few categories. We discussed these concepts at the beginning of the book in the *"Introduction,"* but since that was nearly 200 pages ago, we will review them once again briefly:

a. **Association control** – The alumni association maintains total control of finances. Chapters do not have their own bank accounts and thus do not make payments. Often, these Chapters operate on a net-neutral strategy. These Chapters may or may not be encouraged to raise funds for scholarships. For these Chapters, one of the most valuable sections of the book will be *"Promotion for Maximum Impact."* This will give the Chapter the best chance of reaching that magic participation number critical to covering the costs.

b. **Hybrid control** – Chapters do have Chapter-specific bank accounts but are affiliates of the alumni association and managed largely by the association. There may be one or two accounts, two if operational funds are held separately from scholarship funds. Most of the time, establishing these accounts is done with a specifically identified banking institution (but not exclusively) and using the central alumni association's Employer Identification Number (EIN), but not always. In this approach, the alumni association is responsible for all federal and state filings; however, the Chapters are typically required to keep excellent records and submit them on a routine basis, as determined by the association. Chapters have various degrees of authority to direct the funds in these accounts. They might even have a debit card for more convenient use.

c. **Chapter control** – Chapters have full control of establishing and maintaining bank accounts using their own unique EIN. These Chapters tend to have the greatest need for operational funds, as they do not have access to some of what would be provided if they were legal subordinates of the association, such as insurance coverage. This approach bears the most financial and operational freedom but also the most reporting and compliance responsibility.

Binghamton University Alumni Association operates according to the first category, in which Chapters do not maintain financial accounts. The alumni association will accept event registrations, sign vendor contracts, and make payments for the Chapter's activities.[1]

Fresno State Alumni Association (FSAA) has an organizational structure in which Chapters (chapters, clubs, and networks) are affiliates of the association, illustrating the hybrid scenario. The central alumni association controls the finances, but the Chapters do have a Chapter-specific account with heavy influence on its use. The official handbook states:

> All cash management, disbursement and accounting services shall be handled by the FSAA. The Chapter, Club or Network does not [have] the authority to establish its own, separate bank account.[2]

The handbook goes on to clarify that there actually are two accounts established within the FSAA for each of the Chapters: an operating account and a scholarship account. Chapters have the ability to largely determine how the funds will be allocated to events and activities within guidelines; however, the actual income and payments are processed through the association.[3] For all intents and purposes, the FSAA is in complete control of finances, while the Chapters heavily influence its use.

The University of Tennessee Knoxville (UT Knoxville) Alumni Association is also an example of hybrid control with very limited ability to fundraise for operations. It requires that any Chapter that collects funds must have a checking account in the name of the Chapter but opened using the association's EIN. As such, the Chapter is required to submit an annual financial report.[4]

Just because a bank account exists in a Chapter's name does not mean that the Chapter is authorized to do anything it may wish with that account, especially if it was opened as a legal subordinate of the association, such as in this case. Alumni associations typically have a stance on the receipt of funds for operations. The UT Knoxville Alumni Association clearly states:

> No chapter associated with the Office of Alumni Affairs should be receiving gifts from individuals or organizations for the chapter's general operating funds.[5]

A third example of hybrid control is that of the Syracuse University (SU) Alumni Association. In this situation, approved Chapters are official, IRS-recognized 501(c)(3) tax-exempt entities of the SU Alumni Association. Like UT Knoxville Chapters, they are authorized to open bank accounts with a financial institution of their choosing in their own names but using the EIN of the alumni association. However, in this example, the SU Alumni Association permits Chapters to conduct fundraising within university and IRS guidelines to generate funds for operations. It openly recognizes:

> Along with your dedication, a successful alumni club also needs capital for the day-to-day operations of the club, as well as, for building scholarship and award programs.[6]

Although a bank account is essential for many of the income generating ideas presented, it is not a license to embark on generating income without the blessing of the alumni association—regardless of what college or university your Chapter serves.

A good example of Chapter control is illustrated by the Chapters of the Mississippi State University (MSU) Alumni Association. Each Chapter is encouraged to apply for its own EIN and is self-supporting. The MSU Alumni Association further encourages revenue generation through various means, including auctions, merchandise sales, tournaments, and others. Similar to the attitudes demonstrated by the Stanford Alumni Association (SAA) referenced in the "*Introduction,*" the MSU Alumni Association encourages Chapters with a surplus to use it for the local alumni as one of several options.[7]

It is exceptionally important that a Chapter clearly understands the degrees of freedom in which it has to operate. Financial guidelines and policies are most certainly established by your alumni association and should be adhered to at all times. Please note that the groupings above are loosely assembled and do not cleanly define all Chapter / association relationships. The variations are too numerous to count. For the sake of argument, a framework was required, thus the three buckets presented.

A Checking Account—The Most Basic Requirement

One of the most practical steps in preparing to accept money, be it payments, donations, sponsorships, or other, is the establishment of a Chapter-specific bank account. It is not recommended—or even permitted by most alumni associations—for a Chapter to use a member's personal bank account. This carries serious liability implications, such as unnecessary and inappropriate personal liability, being assumed by the account holder, as well as the potential for Chapter finances to be held hostage by the account holder—not that any devoted alumni would do that.

The Louisiana State University (LSU) Alumni Association, like several alumni associations, is very clear in stating its disapproval of the use of personal accounts:

> Regardless of where you keep your Chapter funds, we insist you do not use your personal bank account.[8]

Although it can often be tempting to process the financial activities of the Chapter through someone's personal bank accounts when the proper channels are less convenient or time consuming to navigate, it is remarkably unwise. Just don't do it. If there are further questions about this practice, simply reach out to any local insurance or financial professional for a conversation—or better yet, to your central alumni association.

Mentioned in the previous subsection, a Chapter may have Chapter-specific bank accounts, or it may not. If it does not, then it still may be possible for the alumni association to accept monies on behalf of the Chapter and earmark them specifically for Chapter use. If the Chapter does have its own bank account(s), it (they) may be through the alumni association or directly on its own. Further, accounts may be either combined or separate when managing operational money vs. scholarship funds.

It is especially beneficial when a Chapter has access to a checking account to support revenue-generation strategies. A checking account opens the doors to the Chapter being able to accept cash, checks (paper or e-check), and electronic transfers. The ability to accept checks simplifies collecting income generated by several of the methods discussed earlier, such as sponsorships, personal donations, and matching gifts. It also enables the Chapter to directly pay for services or to reimburse officers for doing so, typically with a paper or electronic check. Chapter officers, or some subset of the group, might even have a debit card for easier use. This significantly reduces the advanced planning necessary to handle Chapter business and decreases the dependency on the alumni association when executing events and other programs. Accordingly, it steps up the compliance, reporting, and maintenance effort as well.

The Arkansas Alumni Association (AAA) assists Chapters with opening an interest-bearing checking account with First Security Bank of Arkansas. The account is free of monthly fees, includes checks and a debit card, and is managed by the association. One interesting addition is that access to a mobile-banking app has been granted to Chapters.[9]

The Louisiana State University (LSU) alumni Association established very flexible access to Chapter bank accounts. It will either set up an account on behalf of the Chapter to which the Chapter has access to checks to pay bills, or the Chapter is empowered to establish checking and savings accounts at a bank of its choice using its own, Chapter-specific EIN.[10]

When Chapters are opening their own accounts, with or without the association's EIN, it is almost universally accepted to require a minimum of two signatories on the Chapter bank accounts. In many cases, the Chapter President and Treasurer are the two recommended parties, while some scenarios require that one of the two signatories be a representative from the alumni association. Having more than one signatory ensures that the Chapter's banking functions, such as paying bills, are not dependent on the availability and prioritization of a single person. A second overseer also ensures a higher degree of integrity and transparency, minimizing the likelihood of questionable transactions and temptations. From the perspective of the Chapter signatories, not being the sole person responsible for financial accountability can be a comfort.

In the case of the Stanford Alumni Association (SAA), it developed an approach with signatories it deemed helpful in the situation of a defunct Chapter or when officers retire without having passed on the access to the accounts. In addition to the Chapter signatories, two members of the alumni association must also be included as signatories.[11]

When opening a bank account, a Chapter will need to produce the proper paperwork evidencing a business in the state and be prepared to deposit / maintain the minimum balances necessary to avoid fees. Occasionally, an alumni association has made an arrangement with a financial institution in which standard fees have been waived for Chapters. This is generally the case when the Chapters are setting up accounts as a subordinate of the alumni association. Being associated with the alumni association reduces the Chapter's individual risk profile, leading the bank to reduce fees accordingly.

Where possible and cost effective, activating the accounts online and mobile-banking features are of real importance—including appropriate access. In today's world of significant travel, and with many competing priorities, physically going to the bank or even dragging around paper checks that must be handwritten and mailed is not at all reasonable. Most banking institutions do not charge a fee for enabling online access or electronic bill payment, but, just in case, it is a good idea to inquire prior to activating the features.

In short, having access to a bank account makes managing anything financial much easier. Knowing a Chapter's access to either a Chapter-specific checking account or to earmarked funds in the association's account is an important place to start. However a Chapter manages its business, it should never do so through a personal bank account—even if it is unhappy with the approved channels. If the Chapter has the authority to open its own accounts, be mindful of any guidelines regarding number and types of signatories on the account. If none exist, a good rule of thumb is to use the Chapter President and the treasurer.

Valid Business Documentation

Opening any business-related accounts to manage or process money will require proper documentation of a business recognized in your state and by the IRS. At a minimum, the Chapter will need to supply a valid Employer Identification Number (EIN) generated by the IRS.

If the Chapter operates as a subordinate of the alumni association, then the Chapter will either be provided the alumni association's EIN and supporting documentation, or it may need to establish its own EIN. It may also be possible that the alumni association applies for the EIN on behalf of the Chapter.

The University of Florida Alumni Association (UFAA) is an example of the latter. Although each Chapter is required to have its own EIN and bank accounts, the EIN will be obtained through the UFAA.[12]

If the Chapter is independent, it will need to develop and file all appropriate documentation on its own. The next paragraphs help walk a Chapter through what paperwork and steps at a high level would be necessary to become a legal business qualifying for a bank account. We will not venture too deep since each state has different requirements, forms, and processes. This subsection will also not venture past the basic steps necessary to accomplish opening a checking account.

An EIN, also known as a Federal Tax Identification Number (TIN), is a nine-digit number needed for any business, regardless of the type and independent of whether it has or intends to have employees. Just like every legal person in the United States must have a social security number, every legal business must have an EIN. Confirm the Chapter's standing with the alumni association prior to embarking on an organizational or financial strategy. It is likely to have policies in place to assist and / or manage the process.

A Chapter may directly file for an EIN without requiring any prior step and receive its number within minutes. However, should the Chapter have any reason to eventually wish to be its own nonprofit and / or tax-exempt organization or should it specifically be instructed by the alumni association to do so, the Chapter will want to file appropriately in the state prior to filing for a federal EIN.

In the former scenario, if the Chapter simply wishes to obtain an EIN and nothing more, it simply needs to file IRS Form SS-4 online, by fax, or by mail. There is no charge to file for an EIN, and, if done electronically, the EIN can be granted in fifteen minutes or less. Be wary of ads online that charge you to file. The process is quick and easy; there is absolutely no need to pay for assistance. With your Chapter's EIN in hand, it can now open a checking account at a bank.

In the latter scenario, if the Chapter wishes to pursue nonprofit and tax-exempt status or the association guides it down this path, there are several important steps and decisions that must be made prior to filing for the EIN—and they largely happen at the state level. Each state has a different approach and unique requirements; however, there are some commonalities that will be touched upon here.

First, the Chapter will want to have legal rights to its name. Be certain to perform the formal company name search within your Chapter's state (not the state in which the alumni association resides, unless they are the same) prior to submitting any filings. Your central alumni association is likely to have an opinion about the name as well, so be certain to check with your liaison. Often, consideration of the desired website domain name and its availability influences the final determination of the Chapter's name—just a thought worth factoring in.

The Chapter will require the name of a responsible party, sometimes called a registered agent, and a Chapter address. A responsible party must be a resident of the state. The registered agent is the person who is served in the event of legal action or otherwise entitled to receive legal documents on behalf of the Chapter. If the Chapter does not have a specific physical address (PO boxes are not acceptable), the address of the responsible party can be used. Be strategic about this person since your Chapter will not want to refile each time the officers turn over. Choose a person who will have longstanding ties with the Chapter for the foreseeable future. An alternative would be to use a company that acts as a registered agent rather than a person.

One additional high-level decision is that of the Chapter's fiscal year. It is recommended to align the Chapter's fiscal year with that of the alumni association. Most alumni associations have chosen a fiscal year that mirrors that of the academic year, from July 1 to June 30. Others have chosen to align with the calendar year, such as the Texas State Alumni Association, with a fiscal year of January 1 to December 31.[13] Check with the alumni association regarding the official fiscal year to confirm. This date will affect IRS filings. See the later subsection *"State and Federal Tax Implications: Total Annual Receipts and Income Thresholds"* for more on this topic.

The Chapter will also need to know if it plans to pursue designation as nonprofit. The result of this decision impacts the specific forms, required documents, and specific wording that must be understood and included in the Chapter's organizing documents and initial filings. If the Chapter ultimately seeks to be exempt from income tax as a 501(c) entity, then it will need to file upfront as a nonprofit when registering with the state. More information about types and related issues of tax-exempt organizations can be found in the next section, *"State and Federal Tax Implications."*

The next step would be to determine if the Chapter intends to be incorporated or unincorporated. It is recommended that your Chapter seek local professional guidance to clarify the regulations and ramifications. That being said, organization as a corporation is often chosen due to the increased protection from liability and / or when income is expected to be meaningful.

All of the above decisions culminate in the development of the valid business documentation necessary to be a recognized, legal business. These documents are commonly referred to as the "organizing documents." If the Chapter chooses to be a corporation, the organizing documents typically include articles of incorporation that act as a charter to establish the existence of a corporation and, often, bylaws that act as the corporation's operating manual. If the Chapter plans to remain an unincorporated association, the organizing document will most likely be its articles of association, which specify the regulations for the Chapter's operations; the Chapter's purpose; how tasks are to be accomplished within the organization, including the process for appointing directors; and how financial records will be handled.

In either approach—a corporation or an unincorporated association—the organizing documents will require very specific statements regarding the Chapter's purposes and activities, especially if ultimately seeking to be a 501(c)-recognized entity. Your alumni association probably has existing guidance and maybe even sample documents, such as the bylaws, to make the job easier and maintain compliance and consistency with the Chapter network.

The University of Iowa Alumni Association (UIAA) offers clear and detailed guidance on such topics, based on the anticipated size and activities of the Chapters that they call IOWA Clubs. In general, IOWA Clubs are independent from the alumni association; however, they receive significant assistance along the way. The UIAA categorizes these groups into several categories, outlining organizational, legal reporting, tax compliance, UIAA reporting, fiscal responsibility, and federal guidance for each category. They will range from unincorporated associations having only bylaws to more organized nonprofit corporations that are recognized, tax-exempt 503(c)(7) organizations.[14]

Once the Chapter has established its name, determined its structure, and compiled its organizing documents, it can then move forward to file with the state. Generally, there is a small cost to do so. After the documents have been reviewed and processed, the state will likely approve the organization and assign a formation date. Congratulations! The Chapter is a legal entity. Now it can circle back and file for its EIN.

The information presented here was done so to provide a rough understanding of the basic steps to be recognized in your state, then by the IRS, with the specific end goal of establishing the Chapter as a qualified entity to open a bank account. In short, the Chapter will want to:

1. Secure a legal name and appropriate structure through the development of appropriate organizing documents.
2. File and gain recognition with the state as a legal entity (possibly as a nonprofit).
3. File for an EIN with the IRS.
4. Open a checking account.

It may be worth mentioning that at this point the Chapter is recognized by the state and the federal governments as a legal entity—nothing more. No tax exemptions apply, nor do any other special privileges—unless the Chapter did file as a nonprofit entity when submitting its documents to the state. If so, benefits may now expand to include exemption from *state* income tax and possibly other taxes—again, this varies by state.

If the Chapter further desires to be exempt from *federal* income tax and / or it would like to be exempt from paying other *state* taxes, there are a few more steps. The next section, *"State and Federal Tax Implications,"* explores these topics a bit further.

As a reminder, it is possible to seek your Chapter's EIN without first going through the state recognition steps, but it would be ill advised if the Chapter plans to take further steps. Issues arise when the Chapter goes through the process to select a name and files in the state only to find that there is a problem with the initial name chosen. Once a new name is selected, at a minimum, the organizing documents must be updated, possibly triggering the requirement to refile with the state. If so, the filing fee would be required again. Next, a name change must be filed with the IRS, stating the old name and the new name. There is no fee for this change; in fact, there is not even a form. It is done via a simple letter. Luckily, a company name can be changed while keeping the original EIN—it is just more paperwork.

If the Chapter went as far as to open a bank account with the EIN and the now unusable Chapter name, it is a bit more labor intensive. The initial bank accounts must be completely closed and a new set of accounts opened from scratch. Banking practices are less flexible than the IRS EIN recordkeeping, ironically. All of this is to say, save your Chapter the unnecessary hassles, and start with the state filing prior to applying for an EIN.

From a budgeting standpoint, there are a few costs along the way, including organizing fees, annual fees, and change fees. Since they were discussed in the earlier subsection *"Things That Might Need Funding: Behind the Scenes Enhancements,"* I will simply refer you back there for the details.

Once again, each state is unique in how it executes business formation. There are countless variations within each state for steps 1 and 2. Seek central alumni association and professional guidance prior to embarking on any of these paths to ensure your Chapter receives the most explicit, up-to-date, and appropriate guidance for your Chapter and state.

Now that the Chapter has a reasonable understanding of how to establish a Chapter bank account for cash, checks, and electronic transfers, it is time to discuss accounts specifically to enable credit card payments.

Credit Card Payments 101

Several alumni associations provide a mechanism through which Chapters (or technically the alumni association) may capture payments via credit cards. If this describes your circumstances, feel free to skip to the next relevant topic after you have determined what, if anything, the association is charging for use of the system. It may be absorbing the processing fees, or it may be passing them through to the Chapter at some predetermined rate. If you are interested in learning more, let's dive in.

If the Chapter wishes to accept payment for event tickets at the time of registration or other types of payments / contributions online, it will need to explore credit card processing options. There are some important basics to understand. First, there is a very big difference between:

- Orders submitted by alumni online.
- Orders placed over the phone.
- Orders placed in person in which a card is in hand. All three are handled differently by processors and have different pricing.

Orders submitted by alumni online are considered of moderate risk and priced accordingly. These would be orders processed on a website from a computer or using a mobile phone with a mobile payment page. In either case, these orders are submitted directly by the customer using their own credit card.

However, orders placed over the phone are the highest risk and have the most expensive processing fees. An example of a phone order is when an alumnus is in transit and uses the time to call the Chapter in an effort to register for an event. The reason orders over the phone are at such high risk for fraud is that the person technically typing in the credit card information is not the card holder; they cannot see the card at all to confirm that the voice on the other end of the line even has it, much less that it matches that person's identification.

Credit card processors use sophisticated algorithms to detect fraud. When the same computer (or technically the same IP address) is used to enter many different names / addresses / credit card numbers, it sets off a flag, signaling possible fraudulent activity, and shuts down the gateway. To get around that, the credit card processors created a specific processing service to account for this phone order scenario—and they often charge through the roof for it!

Orders taken in person with the credit card in hand are assumed to be the lowest risk scenario and, thus, have a low processing rate. Historically, this has been done by swiping a card. Here is where they may get you, however. In order to swipe cards, the Chapter will need swiping equipment and possibly an app if the swiping is done via a phone or tablet. Depending on the provider, the equipment and / or the apps may have to be purchased on a per-device basis. Sometimes, the swipers are offered at no charge, which means that, typically, the charges for processing the cards will be a little higher. Your Chapter will pay either way. Luckily, this too is already evolving into a more convenient process. Most processing systems now are compatible with your phone's camera and accept a picture taken of the credit card. No longer is swiping technology necessary. Either way, you still have physical access to the credit card in the presence of its owner, so the risk profile is the same as are the fees, typically.

In addition to the three methods of payments discussed above, the credit card processing world also consists of understanding gateways, merchant accounts, and software vendors. The overall concepts are identical to the earlier conversation in the "*Mobile Giving Now for Everyone, Big and Very Small: Cost Considerations*" subsection of the book. Whether credit cards are processed through mobile pages, apps, or websites, the backend processing issues and requirements are the same. To learn more about the need for merchant accounts and other related considerations, refer back to that part of the text.

Luckily, the industry has come a long way in a short period of time. This is much easier today than it was even three years ago. For most alumni Chapter events, taking orders online, selling tickets at the door, and accepting fundraising payments / donations are where the Chapter will experience the highest need for credit cards.

Payment-Processing Options

There are several options for this service. Here are a few to consider—all of which do need evidence of a business to be established. Options range from use-specific vendors, to simple online payment buttons, to broader acceptance of payment types, to existing website-integrated options, to full-service options requiring integration. They range in ease of use, flexibility, and costs.

Since many Chapters might only require payments for event registrations, an event-specific management and payment portal is a consideration. A couple of popular options include Eventbrite and Cvent. In this case, the Chapter would set up the event information and tickets on the event-management site and just link to it. Very little needs to be known at all about what is happening in the background or by whom. These systems are nice because they have added features that support event management, such as capturing names for name tags and reminder notifications, and no need to set up a separate merchant account. The downsides are that pricing is very high, and they only process payments for events and nothing else. By proving a single path, the effort to set them up is low, but they can charge just about anything and get away with it.

For example, at the time of printing, Eventbrite charged 2.5 percent + $0.99 per transaction plus an additional 3 percent. So if your Chapter were selling $20 event tickets, and fifty people registered, your processing fees would amount to about $104.50 of the $1,000 generated. That's about 10.5 percent you are losing. To be fair, they do offer a special 501(c)(3) rate that would drop the fees to $99.50 (10 percent vs. 10.5 percent). It is a very expensive service, but it may be worth the convenience.

Another option is credit-card-less payments offered by few others than PayPal. A very basic PayPal package enables the ability to create a new "button" for each sales item that can be placed on the website. When clicked, the item is paid for by transferring money from the buyer's own PayPal account to the Chapter's PayPal account. The upsides for this approach are that it does not require much technical skill to execute, there is no need for a merchant account, and PayPal is widely trusted. The glaring downsides are that it requires every customer to have a PayPal account from which to pay, there is no option for entering a quantity for an item (like two tickets), the Chapter must transfer money out of the PayPal account and into its checking account from time to time, and it is a high-priced option with very high fees for lesser-used functions such as returns. Though not as high as event management vendors, the pricing still punishes the user for taking the easy way out. Additionally, phone orders, at-the-door processing, quantities of more than one, and variable payments, such as whatever the final price was for an auction item, are not supported—as there are no credit cards used and buttons are specific to one item at a fixed price.

There are several options beyond those above, offering various levels of benefits and support—all at lower pricing. After absorbing the small amount of information presented in this text, you are already armed with more information than the average person and are in a better position to make more cost-effective choices. For example, one such option provides a custom, mobile payment page embracing the payment button concept. It also has a field to enter your own payment, great for use at auctions when final prices are not known in advance. Basic upsides are a much more modern platform, very easy set-up, no technical skill needed, no separate merchant account set-up, revenue automatically deposited in the Chapter's standard checking account (or the association's account), and very low rates. Using the same example above, processing fees would amount to $44.00, or 4.4 percent of the $1,000. There really are no downsides for this type of approach.

From there, pricing can go down even lower, but that typically requires a high volume of transactions, inking a custom contract with a gateway provider / processor, and the addition of monthly fees. This is a very fluid field with services and pricing in constant motion. This overview should arm your leadership with enough information to ask some good questions. If you or your team hits a wall, reach out to us at SACL. We can help you through it, or we can provide access to our specially designed, alumni-Chapter-centric partner solution, often with even better pricing than going direct.

One recommendation I would offer, if feeling ambitious, would be to model your expected types of payments by event or program (membership drive, event tickets, auctions, mobile donations, etc.) and to think through the structure of payments (different ticket options, like member or guest tickets) and the average price for each by event and the approximate number of each. Consider if the items your alumni might be purchasing are fixed fees, like T-shirts, and if they may be purchasing more than one at a time; also consider if purchases may be unknown amounts until the purchase, such as auction winnings. Combine that information with the pricing details provided by each payment processor, and see what is most advantageous for your Chapter's situation on an annual basis. One more thought: if the overlapping costs are not prohibitive, the Chapter might choose to embrace more than one of the payment types above.

The need to accept credit card payments is really a basic requirement these days, whether it is for event tickets, membership dues, scholarship contributions, or something else. But the digital world is so cluttered by players that either confuse would-be clients with a matrix of rates or punish them with ridiculous high pricing. Many Chapters either simply replicate what someone else has already done or throw up their hands and walk away. I get that. The experience was difficult for me as well. That is why I have spent countless hours researching, interviewing, and modeling options—so you don't have to. This is also where my MBA from a finance school goes to work for us all!

60-Second Takeaway

Although strategizing effective ways to generate Chapter income is a worthy pursuit, it should not supersede understanding the flow and costs of receiving and processing the money. This applies to standard checking accounts for processing cash and checks, as well as processors and merchant accounts for credit cards. It all begins with the alumni association and understanding the policies in place. For some Chapters, having their own bank accounts is not an option, but having money earmarked within the central account is. Others have significant influence over Chapter-specific accounts managed by the alumni association, while the remaining Chapters have the flexibility to establish their own independent accounts.

If opening a checking account, the Chapter will need to produce the appropriate paperwork evidencing its recognized-business status, including producing the Chapter's (or association's) EIN at a minimum. If the Chapter has grander plans, it may pursue developing organizing documents and filing in its state for recognition as a legal entity, maybe even as a nonprofit entity.

Once a checking account is established, the Chapter may further consider if enabling alumni payments through online methods with or without credit cards is a priority. If so, there are several tiers of options with varying pricing, breadth of services, and ease of use. Modeling the types, pricing, and quantity of likely transactions, along with processing costs, should drive analysis of the best option. Prudently evaluating the cost of various providers is one important step in demonstrating proper fiduciary responsibility on behalf of the Chapter.

Make It Happen Checklist

☐ Gain clarity regarding the Chapter's ability to either drive revenue into a Chapter-specific checking account or have incoming funds within the association's collective account earmarked for the Chapter's use.

☐ Reach out to the Chapter liaison, and talk through the Chapter leadership's ideas.

☐ If the central alumni association has a pathway established for receiving money, conform to it.

☐ If there is not an established pathway and the central alumni association does not object, proceed with steps to open a checking account.

☐ If the Chapter has no ambition about becoming nonprofit or federally tax exempt, simply file for its EIN.

☐ Otherwise, begin by evaluating the costs associated with becoming a recognized entity and the likely ongoing maintenance costs. If still favorable, continue:

   » Choose a legally available name within the Chapter's state that has a reasonably related website address available.

   » Generate the appropriate organizing documents.

   » File the necessary forms with the state to be recognized as a nonprofit entity.

   » Request an Employer Identification Number (EIN) from the IRS.

☐ Open at least a checking account and possibly a savings account, if appropriate, with a bank.

☐ Update the website with the information on where to mail paper check payments.

☐ If credit card processing is a priority, determine if the association provides a vehicle and at what cost.

☐ If the Chapter will be responsible for the credit card processing, evaluate likely order types, order quantities, and the monetary size of transactions per month and processing costs to select the best processing partner.

☐ Open the appropriate software and merchant accounts, if not already bundled, linking them back to the Chapter's checking account if possible.

☐ The Chapter is ready to accept cash, checks, and credit cards, so put it to work!

State and Federal Tax Implications

Issues of state and federal taxes are complex and vary by widely based factors, including but not limited to the legal status of the alumni association, the legal status of the Chapter, how long the organizations have been in existence, in what state either might reside, what paperwork is filed with what governing bodies, and more. Therefore, there are many variations on these scenarios. The information provided below includes generalizations and is not intended to substitute for guidance from a licensed professional. It should, however, be enough to prepare a Chapter leader to begin an intelligent conversation. Prior to embarking on any strategy with potential state or federal tax implications, seek counsel from the alumni association and a local tax professional.

As referenced briefly in the previous and other sections, it is possible for a qualifying Chapter to:

- Avoid paying income tax to the state and federal governments.
- Receive donations that are deductible from federal income tax by donors.
- Avoid paying sales tax among other taxes to the state.
- Qualify for reduced-rate postage.

A foundational understanding of the basics for this conversation begins with knowing the difference between a *nonprofit* classification and a *tax-exempt* designation. *Nonprofit* is a classification relevant to state laws and regulations. *Tax exempt* is a federal concept managed by IRS regulations. Filing for non-profit status and federal tax exemption are separate and independent processes.

A Chapter may inherit some of the aforementioned benefits from the association, or it may have to establish the right to claim them on its own. If inherited, a Chapter may qualify for any or all of the benefits above through a combination of its legal status as a subordinate of a qualifying central alumni association and the state in which the Chapter resides. If the Chapter operates as an independent organization and wishes to pursue a particular 501(c) status, then it will need to undertake the process largely on its own.

The process to properly file and achieve all bullets listed above can be a bit complicated and circular. However, it can be boiled down to five big, generalized steps, the first two of which have been touched upon in a recent section called "*Collecting and Handling the Money: Valid Business Documentation*":

1. File and become a legal, nonprofit entity in your state (preferably as a corporation, due to added protections and likely income generation in the future)—this step may grant *state income-tax exemption.*
2. File for and receive a federal EIN.
3. Apply for and become an IRS-recognized 501(c)(3) or 501(c)(7)-designated entity (preferably a public charity, when selecting a type)—this bestows the exemption from *federal income tax.*
   » A 501(c)(3)-designated entity is a charitable organization (with respect to Chapters, often organized for charitable and educational purposes). It offers federal tax exemption, plus the benefit of the receipt of tax-deductible donations and the possibility of qualifying for nonprofit postage rates.
   » A 501(c)(7)-designated entity is a federally tax-exempt social club. Contributions received are *not* tax deductible by the donors, and there is no access to reduced postal rates.
4. Return to the state with a 501(c) designation, and file for additional tax benefits, such as a sales tax in some states.
5. Apply for and become approved for *reduced-rate postage* from the US Postal Service, if a 501(c)(3)-designated entity.

Each of the above has financial benefits for the Chapter and, in one case, financial benefits for the alumni. How much depends on the Chapter's behavior and the volume of money flowing through the Chapter, among other factors.

The order of presentation above is important to minimize rework and duplicate costs, in addition to a few being predicated on one earlier in the list. Step 1 should be completed prior to starting Step 2, which must be completed before starting either Steps 3 or 4. Step 3 is recommended to be completed prior to Step 4. Step 5 can begin any time after the completion of Step 3.

Also important is the thought process that goes into deciding to pursue any of the above classifications or designations. Each one brings additional detailed compliance and reporting requirements that, if neglected, can result in revocation of the status and possible penalties. The Chapter leadership should thoroughly vet the opportunities prior to proceeding with any one of them. It is also possible to stop anywhere in the process once the goal has been achieved. For example, maybe the Chapter has no need for the reduced-postage-rate benefit or simply deems that the costs and compliance requirements outweigh the benefit. There is no requirement that the Chapter must pursue it. The Chapter may choose just how far it wishes to go down the state and / or federal pathways.

The next subsections will look at the primary tax considerations affecting Chapter finances from two perspectives: if the Chapter is organizationally part of the central alumni association and if the Chapter is independent. There are several state and federal issues that can be somewhat circular. I will do my best to make the primary concepts as straightforward as possible. Once again, I remind you that this information is not intended to replace professional tax or legal guidance. It is a broad, high-level explanation to assist you in preparing for a conversation with your alumni association and local industry professionals.

501(c)(3) vs. 501(c)(7) and Tax Deductible Donations

TITLE 26, Subtitle A, CHAPTER 1, Subchapter F, PART I, Section 501 of the US Code (Section 501) entitled **Exemption from Tax on Corporations, Certain Trusts, etc.** introduces the general tax-exemption guidelines for organizations. **Publication 557: Tax-exempt Status for Your Organization** specifically documents the rules and procedures for organizations that seek exemption from federal income tax under section 501(a) of the Internal Revenue Code.

If the Chapter is a legal subordinate of the alumni association, it may benefit from the association's tax-exempt status—or it may not. This will be known by the association.

An independent Chapter seeking exemption from state and federal taxes should first establish itself as a nonprofit entity in the state, then determine if it wishes to pursue federal tax-exemption status. A great place to start is with the current revision of IRS **Publication 557** on the IRS website. **Publication 557** discusses several types of tax-exempt organizations. Alumni Chapters typically fall into one of two categories: 501(c)(3) or 501(c)(7).

Per **Publication 557**, an organization may qualify as a 501(c)(3)-tax-exempt organization if it is organized and operated for one or more of the following purposes: religious, charitable, scientific, testing for public safety, literary, educational, fostering national or international amateur sports competition, and / or the prevention of cruelty to children or animals. Examples include nonprofit old-age homes, parent-teacher associations, charitable hospitals, alumni associations, schools, chapters of the Red Cross or the Salvation Army, and churches. Local alumni Chapters can qualify as a Section 501(c)(3) entity if organized and operated for the purpose of advancement of education and possibly charity, depending on your bylaws and activities.

A 501(c)(7) designation describes social and recreational clubs organized specifically for pleasure, recreation, and other similar nonprofit purposes. Per **Publication 557**, examples of typical qualifying organization include college alumni associations not described in Section 501(c)(3); college fraternities and sororities operating chapter houses for students; country clubs; amateur hunting, fishing, tennis, swimming, and other sports clubs; dinner clubs that provide a meeting place, library, and dining room for members; hobby clubs; garden clubs; and variety clubs.

The lines between these two designations seem to be gray with respect to the alumni Chapters. The best determinant is related to the intended and stated purpose(s) of the Chapter. If the primary purpose is to further the educational objectives of the university, then your Chapter may best be classified as a 501(c)(3) organization. Evidence of such intention would include the funding of scholarships, enhancing the student educational experience through welcome and send-off events, and contributions to the university's foundation.

Perhaps the Chapter may have qualifying charitable purposes, such as demonstrated by the Kellogg Network DFW discussed in an earlier section "*Things that Might Need Funding: Stepping Up the Game.*" The Kellogg Network DFW not only has a third-party charitable purpose embedded in its bylaws but also makes good on its intentions by raising money annually for Big Brothers Big Sisters. Otherwise, if the primary purpose is to foster bonding and camaraderie among its members with a specified common interest, then your Chapter may best be classified as a 501(c)(7) organization.

The local Chapters of Harvard alumni are independent from the alumni association. The Harvard Alumni Association (HAA) openly gives these approved organizations the choice as to how to structure their Chapters. They are free to file as nonprofit organizations and free to pursue tax-exempt status as a 501(c) entity. Chapters may choose to apply as a 501(c)(3) or 501(c)(7) organization, or the international equivalent, if they so wish.[1]

Penn Alumni Relations addresses the option of pursuing either a 501(c)(3) designation, a 501(c)(7) designation, or neither, technically leaving the decision up to the Chapters, much like HAA. However, in this case, Penn Alumni Relations does make the following suggestion:

Given the social nature of our regional clubs, 501(c)(7) status is likely the more appropriate choice.[2]

From a different perspective, the West Point Association of Graduates (WPAOG) affords its Chapters the option to pursue or not to pursue recognition as a 501(c)(3) entity without any reference to the typical alternative of a 501(c)(7) designation.[3] It does, however, offer two more options for consideration: designation as a 501(c)(19) or a 501(c)(23), which provide for tax exemption under section 501(a) for organizations that benefit veterans of the United States Armed Forces.[4] The IRS defines a 501(c)(19) organization as

> a post or organization of past or present members of the Armed Forces of the United States, or an auxiliary unit or society of, or a trust or foundation for any such post or organization. [5]

A 501(c)(23) entity is defined as an association organized before 1880, with more than 75 percent of its members as past or present members of the United States Armed Forces, that has a principal purpose of providing insurance and other benefits to veterans or their dependents.[6] This option seems less applicable at face value.

All four designations afford the Chapter tax exemption from federal income tax. The 501(c)(3) designation qualifies Chapters to receive tax-deductible, charitable contributions, such as some membership dues, and opens the door to file for reduced, nonprofit postage. Under certain membership (90 percent of membership must be war veterans) and purpose criteria, contributions made to a 501(c)(19)- or 501(c)(23)-designated entity may also qualify as tax deductible for the donor.[7] It is true, however, that requirements to meet the qualifications for a tax-deductible contribution are more restrictive for these two veterans organizations than for a 501(c)(3) entity. Conversely, under no circumstance is a contribution to a 501(c)(7) Chapter tax deductible for the donor.

Once a Chapter has become a 501(c)-recognized entity, there are several behaviors it has agreed to uphold. A couple such behaviors are keeping accurate accounting books and carefully avoiding any conflict of interest according to the IRS definition. The books are likely to be managed by the Chapter Treasurer, while all officers should keep an eye on such conflicts of interest.

Returning to tax-deductible contributions, contributions to a 501(c)(3) charitable organization are called "charitable contributions"; according to the IRS, a charitable contribution is

> a donation or gift to, or for the use of, a qualified organization. It is voluntary and is made without getting, or expecting to get, anything of equal value.[8]

The IRS provides a guide to better understanding this topic, known as **Publication 526, Charitable Contributions**. Charitable contributions could be cash donations and donations of goods at fair market value, as well as gifts of stock. Memberships, sponsorships, and event tickets, minus any value received in return, could qualify as tax deductible. As the vast majority of income received by the Chapter is likely to be in some form of cash, this discussion will focus on cash transactions. The IRS defines a cash contribution as "paid by cash, check, electronic funds transfer, debit card, credit card or payroll deduction."[9]

The most straightforward example is when alumni make unrestricted cash donations to the Chapter. The donation in its entirety is tax deductible. A contribution made to support the scholarship program is also cleanly tax deductible. Chapter membership dues may or may not be deductible. They would be deductible in entirety if the membership costs $75 or less and the only benefits are free or discounted admission to the events; free or discounted parking; preferred access to goods or services; discounts on the purchase of goods and services; or other intangible benefits, such as offering member spotlights on the web. If the membership costs more than $75 and / or includes more substantial benefits, like a commemorative university coffee table book, a golf shirt, or a complimentary ticket to an event in which food is provided, then the deduction is the result of the membership minus the fairly monetized value of the goods and services received.

If the Chapter is leveraging special events themselves to raise income, then the deductible element is the ticket price minus the value of any and all goods and services received at the event, including but not limited to food and beverage and giveaways such as a book authored by the speaker.

If a Chapter hosts a silent auction and one of the alumni wins a one-week vacation package to Fiji for $1,000, none of the $1,000 is deductible. Since the value of the goods and services cost $2,500 and clearly exceeds what was paid, there is no deduction.

One last example revolves around sponsorships. A sponsorship minus the goods and services included is generally deductible. A sponsorship package might include complimentary tickets to an event, recognition in a slide presentation or from the podium, a table where marketing materials can be displayed, the reception food, and other benefits. In this situation, the deductible portion would be the difference between the sponsorship donation and the value of the reception food plus the specific value attributed to each complimentary event ticket. All of the other benefits listed are intangible.

The responsibility to determine the deductibility of each contribution falls to the Chapter, as does the responsibility to make receipts available. There are some fairly detailed guidelines around when, for how much, and in what form receipts must be made available to the donors. However, it is easier to manage, more considerate, and just good form to provide receipts across the board for any and all payments / contributions / donations made to the Chapter. Then, there is no guesswork.

When providing IRS acceptable receipts for cash items, the Chapter should include the following for each contribution:

- The legal name of the Chapter
- The date of the payment / contribution
- The amount that is deductible

If the Chapter provides receipts at the time of each contribution, all bases on behalf of the Chapter and the alumni are covered regardless of the amount of the individual contribution or cumulative contributions during the tax year. As a courtesy to those supporting the Chapter, it is advisable for the Chapter to do what it can to ensure alumni receive the full allowable tax dedication for their contributions. You want them to want to donate again. Don't let your leadership team's lax behavior be the reason they do not. From there, it is up to the alumni to properly file the charitable contributions on their annual tax returns.

The 501(c)(3) designation not only renders the Chapter exempt from federal income tax and provides access to tax-exempt charitable deductions for donors but also opens the doors to several types of funding not available to others. Earlier in the book, I touched on giving days, matching gifts, and volunteer grants. All three of those are only available to 501(c)(3)-designated organizations. Being classified as a 501(c)(3) entity is not the only criteria, nor does it guarantee a successful outcome; however, it is the first rung on the ladder.

There are some substantial costs associated with the process to file an application for a 501(c)(3) or 501(c)(7) designation. These costs were initially presented in an earlier section, but I will briefly repeat them here. Fees are the same for filing either the IRS Form 1023 or Form 1023-EZ for a 501(c)(3) or for filing IRS Form 1024 for a 501(c)(7) and are based on the Chapter's recent income above or below $10,000. If below that threshold, the charge will be $400; otherwise, pencil in $850.

There is one special exception for very small Chapters. If the Chapter generates less than $5,000 annually, the IRS will waive the need to request a 501(c)(3) determination letter and the fee altogether.[10] The Chapter may simply declare its status. Some Chapters that qualify for this special circumstance still choose to submit a formal application, since it may be challenging for both the Chapter and the donors to reap all of the benefits of the designation without written confirmation from the IRS. The window during which a Chapter may qualify may be small. Once it ramps up a scholarship program or truly embraces strategies presented in the book, that window may start to close rapidly.

Developing and submitting the proper paperwork to have achieved the desired designation is one thing. How the Chapter defined its purpose and behavior on paper in its documents is referred to as having been "organized" for that desired purpose. Then, there is how the Chapter conducts its activities throughout the year, referred to as how it has "operated." At any time, the IRS may review how the Chapter organized itself and has been operating for the past several years to ensure that it continues to meet the qualifications of the tax-exempt designation. The Chapter could fail the test if not in compliance. One way a failure could occur is that the Chapter was organized as a 501(c)(3) to support education but the only Chapter activities were game-watching parties. If the Chapter is organized to support education, then its activities must absolutely reflect that purpose. Funding scholarships and supporting admissions are two possible activities that would evidence the support of education.

If a Chapter were to have its tax-exemption status revoked, there could be serious consequences. Penalties might include the requirement to pay back taxes, the requirement to pay back state income taxes, and the retrospective loss off deductions for alumni donors, to name a few. If a Chapter is not truly formed and operated for a charitable cause or as a social club and cannot comply with bylaws stating that it is, then the pursuit of a 501(c)(3) designation is not the right move for the Chapter.

In short, an independent Chapter interested in seeking federal tax exemption generally decides between a 501(c)(3)-charitable organization, a 501(c)(7)-social club, or, under very unique circumstances, a 501(c)(19)- or 501(c)(23)-veterans organization designation. All but 501(c)(7) entities offer donors that added benefit of tax-deductible charitable contributions.

Although the upside of operating as a 501(c)-recognized entity can be pretty rosy, there are some very real costs, reporting, and compliance issues to consider. Only your Chapter's leadership team will be able to effectively weigh the two sides. If your Chapter is eligible to pursue such a designation, I would suggest it is well worth the time to run the numbers—and seek professional guidance before casting the final vote.

When to Pay Income Tax

In general, there are two primary situations in which income tax applies to Chapters. The first one relates to the actual status and exemptions for which the Chapter qualifies. The second relates to the type of income the Chapter may be generating. In the first scenario, a Chapter will not have to pay state and federal income tax if it falls into one of the following situations:

- It is a complete subordinate of the alumni association and is not responsible for any finances, as they are managed entirely by the association.
- It is an independent Chapter, has been granted a nonprofit, tax-exempt status, and is exempt from paying income or revenue tax federally and within its state—and it did not participate in any activities that would trigger unrelated business income tax.

In most other circumstances, the Chapters will need to pay income tax. Since there are fifty-two states and other jurisdictions, there are likely to be fifty-two different approaches to this topic. The bullets above are very high-level generalizations, but the concepts are reasonable. Some Chapters do not have any individual legal identity at all. The association receives event money and pays for applicable charges out of the single association account. There is no income tax concern of any kind for these Chapters.

While still legal subordinates of the alumni association, other Chapters do have individual, Chapter-specific accounts established under their own EIN or that of the association. Since Chapters in this case are still legal subordinates, they are unlikely to be individually responsible for state income tax—but this is where it starts to get a little murky. Insights from a professional or the association are prudent.

Independent Chapters are likely to be responsible for income or revenue tax unless they have established themselves as an entity exempt from such taxes. The process for doing so varies greatly from state to state, but an important step for the Chapter is to have established itself as a nonprofit entity when filing the forms to become a legally recognized organization. This text has made the assumption from the beginning that if a Chapter were to become a legal entity with the state, it would do so by taking the nonprofit pathway. With respect to other state-specific steps necessary to qualify for income / revenue tax exemption, seek a local tax professional to review your Chapter's situation and local laws and guidelines. From a federal perspective, that was discussed in the previous subsection. Having a 501(c)(3), 501(c)(7), 501(c)(19), or 501(c)(23) designation absolves the Chapter from paying applicable federal income tax—unless it participated in any activities that would trigger unrelated business income tax.

The University of Colorado Boulder (CU Boulder) Alumni Association, founded in 1882 and serving more than 280,000 alumni[11] through more than forty chapters and clubs,[12] frames it nicely for its Chapters. In this case, the Chapters are legally independent from the alumni association. Chapters have the option to structure their organizations as they see fit. Some Chapters have filed as a nonprofit at the state level and stopped there; some have taken it further and have become a 501(c)(3)-tax-exempt organization at the federal level. For those Chapters that have *not* sought any form of income-tax exemption, the CU Boulder Alumni Association reminds them:

> Any revenue taken in by the chapter or club may be considered taxable income at the state or federal level, and the chapter or club leadership is responsible for filing state and federal tax returns on its income. The University of Colorado Boulder and the CU-Boulder Alumni Association cannot be held responsible for any tax liability accrued by chapters or clubs. Chapters and clubs should build funds into their operating budget to help cover these liabilities.[13]

Interestingly, the CU Boulder Alumni Association does offer an out to those Chapters. If the Chapters were to process their own revenue (ticket sales, sales of merchandise, etc.) through a payment-processing vendor like Eventbrite, the Chapters would be responsible for filing the IRS Form 1099-K, Payment Card and Third-party Network Transactions. Instead, if they choose to use the association's payment-processing system for collecting revenue, it would eliminate the Chapter tax liability. In other words, since the alumni association directly received the payments, the association would be responsible for accounting for the income rather than the Chapter. One twist to leveraging this loophole is that the money collected by the CU Boulder Alumni Association on behalf of the Chapter cannot be transferred into the Chapter's control following the event or program. It must remain with the alumni association until directly paid out to a vendor on the Chapter's behalf.[14]

The second issue presented relates to taxable "unrelated business income" for nonprofit, tax-exempt organizations. Not only does this concept apply at the state level, it will also affect federal income taxes. According to the IRS:

For most organizations, an activity is an unrelated business (and subject to unrelated business income tax) if it meets three requirements: It is a trade or business, it is regularly carried on, and it is not substantially related to furthering the exempt purpose of the organization.[15]

One example would be an alumni Chapter selling advertising space in the Chapter newsletters. This advertising income would be considered unrelated taxable income, likely for the state and certainly by the IRS. If unrelated business income taxes are applicable, plan to make payments on a quarterly basis once the estimated taxes reach $500. There are a few exceptions and lots of grey space related to this topic, so I will leave it there for you to sort out with a local professional. Federally, the IRS offers additional information in its **Publication 598: Tax on Unrelated Business Income of Exempt Organizations**. This is an excellent topic for which to seek the advice of the alumni association and a local tax professional. Just be aware that state and / or federal taxes may be a consideration for your Chapter when building a budget.

A Closer Look at Tax-Free Purchases

It is possible through various channels that a Chapter may be exempt from paying state sales and any one or more of the following: property tax, franchise taxes, and other taxes. For the immediate discussion, we will focus on sales tax since it is a more universally common benefit across the United States. This can be especially meaningful when residing in states levying the highest sales taxes, such as Louisiana (9.98 percent), Tennessee (9.46 percent), Arkansas (9.3 percent), Alabama (9.01 percent), and Washington (8.92 percent).[16]

The Chapter needs to spend as little money as possible while executing revenue-generating efforts. As discussed earlier in the text, just as important as generating income is the effort to minimize necessary costs. One area in which to focus on minimizing costs is state sales tax. The Chapter has nothing to show for money spent on paying sales tax. Don't do it if you do not have to.

Just as a clarification, sales tax is a state tax issue and is unrelated to federal IRS tax-exemption status. Chapters may benefit from sales-tax exemption if a Chapter is a legal subordinate of a central alumni association qualifying for a sales-tax exemption, in which the exemption may be passed down to Chapters that are either: (a) in the same state or (b) in selected states through waivers.

Just because a Chapter is a legal subordinate of the central alumni association does not grant automatic exemption from paying sales tax. First, the central alumni association must *qualify* for the state tax exemption itself; not all do. For example, the Louisiana State University (LSU) Alumni Association is not exempt from paying sales tax.[17] Even if its alumni Chapters were legal subordinates of the association (which they are not), it does not have the privilege to pass down to them.

Next, if the sales-tax exemption does *exist* and *is* transferrable, the Chapter must typically be in the same state as the alumni association. The Sul Ross State University Alumni Association, representing its 23,000 alumni and twelve chapters and groups[18] located in the State of Texas, addresses this issue in its Chapter handbook when it writes:

> The University tax-exempt, not-for-profit status only covers goods and services purchased in Texas.[19]

Another similar situation with a twist can be found with the University of Florida Alumni Association (UFAA), which is a recognized, nonprofit organization qualified for sales-tax exemption in its home state of Florida. The exemption does pass down to the alumni Chapters located in Florida. The UFAA recommends to out-of-state Chapters that they must file independently for sales-tax exemption with their states.[20]

The last scenario resulting in sales-tax exemption is related to waivers. For example, the Stanford Alumni Association (SAA) located in California holds a waiver on sales tax in Massachusetts and Washington, DC. This means that subordinate Chapters in those states can also waive sales tax on purchases in support of engaging local alumni in those states.[21]

The Johns Hopkins Alumni Association (JHAA) has actually gone through the process to qualify for sales-tax exemption in thirty-two states. Therefore, its Chapters, which are extensions of the alumni association, are also eligible to benefit from its sales-tax exemption in those thirty-two states.[22]

One additional point related to the validity of sales-tax exemption is predicated on the purpose of the purchase. The products purchased must be for use in supporting the mission of the Chapter. If the Chapter runs a little side business to raise money, purchases to support the side business are not exempt from sales tax. For example, several alumni operate a very small flower service around the holidays, which benefits the Chapter. Supplies purchased for the flower business are not exempt from sales tax, and the income generated is not exempt from income tax.

Lastly, it is the responsibility of any organization exempt from sales tax to supply proof for the retailer's records. In some cases, the state provides a form that is required to be completed and left with the retailer. Some companies have chosen to approach the situation more efficiently, eliminating the physical paperwork while still maintaining the necessary records to justify the reduced sales tax it will be reporting to the state. Office Depot is one such company. If you present your sales-tax-exemption paperwork to a cashier, you are invited to open a nonprofit account. Going forward, each subsequent purchase for the Chapter will simply be linked with the nonprofit account, negating the need for hardcopy printouts each time.

It goes without saying that the tax relationships between the Chapter, the alumni association, and each state are not standard or formulaic. One thing is for certain, however, and that is that your alumni association will be fully aware of if and how your Chapter may benefit from any sales-tax exemption. Your first stop should be your alumni Chapter liaison.

In order for the Chapter to maximize the sales-tax-exemption benefit, it is important that all officers and representatives that will be making purchases or establishing contracts for goods or services on behalf of the Chapter are aware of the sales-tax exemption. They should also have easy access to the state-supplied verification form or the retailer-specific account numbers necessary to enable the exemption to be applied.

In short, it is possible that a Chapter may not be required to pay sales tax, by way of its relationship with the association or on a Chapter's own merit. If that is the case, be certain your Chapter leadership team is aware, can identify applicable purchases, and has the information / tools / paperwork to utilize the benefit when the opportunity presents itself.

Total Annual Receipts and Income Thresholds

One last overarching topic we will discuss revolves around a Chapter's total income. All recognized businesses are required to file annual returns with the federal government. If the Chapter is a 501(c)(3)-, 501(c)(7)-, 501(c)(19)-, or 501(c)(23)-tax-exempt organization, it will be required to file some variation of IRS Form 990. If the Chapter is legally a subordinate of the central alumni association, the central alumni association most likely handles the IRS filings. In that case, the Chapter simply needs to work with the association to provide any material it may need.

On the other hand, Chapters that are independent from the central alumni association are required to handle IRS filings and compliance on their own. This section is geared toward those Chapters. The IRS Form 990 is the annual return document required for most organizations exempt from income tax under section 501(a), which includes 501(c) organizations. Thus, all four 501(c)-designated entities discussed are required to file an IRS Form 990 annually. There are several versions of the Form 990 as follows:

- Form 990, *Return of Organization Exempt from Income Tax*
- Form 990-EZ, *Short Form Return of Organization Exempt from Income Tax*
- Form 990-N (also called the Form 990 e-postcard)
- Form 990-PF, *Return of Private Foundation or Section 4947(a)(1) Nonexempt Charitable Trust Treated as a Private Foundation*
- A series of individual, applicable schedules

It is unlikely that the Chapter is categorized as a private foundation (Chapters are typically public charities), so that eliminates the Form 990-PF from this discussion. The determination of which version of the form is required largely depends on the income the Chapter receives and the assets it has. The IRS refers to such income as "gross receipts." According to the IRS:

> *Gross receipts* are the total amounts the organization received from all sources during its annual accounting period, without subtracting any costs or expenses.[23]

As the specific form to be filed is significantly dependent on income, growing the Chapter's income as discussed in this book might reasonably have an impact on the Chapter's typical tax filings. The following table lists the filing thresholds for the Form 990 series.

Gross Receipts (All Income)		Total Assets	Form
Normally ≤ $50,000	and	Any	990-N
< $200,000	and	< $500,000	990-EZ or 990
≥ $200,000	and	≥ $500,000	990

Most Chapters fall into the $50,000 or less income category, thus only needing to file the Form 990-N. Its filing process is online and quick, requiring only minimal information about the organization and taking only minutes. Although it is quick and easy, it is not optional. Should the Chapter neglect to file for three years, it will lose its tax-exempt status altogether. This would be a disaster. The Chapter would be subject to penalties and back taxes to the IRS and to the state. If a 501(c)(3), donors would be subject to the deductions becoming invalid. Thus, do not overlook filing the form.

If the Chapter falls into the category requiring a Form 990-EZ, there is a significant step-up in the filing effort and information disclosed. This form requires a breakdown of programs performed as well as officers and directors by name, accompanied by other details. It is important to note that all Form 990s submitted to the IRS are public information. Accordingly, all information submitted on such forms is available to anyone looking.

From that perspective, the Chapter should be aware of its income and how it might impact tax filing. For example, a Chapter partners with another tax-exempt organization to raise money for inner-city youth education. This Chapter is fairly active and typically experiences a total income of $35,000 per year from events and for scholarships. During this specific event, $20,000 is expected to be raised for inner-city youth. From a tax perspective, it might be strategic to allow the cash to be accepted directly by the partnering charity rather than collecting it through the Chapter and passing it on to the charity. In one situation, the Chapter is qualified to file a simple Form 990-N, and in the other, it must complete the more invasive and revealing Form 990-EZ and very possibly additional schedules as applicable.

The jump from filing the Form 990-EZ to the full Form 990 is equally as unpleasant for those Chapters hovering near total income of $200,000. The first time is the worst, though. From that point on, they have a foundation from which to work.

Of course, the Chapter should file the most appropriate form as outlined by the IRS. This guide simply presents the impact that growing a Chapter's income in a particular way may have on filing an annual tax return. If the Chapter finds itself with an annual income nearing the $50,000 or $200,000 thresholds, it would be prudent for the leadership to evaluate the budget and revenue plans with a local tax or finance professional—ideally found within the pool of alumni.

There is one more topic that is worth mentioning here related to filing IRS Form 1099. Any business, including tax-exempt organizations, is required to file a Form 1099 anytime it has paid out $600 or more annually to: a person who is not a Chapter employee; any attorney or law firm; someone receiving prizes and awards; and others based on a list of criteria. A Form 1099 is not required if the recipient of the payment was a corporation or qualifies under one of the other approved exceptions. In most cases, the Chapter will be required to file Form 1099 by January 31 each year.[24] Conveniently, the need to file a Form 1099 does not affect the form required for the Chapter's annual return. For example, a Chapter that paid $1,200 to an attorney for assistance with its organizing documents would be required to file a Form 1099 for that service. Since that Chapter only had annual receipts of $22,000, it is still qualified to submit the Form 990-N. One does not impact the other.

The filing deadline for 990s is the fifteenth day of the fifth month after the end of the organization's fiscal year. In most cases for Chapters, that would mean that the fiscal year would end on June 30 if aligned with the academic year, and the 990 filing deadline would be November 15. It is possible to get a six-month extension without penalty upon request, however.

Any Chapter that is recognized as a legal entity will have to file annual returns, regardless of whether taxes are owed. Chapters that exist as legal entities of the central alumni association can breathe easy as long as requested documentation has been submitted to the alumni association. Independent Chapters are required to file on their own. Fortunately, most simply file the 990-N in minutes—even when operating a highly functioning and professional Chapter. The hassles of filing once a year are often significantly outweighed by the benefits—but that is up to your Chapter to decide.

60-Second Takeaway

Issues of state and federal taxes are complex and vary widely. Accordingly, seek counsel from the alumni association and / or a local tax professional prior to embarking on any strategy with any potential tax implications. With the appropriate recognition, Chapters may benefit from state and federal income tax and state sales-tax exemptions, tax-free donations, and reduced-rate postage.

These benefits may be passed down through the association or, for independent Chapters, filed for on their own.

For alumni Chapters, federal income-tax exemption is granted following an application for recognition as a 501(c)(3), 501(c)(7), 501(c)(19), or 501(c)(23) entity. All four designations are afforded federal income-tax exemption. All but the 501(c)(7) designation affords the possibility of tax-deductible contributions for donors. Only the 501(c)(3) designation permits the possibility of reduced-rate postage. Be certain the Chapter is consistent, timely, and accurate with properly documented donor receipts. At the state level, a Chapter may qualify for both income- and sales-tax exemption on qualified monies. Ensure that the Chapter leaders are aware of the sales-tax exemption and prepared to take advantage of any potential savings. Also, be cognizant of possible taxes associated with unrelated business taxable income.

All businesses are required to file IRS Form 1099, generally when paying for services over $600 annually other than to corporations. All 501(c)-recognized organizations file IRS Form 990s annually. Be prepared with the documentation needed by the association or to file on your own. There are real costs associated with filing and compliance requirements for maintaining a federal tax exemption, but the benefits may outweigh the costs.

Make It Happen Checklist

☐ Understand whether your Chapter is responsible for filing any annual state and / or federal tax / information returns or if the alumni association takes care of all such details.

☐ Independent Chapters, evaluate the costs and benefits related to applying for and maintaining all possible tax-exemption designations for maximum tax benefit.

☐ Seek guidance from the alumni association and a local tax professional prior to making a decision.

☐ If approved, apply for nonprofit status with the state.

☐ Apply for 501(c)(3), 501(c)(7), 501(c)(19), or 501(c)(23) status with the IRS, based on how the Chapter is to be organized and operated.

☐ Complete any final state tax exemptions based on having achieved an IRS tax-exempt designation.

☐ Follow through with filing for reduced postage rates if applicable.

☐ When maintaining any 501(c) status:

» Ensure the Chapter continues to operate in alignment with the Chapter's bylaws.

» Be aware of properly accounting for unrelated taxable income.

» File all appropriate IRS Forms 1099.

» Commit to filing the proper Form 990 annually, being mindful of when Chapter income begins to approach the next threshold for the next, more involved Form 990.

☐ If the Chapter is specifically a 501(c)(3), 501(c)(19), or 501(c)(23):

» Make it known to the alumni that donations, contributions, and payments are partially to fully tax deductible—often.

» For every item sold (event tickets, memberships, sponsorships, etc.), the Chapter leadership should establish the reasonable amount that is tax deductible.

» The Chapter should also provide a proper receipt at the time of payment.

☐ With respect to state sales tax, determine if the Chapter inherits sales-tax exemption from the alumni association, if the Chapter qualifies on its own merit, or if it must apply to qualify.

☐ If the Chapter is a legal subordinate of the alumni association, ensure that all requested financial forms and files are provided promptly so that the association may properly file its annual returns.

☐ If the Chapter needs assistance distilling the tax information down to what is relevant for alumni Chapters, managing the process or preparing for tax filings, it should consider seeking guidance.

Why It's Worth Every Minute

To some, the ideas, guidelines, and parameters presented in this book may seem a bit arduous. The fact is, these thoughts, discussions, and options actually make the experience more transparent and easier. There are already tens of thousands of volunteers so dedicated that they push through even without the added materials and support. Those alumni leaders know a secret shared by anyone who has stepped into the shoes of an alumni volunteer—and that is the unconditional, timeless power of the alumni bond pulsing throughout the entire network.

How many times in life does a person truly have the opportunity to positively impact the careers, the families, and the hopes and dreams of others? Not many . . . Unless you choose to embrace a role like one in alumni leadership. Those who step up to the plate have the unmistakable opportunity to cultivate a community, generate occasions, and foster relationships that may spark at any moment, changing the course of someone's life forever. Maybe an alumnus meets his future bride that night at the tailgate, or maybe an entrepreneurial alumna connects with just the right investor to make her vision a reality, or, just maybe, you meet your next best friend who holds you up when things do not go as planned. Alumni leaders both in the trenches and at the alumni association get to be in the business of making life for everyone around so much more successful, rewarding, and filled with joy.

In my life, a single moment of alumni connection changed it forever. Let me share a bit of background to give the experience more context. My mother grew up with her three older siblings on a Wisconsin farm among swarms of hard-working relatives within a peaceful, happy, buzzing community. My father, more of a city boy, was raised with his younger sister in a much more industrial part of the country, a small mill town south of Pittsburgh. They met when both my mother's career in cosmetology and my father's undergraduate studies in nuclear engineering took them to Madison, Wisconsin. Over the years and a few degrees later, my father became part of the booming oil and gas industry, and our family moved several times between Pennsylvania and Texas, spending the majority of the time in a Dallas suburb.

With that foundation laid, fast forward to the end of my MBA studies, when I was nearing graduation and exploring several exciting domestic job opportunities with promising careers. I longed for the chance to better understand global business, but I was not ready for anything drastic . . . Then along came Barry Wilson. Mr. Wilson was then a senior Vice President at Medtronic and the President of Medtronic International, based in Switzerland. As a prominent Wharton alumnus, he was in Philadelphia to be the honored keynote speaker for a global conference. While in town, he took time to meet with three of us who had been interns with Medtronic over the summer.

Much to my surprise, this exceptionally busy and direct man had taken the time to become familiar with our internship projects, read our performance reviews, and interviewed our managers prior to his trip. When we had a moment to talk privately, Mr. Wilson very pointedly asked why I had not accepted Medtronic's employment offer. Politely, I explained that although I would be so very fortunate to work for such an amazing, innovative company, I was still exploring other opportunities to work internationally for a short spell of about six months. Mr. Wilson flat-out stated that Medtronic did not support international assignments for any position below that of a Vice President, and even then, only for periods of three and five years. Well, that was that, and the conversation abruptly ended. What had I done? Was my offer about to be rescinded?

Quite the opposite. Two weeks later, Medtronic reached out with the most unexpected arrangement. They offered an unprecedented six-month assignment in Europe under the sponsorship of Barry Wilson as part of the package. I leapt at the opportunity! After one year at corporate headquarters in Minneapolis, Minnesota, my expatriate assignment began, for which I was based in the village of Morges on the banks of Lake Geneva. I was remarkably fortunate: not only was my sponsor truly engaged and the entire environment a learning opportunity but the local team was receptive, welcoming, and open to coaching this newly minted MBA in the ways of European business. Six Medtronic colleagues at the European headquarters in particular were incredibly influential:

- My immediate supervisor, then the Vice President of the neurological division and a fellow American expatriate.
- The Italian director of the deep brain stimulation division, who has remained an amazing friend and teacher before and after I had the honor of working for him directly.
- The Lebanese, Senegalese, and Swiss director of business development and fellow Wharton alumnus, who I affectionately recall emphasized

the proper pronunciation of his beautiful baby boy's name as "Jad," not "Jihad."

- Another American expatriate in the legal department, who introduced me to so very much, including my favorite Swiss pastry and how to order a turkey in Switzerland.
- One more Italian, a business-development manager who made every one of my American guests feel like they were royalty and whose whole family embraced this outsider with open arms.
- A one-of-a-kind Dutchman and brilliant scientist, who welcomed me with such warmth and was instrumental in my country-by-country integration with co-workers and customers alike.

I cannot even begin to share the impact those six, Mr. Wilson, and others had on my professional growth! Additionally, this is where an earlier introduction to a true visionary in the field of medicine evolved into one of my most significant mentors. Prof. Alim Louis Benebid, a brilliant neurosurgeon practicing in France, was considered the "Father of Deep Brain Stimulation" and had been nominated for the Nobel Prize in Physiology or Medicine for his discovery. He was integral to my internship research project and, again, to my new role in Europe.

The impact on my personal life was not any less influential. Although unexpected for an expatriate in Europe, a temporary person with a short, finite end to physical presence, I was blessed to have developed some of my strongest relationships. I met one of my very best friends during that time. We danced on the beach at her wedding just a few short years ago, and I have now permanently become fused with her family as the joyous godmother to one of her beautiful and talented daughters. In fact, a little-known fact is that in celebration of her baptism, the godfather, a local Swiss dairy farmer, named one of his cows after her and another after me!

Three years after I landed at the Geneva airport for the first time, following a promotion and two extensions, I returned to the United States, changed forever. Such an amazing opportunity could not have happened without the almost palpable power of the alumni connection. Prior to meeting Mr. Wilson that day on campus, our paths had never intersected. It was the commonality of our alma mater that brought us together and the alumni connection that drove the extraordinary steps that followed.

Much of who I am today—my willingness to take risks, the broader understanding with which I see people and their behaviors, and my greater appreciation for the glorious differences of life—largely stems from that unparalleled experience fueled by the incredible people who filled it. Mr. Wilson and I still maintain a cherished relationship, as I do with several others who were and continue to be so meaningful. It was an honor sitting alongside his wife to watch Prof. Benabid accept a Lifetime Achievement Award from the US Department of Health and Human Services, as well as, later, the Lasker Prize just a couple of years ago in New York. My Italian colleague, then manager, is a lasting friend who will stand the test of time. And my goddaughter continues to grow into a spirited and curious young lady, just like her mom! I look forward to being her guide when she and her sister visit the United States for the first time.

That is just one of my personal experiences illustrating the enormity and power of the alumni network. I will bet that you have a meaningful personal connection, a job opportunity, or a spiritual awakening as a result of another alumna / alumnus in your life. What a gift and a privilege it is to be a small part of helping others find those magical moments, those undeniable inflection points. As volunteer alumni Chapter leaders, we have the honor of doing just that. We have an impact by crafting the environments that foster countless chance, life-altering meetings.

The role as an alumni leader can be challenging at times, for reasons presented at the beginning of this book—largely because each leader has to start from square one to develop a system, often by brute force, that works for him or her. This is a new day. *Fully Funded* and SACL have done much of the work for you, for your alumni Chapter, and for your association to remove or minimize many of those challenges, leaving only the most enjoyable parts behind. Having the privilege to be a positive, meaningful player in the lives of so many fellow alumni—even without the much-appreciated resources and guidance from the Chapter perspective now available—is a labor of love and worth every minute.

About the Society for Alumni Club Leadership (SACL)

The Society for Alumni Club Leadership (SACL) serves the grassroots efforts of volunteer alumni leaders—either through partnerships with the central alumni association or directly—to facilitate highly functioning Chapters and thriving networks. It is hyper-focused on making the role of local alumni chapter / club / group leaders remarkably enjoyable, successful, and sustainable.

SACL offers a subscription-based, turnkey, online back office, further complemented by specialty services on an as-needed basis. As part of a subscription, groups will access a server for file management, centralized vendor contacts, chapter-specific calendaring tool, and a wealth of sample documents and templates. Additionally, subscribers benefit from the Alumni Leadership Education Series, a vital part of the services offering targeted materials to prepare and guide today's alumni club leaders to triumph over the various challenges they face—without having to reinvent the wheel. Selected specialty services include shouldering the Chapter's repetitive tasks and administrivia through the Remote Chapter Assistant (RCA); facilitating mobile giving and credit card transactions at unheard-of pricing; offering customizable, templated Web pages; and channeling one-off Chapter and association insurance solutions; among others.

Through the personalized ClubHub, each Chapter leader is able to access the tools, services, and guidance to enhance survival—and, more intentionally, enable the Chapter to flourish. SACL brings together the best practices of countless clubs and associations, positively impacts the morale of leaders, and reduces the volunteer's day-to-day operational burden through affordable turnkey programs and tools. The benefits are magnified when the alumni association unleashes the services in a consistent strategy across the chapter network.

SACL is the pioneer in providing the infrastructure, tools, and coaching necessary to successfully operate and manage local alumni clubs from inception. SACL is driving thriving networks!

Appendix—Free SACL Tools and Resources Available to Readers

Access to these tools is available for free to all those who purchase this book, as a gesture of appreciation.

1. **Chapter Budgeting Template** – A tool to assist in modeling Chapter budgets. Categories, sub-categories, and payment timing elements have been outlined, allowing the Chapter to complete only what is applicable. The resulting totals should provide some clarity into how robust of an income plan the Chapter should push.

2. **Head Shot Dos and Don'ts** – This guide will provide essential recommendations that will make the difference between photos cluttered with distractions and impressive images that allow your alumni's dynamic personalities to be the focal point.

3. **List of Community Giving Days** – I have compiled a list of communities that host giving days around the country, with contact links and a few statistics for your reference.

Notes

Preface

1 Calculated from census and other data:
   - » Population number: "U.S. and World Population Clock," United States Census Bureau, accessed February 13, 2017, https://www.census.gov/popclock.
   - » Percent over age twenty-five: "Population Distribution by Age," Kaiser Family Foundation, accessed February 13, 2017, http://kff.org/other/state-indicator/distribution-by-age/?currentTimeframe=0.
   - » Percent alumni and percent with degrees: Camille L. Ryan and Kurt Bauman, *Educational Attainment in the United States: 2015*, United States Census Bureau, March 2016, accessed February 13, 2017, http://www.census.gov/content/dam/Census/library/publications/2016/demo/p20-578.pdf.

2 "Fast Facts," National Center for Education Statistics (NCES) Home Page, a part of the U.S. Department of Education, accessed May 22, 2017, https://nces.ed.gov/fastfacts/display.asp?id=84.

3 Council for Aid to Education, "Colleges and Universities Raise $41 Billion in 2016," news release, February 7, 2017, accessed February 13, 2017, http://cae.org/images/uploads/pdf/VSE-2016-Press-Release.pdf.

4 Evan Shelan (CEO of eZforex and alumnus of the Wharton School at the University of Pennsylvania), interview, October 29, 2016.

5 Council for Aid to Education, "Colleges and Universities Raise $41 Billion in 2016," news release, February 7, 2017, accessed February 13, 2017, http://cae.org/images/uploads/pdf/VSE-2016-Press-Release.pdf.

6 Melissa Dawn Newman, "Determinants of alumni membership in a dues-based alumni association" (doctoral dissertation, University of Louisville, 2009), http://ir.library.louisville.edu/etd/1052/.

7 Annual Giving Network, *2014 Survey Report*, 2, accessed February 13, 2017, https://annualgiving.com/wp-content/uploads/2014/09/AGN-2014-Survey-Report.pdf.

8 Ibid.

9 Council for Aid to Education, "Colleges and Universities Raise $41 Billion in 2016," news release, February 7, 2016, http://cae.org/fundraising-in-education/survey-results-other-research/annual-press-release.

10 Andrew Cafourek (CEO of Alumni Spaces) and Bill Moakley (University of Oklahoma Alumni Association), "Your Chapters Have Spoken! Here's What They Said" (presentation, first presented during the CASE IV District Conference "Destination: Engagement," Fort Worth, Texas, March 5, 2017).

11   Kirk Purdom (Executive Director, Ole Miss Alumni Association), phone interview, February 27, 2017.

12   Alumni Association of the University of Mississippi, *Club Leadership Handbook*, 7, http://www.olemissalumni.com/wp-content/uploads/2016/02/Leadership-Handbook-2.19.16_revised_b.pdf.

Introduction

1   Marquette University Alumni Association, *Alumni Engagement and Outreach Volunteer Manual*, 1, accessed February 9, 2017, http://muconnect.marquette.edu/Document.Doc?id=16.

2   "Clubs & Chapters," MU Connect, last modified 2017, accessed February 9, 2017, http://www.marquette.edu/alumni/clubschapters-index.php#reg.

3   "About MUAA," MU Connect, last modified 2017, accessed February 9, 2017, http://www.marquette.edu/alumni/about-index.php.

4   Marquette University Alumni Association, *Alumni Engagement and Outreach Volunteer Manual*, 13, accessed February 9, 2017, http://muconnect.marquette.edu/Document.Doc?id=16.

5   "Community Home," Nebraska Alumni Association, last modified 2016, http://www.huskeralum.org/s/1620/start.aspx.

6   "Groups & Chapters," Nebraska Alumni Association, last modified 2016, http://www.huskeralum.org/s/1620/social.aspx?sid=1620&gid=1&pgid=386.

7   Nebraska Alumni Association, *Chapter & Groups Leader Manual*, 13, http://www.huskeralum.org/s/1620/images/editor_documents/Chapters_and_groups/Chapter_and_group_manual_rev._2016.pdf.

8   "Find a Seminole Club or Chapter," Florida State University Alumni Association, http://alumni.fsu.edu/community/seminole-clubs/find.

9   "Alumni Networks," Florida State University Alumni Association, http://alumni.fsu.edu/community/alumni-networks.

10   Stanford Alumni Association, *Stanford Club Leaders Handbook*, 56, April 6, 2011, https://alumni.stanford.edu/content/groups/docs/2011_Club_Handbook.pdf.

11   Council for Aid to Education, "Colleges and Universities Raise $41 Billion in 2016," news release, February 7, 2016, http://cae.org/fundraising-in-education/survey-results-other-research/annual-press-release.

Things That Might Need Funding

1   "Membership," Stay Connected to the U, 2017, accessed January 26, 2017, https://umnalumni.org/membership/.

2   Gretchen Ambrosier (Vice President of Engagement, University of Minnesota Alumni Association), phone interview, January 27, 2017.

3   University of Minnesota Alumni Association, *Volunteer Resource Guide*, 6, http://www.minnesotaalumni.org/s/1118/images/editor_documents/volunteer_resource_guide_draft_3_bb.pdf?sessionid=021b4e97-a827-44a3-8fc2-b4331d702c2b.

4   Brandon Maske (Assistant Director of Constituent Engagement, Iowa State University Alumni Association), phone interview, January 10, 2017.

5   Iowa State University Alumni Association, *National Clubs Program Handbook*, 2015, 7, https://www.google.com/url?sa=t&rct=j&q=&esrc=s&source=web&cd=1&ved=0ahUKEwiM1-vGmJrTAhXBMG-MKHc6sCb8QFggfMAA&url=http%3A%2F%2Fwww.isualum.org%2Fmedia%2Fcms%2FClub_Handbook_FY16_CAEF7FE23450D.docx&usg=AFQjCNFfipCtmRyc__y_O9bmxbVvntS8XA&sig2=MEPL6o3Ph2JS-LHgrn_oOQ&cad=rja.

6   Sarah Brokamp (Coordinator of Alumni & Annual Giving, Bowling Green State University Alumni Association), phone interview, January 27, 2017.

7   "Regional Networks," Bowling Green State University, accessed February 12, 2017, https://www.bgsu.edu/alumni/get-involved/regional-networks.html.

8   Melissa McClellen (Director of Clubs) and David Overstreet (Director of Administration and Operations, Florida State University Alumni Association), phone interview, January 10, 2017.

9   "Find a Seminole Club or Chapter," Florida State University Alumni Association, accessed February 12, 2017, http://alumni.fsu.edu/community/seminole-clubs/find.

10   Andrew Cafourek (CEO of Alumni Spaces) and Bill Moakley (University of Oklahoma Alumni Association), "Your Chapters Have Spoken! Here's What They Said" (presentation, first presented during the CASE IV District Conference "Destination: Engagement," Fort Worth, Texas, March 5, 2017).

11   Ibid.

12   Ibid.

13   Ashley McBride (Constituent Relations, Georgia State University Alumni Association), phone interview, January 26, 2017.

14   Georgia State University Alumni Association, *Georgia State University Alumni Networks Manual*, 18, accessed January 26, 2017, http://www.pantheralumni.com/s/1471/images/gid2/editor_documents/alumni_networks/gsu_network_leaders_manual_-_2017.pdf.

15   Teresa Harder (Director of Regional Alumni Programs, Boise State Alumni Association), phone interview, January 18, 2017.

16   Boise State Alumni Association, *Boise State University Alumni Association Regional Programs Handbook*, 15, https://alumni.boisestate.edu/wp-content/uploads/2016/07/Chapter_Club_Bronco-Contact-Handbook_2016_Final.docx.

17   "Facts," Wisconsin Alumni Association, 2017, http://www.uwalumni.com/about/facts.

18   Wisconsin Alumni Association, *Chapter Leader Handbook*, 10, http://www.uwalumni.com/wp-content/uploads/Chapter_Leader_Handbook_2016.pdf.

19   "Chapter Scholarships," Wisconsin Alumni Association, 2017, http://www.uwalumni.com/chapters-groups/scholarships.

20   "University of Iowa Alumni Association," University of Iowa Alumni Association,

2017, http://www.iowalum.com.

21 "U.S. IOWA Clubs and Contacts," University of Iowa Alumni Association, 2017, http://www.iowalum.com/clubs/locations.cfm.

22 University of Iowa Alumni Association, *Recognized IOWA Club Handbook*, 14, http://www.iowalum.com/clubs/pdf/Handbook.pdf.

23 "Who We Are," Arkansas Alumni, University of Arkansas, accessed January 26, 2017, http://www.arkansasalumni.org/s/1429/index.aspx?sid=1429&gid=1&pgid=3547.

24 Teri Dover (Director, Membership & Marketing) and Shanna Bassett (Associate Director, Membership & Marketing, Arkansas Alumni Association), phone interview, January 26, 2017.

25 Arkansas Alumni, *Chapter Guidebook 2016-2017*, 12–14, accessed January 26, 2017, http://www.arkansasalumni.org/s/1429/images/editor_documents/Chapters/2016-2017_Chapter_guidebook-min__1_.pdf.

26 Ibid.

27 Tricia Reviera (Senior Executive Director and Director of Alumni Engagement, Indiana University [IU] Alumni Association), phone interview, January 19, 2017.

28 Ibid.

29 Ibid.

30 "The History of the Alumni Association," Mississippi State University Development and Alumni, accessed February 9, 2017, http://www.alumni.msstate.edu/s/811/alumni/interior.aspx?sid=811&gid=1&pgid=271.

31 Mississippi State University Alumni Association, *2015 Chapter Handbook*, 17, http://www.alumni.msstate.edu/s/811/images/editor_documents/Chapter_handbook/Chapter_handbook_2015v2.pdf.

32 "Chapter Scholarships," Mississippi State University Development and Alumni, accessed February 9, 2017, http://www.alumni.msstate.edu/s/811/alumni/interior.aspx?sid=811&gid=1&pgid=703.

33 Iowa State University Alumni Association, *National Clubs Program Handbook*, 8, http://www.isualum.org/media/cms/Club_Handbook_FY16_0C14FC80760B3.pdf.

34 Mitchell Tsai (Chapter President, Wharton Club of Houston), interview, December 14, 2016.

35 "Chapters & Networks," Texas Exes, Ex-Students' Association of the University of Texas, https://texasexes.org/Chapters-networks.

36 Texas Exes, Ex-Students' Association of the University of Texas, *2016-2017 Chapter Handbook*, 4, https://www.texasexes.org/sites/default/files/uploads/chapter_leader_handbook_2016-2017.pdf.

37 "Clubs & Groups," Kellogg Alumni Network, Kellogg School of Management, Northwestern University, accessed February 13, 2017, http://alumni.kellogg.northwestern.edu/clubs.

38 "Alumni Network," Kellogg School of Management, Northwestern University,

accessed February 12, 2017, http://www.kellogg.northwestern.edu/programs/full-time-mba/career-path/alumni-network.aspx.

39 Sean Lofgren (Board Member and Past President, Kellogg Network DFW), interview, October 19, 2016.

40 "About," Dartmouth Alumni, Trustees of Dartmouth College, 2017, http://alumni.dartmouth.edu/home/about.

41 Dartmouth College Office of Alumni Relations, *Operating Guidelines and Recommended Best Practices for Recognized Alumni Clubs, Affiliated Groups, and Shared Interest Groups*, 15, 2016–2017, http://alumni.dartmouth.edu/sites/alumni/files/Files/operatingguidelines2017.pdf, p. 15.

42 "About Us," ASU Alumni Association, Arizona State University, accessed February 12, 2017, https://alumni.asu.edu/about.

43 "Our Story," Pat Tillman Foundation, accessed February 13, 2017, http://pattillmanfoundation.org/our-story.

44 ASU Alumni, *Fall Forum for Chapter & Club Leaders*, 26, October 21, 2016, accessed February 13, 2017, https://www.dropbox.com/s/1kr4t4vmz2bml7s/PPT%20for%20Chapter%20Conference.pptx?dl=0.

45 University of Delaware Office of Alumni Relations, *Alumni Club Leaders Handbook*, 9, http://www.udconnection.com/getattachment/6de08a0a-c388-4285-a495-6839d93f7ec3/UD-Leadership-Handbook.aspx.

46 Justine Tally-Beck (Director, Alumni Relations, University of Delaware Office of Development and Alumni Relations), phone interview, January 23, 2017.

47 John Young (Director of Alumni Chapters, University of Tennessee, Knoxville [UT Knoxville] Office of Alumni Affairs), phone interview, April 3, 2017.

48 University of Tennessee, Knoxville, *Alumni Chapter Manual*, 25, accessed February 13, 2017, http://alumni.utk.edu/s/1341/images/gid2/editor_documents/Chapters/2016_Chapter_manual_for_web.pdf.

49 James Stofan (Vice President for Alumni Relations, and Jered Bocage, Director of Alumni Programs, Tulane Alumni Association), phone interview, January 25, 2017.

50 "Tulane Alumni Association – Community Home," Tulane University Office of Alumni Relations, 2016, http://alumni.tulane.edu/s/1586/Alumni/16/home.aspx?gid=3&pgid=61.

51 Tulane University Office of Alumni Relations, *Tulane Alumni Association Club Handbook*, 34, June 27, 2016, http://alumni.tulane.edu/s/1586/images/gid3/editor_documents/taa_board_/2016_summer_meeting/1_-_2016_taa_club_handbook.pdf?sessionid=c295ecb2-461a-4202-a557-bd39aca3626d.

52 Nebraska Alumni Association, *Chapter & Groups Leader Manual*, 15–17, http://www.huskeralum.org/s/1620/images/editor_documents/Chapters_and_groups/Chapter_and_group_manual_rev._2016.pdf.

53 "Chapters," LSU Alumni Association, 2017, http://www.lsualumni.org/Chapters.

54 "LSU Alumni Association," LSU Alumni Association, 2017, http://www.

lsualumni.org/.

55 "Tulane Alumni Association – Community Home," Tulane University Office of Alumni Relations, 2016, http://alumni.tulane.edu/s/1586/Alumni/16/home.aspx?gid=3&pgid=61.

56 LSU Alumni Association, *General Liability Coverage: LSU Alumni Association's Recognized Alumni Chapters*, http://www.lsualumni.org/Images/Interior/Chapters/Chapter_liability.pdf.

57 "Clubs & Shared Interest Groups," Harvard Alumni, 2017, accessed February 9, 2017, https://alumni.harvard.edu/haa/clubs-sigs.

58 Harvard Alumni Association, Clubs & Shared Interest Groups Office, *HAA Club Officer Handbook: How to Start or Revive a Harvard Club*, 19–22, http://alumni.harvard.edu/sites/default/files/page/files/haa-club-officer-handbook1.pdf.

59 Stanford Alumni Association, *Stanford Club Leaders Handbook*, 54, April 6, 2011, https://alumni.stanford.edu/content/groups/docs/2011_Club_Handbook.pdf.

60 BYU Alumni, *BYU Alumni Database Totals*, March 3, 2016, http://alumni.byu.edu/sites/default/files/about/alumni-docs/alumni_data_april_2016_002.pdf.

61 Wendy Hudson (Director, Alumni Relations, Brigham Young University), phone interview, February 24, 2017.

62 Ibid.

63 Arkansas Alumni, *Chapter Guidebook 2016-2017*, 7, accessed January 26, 2017, http://www.arkansasalumni.org/s/1429/images/editor_documents/Chapters/2016-2017_Chapter_guidebook-min__1_.pdf.

64 Texas State Alumni Association, *2015 Annual Report*, 23, 2015, http://alumni.txstate.edu/file/Alumni-Annual-Report_2015.pdf.

65 Texas State Alumni Association, *Alumni Chapter Operational Guidelines*, 11, August 31, 2014, http://alumni.txstate.edu/file/Chapter-Operational-Guidelines-Final---Starting-a-new-Chapter.pdf.

66 Kevin Lobdell (Associate Director of Alumni Engagement, Binghamton University Alumni Association), phone interview, January 18, 2017.

67 Ibid.

68 Michael Fahey (Managing Director, State Relations, Alumni Relations and Engagement, Wisconsin Alumni Association), phone interview, January 19, 2017.

69 Rosalind Muchiri (Director of Alumni Relations & Annual Giving, Bowie State University National Alumni Association), phone interview, January 27, 2017.

70 "HBCU Alumni Leaders Conference," Bowie State University, 2017, accessed February 13, 2017, https://www.bowiestate.edu/about/calendar/details/hbcu-alumni-leaders-conference/2016-08-06.

71 Rosalind Muchiri (Director of Alumni Relations & Annual Giving, Bowie State University National Alumni Association), phone interview, January 27, 2017.

72 "Alumni Clubs," Purdue Alumni Association, accessed April 10, 2017, http://purdue.imodules.com/s/1461/alumni/index.aspx?sid=1461&gid=1001&pgid=320.

73 Purdue Alumni Association, *Club Handbook: A Guide to Sanctioning Your Club*, 8, July 27, 2015, http://purdue.imodules.com/s/1461/images/gid1001/editor_documents/club/club_handbook_2015-16.pdf.

74 Texas Secretary of State, *Form 202—General Information (Certificate of Formation – Nonprofit Corporation)*, 4, https://www.sos.state.tx.us/corp/forms/202_boc.pdf, p. 4.

75 "How to Form a Nonprofit Organization in New York State," The State of New York, accessed February 12, 2017, https://www.ny.gov/new-york-state-nonprofit-coordination-unit/how-form-nonprofit-organization-new-york-state.

76 Florida Department of State, Division of Corporations, *Form CR2E006: Instructions for Not for Profit Articles of Incorporation*, September 2016, accessed February 12, 2017, http://form.sunbiz.org/pdf/cr2e006.pdf.

77 Department of the Treasury, Internal Revenue Service, *Publication 557: Tax-Exempt Status for Your Organization*, 3, last modified January 2017, https://www.irs.gov/pub/irs-pdf/p557.pdf.

78 Department of the Treasury, Internal Revenue Service, *Form 8717: User Fee for Exempt Organization Determination Letter Request*, last modified September 2015, https://www.irs.gov/pub/irs-pdf/f8718.pdf.

79 "Public Charity – Tax Exemption Application," Internal Revenue Service, January 26, 2017, accessed February 23, 2017, https://www.irs.gov/charities-non-profits/charitable-organizations/public-charity-exemption-application.

80 Illinois Secretary of State, *Form NFP 114.05: Domestic/Foreign Corporation Annual Report*, last modified October 2014, accessed February 12, 2017, http://www.cyberdriveillinois.com/publications/pdf_publications/nfp11405.pdf.

81 "Filing Requirements – Form 199, Exempt Organization Annual Information," Franchise Tax board, the State of California, 2017, accessed February 12, 2017, https://www.ftb.ca.gov/businesses/Exempt-Organizations/Filing-Requirements-Form-199.shtml.

82 Florida Department of State, Division of Corporations, *Form CR2E044: Transmittal Letter*, May 2013, accessed February 12, 2017, http://form.sunbiz.org/pdf/cr2e044.pdf.

83 Florida Department of State, Division of Corporations, *Form CR2E045: Cover Letter*, March 2012, accessed February 12, 2017, http://form.sunbiz.org/pdf/cr2e045.pdf.

84 Commonwealth of Kentucky, Alison Lundergan Grimes, Secretary of State, Division of Business Filings, *Statement of Change: Principal Office Address, Registered Agent and/or Registered Office Address*, accessed February 12, 2017, http://www.sos.ky.gov/bus/business-filings/Forms/Documents/PORAROChange.PDF.

85 Harvard Alumni Association, Clubs & Shared Interest Groups Office, *HAA Best Practices Handbook*, 2, http://alumni.harvard.edu/sites/default/files/page/files/HAA%20Club%20and%20SIG%20Best%20Practices_1.pdf.

86 "About Us," United States Naval Academy Alumni Association and Foundation,

2012, accessed February 17, 2017, http://www.usna.com/page.aspx?pid=204.

87 Lt. Col. Junior Ortiz (Vice President of Programs for the US Naval Academy Alumni Association of North Texas), interview, December 14, 2016.

88 Nebraska Alumni Association, *Chapters & Groups Leader Manual*, 11, http://www.huskeralum.org/s/1620/images/editor_documents/Chapters_and_groups/Chapter_and_group_manual_rev._2016.pdf.

89 "Join an Alumni Group," Penn State Alumni Association, accessed February 13, 2017, http://alumni.psu.edu/groups.

90 "Alumni Association Overview," Penn State Alumni Association, accessed February 13, 2017, http://alumni.psu.edu/about_us/overview.

91 Penn State Alumni Association, *Chapter Leaders Resource Guide*, 12, June 2014, http://alumni.psu.edu/groups/volunteer/ChapterLeadersResourceGuide.pdf.

Coveted Resources from the Central Alumni Association

1 "Find Your Community," American University Alumni Association, accessed May 29, 2017, http://alumniassociation.american.edu/s/1395/index1col-social.aspx-?sid=1395&gid=1&pgid=331&_ga=2.185503785.1818743997.1496114965-1448341942.1487041856.

2 American University Office of Alumni Relations, *Alumni Volunteer Handbook*, 15, http://alumniassociation.american.edu/s/1395/images/editor_documents/volunteer_handbook/2013_alumni_volunteer_guide.hyperlinked.pdf.

3 "About the UK Alumni Association," University of Kentucky Alumni Association, 2017, accessed February 13, 2017, http://www.ukalumni.net/s/1052/semi-blank-noimg.aspx?sid=1052&gid=1&pgid=304.

4 University of Kentucky Alumni Association, *UK Alumni Association Club Resources Survey*, 5, April 12, 2016, http://www.uky.edu/Alumni/web/2016/Club%20Resources%20and%20Programs%20Survey%20Summary%20by%20volunteers%20ppt%204_12_16.pptx.

5 "FAQs," UNC General Alumni Association, 2017, accessed February 13, 2017, https://alumni.unc.edu/about-the-gaa/faqs.

6 "What is the GAA," UNC General Alumni Association, 2017, accessed February 13, 2017, https://alumni.unc.edu/about-the-gaa/what-is-the-gaa.

7 UNC General Alumni Association, *Handbook for Club Leaders*, 25–26, October 2016, https://alumni.unc.edu/wp-content/uploads/2016/10/Oct2016Handbook.pdf.

8 Ibid.

9 Ibid.

10 University of Tennessee, Knoxville, *Alumni Chapter Manual*, 39, accessed February 13, 2017, http://alumni.utk.edu/s/1341/images/gid2/editor_documents/Chapters/2016_Chapter_manual_for_web.pdf.

11 Ibid., 20.

12 Mari Meyer (Senior Associate Director, Global Engagement, the University of

Chicago Alumni Association), phone interview, February 1, 2017.

13 University of Chicago Alumni Association, *Volunteer Handbook*, 19, March 2012, https://alumniandfriends.uchicago.edu/sites/default/files/volunteer_handbook.pdf.

14 Jodi Kaplan (Senior Director, Alumni Relations, Office of Alumni Relations, University of Connecticut [UCONN] Alumni Association), phone interview, February 15, 2017.

15 "Alumni Networks," UConn Alumni, University of Connecticut, accessed February 14, 2017, http://uconnalumni.com/community/alumni-networks/.

16 "Affinity Groups," UConn Alumni, University of Connecticut, accessed February 14, 2017, http://uconnalumni.com/community/affinity-groups/.

17 "Alumni Networks," UConn Alumni, University of Connecticut, accessed February 14, 2017, http://uconnalumni.com/community/alumni-networks/.

18 "About the UA Alumni Association," UA Alumni Association, 2017, accessed February 12, 2017, http://arizonaalumni.com/connect/about-ua-alumni-association.

19 Judy Frederick (Senior Director of Administration and Finance and Associate Executive Director MCV Alumni Association of VCU) and Amy Grey (Interim Senior Director, Outreach and Engagement, VCU Alumni), phone interview, February 1, 2017.

20 "Your Alumni Association," Johns Hopkins Alumni Association, accessed February 14, 2017, https://alumni.jhu.edu/alumniassociation.

21 "About Us," Alumni Association of the University of Michigan, accessed February 14, 2017, http://alumni.umich.edu/about-us/. Accessed 14 February 2017.

22 "Club Websites," Alumni Association of the University of Michigan, accessed May 30, 2017, http://clubs.alumni.umich.edu/clubleaders/club_websites?_ga=2.168794658.287040746.1496179900-2056333311.1483038319.

23 "About the Association," Wellesley College, accessed February 13, 2017, http://www.wellesley.edu/alumnae/about#QK3DrO4hbDTrIDtj.97.

24 "Classes, Clubs, & Groups," Wellesley College, accessed February 13, 2017, http://www.wellesley.edu/alumnae/groups#yYUXbVK0rgqz50Ps.97.

25 "UHAA About/History," UH Alumni, 2017, https://uhalumni.org/uhaa/history.

26 "Financing a Chapter," UH Alumni, 2017, https://uhalumni.org/uhaa/Chapters/financing.

27 University of Georgia Alumni Association, *UGA Alumni Chapter Leader Playbook*, 5, 2016, https://alumni.uga.edu/wp-content/uploads/Alumni_Handbook_2016.pdf.

28 "About the UGA Alumni Association," UGA Alumni, accessed March 31, 2017, https://alumni.uga.edu/about-uga-alumni-association/.

29 University of Georgia Alumni Association, *UGA Alumni Chapter Leader Playbook*, 34–35, 2016, https://alumni.uga.edu/wp-content/uploads/Alumni_Handbook_2016.pdf.

30 "The University of Florida Alumni Association," University of Florida Alumni Association, 2016, http://connect.ufalumni.ufl.edu/about/about-ufaa.

31 University of Florida Alumni Association, *Gator Club and Affiliate Group Leaders Handbook*, pp. 63 and 12, https://www.ufalumni.ufl.edu/gatorclubs/admin/docs/dl/?file=218.

32 Florida State University Alumni Association, *Operation Club*, 3, January 2015, http://alumni.fsu.edu/sites/alumni.fsu.edu/files/documents/Community/Clubs/Financials/Operation_Club_FAQ_Jan_2015.pdf.

33 Andrew Cafourek (CEO of Alumni Spaces) and Bill Moakley (University of Oklahoma Alumni Association), "Your Chapters Have Spoken! Here's What They Said" (presentation, first presented during the CASE IV District Conference "Destination: Engagement," Fort Worth, Texas, March 5, 2017).

34 "Club Funding & Funds," Alumni Association of the University of Michigan, accessed May 30, 2017, http://clubs.alumni.umich.edu/clubleaders/funding_funds.

35 Steve Burns (Director of Global Engagement, University of Michigan Alumni Association), phone interview, February 21, 2017.

36 Arkansas Alumni, *Chapter Guidebook 2016-2017*, 6, accessed January 26, 2017, http://www.arkansasalumni.org/s/1429/images/editor_documents/Chapters/2016-2017_Chapter_guidebook-min__1_.pdf.

37 Wendy Hudson (Director, Alumni Relations, Brigham Young University), phone interview, February 24, 2017.

38 Ryan Chreist (Assistant Vice Chancellor and Executive Director, University of Colorado Boulder Alumni Association), interview, January 24, 2017.

39 Alumni Association, University of Colorado Boulder, *Alumni Chapter Manual and Memorandum of Understanding*, 17, http://www.colorado.edu/alumni/sites/default/files/attached-files/alumni_chapter_manual_and_memorandum_of_understanding.pdf.

40 Penn State Alumni Association, *Chapter Leaders Handbook*, 12, http://www.alumni.psu.edu/groups/volunteer/volunteer-toolkit/archives/handbook.PDF.

41 LSU Alumni Association, *Chapter Guidelines Booklet*, 7, 2016, http://www.lsu-alumni.org/Images/Interior/Chapters/2016Chapter%20guidelines.compressed.pdf.

42 Boise State Alumni Association, *Boise State University Alumni Association Regional Programs Handbook*, pp. 9 and 15, 2016, https://alumni.boisestate.edu/wp-content/uploads/2013/10/Chapter_Club_Bronco-Contact-Handbook_2016-GS-HC-4-22-16_PDF.pdf.

43 Matthew Wilson (Associate Vice President, Alumni Community Development, University of Illinois Alumni Association), phone interview, January 17, 2017.

44 "2016 Alumni Leadership Conference," Illinois Alumni, University of Illinois Alumni Association, https://illinoisalumni.org/events/2016-alumni-leadership-conference.

45 David Bambrey (Senior Director of Campus Relations, Alumni) and Dawn Werry (Senior Director, External Relations, Ohio University Alumni Association),

phone interview, February 2, 2017.

46 "Alumni Leaders Conference," Ohio University, 2017, https://www.ohio.edu/alumni/already-involved/alumni-leaders-conference.cfm.

47 David Bambrey (Senior Director of Campus Relations, Alumni) and Dawn Werry (Senior Director, External Relations, Ohio University Alumni Association), phone interview, February 2, 2017.

48 "Networks," MIT Alumni Association's Infinite Connection, https://alum.mit.edu/networks.

49 "MIT Alumni Leadership Conference — Sept. 15–16, 2017," MIT Alumni Leadership Conference, https://alc.mit.edu/.

50 "Frequently Asked Questions," MIT Alumni Leadership Conference, https://alc.mit.edu/faq/#Q_4.

51 Lauren Wojtkun (Director of Volunteer Training and Development, Massachusetts Institute of Technology Alumni Association), phone interview, February 27, 2017.

52 Denise Smith (Director of Alumni Relations, Truman State University Alumni Association), phone interview, February 1, 2017.

53 Truman State University Alumni Association Board of Directors, *Travel Stipend Policy & Reimbursement Form*, August 2013, http://www.truman.edu/wp-content/uploads/2014/09/Travel-Stipend-Form-Chapter-Representatives.pdf.

54 "About Us," Villanova University Alumni Association, Families and Friends, 2013, accessed February 14, 2017, http://alumni.villanova.edu/s/1695/alumni/index.aspx?sid=1695&gid=2&pgid=1059.

55 Villanova University Alumni Association, *2016 Volunteer Leaders Conference Reimbursement Details*, http://alumni.villanova.edu/s/1695/images/gid2/editor_documents/vlc_docs/2016_vlc_reimbursement_details.pdf.

56 Kelly Dubbs (Assistant Director of Student and Alumni Program Engagement, Villanova University Alumni Association), phone interview, October 27, 2016.

57 Nebraska Alumni Association, *Chapters & Groups Leader Manual*, 5, http://www.huskeralum.org/s/1620/images/editor_documents/Chapters_and_groups/Chapter_and_group_manual_rev._2016.pdf.

58 Katheryn Greenwade (Vice President, the Association of Former Students of Texas A&M University), phone interview, January 19, 2017.

59 "Coach's Night," The Association of Former Students of Texas A&M, 2017, http://www.aggienetwork.com/events/coachsnight.aspx.

60 University of Florida Alumni Association, *Gator Club and Affiliate Group Leaders Handbook*, 59, https://www.ufalumni.ufl.edu/gatorclubs/admin/docs/dl/?file=218.

61 Bowling Green State University Alumni, *Volunteer Handbook for Alumni Affinity Groups*, 7, https://www.bgsu.edu/content/dam/BGSU/alumni/documents/affinity/Affinity-Group-Handbook.pdf.

62 Sarah Brokamp (Coordinator of Alumni & Annual Giving, Bowling Green State

University Alumni Association), phone interview, January 27, 2017.

63 "Award-Winning Minneapolis Event Venue: McNamara Alumni Center," McNamara Alumni Center, accessed January 26, 2017, https://mac-events.org.

Chapter Memberships—Great Foundational Income

1 Faith Ward (Director of Alumni Affairs, Troy University Alumni Association), phone interview, February 1, 2017.

2 Troy University Alumni Association, *Alumni Leadership*, 6, accessed February 12, 2017, http://www.troy.edu/alumni/assets/documents/Alumni-Chapter-Manual.pdf.

3 Penn State Alumni Association, *Chapter Leaders Resource Guide*, 7–8, June 2014, http://alumni.psu.edu/groups/volunteer/ChapterLeadersResourceGuide.pdf.

4 Pauline Saraceni (Assistant Director of Alumni Affairs, Syracuse University Office of Alumni Engagement), phone interview, January 5, 2017.

5 Syracuse University Office of Alumni Relations, *SU Alumni Club Manual*, October 2013, http://alumni.syr.edu/wp-content/uploads/2017/01/2013-Club-Manual-final-updated-2.14docx.pdf.

6 Ibid., pp. 6 and 17.

7 West Point Association of Graduates, *Society Leader Guide 2016*, 9, http://www.westpointaog.org/file/societyleadershandbook.pdf.

8 "Reconnect with Grads," West Point Association of Graduates, accessed February 14, 2017, http://www.westpointaog.org/reconnectwithgrads.

9 West Point Association of Graduates, *Society Leader Guide 2016*, 10–11, http://www.westpointaog.org/file/societyleadershandbook.pdf, pp. 10, 11.

10 Iowa State University Alumni Association, *National Clubs Program Handbook*, 7, http://www.isualum.org/media/cms/Club_Handbook_FY16_0C14FC80760B3.pdf.

11 "Benefits of Membership," Auburn Alumni Association, accessed February 14, 2017, http://www.alumni.auburn.edu/benefits-of-membership/.

12 "Auburn Clubs," Auburn Alumni Association, accessed May 30, 2017, http://www.alumni.auburn.edu/clubs/.

13 "Auburn Clubs," Auburn Alumni Association, accessed February 14, 2017, http://www.alumni.auburn.edu/clubs/#resources.

14 University of Tennessee, Knoxville, *Alumni Chapter Manual*, 13, accessed February 13, 2017, http://alumni.utk.edu/s/1341/images/gid2/editor_documents/Chapters/2016_Chapter_manual_for_web.pdf.

15 Penn Alumni Regional Clubs, *The Penn Alumni Regional Clubs Handbook*, 2, accessed February 13, 2017, http://viewer.zmags.com/publication/72f0b1ed#/72f0b1ed.

16 Ibid., 4.

17 Ibid., 7.

18 LSU Alumni Association, *Chapter Guidelines Booklet*, pp. 2 and 8, 2016, http://

www.lsualumni.org/Images/Interior/Chapters/2016Chapter%20guidelines.compressed.pdf.

19 Syracuse University Office of Alumni Relations, *SU Alumni Club Manual*, 6–7, October 2013, http://alumni.syr.edu/wp-content/uploads/2017/01/2013-Club-Manual-final-updated-2.14docx.pdf.

20 "Chapters," US Air Force Academy AOG & Endowment, accessed February 23, 2017, http://www2.usafa.org/group/Chapters.

21 Association of Graduates, United States Air Force Academy, *2016–2017 Chapter Handbook*, 6–7, http://www2.usafa.org/Documents/AOG%20Chapters/ChapterHandbook2016PrintFile.pdf.

22 "Alumni Chapter Membership," Truman State University, 2017, accessed February 14, 2017, https://secure.truman.edu/alumni-s/membership_upay.asp.

23 Alumni Association of the University of Mississippi, *Club Leadership Handbook*, 7, http://www.olemissalumni.com/wp-content/uploads/2016/02/Leadership-Handbook-2.19.16_revised_b.pdf.

24 Pew Research Center, *Parent of children under 18 – Religion in America*, accessed March 31, 2017, http://www.pewforum.org/religious-landscape-study/parent-of-children-under-18.

Sponsorships Loved Far and Wide

1 Virginia Commonwealth University Alumni, *VCU Alumni Chapter Toolkit*, 8, https://www.vcualumni.org/media/ADVSRV/alumni/files/VCUAlumniChapterToolkit.pdf.

2 Georgia State University Alumni Association, *Georgia State University Alumni Club and Chapter Manual*, 12, http://netcommunity.gsu.edu/NetCommunity/Document.Doc?id=558.

3 University of Georgia Alumni Association, *UGA Alumni Chapter Leader Playbook*, 32, 2016, https://alumni.uga.edu/wp-content/uploads/Alumni_Handbook_2016.pdf.

4 "Financial Policies," Johns Hopkins Alumni Association, https://alumni.jhu.edu/financialpolicies.

5 Binghamton University Alumni Association, *Regional Chapter and Affinity Group Handbook*, 20, https://www.binghamton.edu/alumni/events-chapters/Regional%20Chapter%20and%20Affinity%20Group%20Handbook%20-%20April%202015.pdf.

6 Georgia State University Alumni Association, *Georgia State University Alumni Club and Chapter Manual*, 12, http://netcommunity.gsu.edu/NetCommunity/Document.Doc?id=558.

7 Nebraska Alumni Association, *Chapters & Groups Leader Manual*, 18, September 2013, http://www.huskeralum.org/s/1620/images/editor_documents/Chapters_and_groups/leader_-_manual.pdf.

8 University of Florida Alumni Association, *Gator Club and Affiliate Group Leaders*

Handbook, 33, https://www.ufalumni.ufl.edu/gatorclubs/admin/docs/dl/?-file=218.

9   Greg Schwartz (Sponsorships Co-Chair and Past President, Harvard Business School Club of Dallas), interview, February 15, 2017.

10 Stacie Hyatt, *Wharton Club of Dallas–Fort Worth, Celebrating 30 Years 1981–2011* (January 12, 2011).

Traditional and Not-So-Traditional Fundraising

1   Wendy Hudson (Director, Alumni Relations, Brigham Young University), phone interview, February 24, 2017.

2   Federal Reserve System, *The 2013 Federal Reserve Payments Study,* 46, July 2014, accessed February 19, 2017, https://www.frbservices.org/files/communications/pdf/general/2013_fed_res_paymt_study_detailed_rpt.pdf.

3   Board of Governors of the Federal Reserve System, *The Federal Reserve Payments Study 2016,* 2, December 2016, accessed February 18, 2017, https://www.federalreserve.gov/newsevents/press/other/2016-payments-study-20161222.pdf.

4   Board of Governors of the Federal Reserve System, *Consumers and Mobile Financial Services 2016,* 1, March 2016, accessed February 18, 2017, https://www.federalreserve.gov/econresdata/consumers-and-mobile-financial-services-report-201603.pdf.

5   Ibid.

6   First Data, *There's No Slowing Down Millennials,* 3, accessed February 18, 2017, https://www.firstdata.com/content/dam/FirstData/fdc_site/homepage_v2/millennials/images/millennial-white-paper-FNL.pdf.

7   WePay, "WePay's Small Business Payments Survey Data Suggests the Death of Checks," news release, June 20, 2013, accessed February 19, 2017, http://www.marketwired.com/press-release/wepays-small-business-payments-survey-data-suggests-the-death-of-checks-1804103.htm.

8   Board of Governors of the Federal Reserve System, *Consumers and Mobile Financial Services 2016,* 76–77, March 2016, accessed February 18, 2017, https://www.federalreserve.gov/econresdata/consumers-and-mobile-financial-services-report-201603.pdf.

9   University of Georgia Alumni Association, *UGA Alumni Chapter Leader Playbook,* pp. 12 and 42, 2016, https://alumni.uga.edu/wp-content/uploads/Alumni_Handbook_2016.pdf.

10 University of Florida Alumni Association, *Gator Club and Affiliate Group Leaders Handbook,* 27, https://www.ufalumni.ufl.edu/gatorclubs/admin/docs/dl/?-file=218.

11 Courtney Roehling (Vice President of Engagement, Ex-Students' Association of the University of Texas), phone interview, January 6, 2017.

12 West Point Association of Graduates, *Society Leader Guide 2016,* 11, http://www.westpointaog.org/file/societyleadershandbook.pdf.

13   Purdue Alumni Association, *Appendix J: Auctions and Raffles as Fundraisers*, accessed February 19, 2017, http://purdue.imodules.com/s/1461/images/editor_documents/club/appendixj.pdf.

14   Bowling Green State University Alumni, *Auction, Raffle, and Banquet Fundraiser Procedures*, 1, 2016, https://www.bgsu.edu/content/dam/BGSU/alumni/documents/Auction-FundRaiser-Banquet-Procedures.doc.

15   Sarah Brokamp (Coordinator of Alumni and Annual Giving, Bowling Green State University Alumni Association), phone interview, January 27, 2017.

16   "Crowdfunding Industry Statistics 2015 2016," CrowdExpert.com, accessed February 19, 2017, http://crowdexpert.com/crowdfunding-industry-statistics.

17   Andre Bourque, "Are Millennials the Most Generous Generation?," *Entrepreneur*, March 29, 2016, accessed February 19, 2017, https://www.entrepreneur.com/article/271466.

18   Aaron Smith, "Shared, Collaborative and On Demand: The New Digital Economy," Pew Research Center, news release, May 19, 2016, 2, http://www.pewinternet.org/files/2016/05/PI_2016.05.19_Sharing-Economy_FINAL.pdf.

19   Ibid., 12.

20   Ibid., 44.

21   Ibid., 43.

22   Architect Staff, "Michael Graves, Dead at 80," *Architect Magazine*, March 12, 2015, http://www.architectmagazine.com/design/michael-graves-dead-at-80_o.

23   Mitch Lipka, "Crowdfunding for a Good Cause Gets Cheaper," *Time*, January 16, 2015, accessed February 19, 2017, http://time.com/money/3670895/crowdfunding-personal-fundraising-fees.

24   "Crowdfunding 101," Crowdfunding Strategy & Information, 2016, accessed February 19, 2017, http://crowdfundingstrategy.net/beforeyoucrowdfundtips.

25   Jamie L., "Mobile Fundraising Statistics," @Pay, January 21, 2016, accessed February 19, 2017, https://www.atpay.com/mobile-fundraising-statistics.

26   "Alumni – VOLStarter," University of Tennessee, Knoxville, https://volstarter.utk.edu.

27   University of Tennessee, Knoxville, *Alumni Chapter Manual*, 34, accessed February 13, 2017, http://alumni.utk.edu/s/1341/images/gid2/editor_documents/Chapters/2016_Chapter_manual_for_web.pdf.

28   "Who Are UMSL Alumni?," University of Missouri–St. Louis Office of Alumni Engagement, 2016, accessed March 1, 2017, http://www.umslalumni.org/s/260/alumni/index.aspx?sid=260&gid=1001&sitebuilder=1&pgid=1259. Accessed 1 March 2017.

29   "Chapters, Networks, and Groups," University of Missouri–St. Louis Office of Alumni Engagement, 2016, accessed March 1, 2017, http://www.umslalumni.org/s/260/alumni/index.aspx?sid=260&gid=1001&pgid=1149.

30   "Give," University of Missouri–St. Louis, accessed March 1, 2017, https://crowdfund.umsl.edu.

31 "UMSL Marketing Advisory Board Scholarship Fund 2016," University of Missouri–St. Louis, accessed March 1, 2017, https://crowdfund.umsl.edu/project/2850.

32 University of Iowa Alumni Association, *Recognized IOWA Club Handbook*, 10, http://www.iowalum.com/clubs/pdf/Handbook.pdf.

33 "Raffles in Texas: Know the Law," Texas Attorney General Ken Paxton, May 10, 2010, https://www.texasattorneygeneral.gov/alerts/alerts_view_alpha.php?id=58&type=1.

34 University of Minnesota Alumni Association, *Volunteer Resource Guide*, 6, http://www.minnesotaalumni.org/s/1118/images/editor_documents/volunteer_resource_guide_draft_3_bb.pdf?sessionid=a2fe66da-7905-4300-957f-83d56c22a316.

35 Syracuse University Office of Alumni Relations, *SU Alumni Club Manual*, 17, October 2013, http://alumni.syr.edu/wp-content/uploads/2017/01/2013-Club-Manual-final-updated-2.14docx.pdf.

36 University of Florida Alumni Association, *Gator Club and Affiliate Group Leaders Handbook*, 34, https://www.ufalumni.ufl.edu/gatorclubs/admin/docs/dl/?file=218.

37 "Fayette County UK Alumni Club 2016 City Par-3 Championship," University of Kentucky Alumni Association, 2017, http://www.ukalumni.net/s/1052/semi-blank-noimg.aspx?sid=1052&pgid=7058&gid=1&cid=12770&ecid=12770&post_id=0.

38 Jim Richardson (President of the University of Kentucky [UK] Fayette County Alumni Club), phone interview, October 18, 2016.

39 "Ole Miss – New Orleans SEC Tennis Tournament," Ole Miss Alumni Association, accessed February 19, 2017, http://rebelnetwork.olemissalumni.com/s/1605/alumni/rd/2-col.aspx?sid=1605&gid=2&pgid=2361&content_id=1608.

Mobile Giving Now for Everyone, Big and Very Small

1 Amy Gahran, "Donating to Charity by Text Message: Lessons from Haiti," CNN, January 12, 2012, accessed February 19, 2017, http://www.cnn.com/2012/01/12/tech/mobile/charity-donations-text-messages.

2 "Mobile Giving Foundation," Mobile Giving Foundation, 2017, http://www.mobilegiving.org.

3 Jamie L., "Mobile Fundraising Statistics," @Pay, January 21, 2016, accessed February 19, 2017, https://www.atpay.com/mobile-fundraising-statistics/. Accessed 19 February 2017.

4 Achieve, *Cause, Influence & the Next Generation Workforce: The 2015 Millennial Impact Report*, pp. 9 and 26, 2015, http://fi.fudwaca.com/mi/files/2016/07/2015-MillennialImpactReport_01.pdf.

5 "Google," Google.com, https://www.google.com.

6 "Carry The Load," Carry The Load, http://www.carrytheload.org/site/

PageServer?pagename=home.

7   Association of Graduates, United States Air Force Academy, *2016–2017 Chapter Handbook*, 26–27, http://www2.usafa.org/Documents/AOG%20Chapters/ChapterHandbook2016PrintFile.pdf.

General Events Are Still the Workhorse

1   Andrew Cafourek (CEO of Alumni Spaces) and Bill Moakley (University of Oklahoma Alumni Association), "Your Chapters Have Spoken! Here's What They Said" (presentation, first presented during the CASE IV District Conference "Destination: Engagement," Fort Worth, Texas, March 5, 2017).

2   Tulane University Office of Alumni Relations, *Tulane Alumni Association Club Handbook*, 31, June 27, 2016, http://alumni.tulane.edu/s/1586/images/gid3/editor_documents/taa_board_/2016_summer_meeting/1_-_2016_taa_club_handbook.pdf?sessionid=37ce688f-3809-4ec3-afb4-43efc5fcb58a.

3   University of Minnesota Alumni Association, *Volunteer Resource Guide*, 6, http://www.minnesotaalumni.org/s/1118/images/editor_documents/volunteer_re-source_guide_draft_3_bb.pdf?sessionid=a2fe66da-7905-4300-957f-83d56c2 2a316.

4   "The Restriction of Political Campaign Intervention by Section 501(c)(3) Tax-Exempt Organizations," Internal Revenue Service, September 13, 2016, accessed February 19, 2017, https://www.irs.gov/charities-non-profits/charitable-organizations/the-restriction-of-political-campaign-intervention-by-section-501-c-3-tax-ex-empt-organizations.

5   "SEC Alumni and Fans of Boston," Facebook, accessed February 19, 2017, https://www.facebook.com/SECboston/about/?ref=page_internal.

6   Binghamton University Alumni Association, *Regional Chapter and Affinity Group Handbook*, 16, https://www.binghamton.edu/alumni/events-chapters/Regional%20Chapter%20and%20Affinity%20Group%20Handbook%20-%20April%202015.pdf.

7   American University Office of Alumni Relations, *Alumni Volunteer Handbook*, 26, http://alumniassociation.american.edu/s/1395/images/editor_documents/volunteer_handbook/2013_alumni_volunteer_guide.hyperlinked.pdf.

8   University of Illinois Alumni Association, *Event Rental*, 1–2, http://uialumniasso-ciation.org/wp-content/uploads/sites/5/2015/10/Event-Rental.pdf.

9   "Club Leaders Toolbox," Association of Yale Alumni, accessed February 15, 2017, http://www.aya.yale.edu/content/club-leaders-toolbox.

10   Nory Babbitt (Senior Director for Club and Association Relations, Association of Yale Alumni), phone interview, February 15, 2017.

11   "The Yale Club of New York City," The Yale Club of New York City, accessed February 15, 2017, http://www.yaleclubnyc.org.

12   "Yale Club Membership Information," The Yale Club of New York City, accessed February 15, 2017, http://www.yaleclubnyc.org/membership.

13 "Louisiana Chapters," Southern University Alumni Federation, accessed May 30, 2017, http://www.sualumni.org/page/LouisianaChapters.

14 "Out of State Chapters," Southern University Alumni Federation, accessed May 30, 2017, http://www.sualumni.org/page/OutofStateChapters.

15 "Southern University Alumni Federation," Southern University Alumni Federation, accessed February 19, 2017, http://www.sualumni.org.

16 "Crawfish Boil & Fish Fry," Southern University Alumni, Houston Chapter, accessed February 19, 2017, http://www.houstonjaguars.com/crawfish-boil-fish-fry.

17 "Local Chapters," Campbell University Alumni Association, accessed February 19, 2017, http://alumni.campbell.edu/s/881/index.aspx?sid=881&gid=1&pgid=995.

18 Michael Little (Director of Alumni Engagement, Campbell University Alumni Association), phone interview, March 2, 2017.

19 "Cape Fear Chapter Hosts BBQ on the Beach," Campbell University Alumni Association, accessed February 19, 2017, http://alumni.campbell.edu/s/881/index.aspx?sid=881&gid=1&pgid=252&cid=4432&ecid=4432&ci-id=11533&crid=0.

20 Kevin Stokes (Regional and Chapter Program Manager, University of Utah Alumni Association), phone interview, February 24, 2017.

21 "Lake Accotink Picnic," Washington, DC Chapter – University of Utah Alumni Association, accessed February 20, 2017, http://www.uofudc.com/lake-accotink-picnic.html.

22 "Chapters," Virginia Tech Alumni Association, last modified 2017, accessed February 20, 2017, http://www.alumni.vt.edu/Chapters.html.

23 "Factbook: About the University," Virginia Tech, last modified 2017, accessed February 20, 2017, https://www.vt.edu/about/factbook.html.

24 "July 2016 Newsletter," Viginia Tech Alumni Association – Seattle Chapter, last modified July 25, 2016, accessed February 20, 2017, https://seattlehokies.wordpress.com/2016/07/25/july-newsletter.

25 "2016 Army/Navy Game Party (Palo Alto)," SF Bay Area Chapter US Naval Academy Alumni Association, accessed February 20, 2017, https://s07.123signup.com/servlet/SignUpMember?PG=1531170182300&P=15311701911431419000&Info.

26 Florida State University Alumni Association, *2016–2017 Seminole Club® Handbook*, 39, http://alumni.fsu.edu/sites/alumni.fsu.edu/files/2016%20Seminole%20Club%20Handbook1.pdf.

27 Tulane University Office of Alumni Relations, *Tulane Alumni Association Club Handbook*, 46, June 27, 2016, http://alumni.tulane.edu/s/1586/images/gid3/editor_documents/taa_board_/2016_summer_meeting/1_-_2016_taa_club_handbook.pdf?sessionid=c295ecb2-461a-4202-a557-bd39aca3626d.

28 Amy Simonini (Assistant Director, University of Rhode Island Alumni Association), phone interview, February 27, 2017.

29 Jenny Kieta Cox (Director, Alumni Relations, Texas Christian University [TCU]

Alumni Relations), phone interview, 18 January 2017.

30 "Chapter Cities," Texan Christian University Alumni Association, last modified 2017, https://alumni.tcu.edu/new/Chapter-cities.

31 TCU Alumni Association, *Chapter Handbook 2011*, 23, https://www.google.com/url?sa=t&rct=j&q=&esrc=s&source=web&cd=1&ved=0ahUKEwjqlqLzo5rU-AhWCwVQKHRwiDKMQFggoMAA&url=http%3A%2F%2Fwww.froglinks.com%2Fs%2F441%2Fimages%2Feditor_documents%2F-ChapterGroupNetwork%2FTCUChapterGroupNetwork_Handbook.docx&usg=AFQjCNF9n50F6RZN3gaowlN4aYe4wJxdPQ&sig2=A8Yz-Tys12mkI2Lq4dMgXEQ&cad=rja.

Giving Days Are Sweeping the Country

1 "Give Local Greater Waterbury and Litchfield Hills," Connecticut Community Foundation, last modified 2017, http://www.conncf.org/nonprofits/give-local.

2 "#NTXGiving Day," Communities Foundation of Texas, last modified 2017, accessed March 1, 2017, https://northtexasgivingday.org.

3 Ibid.

4 Nicole Neroulias Gupte, "Community Foundations, Nonprofits Prep for 2016 Giving Days," *Philanthropy Northwest* (blog), April 6, 2016, accessed March 1, 2017, https://philanthropynw.org/news/community-foundations-nonprofits-prep-2016-giving-days.

5 "GiveBIG 2016 Exceeds Goals - Delivers Lift for Many Local Nonprofits," *Impact* (blog), Seattle Foundation, June 14, 2016, accessed March 1, 2017, https://www.seattlefoundation.org/Blog/GiveBIG-2016-Exceeds-Goal.

6 Sacramento Region Community Foundation, *BIG Day of Giving 2016 Post-Event Report*, http://www.sacregcf.org/srcf/assets/BIG%20Day%20of%20Giving%20 2016%20Post%20Event%20Report.pdf.

7 "Giving Tuesday," Giving Tuesday, https://www.givingtuesday.org/.

8 Ben Libman, "Fourth Annual Columbia Giving Day Raises Nearly $13 Million," *Columbia Daily Spectator*, October 22, 2015, http://columbiaspectator.com/news/2015/10/22/fourth-annual-columbia-giving-day-raises-nearly-13-million.

9 Yeewen New, "Columbia Raises Record-High $14.5 Million on Giving Day," *Columbia Daily Spectator*, November 14, 2016, http://columbiaspectator.com/news/2016/10/27/columbia-raises-record-high-145-million-giving-day.

10 "Columbia Giving Day 2016: Thank you!," YouTube video, 1:26, posted by "columbiagivingday," October 26, 2016, https://youtu.be/i1zP_1j72Fg.

11 Purdue University, "Purdue Day of Giving Raises Record $13.7 Million in 24 Hours; Largest Total for Single-Day Campaign in Higher Ed," news release, April 30, 2015, http://www.purdue.edu/newsroom/releases/2015/Q2/purdue-day-of-giving-raises-record-13.7-million-in-24-hours-largest-total-for-single-day-campaign-in-higher-ed.html.

12 Purdue University, "Purdue Day of Giving Shatters Its Own Record, Raising

$18.3 Million in 24-Hour Higher-Ed Campaign," news release, April 28, 2016, https://www.purdue.edu/newsroom/releases/2016/Q2/purdue-day-of-giving-shatters-its-own-record,-raising-18.3-million-in-24-hour-higher-ed-campaign. html.

13 "Purdue Day of Giving 2016 Thank You," YouTube video, 1:17, posted by "Purdue University," April 28, 2016, https://youtu.be/eNyJWcV4P0M.

Matching Gifts—Big Money Left on the Table

1 Steve Delfin, "Engagement: From Strategy to Success," *America's Charities Blog*, June 1, 2015, https://www.charities.org/news/blog/engagement-strategy-success.

2 "1% Companies," Pay It Forward Foundation, last modified 2017, http://www. payitforward.foundation/pages/1-companies.

3 "Matching Gift and Corporate Giving Statistics," Double the Donation, last modified January 2017, https://doublethedonation.com/matching-grant-re-sources/matching-gift-statistics/.

4 CECP, *Giving in Numbers: 2016 Edition*, 21, 2016, http://cecp.co/wp-content/ uploads/2016/11/GIN2016_Finalweb.pdf?redirect=no.

5 "Matching Gifts," GE Sustainability, last modified 2017, http://www.gefounda-tion.com/giving-programs/matching-gifts/.

6 "Employee Participation," ExxonMobil, last modified 2017, http://corporate. exxonmobil.com/en/community/worldwide-giving/employee-giving/overview.

7 Adam Weinger, "Seven Companies with the Most Unique Matching Gift Programs for Employees," *Triple Pundit*, February 25, 2014, http://www.triplepundit. com/2014/02/seven-companies-unique-matching-gift-programs-employees/.

8 GE Foundation, *GE Foundation Matching Gifts Program*, 1, http://dsg. files.app.content.prod.s3.amazonaws.com/gesustainability/wp-content/up-loads/2017/05/09125207/MG-guidelines-for-1-1-15.pdf.

9 "Matching Gifts Program," Bank of America, last modified 2017, http://about. bankofamerica.com/en-us/global-impact/matching-gifts-features-and-eligibility. html#fbid=KeEoOK05J8F.

10 Apple Inc., *Apple Matching Gifts Program*, 2014, http://forms.matchinggifts.com/ AppleGuide.pdf.

Volunteer Grants Are Easy Money for Chapter Leaders

1 CECP, *Giving in Numbers: 2016 Edition*, 21, 2016, http://cecp.co/wp-content/ uploads/2016/11/GIN2016_Finalweb.pdf?redirect=no.

2 Adam Weinger, "Volunteer Grant Programs: A Mutually Beneficial Collaboration Between Nonprofits and Corporations," *Triple Pundit*, May 27, 2014, http://www.triplepundit. com/2014/05/volunteer-grant-programs-mutually-beneficial-collaboration-nonprofits-cor-porations/.

3 CECP, *Giving in Numbers: 2016 Edition*, 7, 2016, http://cecp.co/wp-content/ uploads/2016/11/GIN2016_Finalweb.pdf?redirect=no.

4   "Matching Gift and Corporate Giving Statistics," Double the Donation, last modified January 2017, https://doublethedonation.com/matching-grant-re-sources/matching-gift-statistics/.

5   "Deloitte Volunteer Impact Research," Deloitte, https://www2.deloitte.com/us/en/pages/about-deloitte/articles/citizenship-deloitte-volunteer-impact-research.html.

6   "Microsoft's 2016 Giving Results," Microsoft, last modified 2017, accessed April 2, 2017, http://www.microsoft.com/about/philanthropies/our-employees/em-ployee-giving.

7   Verizon, *Volunteer Incentive Program (VIP)*, last modified January 2017, http://www.verizon.com/about/sites/default/files/Volunteer-Incentive-Program-Rules.pdf.

8   "Give Back," Pfizer Plus, last modified 2017, http://www.pfizerplus.com/gi/vol-unteer_program.aspx.

9   "Employee Programs," AmeriGives, Kimberly-Clark Foundation, Inc., last mod-ified October 11, 2015, https://new.givingprograms.com/kcc.

10   "Volunteer Grants," Bank of America, last modified 2017, http://about.ban-kofamerica.com/en-us/global-impact/volunteer-grants-features-and-eligibility.html#fbid=KeEoOK05J8F.

11   "Individual Volunteer Involvement Program Guidelines," ExxonMobil, https://secure3.easymatch.com/ExxonMobilVIP/CustomerContent/common/Guidelinesivip.asp.

Promotion for Maximum Impact

1   Andrew Cafourek (CEO of Alumni Spaces) and Bill Moakley (University of Oklahoma Alumni Association), "Your Chapters Have Spoken! Here's What They Said" (presentation, first presented during the CASE IV District Conference "Destination: Engagement," Fort Worth, Texas, March 5, 2017).

2   Georgia State University Alumni Association, *Georgia State University Alumni Networks Manual*, 12, accessed January 26, 2017, http://www.pan-theralumni.com/s/1471/images/gid2/editor_documents/alumni_networks/gsu_network_leaders_manual_-_2017.pdf.

3   Texas State Alumni Association, *Alumni Chapter Operational Guidelines*, 11, August 31, 2014, http://alumni.txstate.edu/file/Chapter-Operational-Guidelines-Final---Starting-a-new-Chapter.pdf.

4   Neil Patel, "How to Reach Baby Boomers, Gen-Xers and Millennials with Your Online Marketing," *Quick Sprout Blog*, July 8, 2016, https://www.quicksprout.com/2016/07/08/how-to-reach-baby-boomers-gen-xers-and-millennials-with-your-online-marketing.

5   Eileen Patten and Richard Fry, "How Millennials Today Compare with Their Grandparents 50 Years Ago," *Fact Tank* (blog), Pew Research Center, March 19, 2015, http://www.pewresearch.org/fact-tank/2015/03/19/

how-millennials-compare-with-their-grandparents/#!6.

6   Pew Research Center, *Millennials in Adulthood*, 4, 6–7, 10–11, March 7, 2014, http://www.pewsocialtrends.org/2014/03/07/millennials-in-adulthood.

7   Neil Patel, "How to Reach Baby Boomers, Gen-Xers and Millennials with Your Online Marketing," *Quick Sprout Blog*, July 8, 2016, https://www.quicksprout.com/2016/07/08/how-to-reach-baby-boomers-gen-xers-and-millennials-with-your-online-marketing.

8   Adestra, *2016 Consumer Adoption & Usage Study*, 5, http://www.adestra.com/resources/downloadable-reports/consumer-adoption-and-usage-study.

9   Yahoo!, *Generation X: America's most Influential Generation*, 3, https://ad-marketing.yahoo.net/rs/118-OEW-181/images/AT%20Yahoo%20-%20Gen%20X_America%27s%20Most%20Influential%20Generation.pdf.

10 Rieva Lesonsky, "Gen X: How to Market to the Forgotten Generation," *OPEN Forum* (blog), American Express, September 15, 2014, https://www.americanexpress.com/us/small-business/openforum/articles/gen-x-how-to-market-to-the-forgotten-generation.

11 Yahoo!, *Generation X: America's most Influential Generation*, 11, https://ad-marketing.yahoo.net/rs/118-OEW-181/images/AT%20Yahoo%20-%20Gen%20X_America%27s%20Most%20Influential%20Generation.pdf.

12 Ibid., 15.

13 Ibid., 16.

14 Ibid., 18.

15 comScore, Inc., *2016 U.S. Cross-Platform Future in Focus* (2016), 7, 23.

16 Andrew Perrin, Pew Research Center, *Social Media Usage: 2005–2015*, 4, October 8, 2015, http://www.pewinternet.org/2015/10/08/social-networking-usage-2005-2015.

17 "How Digital Behavior Differs Among Millennials, Gen Xers and Boomers," eMarketer, March 21, 2013, https://www.emarketer.com/Article/How-Digital-Behavior-Differs-Among-Millennials-Gen-Xers-Boomers/1009748.

18 Richard Fry, "Millennials Overtake Baby Boomers as America's Largest Generation," *Fact Tank* (blog), Pew Research Center, April 25, 2016, http://www.pewresearch.org/fact-tank/2016/04/25/millennials-overtake-baby-boomers/.

19 Sally Kane, "Baby Boomers in the Workplace," The Balance, February 22, 2017, https://www.thebalance.com/baby-boomers-2164681.

20 Pew Research Center, *Millennials in Adulthood*, 14, March 7, 2014, http://www.pewsocialtrends.org/2014/03/07/millennials-in-adulthood.

21 Ibid., 13.

22 Ibid., 7.

23 Merrill Lynch, *Leisure in Retirement: Beyond the Bucket List* (Bank of America Corporation, 2016).

24 The Neilsen Company & BoomAgers LLC, *Introducing Boomers: Marketing's Most Valuable Generation*, 4, 2012, http://www.nielsen.com/content/dam/corporate/

us/en/reports-downloads/2012-Reports/nielsen-boomers-report-082912.pdf.

25 Jackie Crosby, "Don't Call Us Old: Baby Boomers Reject Traditional Terms for Aging," *Star Tribune*, March 30, 2015, http://www.startribune.com/don-t-call-us-old-baby-boomers-reject-traditional-terms-for-aging/293835401/.

26 Merrill Lynch, *Giving in Retirement: America's Longevity Bonus*, 5, https://mlaem.fs.ml.com/content/dam/ML/Articles/pdf/ML_AgeWave_Giving_in_Retirement_Report.pdf.

27 Merrill Lynch, *Leisure in Retirement: Beyond the Bucket List* (Bank of America Corporation, 2016), 11.

28 Jim Harter and Sangeeta Agrawal, "Many Baby Boomers Reluctant to Retire," Gallup, January 20, 2014, http://www.gallup.com/poll/166952/baby-boomers-reluctant-retire.aspx.

29 Adestra, *2016 Consumer Adoption & Usage Study*, 4, 14, 16, http://www.adestra.com/resources/downloadable-reports/consumer-adoption-and-usage-study.

30 Pamela Lockard, "The Truth About Baby Boomers and Social Media," *DMN3* (blog), July 1, 2015, https://www.dmn3.com/dmn3-blog/boomers-and-social-media.

31 Andrew Cafourek (CEO of Alumni Spaces) and Bill Moakley (University of Oklahoma Alumni Association), "Your Chapters Have Spoken! Here's What They Said" (presentation, first presented during the CASE IV District Conference "Destination: Engagement," Fort Worth, Texas, March 5, 2017).

32 Chad S. White, "2016 Mobile-Friendly Email & Landing Page Trends [Infographic]," *Litmus* (blog), August 1, 2016, https://litmus.com/blog/2016-mobile-friendly-email-landing-page-trends-infographic.

33 Kerry Jones, "The Generational Content Gap: How Different Age Groups Consume Content," *Marketing Land*, August 18, 2015, http://marketingland.com/generational-content-gap-how-different-age-groups-consume-content-138810.

34 Kayla Lewkowicz, "Surprise! Millennials Love Email Just As Much As Everybody Else," *Litmus* (blog), April 27, 2016, https://litmus.com/blog/surprise-millennials-love-email-just-as-much-as-everybody-else.

35 Daniel Burstein, "Marketing Research Chart: Do Different Age Groups Prefer Different Channels?," *MarketingSherpa Blog*, March 10, 2015, https://www.marketingsherpa.com/article/chart/channels-preferred-by-age-groups.

36 Giselle Abramovich, "Survey: Email Is Evolving And Time Spent With It Growing," *CMO.com*, October 3, 2016, http://www.cmo.com/adobe-digital-insights/articles/2016/9/30/adobe-email-survey-2016.html#gs.yI5oTfs.

37 Adestra, *2016 Consumer Adoption & Usage Study*, 3, http://www.adestra.com/resources/downloadable-reports/consumer-adoption-and-usage-study.

38 Ibid., 14.

39 Ibid., 16.

40 Ibid., 21.

41 Chad S. White, "2016 Mobile-Friendly Email & Landing Page Trends

[Infographic]," *Litmus* (blog), August 1, 2016, https://litmus.com/blog/2016-mobile-friendly-email-landing-page-trends-infographic.

42 Andrew Cafourek (CEO of Alumni Spaces) and Bill Moakley (University of Oklahoma Alumni Association), "Your Chapters Have Spoken! Here's What They Said" (presentation, first presented during the CASE IV District Conference "Destination: Engagement," Fort Worth, Texas, March 5, 2017).

43 Adestra, *2016 Consumer Adoption & Usage Study*, 40, http://www.adestra.com/resources/downloadable-reports/consumer-adoption-and-usage-study.

44 Matthew D. Schulz (Director of Engagement, Fresno State Alumni Association), phone interview, February 2, 2017.

45 Andrew Cafourek (CEO of Alumni Spaces) and Bill Moakley (University of Oklahoma Alumni Association), "Your Chapters Have Spoken! Here's What They Said" (presentation, first presented during the CASE IV District Conference "Destination: Engagement," Fort Worth, Texas, March 5, 2017).

46 Stanford Alumni Association, *Stanford Club Leaders Handbook*, 24–25, April 6, 2011, https://alumni.stanford.edu/content/groups/docs/2011_Club_Handbook.pdf.

47 Florida State University Alumni Association, *2016–2017 Seminole Club® Handbook*, 25, http://alumni.fsu.edu/sites/alumni.fsu.edu/files/2016%20Seminole%20Club%20Handbook1.pdf.

48 Andrew Cafourek (CEO of Alumni Spaces) and Bill Moakley (University of Oklahoma Alumni Association), "Your Chapters Have Spoken! Here's What They Said" (presentation, first presented during the CASE IV District Conference "Destination: Engagement," Fort Worth, Texas, March 5, 2017).

49 David Daniels, The Relevancy Group, LLC, *Exploring the Benefits of Real-Time Email*, 4, http://www.realtime.email/wp-content/uploads/2014/12/Exploring-The-Benefits-of-Realtime-Email-The-Relevancy-Group-Liveclicker-1.pdf.

50 Adestra, *2016 Consumer Adoption & Usage Study*, 9, http://www.adestra.com/resources/downloadable-reports/consumer-adoption-and-usage-study.

51 Ibid., 40.

52 David Daniels, The Relevancy Group, LLC, *Exploring the Benefits of Real-Time Email*, http://www.realtime.email/wp-content/uploads/2014/12/Exploring-The-Benefits-of-Realtime-Email-The-Relevancy-Group-Liveclicker-1.pdf.

53 Andrew Perrin, Pew Research Center, *Social Media Usage: 2005–2015*, 6, October 8, 2015, http://www.pewinternet.org/files/2015/10/PI_2015-10-08_Social-Networking-Usage-2005-2015_FINAL.pdf.

54 Ibid., 4.

55 Statista, *Percentage of U.S. Population Who Currently Use Any Social Media from 2008 to 2017*, https://www.statista.com/statistics/273476/percentage-of-us-population-with-a-social-network-profile/.

56 Daniel Burstein, "Marketing Research Chart: How Do Customers Want to Communicate?," *MarketingSherpa Blog*, February 3, 2015, http://www.

marketingsherpa.com/article/case-study/customer-communication-by-channel.

57 Daniel Burstein, "Marketing Research Chart: Do Different Age Groups Prefer Different Channels?," *MarketingSherpa Blog*, March 10, 2015, https://www.marketingsherpa.com/article/chart/channels-preferred-by-age-groups.

58 "Company Info," Facebook, accessed February 21, 2017, http://newsroom.fb.com/company-info.

59 "U.S. and World Population Clock," United States Census Bureau, accessed February 21, 2017, http://www.census.gov/popclock.

60 Pew Research Center, *Mobile Messaging and Social Media 2015*, 3, August 19, 2015, http://www.pewinternet.org/files/2015/08/Social-Media-Update-2015-FINAL2.pdf.

61 Ibid., 3.

62 Statista, *Leading Social Media Websites in the United States in November 2016, Based on Share of Visits*, https://www.statista.com/statistics/265773/market-share-of-the-most-popular-social-media-websites-in-the-us/.

63 Pew Research Center, *Mobile Messaging and Social Media 2015*, 10, August 19, 2015, http://www.pewinternet.org/files/2015/08/Social-Media-Update-2015-FINAL2.pdf.

64 comScore, Inc., *2016 U.S. Cross-Platform Future in Focus* (2016), 34.

65 Andrew Cafourek (CEO of Alumni Spaces) and Bill Moakley (University of Oklahoma Alumni Association), "Your Chapters Have Spoken! Here's What They Said" (presentation, first presented during the CASE IV District Conference "Destination: Engagement," Fort Worth, Texas, March 5, 2017).

66 James B. Stewart, "Facebook has 50 Minutes of Your Time Each Day. It Wants More.," Common Sense, *New York Times*, May 5, 2016, https://www.nytimes.com/2016/05/06/business/facebook-bends-the-rules-of-audience-engagement-to-its-advantage.html?_r=0.

67 Pew Research Center, *Mobile Messaging and Social Media 2015*, 10, August 19, 2015, http://www.pewinternet.org/files/2015/08/Social-Media-Update-2015-FINAL2.pdf, p. 10.

68 Association of Yale Alumni, *Setting Up Social Media for Your Yale Alumni Organization & Encouraging Social Sharing About Your Events*, accessed February 21, 2017, https://www.dropbox.com/s/2zud5oz35mpu5fi/Setting%20Up%20Social%20Media%20for%20Alumni%20Groups%2004.12.16.pdf?dl=0.

69 Laura Weekley (Senior Director, Alumni Relations, Emory Alumni Association), phone interview, January 24, 2017.

70 Emory Alumni Association, *Chapter Social Media Overview & Facebook Guidelines*, http://www.alumni.emory.edu/_includes/documents/sections/volunteer/socielmediaoverview.pdf.

71 Kelly Davis (Director of Alumni Relations, Arkansas Tech University Alumni Association), phone interview, January 25, 2017.

72 Arkansas Tech University Alumni Association, *Arkansas Tech University Alumni*

Association Chapter Development Handbook, 11–12, accessed January 26, 2017, http://www.techties.atu.edu/s/978/images/editor_documents/Chapters/atu_Chapter_handbook__050514_.pdf?sessionid=6c34fa41-8eda-420c-9e96-12904 818bc28.

73   Marquette University Alumni Association, *Alumni Engagement and Outreach Volunteer Manual*, 17, accessed February 9, 2017, http://muconnect.marquette.edu/Document.Doc?id=16.

74   "Marketing & Communications 101," Penn Alumni, http://www.alumni.upenn.edu/s/1587/gid2/16/interior_1col.aspx?sid=1587&gid=2&pgid=9186.

75   "About Us," LinkedIn, accessed February 21, 2017, https://press.linkedin.com/about-linkedin.

76   Ibid.

77   Pew Research Center, *Mobile Messaging and Social Media 2015*, 13, August 19, 2015, http://www.pewinternet.org/files/2015/08/Social-Media-Update-2015-FINAL2.pdf.

78   comScore, Inc., *2016 U.S. Cross-Platform Future in Focus* (2016), 34.

79   Pew Research Center, *Mobile Messaging and Social Media 2015*, 15, August 19, 2015, http://www.pewinternet.org/files/2015/08/Social-Media-Update-2015-FINAL2.pdf.

80   Andrew Cafourek (CEO of Alumni Spaces) and Bill Moakley (University of Oklahoma Alumni Association), "Your Chapters Have Spoken! Here's What They Said" (presentation, first presented during the CASE IV District Conference "Destination: Engagement," Fort Worth, Texas, March 5, 2017).

81   "Groups – Overview," LinkedIn Help, last modified 2017, https://www.linkedin.com/help/linkedin/answer/1164/groups-getting-started?lang=en.

82   Villanova University Alumni Association, *VUAA Chartered Organizations Guidebook*, L, last modified fall 2016, http://alumni.villanova.edu/s/1695/images/gid2/editor_documents/volunteer_resources/vuaa_chartered_organizations_guidebook_-_fall_2016_edition.pdf.

83   Binghamton University Alumni Association, *Regional Chapter and Affinity Group Handbook*, 15, https://www.binghamton.edu/alumni/events-chapters/Regional%20Chapter%20and%20Affinity%20Group%20Handbook%20-%20 April%202015.pdf.

84   Wisconsin Alumni Association, *Chapter Leader Handbook*, 4, http://www.uwalumni.com/wp-content/uploads/Chapter_Leader_Handbook_2016.pdf.

85   Daniel Burstein, "Marketing Research Chart: How Do Customers Want to Communicate?," *MarketingSherpa Blog*, February 3, 2015, http://www.marketingsherpa.com/article/case-study/customer-communication-by-channel.

86   Neil Patel, "How to Reach Baby Boomers, Gen-Xers and Millennials with Your Online Marketing," *Quick Sprout Blog*, July 8, 2016, https://www.quicksprout.com/2016/07/08/how-to-reach-baby-boomers-gen-xers-and-millennials-with-your-online-marketing.

87 Adestra, *2016 Consumer Adoption & Usage Study*, 43, http://www.adestra.com/resources/downloadable-reports/consumer-adoption-and-usage-study.

88 Statista, *Most Famous Social Network Sites Worldwide as of April 2017, Ranked by Number of Active Users (in Millions)*, https://www.statista.com/statistics/272014/global-social-networks-ranked-by-number-of-users/.

89 Twitter, *Q3 2016 Earnings Report*, 4, http://files.shareholder.com/downloads/AMDA-2F526X/3143820223x0x913986/54A7EF6C-F9C3-44C7-BF3C-D4A921452DFA/Q3_16_Earnings_Slides.pdf.

90 Pew Research Center, *Mobile Messaging and Social Media 2015*, 8, August 19, 2015, http://www.pewinternet.org/files/2015/08/Social-Media-Update-2015-FINAL2.pdf.

91 Ibid., 14.

92 Ibid., 15.

93 Statista, *Leading Social Media Websites in the United States in November 2016, Based on Share of Visits*, https://www.statista.com/statistics/265773/market-share-of-the-most-popular-social-media-websites-in-the-us/.

94 comScore, Inc., *2016 U.S. Cross-Platform Future in Focus* (2016), 34.

95 Andrew Cafourek (CEO of Alumni Spaces) and Bill Moakley (University of Oklahoma Alumni Association), "Your Chapters Have Spoken! Here's What They Said" (presentation, first presented during the CASE IV District Conference "Destination: Engagement," Fort Worth, Texas, March 5, 2017).

96 Tufts University Alumni Association, *Tufts Alumni Volunteer Handbook*, 46, http://tuftsalumni.org/pdfs/Tufts_Alumni_Volunteer_Handbook.pdf.

97 Ibid., 47.

98 Iowa State University Alumni Association, *National Clubs Program Handbook*, 12, http://www.isualum.org/media/cms/Club_Handbook_FY16_0C14FC80760B3.pdf.

99 Virginia Commonwealth University Alumni, *VCU Alumni Chapter Toolkit*, 11, https://www.vcualumni.org/media/ADVSRV/alumni/files/VCUAlumniChapterToolkit.pdf.

100 "Text Messaging Marketing," CallFire, accessed February 21, 2017, https://www.callfire.com/text-messaging-marketing.

101 Daniel Burstein, "Marketing Research Chart: How Do Customers Want to Communicate?," *MarketingSherpa Blog*, February 3, 2015, http://www.marketingsherpa.com/article/case-study/customer-communication-by-channel.

102 Daniel Burstein, "Marketing Research Chart: Do Different Age Groups Prefer Different Channels?," *MarketingSherpa Blog*, March 10, 2015, https://www.marketingsherpa.com/article/chart/channels-preferred-by-age-groups.

103 Andrew Cafourek (CEO of Alumni Spaces) and Bill Moakley (University of Oklahoma Alumni Association), "Your Chapters Have Spoken! Here's What They Said" (presentation, first presented during the CASE IV District Conference "Destination: Engagement," Fort Worth, Texas, March 5, 2017).

104 University of Iowa Alumni Association, *Recognized IOWA Club Handbook*, 9, http://www.iowalum.com/clubs/pdf/Handbook.pdf.

105 TCU Alumni Association, *Chapter Handbook 2011*, 30, https://www.google.com/url?sa=t&rct=j&q=&esrc=s&source=web&cd=1&ved=0ahUKEwjqlqLzo5rU-AhWCwVQKHRwiDKMQFggoMAA&url=http%3A%2F%2Fwww.froglinks.com%2Fs%2F441%2Fimages%2Feditor_documents%2F-ChapterGroupNetwork%2FTCUChapterGroupNetwork_Handbook.docx&usg=AFQjCNF9n50F6RZN3gaowlN4aYe4wJxdPQ&sig2=A8Yz-Tys12mkI2Lq4dMgXEQ&cad=rja.

106 UNC General Alumni Association, *Handbook for Club Leaders*, 12, October 2016, https://alumni.unc.edu/wp-content/uploads/2016/10/Oct2016Handbook.pdf

107 "Diversity at Wharton," The Wharton School, accessed February 21, 2017, https://mba.wharton.upenn.edu/diversity-at-wharton.

108 UNC General Alumni Association, *Handbook for Club Leaders*, 23, October 2016, https://alumni.unc.edu/wp-content/uploads/2016/10/Oct2016Handbook.pdf.

109 Daniel Burstein, "Marketing Research Chart: How Do Customers Want to Communicate?," *MarketingSherpa Blog*, February 3, 2015, http://www.marketingsherpa.com/article/case-study/customer-communication-by-channel.

110 Daniel Burstein, "Marketing Research Chart: Do Different Age Groups Prefer Different Channels?," *MarketingSherpa Blog*, March 10, 2015, https://www.marketingsherpa.com/article/chart/channels-preferred-by-age-groups.

111 "About ASU Magazine," ASU Magazine, https://magazine.asu.edu/about.

112 Daniel Burstein, "Marketing Research Chart: How Do Customers Want to Communicate?," *MarketingSherpa Blog*, February 3, 2015, http://www.marketingsherpa.com/article/case-study/customer-communication-by-channel.

113 Daniel Burstein, "Marketing Research Chart: Do Different Age Groups Prefer Different Channels?," *MarketingSherpa Blog*, March 10, 2015, https://www.marketingsherpa.com/article/chart/channels-preferred-by-age-groups.

114 Adestra, *2016 Consumer Adoption & Usage Study*, 5, http://www.adestra.com/resources/downloadable-reports/consumer-adoption-and-usage-study.

115 University of Delaware Office of Alumni Relations, *Alumni Club Leaders Handbook*, 21, http://www.udconnection.com/getattachment/6de08a0a-c388-4285-a495-6839d93f7ec3/UD-Leadership-Handbook.aspx, p. 21.

116 "Alumni Chapters," St. Bonaventure University, accessed January 26, 2017, https://www.sbu.edu/alumni/alumni-Chapters.

117 St. Bonaventure University, *Handbook for Chapter Leaders*, 4, accessed January 26, 2017, http://www.sbu.edu/sbucustom/alumni/Chapter_Leader_Handbook_Final.pdf.

118 Ibid., 7.

119 "What We Do," Duke Alumni Association, https://alumni.duke.edu/what-we-do.

120 "Volunteer Resources," Duke Alumni Association, https://alumni.duke.edu/volunteer/volunteer-resources.

121 "School Groups," Duke Alumni Association, https://alumni.duke.edu/all_ groups?qt-home_groups_logged_out=0.

122 "Affinity Groups," Duke Alumni Association, https://alumni.duke.edu/affinity-groups.

123 "School Groups," Duke Alumni Association, https://alumni.duke.edu/all_ groups?qt-home_groups_logged_out=3.

124 "Chapters & Clubs," Alumni Association, University of Colorado Boulder, accessed May 30, 2017, http://www.colorado.edu/alumni/chapters-clubs.

125 Marquette University Alumni Association, *Alumni Engagement and Outreach Volunteer Manual*, 9, accessed February 9, 2017, http://muconnect.marquette. edu/Document.Doc?id=16.

126 Dartmouth College Office of Alumni Relations, *Operating Guidelines and Recommended Best Practices for Recognized Alumni Clubs, Affiliated Groups, and Shared Interest Groups*, 17, 2016–2017, http://alumni.dartmouth.edu/sites/alumni/files/Files/operatingguidelines2017.pdf.

127 Andrew Cafourek (CEO of Alumni Spaces) and Bill Moakley (University of Oklahoma Alumni Association), "Your Chapters Have Spoken! Here's What They Said" (presentation, first presented during the CASE IV District Conference "Destination: Engagement," Fort Worth, Texas, March 5, 2017).

128 "The Association," myNotreDame, last modified 2017, http://my.nd.edu/s/1210/ myND/interior-2col.aspx?sid=1210&gid=1&pgid=18704.

129 Syracuse University Office of Alumni Relations, *SU Alumni Club Manual*, 12, October 2013, http://alumni.syr.edu/wp-content/uploads/2017/01/2013-Club-Manual-final-updated-2.14docx.pdf.

130 "Texas Exes Rocky Mountain Chapter," Meetup, https://www.meetup.com/ Texas-Exes-Rocky-Mountain-Chapter/.

131 "Colorado Duke University Alumni Chapter (Denver, CO)," Meetup, https:// www.meetup.com/Colorado-Duke-University-Alumni-Chapter/.

132 Marquette University Alumni Association, *Alumni Engagement and Outreach Volunteer Manual*, 18, accessed February 9, 2017, http://muconnect.marquette. edu/Document.Doc?id=16.

133 Penn State Alumni Association, *Chapter Leaders Resource Guide*, 40, June 2014, http://alumni.psu.edu/groups/volunteer/ChapterLeadersResourceGuide.pdf.

134 University of Kentucky Alumni Association, *2016–2017 Alumni Club Leaders Handbook*, 36, http://www.uky.edu/Alumni/web/2016/Leadershipmanual.pdf.

135 "Marketing & Communications Specialist," Alumni Association of the University of Michigan, last modified 2017, http://alumni.umich.edu/clubs-and-groups/ club-leader-resources/marketing-communications/.

136 Alumni Association of the University of Mississippi, *Club Leadership Handbook*, 11, http://www.olemissalumni.com/wp-content/uploads/2016/02/Leadership-Handbook-2.19.16_revised_b.pdf.

137 Andrew Cafourek (CEO of Alumni Spaces) and Bill Moakley (University of

Oklahoma Alumni Association), "Your Chapters Have Spoken! Here's What They Said" (presentation, first presented during the CASE IV District Conference "Destination: Engagement," Fort Worth, Texas, March 5, 2017).

138 comScore, Inc., *2016 U.S. Cross-Platform Future in Focus* (2016), 23.

139 Daniel Burstein, "Marketing Research Chart: Do Different Age Groups Prefer Different Channels?," *MarketingSherpa Blog*, March 10, 2015, https://www.marketingsherpa.com/article/chart/channels-preferred-by-age-groups.

140 Ibid.

141 Laura Kenny, "Try It: Can You Hear These Sounds Only Young People Hear?," Yahoo Health, March 13, 2015, accessed February 22, 2017, https://www.yahoo.com/beauty/try-it-can-you-hear-these-sounds-only-young-112627654778.html.

142 "Age-Related Hearing Loss – Prebyacusis," Hear-it.org, accessed February 22, 2017, http://www.hear-it.org/Age-related-hearing-loss.

143 University of Chicago Alumni Association, *UChicago Alumni Volunteer Guide for Writing Social Media Content*, 2, http://kintera.org/atf/cf/%7B25c2541e-96eb-4e70-947f-aba13cd89dcd%7D/VOUNTEERGUIDE-WRITINGSOCIALMEDIACONTENT.PDF?_ga=1.156212466.871611558.1483022425.

144 Penn State Alumni Association, *Chapter Leaders Resource Guide*, 38, June 2014, http://alumni.psu.edu/groups/volunteer/ChapterLeadersResourceGuide.pdf.

145 Liz Conwell (Alumni Relations Manager, Grand Canyon University Alumni Association), phone interview, January 25, 2017.

146 Grand Canyon University Alumni, *Alumni Chapter Handbook*, 8, accessed January 26, 2017, http://alumni.gcu.edu/Documents/Alumni/Alumni-Chapter-Handbook.pdf.

Collecting and Handling the Money

1 Binghamton University Alumni Association, *Regional Chapter and Affinity Group Handbook*, 14, https://www.binghamton.edu/alumni/events-chapters/Regional%20Chapter%20and%20Affinity%20Group%20Handbook%20-%20April%202015.pdf.

2 Fresno State Alumni Association, *Chapters, Clubs & Networks Handbook*, 10, last modified March 8, 2014, accessed February 12, 2017, https://www.fresnostate.edu/alumni/documents/01_Chapters%20Clubs%20Networks%20Handbook.pdf.

3 Ibid., 11.

4 University of Tennessee, Knoxville, *Alumni Chapter Manual*, 39, accessed February 13, 2017, http://alumni.utk.edu/s/1341/images/gid2/editor_documents/Chapters/2016_Chapter_manual_for_web.pdf.

5 Ibid., 27.

6 Syracuse University Office of Alumni Relations, *SU Alumni Club Manual*, pp. 9 and 16–17, October 2013, http://alumni.syr.edu/wp-content/

uploads/2017/01/2013-Club-Manual-final-updated-2.14docx.pdf.

7   Mississippi State University Alumni Association, *2015 Chapter Handbook*, 14,
    http://www.alumni.msstate.edu/s/811/images/editor_documents/Chapter_
    handbook/Chapter_handbook_2015v2.pdf.

8   LSU Alumni Association, *Chapter Guidelines Booklet*, 9, 2016, http://www.lsu-
    alumni.org/Images/Interior/Chapters/2016Chapter%20guidelines.compressed.
    pdf.

9   Arkansas Alumni, *Chapter Guidebook 2016-2017*, 7, accessed January 26,
    2017,   http://www.arkansasalumni.org/s/1429/images/editor_documents/
    Chapters/2016-2017_Chapter_guidebook-min__1_.pdf.

10 LSU Alumni Association, *Chapter Guidelines Booklet*, 9, 2016, http://www.lsu-
    alumni.org/Images/Interior/Chapters/2016Chapter%20guidelines.compressed.
    pdf.

11 Stanford Alumni Association, *Stanford Club Leaders Handbook*, 54, April 6, 2011,
    https://alumni.stanford.edu/content/groups/docs/2011_Club_Handbook.pdf.

12 University of Florida Alumni Association, *Gator Club and Affiliate Group Leaders
    Handbook*,   27,   https://www.ufalumni.ufl.edu/gatorclubs/admin/docs/dl/?-
    file=218, p. 27.

13 Texas State Alumni Association, *Alumni Chapter Operational Guidelines*, 9, August
    31, 2014, http://alumni.txstate.edu/file/Chapter-Operational-Guidelines-Final--
    -Starting-a-new-Chapter.pdf.

14 University of Iowa Alumni Association, *Recognized IOWA Club Handbook*, 3–4,
    http://www.iowalum.com/clubs/pdf/Handbook.pdf.

State and Federal Tax Implications

1   Harvard Alumni Association, Clubs & Shared Interest Groups Office, *HAA Club
    Officer Handbook: How to Start or Revive a Harvard Club*, 15–17, http://alumni.
    harvard.edu/sites/default/files/page/files/haa-club-officer-handbook1.pdf.

2   Penn Alumni Regional Clubs, *The Penn Alumni Regional Clubs Handbook*, 9,
    http://viewer.zmags.com/publication/72f0b1ed#/72f0b1ed.

3   West Point Association of Graduates, *Society Leader Guide 2016*, 11, http://www.
    westpointaog.org/file/societyleadershandbook.pdf.

4   West Point Association of Graduates, *Applying for Tax Exempt Status*, 2017,
    https://www.westpointaog.org/file/ApplyingforTaxExemptStatus.pdf.

5   "Internal Revenue Manual – 7.25.19 Veterans' Organizations," Internal Revenue
    Service, accessed February 23, 2017, https://www.irs.gov/irm/part7/irm_07-025-
    019.html.

6   "Veterans' Organizations," Internal Revenue Service, accessed April 12, 2017,
    https://www.irs.gov/charities-non-profits/other-non-profits/veterans-organiza-
    tions.

7   "Internal Revenue Manual – 7.25.19 Veterans' Organizations," Internal
    Revenue Service, accessed February 23, 2017, https://www.irs.gov/irm/part7/

irm_07-025-019.html.

8 Department of the Treasury, Internal Revenue Service, *Publication 526: Charitable Contributions*, 2, January 19, 2017, https://www.irs.gov/pub/irs-pdf/p526.pdf.

9 Ibid., 17.

10 "Public Charity – Tax Exemption Application," Internal Revenue Service, last modified January 26, 2017, accessed February 23, 2017, https://www.irs.gov/charities-non-profits/charitable-organizations/public-charity-exemption-application.

11 "About," Alumni Association, University of Colorado Boulder, accessed February 12, 2017, http://www.colorado.edu/alumni/about.

12 "Chapters & Clubs," Alumni Association, University of Colorado Boulder, accessed February 12, 2017, http://www.colorado.edu/alumni/connect/Chapters-clubs.

13 Alumni Association, University of Colorado Boulder, *Alumni Chapter Manual and Memorandum of Understanding*, 19, http://www.colorado.edu/alumni/sites/default/files/attached-files/alumni_chapter_manual_and_memorandum_of_understanding.pdf.

14 Ibid., 19–20.

15 "Unrelated Business Income Defined," Internal Revenue Service, last modified November 7, 2016, https://www.irs.gov/charities-non-profits/unrelated-business-income-defined.

16 Jennifer Larino, "Louisiana Has the Highest Sales Tax Rate in America," *Times-Picayune*, January 31, 2017, accessed February 23, 2017, http://www.nola.com/business/index.ssf/2017/01/louisiana_highest_sales_tax_ra.html.

17 LSU Alumni Association, *Chapter Guidelines Booklet*, 9, 2016, http://www.lsu-alumni.org/Images/Interior/Chapters/2016Chapter%20guidelines.compressed.pdf.

18 Aida Luevanos (Director, Sul Ross State University Alumni Association), phone interview, January 25, 2017.

19 Sul Ross State University Alumni Association, *Regional Chapter Handbook*, 11, last modified fall 2014, http://www.sulross.edu/sites/default/files//sites/default/files/users/docs/alumni_rel/sul_ross_alumni_chapter_handbook2.pdf

20 University of Florida Alumni Association, *Gator Club and Affiliate Group Leaders Handbook*, 27, https://www.ufalumni.ufl.edu/gatorclubs/admin/docs/dl/?file=218.

21 Stanford Alumni Association, *Stanford Club Leaders Handbook*, 59, April 6, 2011, https://alumni.stanford.edu/content/groups/docs/2011_Club_Handbook.pdf.

22 "Financial Policies," Johns Hopkins Alumni Association, https://alumni.jhu.edu/financialpolicies.

23 "Gross Receipts Defined," Internal Revenue Service, last modified November 6, 2012, https://www.irs.gov/charities-non-profits/gross-receipts-defined.

24 "Form 1099-MISC, Miscellaneous Income," Internal Revenue Service, last modified September 6, 2016, https://www.irs.gov/uac/about-form-1099misc.

About the Author

Stacie Hyatt, author, speaker, President, and CEO of the Society for Alumni Club Leadership (SACL), is wildly passionate about volunteer alumni leaders and the success of each network. Her enthusiasm precipitates from personal experiences and witnessing how often lives and careers are completely transformed, sometimes through just a single alumni interaction.

She has served in leadership roles for the Wharton Club of Dallas–Fort Worth as President and Vice President of Programs, is currently on its board of directors, and has been a repeat Wharton Global Clubs Conference speaker. Together with the dedication of the entire local leadership team and the club's liaison, she led the club during its most dynamic era, in which dues-paying membership was at its highest and marquee events were most attended.

Building on her passion, she partnered with local leaders from other alumni Chapters to co-found the Dallas Business Club (DBC) in 2006, an association that has grown to represent more than twenty-five local MBA alumni clubs and tens of thousands of local alumni.

Through personal experience coupled with exposure to the vast network of DBC alumni club officers, Stacie has developed unique expertise in establishing, managing, and growing alumni clubs. She brings efficient clarity to areas including leadership structure, volunteer recruiting, incorporation documentation, state and federal nonprofit and tax-exemption designations, bylaws and governance, procedures and policies, tax reporting and filings, risk assessment and mitigation, insurance coverage, program development, event planning and execution, communications and promotion, sponsorships, new alumni integration, club revitalization, and much more.

Prior to her full-time dedication to alumni leadership, Stacie was a successful international sales, marketing, and product development executive in the global medical and research technology sectors with companies such as Medtronic and St. Jude Medical. She earned her MBA from the Wharton School at the University of Pennsylvania and a BS in bioengineering from Texas A&M University, where she served academia through the industry advisory boards for both the Dwight Look College of Engineering and the Department of Biomedical Engineering. Stacie's commitment to her community extends beyond academics into active leadership of and participation in professional, humanitarian, and women's organizations such as the Tech Titans, the Salvation Army, and the Executive Women's Roundtable, among others.